THE AMERICAN MIDDLE SCHOOL
An Organizational Analysis

A BLAISDELL BOOK IN EDUCATION

CONSULTING EDITOR

John I. Goodlad, University of California at Los Angeles

The American Middle School

AN ORGANIZATIONAL ANALYSIS

Samuel H. Popper

UNIVERSITY OF MINNESOTA

BLAISDELL PUBLISHING COMPANY
A Division of Ginn and Company
WALTHAM, MASSACHUSETTS • TORONTO • LONDON

To

Evelyn, Steven, and Janet

**With deep feeling for the
many leaves of absence from
family activities during the
writing of this book**

FOREWORD

Professor Popper's central thesis is that "pressures of culture" and "the human condition at the onset of adolescence" call for a period of schooling which is neither elementary nor secondary but a distinctive phase between the two. The unique functions of this phase are dissipated in 8-4 and 6-6 patterns of school organization, with the concerns of elementary education prolonged unduly in the former and those of high school education predominating too early in the latter. Given the present state of knowledge about human development, a middle school should be identified in a 6-3-3 plan of organization. It should be fully institutionalized in its own physical environment by a principal and teachers who have internalized the paramount value of optimum human development at the onset of puberty, and through a program geared specifically to the concerns of early adolescents and to the impact of society upon them. Such a school exists, more often than not, in name only.

The persisting malaise of the middle school movement—now more than a half-century old in the United States—lies not in concept but in practice, according to Professor Popper. Many of the guiding ideas were clearly enunciated by Superintendent Frank F. Bunker when he opened his first middle schools in 1910 at Berkeley. These ideas have been reiterated, refined, and expanded, with the body of theoretical-deductive evidence becoming more impressive and compelling. But the middle school has not yet come into its own. Professor Popper recalls the Myth of Sisyphus. Zeus had condemned Sisyphus to Hades where he was destined to forever roll a heavy stone up a steep hill only to have it roll down again whenever the summit was reached. Fortunately, in the case of the American middle school, the stone always comes to a stop before it reaches the base of the hill. And, happily, the lot of those who toil in and for the middle school is decidedly better than what we might perceive it to be in Hades, with or without the pushing of stones!

Professor Popper, then, is no dispassionate observer in his chronicling of the trials and tribulations of this middle school. Nor is he dull. He justifies the need for, and specifies the nature of, the legitimatizing of institutions by taking us through the labyrinths of Parsonian theory—no mean feat, the reader will recognize. He documents growing recognition of the need for this new school against a background of social evolution in nineteenth-century America. And he explores the thesis that adequate institutionalization of the middle school was thwarted largely by a twentieth-century retreat to technicism in public education and the "cult of efficiency" embraced by administrators who perceived themselves as business executives rather than as educational leaders. Throughout, the pages are enriched by intriguing glimpses into the lives and ideas of Herbert Spencer, John D. Rockefeller, Oliver Wendell Holmes, Jr., Frederick Jackson Turner, Charles A. Beard, Samuel Sidney McClure, Francis Wayland Parker, Nicholas Murray Butler, Charles William Eliot, William James, John Dewey, Edward L. Thorndike, and Superintendents William T. Harris, William H. Maxwell, W. A. Greeson, and many more.

The canvas is a large one and his strokes are broad. The artillery called up—particularly in the organizational aspects of his treatise—is so formidable that one wishes Professor Popper had brought the whole of precollegiate education within range. Those advocates of K-12 plans, in which the phases of schooling tend to lose their organizational identity in provisions for continuous pupil progress, will want to query Professor Popper on the articulation-separation balance he considers essential to fulfilling the middle school's functions.

This is not a "methods" book. But no truly meaningful technology for educating early adolescent boys and girls can be developed until we are clear on the functions of the middle phase of schooling.

Professor Popper's volume now becomes a fitting companion to an

THE AMERICAN MIDDLE SCHOOL

An Organizational Analysis

CONTENTS

Secretary, American Association of School Administrators, delightful story teller that he is, helped at the earliest stage of the manuscript with his tale of Leonardo Da Vinci and the monks' criticism of the "Last Supper." And I shall be everlastingly grateful to my friend Glenn F. Varner, champion of middle school education, for having alerted me to the difficult predicament of the American middle school. A scholarly effort is always helped by the support of good library resources. Staff personnel of the Fifth Avenue branch of the New York City Public Library and the Walter Library of the University of Minnesota have been unstinting in their proffer of assistance.

Valuable assistance was given by the Blaisdell Publishing Company, especially through their Consulting Editor, Dr. John I. Goodlad, and a very skillful crew of editorial and production personnel.

Acknowledgment is also made to publishers who have granted permission to quote generously from their copyrighted sources and who are cited in the book. I am especially beholden to the publisher and editor of *School Management* for permission to use the superb sketches by Mr. C. William Brubaker of Perkins and Will.

Mr. Eldon J. Null helped to hasten the manuscript to completion by relieving me of time-consuming chores. Mrs. Ruth Roston undertook the onerous task of gremlin hunting in the typed manuscript. I am obligated to both.

The greatest pleasure of all is to acknowledge the help of my wife, Evelyn. Merely dedicating this book to her and to our children is a grossly inadequate expression of my feelings.

Should the reader find cause to fault the book despite such generous assistance, I alone am culpable.

S. H. P.

ACKNOWLEDGMENTS

It is difficult to conceive of any intellectual endeavor which may be said to be free altogether from indebtedness to others. Had the ideas of Talcott Parsons, Robert K. Merton, Philip Selznick, and other social scientists not been available, this book would very likely have been of a different character.

Closer to home, I stand indebted to the following for their criticism of those parts of the manuscript each has read: Professor Ayers Bagley, Department of History and Philosophy of Education, University of Minnesota; Professor Luvern L. Cunningham, Director of the Midwest Administration Center, University of Chicago; Professor Edward Gross, Department of Sociology, University of Minnesota. My sometime active collaboration with the latter two will remain a deeply cherished experience.

Discussions with Professor Timothy L. Smith, Department of History, University of Minnesota; Professor John E. Bicknell, Department of Educational Psychology, University of Alberta; Roy O. Isacksen, Principal, Como Park Junior High School; and Professor Emma M. Birkmaier, Head, Department of Modern Languages, University High School of the College of Education, University of Minnesota, have been of inestimable value. Dr. William J. Ellena, Associate Executive

the legitimizing value of a middle school—its claim to the right of existence—has to be defined. Such a definition is precisely the desideratum of this book.

SAMUEL H. POPPER

Minneapolis, Minn.

ingly for a view of the early adolescent in American culture and within the client system of public school organization. Early adolescence is taken to mean, as it has been since the inception of the American middle school, the years from about 12 to 15: the so-called "awkward age." The burden of the chapter, in short, is to explore cultural conditions which make necessary a special school for early adolescents in American society.

The final chapters reaffirm the larger social value of the American middle school. It is proposed that its unhappy past can well serve as prologue to a brighter future, provided we cast out from the middle school what has become functionally obsolescent. A revitalization program is then proposed for the middle school of tomorrow.

It is now opportune to make explicit an awareness that much of what is contained in this analysis of the American middle school organization has relevance, to a greater or lesser degree, for all units of the public school system. Indeed, tools of analysis which have been employed here for the middle school would serve equally well for an analysis of *any other unit* of public school organization, including *the system itself*. But because my intellectual interest here is in the larger theoretical problem of middle school legitimation, it seemed unwise to risk a blurring of the focus with distracting analytical references to other units of public school organization. Moreover, it is altogether of value to recognize that analytical scholarship in educational administration need not have a "boxed-in look" when it focuses on a micro unit of school organization.

Also, as the reader will discover, my subject is complex. An analytical treatment of a complex subject does not lend itself to simple narrative exposition. The reader will be well served, therefore, to keep in his "mind's eye" the notion of a cognitive map which projects different ways of looking at a middle school organization. Theoretical and empirical sources integrate these perspectives in a composite projection of the subject. Careful concentration on integrating threads should reward the reader with deeper insights into the *differentiated function* of the American middle school in the process of socialization.

More than anything else, the American middle school is now in desperate need of revitalization in a modern idiom. The task is Gargantuan and it will require the active participation of local and state school board members, school administrators, teachers, guidance counselors, and middle school specialists in schools of education. But first,

The impact of social reconstruction returns the discourse to the school as a formal organization. It is now examined as a type of bureaucratic structure.

Max Weber's machine model for explaining one type of social order in modern society, informal organization, modern-day orientations to the management of complex organizations, and other relevant concepts are brought into the discussion. Parsons' theoretical view of three primary functional subsystems in the division of labor of complex organizations rounds out the discussion of formal organization.

All of the foregoing is then used as a cognitive map for an analysis of what has gone wrong in the American middle school. How is it that the separately-housed middle school unit, which by a 1958 count of the U.S. Office of Education constituted 20.6 percent of all secondary schools in the nation, and which enrolled 25.0 percent of the nation's secondary school pupils, should today be afflicted by problems which stem largely from an ambiguous legitimation? A general overview of salient middle school problems is then coupled with an attempt to pinpoint their sources.

A treatment of the middle school program—the technology with which a middle school organization attains its goal—is set within an evolutionary context. Although this is not meant as a curriculum book, it seemed necessary to cite ancestral influences of the middle school program and early attempts to institutionalize it. The question of whether scholastic achievement is thwarted in a modern-day middle school by a dominant psychosocial orientation to early adolescent education, as some have claimed it is indeed, is explored in the light of an intensive statistical evaluation of academic gain on standardized tests that have been made of a middle school program in a large city school system. It is the only intensive evaluation of its kind known to me and it is used in accordance with Occam's rule of parsimony.

One chapter is devoted entirely to the early adolescent pupil. The public school organization exists after all as a service organization of the type which Talcott Parsons classifies as "pattern-maintenance." Its outputs, from the point of view of society, contribute to a reaffirmation of the integrity of the institutionalized value system. It renders a service to pupils at various stages of maturation by training them in skills they will need as adults and strives to inculcate in them a commitment to the broad values of society. The fields of psychology, physiology, sociology, and anthropology have been drawn upon accord-

gateway to intensive study of middle school structure and process. It is assumed, moreover, that anyone who has a professional interest in the middle school will welcome further exploration in those social science sources from which sensitizing concepts may be drawn for knowing its larger cultural purpose in society. Ample footnote references have been provided for this purpose.

The following are the main structural elements of the book. At the outset, the middle school is presented in overview fashion as a functionally differentiated unit of the superordinate public school system. Its emergence in the larger system of public school organization at about 1910 is explained as a direct consequence of a secondary differentiation: early adolescent pupils were now defined as a special category of public school clients.

The concept of functional value is then used as a bridging theme in a first treatment of the middle school as a social system which is structured as a formal organization. This leads directly to a definition of the middle school's discrete goal in public school organization. I categorize this as its "paramount goal." It seemed necessary in the interest of analytical clarity to prepare such a foundation for the goal definition because, as an organizational unit of a rationalistic system, the differentiated function of the middle school goal must be shown to also possess means value—functional value—for goal attainment by the superordinate system.

The obligation of school administrators to institutional leadership comes in for much attention. Here, the middle school is viewed as an implementing instrument of the institution we know as public education. Talcott Parsons' theoretical explication of the institutionalization of values and the legitimation of action systems by society is used as a context for the discussion.

For an institutional treatment of the middle school, the historical setting in which it emerged on the American scene had to be sketched on a large canvas. An analysis of any cultural system without a return to the historical imperatives which propelled it into existence is sterile of cognitive value in the present. Therefore, layers of the past are turned up to expose those social exigencies which had propelled a middle school in the United States into existence. The focal point of the canvas is society in the throes of social reconstruction and its impact on public education. Relevant events and characters of the *milieu* following 1865 are treated in measured detail.

paramount valuation in middle school education did shift to the affec-tive domain. An analysis and explication of the cultural thrusts which account for its radical adaptation in American society is, therefore, the burden of this book.

Its pioneers in the United States meant the middle school to serve as a transitional unit between childhood education in the elementary school and later adolescent education in the high school. Pupils in-between these two stages of maturation, standing at the threshold of puberty, were to be assigned to a middle school. Because of historical accident and tradition, but not out of any substantive relevance to the American adaptation of the middle school concept, this unit of public school organization today is more commonly known as a junior high school.

Only in the United States and Canada is the middle school unit called a junior high school. But even in the United States, there is a growing inclination to dissociate the misapplied name of junior high school from early adolescent education. The institutional authority of the American middle school resides, after all, with the social value in the educative process to which it gives expression and not with the name by which it is called. Therefore, in an institutional frame of reference, physiological and psychological science alone possess the necessary com-petence to set the functionally appropriate period of socialization for this unit of school organization.

My purpose overall is to project the American middle school organiza-tion in a wide-angled theoretical perspective. A form of structural-functional analysis seemed to me the methodological strategy best suited for this purpose. The organization of the middle school is mapped, therefore, in the following three projections of system: as a mechanistic system, as a psychological system, and as a cultural system. The same organization is viewed from three perspectives of system analysis.

Best results will be obtained from the book by those who have a background in social and behavioral science. The sociology of organ-izations—and more particularly Talcott Parsons' general theory of social systems—the social history of the United States since 1865, cultural anthropology, and social psychology are especially recommended as profitable areas for cultivation. It was never my intention that this book should contain all there is to be known about middle school organization. Quite the contrary, a book of this kind serves best as a

PREFACE

What over the years we have come to know as the Junior High School is institutionally America's Middle School. What is at issue now in professional dialogue is not whether there shall be a junior high school or a middle school, a semantic distinction without a difference, but rather which grades are functionally appropriate for this unit of public school organization.

From the perspective of organization theory, and out of a concern for the human condition in American society at early adolescence, a meaningful resolution of this issue has to begin with a rigorous definition of the *differentiated function* that is expected of a middle school in the division of labor of a public school system. Otherwise, we shall continue to mismanage the middle school as a formal system, do it violence as a social system, and abuse its uniqueness as an institutional, or cultural, system.

For in point of fact, the concept of a middle school is not of American origin. Middle schools were in existence before they were added to the structure of public school organization in the United States. However, the United States was the first cultural system to make dominant a *psychosocial orientation* in middle school structure and process. The learning of cognitive skills was by no means neglected, but the

earlier book in this series, *The Secondary Phase of Education* (1965) by Lawrence W. Downey, in the quest for more precise conceptualization of our schools as social institutions. Both are testimony to the fact that education is, indeed, a legitimate, demanding field of study.

JOHN I. GOODLAD

1

THE FIRST MIDDLE SCHOOLS

The Association for Supervision and Curriculum Development published in 1961 a landmark position statement on the American middle school. It was endowed with institutional insight and it was forward looking. We shall return more than once to this remarkable statement. However, one of its observations is relevant now. The report notes:[1]

> As an institution under pressure to change, without a clear mandate regarding function, purpose, or structure, the junior high school imposes special burdens upon its staff members as well as upon its students.

The foregoing expresses with singular conciseness the so-called problem of the modern middle school. However, it should not be overlooked that the reference to "an institution under pressure to change" has significant relevance today, in one measure or another, for all of the institutional network of society.

For, like it or not, changes are occurring at breathtaking speed in every sector of American society. It is widely acknowledged that spec-

[1] Jean D. Grambs, Clarence G. Noyce, Franklin Patterson, and John Robertson, *The Junior High School We Need* (Washington, D.C.: Association for Supervision and Curriculum Development, 1961), p. 12.

3

tacular achievements in the sciences, and, therefore, the technologies which evolve from these sciences, are responsible for the accelerated pace of change. Heraclitus of Ephesus from Asia Minor, so it would seem, was right after all when he insisted that all things change and constancy is an illusion.

The nuclear bomb is, certainly in the popular domain, the single most dramatic manifestation of recent successes in the physical sciences which have accelerated the pace of change. Less well known to the larger public, however, are the forward strides that have been attained at the same time in the social and behavioral sciences. But in the main, thrusts in both the physical and human sciences have come from the exigencies of World War II.

Newspapers and popular journals have reported many times over the extensive involvement of physical scientists in the war effort. Not so well publicized has been the involvement in war programs of social and behavioral scientists. As Andrew W. Halpin put it with characteristic verve:[2]

> The war forced social scientists out of their laboratories; psychologists, sociologists, and anthropologists had to tackle a whole range of new problems, and their research was supported on a scale previously unknown in those disciplines. In effect, the social scientists were told—in the colloquialism of the poker table—to "put up or shut up." They "put up." During the war years social science research came into its own and achieved a new maturity.

From the empirical social science research of World War II years have come methodological innovations for studying complexities of the social and psychological systems of individuals and groups. The work of the Research Branch of the Information and Education Division of the United States Army is illustrative.

The Research Branch was assembled in 1941. Its technical civilian director through the war years was the late Harvard sociologist Samuel A. Stouffer. Its mission was to measure and report different aspects of troop morale in branches of the United States Army. Many field investigations were performed in the course of the mission. But in order to attain maximum usefulness from the collected data, social scientists had to devise new instruments for measuring, among other things, both the direction and intensity of group attitudes. Out of

2 "Editor's Introduction" in Andrew W. Halpin (ed.), *Administrative Theory in Education* (Chicago: University of Chicago Midwest Administration Center, 1958), p. ii.

these wartime studies of the American soldier came refinements in scale construction and scalogram analysis. The Guttman Scale and Paul F. Lazarsfeld's latent structure analysis are cases in point.[3]

Not alone were older methodologies refined and new ones devised for war-related social science research, but an added windfall accrued to social sciences from postwar reassessments of data gathered in the military establishment during the war years. Out of such reassessments, for example, were gained fresh insights into the sociology of primary group behavior and reference group theory.[4]

With no "bang" of an exploding nuclear force to herald their achievements, social scientists nonetheless have pushed the human sciences, as Halpin put it, to "a new maturity"; a maturity which has opened new vistas on destructive conflict in social systems and on techniques for effecting greater human cooperation in interaction. When it is contemplated how social and technical engineering depend upon advancements in the respective sciences from which they stem, little wonder that change—ubiquitous and continuing change—should have become the hallmark of modern life.

But what has all of this to do with the middle school organization or, for that matter, with school administration?

Warrant for the foregoing exposition on change is the certainty that whatever change is destined to occur in the American middle school will be a consequence of how this unit of public school organization is perceived by school administrators. Moreover, because administrative decision making is a product of social process, the focus on postwar developments in the social sciences is altogether warranted. Within such a frame of reference, administration, that is, administration *qua* administration, and never mind the adjective which precedes the noun, is essentially a type of social engineering which draws upon the social sciences in the same manner as technical engineering draws upon the physical sciences.

Recent developments in educational administration provide an

---

[3] The fascinating war activities of the Research Branch are described in four volumes which have been published by the Princeton University Press in a series known as *Studies in Social Psychology in World War II*. The more popular reference to this series is "The American Soldier."

The Likert scale was already in use before the war, but wartime refinements gave to this measuring technique a wider statistical latitude.

[4] For an illustration of such a reassessment of wartime military research, look in Robert K. Merton and Paul F. Lazarsfeld, eds., *Continuities in Social Research: Studies in the Scope and Method of "The American Soldier"* (New York: The Free Press, 1950).

illustration of the latter point. School administration, as a field of professional study, has been transformed dramatically in recent years. Its conceptual posture, and consequently the research and literature of educational administration, has since the end of World War II assumed a bolder stance. It is no accident at all that transformations in educational administration evolved in a parallel fashion with rising levels of sophistication in the social and behavioral sciences.

Structural manifestations of the postwar turn in educational administration can be seen in the formation of such organizations as the National Conference for Professors of Educational Administration (NCPEA, established in 1947), the Cooperative Program in Educational Administration (CPEA, first support given by the W. K. Kellogg Foundation in 1950), the University Council for Educational Administration (UCEA, established in 1956, also with a grant from the W. K. Kellogg Foundation), the Committee for Advancement of School Administration of the American Association of School Administrators (CASA, established in 1955), and the revised preparation programs for all levels of school administration at major universities.[5]

Out of all this postwar activity in educational administration has come change; so much so, that by the mid-fifties Daniel E. Griffiths was moved to begin his book, *Human Relations in School Administration,* with the observation: "We are now in the midst of the greatest period of change in school administration since its origin in American education."[6]

Imperatives for Conceptual Clarity

More than anything else, the American middle school of today is sorely in need of institutional definition. People generally have no difficulty in defining an elementary school or a high school, but the search for a middle school definition puts them under an exhausting strain. Even one so eminent and erudite as Charles H. Judd wrote in 1923: "The junior high school is not an institution with fixed pur-

---

[5] For a more detailed account of some of these developments see Hollis A. Moore, Jr., *Studies in School Administration* (Washington, D.C.: American Association of School Administrators, 1957); see also Halpin, "The Development of Theory in Educational Administration," *Administrative Theory in Education,* pp. 1–11.

[6] Daniel E. Griffiths, *Human Relations in School Administration* (New York: Appleton-Century-Crofts, Inc., 1956), p. 3. Copyright © 1956, Appleton-Century-Crofts, Inc. Both the title and content of this book at once reflect the modern mood of educational administration.

poses and definable content."[7]   Such a view of the American middle school is, in sociological terms, a denial of its essential characteristics as a cultural system and as a rational system.

The very misappellation by which this school has come to be known is symptomatic of the confusion that surrounds its dominant organizational purpose.   Too many people—professionals and laymen alike— have come to regard the middle school as a high school in miniature; a thing it was never meant to be.

There were those who rejected the name of junior high school from the beginning.   Many schoolmen preferred intermediate school as the name of America's school for early adolescents.   They were exceedingly apprehensive of misleading inferences in the junior high school label.

They were afraid the dominant organizational purpose of the middle school would be taken to be the preparation of pupils for high school and it would thereby invite curricular and administrative overlordship by the latter.   An anticipated imitation of the high school by "junior," and resulting difficulties in attracting teachers to the middle school, was also captured by these schoolmen in their vision of the future.   But once a number of large city school systems took the name of junior high school, other systems followed without speculating about dire latent consequences.[8]

One place where conceptual confusion about the middle school has been hurting most particularly is in teacher preparation programs, especially those of larger university systems.   For years now, middle school principals in every section of the country have been crying at the gates of colleges of education: "Give us teachers who are specially prepared to teach our early adolescent pupils."   But to no avail!

Colleges of education acknowledge gladly their obligation to prepare teachers for diverse instructional roles in the nation's schools.   They insist at the same time that this obligation extend mostly to the preparation of teachers for the kindergarten, elementary school, and the high school.   When pressed particularly about the middle school, they claim that they are indeed preparing middle school teachers, but as an adjunct of preparation programs for high school teachers.

---

[7] Charles H. Judd, "Fundamental Educational Reforms," *Elementary School Journal*, Vol. XXIII, January 1923, p. 339.   Hereafter cited as Judd, "Fundamental Educational Reforms."   Published by the University of Chicago Press.

[8] See the enlightening discussion of this problem in Calvin Olin Davis, *Junior High School Education* (New York: World Book Co., 1926), pp. 9–11.

Here precisely is the rub! A middle school is neither an elementary school nor a high school: it is a *functionally differentiated unit* of the larger public school organization. Its formal structure is as definable in cogent sociological and pedagogical terms as are the units we call the elementary school and high school. Nevertheless, school administrators insist, and with justifiable professional chagrin, that most colleges of education *do not* prepare teachers for the middle school organization. Chapter 11 will treat in greater detail the consequence of this attitude toward the middle school in teacher education.

Only through a commandingly cogent reassertion of its institutional and organizational values can the American middle school hope to escape from this malaise. It is, therefore, altogether imperative that an analytical distinction be made between the paramount middle school goal and functional patterns in the unit; that is to say, the means of attaining that goal. As a first step, let it be clearly marked that no substantive meaning attaches to the name *junior high school*. The name is an accident of history. Values, components of organization, and educative process are the important variables in such a distinction.

Next, a cognitive map of the middle school organization is required. In the construction of such a map, more than anything else it is necessary to keep in sharp focus the distinctive institutional purpose of the American middle school. Once that is in focus, whether a middle school shall be a two-, three-, or four-year structure, or even a non-graded structure, is a matter which has to be in harmony with this institutional purpose. Put in another way: because the distinctive institutional purpose of the American middle school is for early adolescent education, physiological and psychological science alone possess the necessary competence for setting the functionally appropriate period of socialization for this unit of public school organization.

A cognitive map of the middle school organization moreover should facilitate the development of effective administrative and technological processes for the unit. For one thing, experimentation with educative process need not be inhibited by ambiguity about its paramount organizational goal. For another, a reliable orientation to its structure and process ought to be comforting to an administrator who has to establish a middle school program in a 6-6 school organization of a sparsely populated community with a low school enrollment and a narrow tax base. In the main, and regardless of the system's organizational pattern, how a middle school program will fare in the hands of an administrator turns on his understanding of the middle school's institutional purpose in American culture. It is a fact which has been verified again and again by middle school experience ever since the unit took permanent hold in American society early in the twentieth century. The manner of its appearance on the educational landscape in the United States is, therefore, an appropriate first datum for mapping the American middle school.

The Middle School Takes Hold

Three movements converged at the twilight of the nineteenth century and widened the base of educational opportunity in the United States. These movements acquired great momentum in the nascent industrial and urban environment of the post-Civil War period.

Because the first of these movements pervaded every sector of the American social system, many regard it as the fountainhead of the other two. Its substance was a vigorous reassertion, in the new era of factories and cities, of those humanistic-democratic values for which the Fathers of the Republic had risked life and freedom. The second of the movements took the form of a dynamic new interest in the scientific study of man's social and psychological behavior. Out of the latter stemmed, among others, the child-study movement. This, then, was the third of these movements. Its driving purpose was the scientific study of child growth and development.

As the combined thrust of these movements impinged upon the institution of public education, adaptive innovations became necessary in American public school organizations, whose cultural mission it is to fulfill the social values of universal public education. The appearance of the modern middle school at about 1910 was a structural manifestation of but one of several such adaptations in the implementing system of public education. It was, and we shall return to this theme later, the last major outcome of a revitalization movement in American education.

The so-called junior high school of the 1910 period was in point of fact an American borrowing of a European idea. Denmark, following in the path of Nikolai F. S. Grundtvig's pedagogical humanism, established a middle school in 1903 as a means of widening the base of educational opportunity in that country.[9]

A political upheaval in Denmark brought to power in 1901 a liberal government which adopted a parliamentary system. Up to that time, Denmark's national system of education consisted of two separate school organizations: an elementary school and a secondary school. Only a small fraction of the elementary school enrollment went on to secondary education. However, the passage of a Higher Education Act in 1903 established a middle school in urban school systems to encourage larger numbers of elementary school pupils on to the secondary school.

But unlike the middle school in the United States, the Danish middle school was bifurcated. One branch, *the examination middle school,* was given a pronounced academic character and its curriculum was made subject to the external control of the high school. Another branch, *the prevocational middle school,* was given a vocational character and it had exclusive internal control over its curriculum.[10]

The middle school in the United States was also set between the elementary and high school units. However, two characteristics distinguished it—indeed made it unique—from the European model: its orientation to structure and process was dominantly fixed on the psychological and social conditions of early adolescents in American culture and no attempt was made to bifurcate the curriculum.

Although 1910 is usually given as the year of the first American middle school, there is evidence of some earlier experiences with the middle school concept in the United States. One historical reference makes mention of a "junior high school" as early as 1884, but nothing else seems to be known about it.[11] Richmond, Indiana, is said to have had in 1895 a "distinct unit of the city school" set apart for seventh and eighth graders.[12] Also, the State of Florida is known to have paid state aids early in the twentieth century for the operation of "junior high schools."

An official record is extant which shows that the State of Florida provided such financial aid to forty-seven "junior high schools" during the

[9] For the pedagogical ideas of Nicolai Frederik Severin Grundtvig see Olive Dame Campbell, *The Danish Folk School* (New York: The Macmillan Company, 1928).
[10] See *World Survey of Education* (Paris: UNESCO, 1955), p. 188.
[11] *Proceedings of the Twenty-first Annual Meeting of the North Central Association of Colleges and Secondary Schools,* 1916, p. 175. Hereafter cited as *Proceedings,* NCA.
[12] N. C. Heironomous, "Is This the Earliest Known Junior High School?" *The Clearing House,* Vol. 14, May 1940, p. 518.

school year 1903–04. Moreover, the State Legislature of Florida in 1905 enacted enabling legislation for the establishment of an additional sixty-five such schools.[13]

However, a check of the record by Thomas D. Bailey, erstwhile Superintendent of Public Instruction for the State of Florida, led him to conclude: "(1) that the legislature designated the ninth and tenth grades as junior high grades, (2) that the junior high school offered the curriculum adopted for the first two grades of the secondary school. . . ."[14] The State Legislature of Florida, it seems, had in fact enacted enabling legislation for a bifurcated high school system: one division was called "junior high school" and the other "senior high school." The former was made a terminal school and took the first two grades only of a four-year secondary school curriculum, whereas the latter offered all four grades.[15]

Berkeley, California, is generally credited with having opened the first developed middle schools in the United States. Superintendent Frank Forest Bunker in 1909 had laid a proposal before the Berkeley Board of Education which called for a reorganization of that city's school system to a 6-3-3 structural pattern. According to Bunker: "The plan proposed that, at or near the center of each geographical quarter of the city, there should be erected a separate building, adapted particularly to the needs of the seventh, eighth, and ninth grades of the section."[16]

Two such schools were opened in Berkeley during 1910; both were called Introductory High School. Columbus, Ohio, about the same time, opened a three-year school for early adolescents and called it Junior High School. Grand Rapids, Michigan, opened one such three-year school in 1911, as did Los Angeles, and in rapid succession a number of other larger city school systems opened such schools.[17]

Most of these were established as three-year schools. Some were opened as one-, two-, four-, and even five-year structures. These

---

[13] Charles Maphis, "A Decade of Growth," *Proceedings of the Nineteenth Annual Meeting of the Association of Colleges and Preparatory Schools of the Southern Association,* 1913, p. 52.

[14] Letter from Thomas D. Bailey to author, May 7, 1963.

[15] Thomas Everette Cochran, *History of Public-School Education in Florida,* Bulletin, 1921, No. 1, p. 129. Quoted in enclosure with letter from Thomas D. Bailey.

[16] Frank Forest Bunker, *Reorganization of the Public School System,* Bureau of Education, Department of Interior, Bulletin, 1916, No. 8 (Washington, D.C.: Government Printing Office, 1916), p. 87.

[17] *Proceedings,* NCA, 1914, p. 22.

schools were sometimes named after a celebrated local, or national, figure, but more often they were called Intermediate School, Sub-High School, Upper Grammar School, Departmental School, Higher Primary School, and variations thereof. It is significant, in regard to the middle school concept, that the early literature reveals a common tendency of authors to use interchangeably the names of Intermediate School and Junior High School.

But regardless of name or organizational pattern, there was a wide-based consensus among its early sponsors that the differentiated function of the new organizational unit was to provide "a suitable educational environment" for early adolescents.[18] The early sponsors were satisfied that the idea of a middle school was pedagogically sound and that a separate unit of school organization was the appropriate administrative mechanism for implementing it. Quite typical of this sentiment was the view of Charles Hughes Johnston, who, as Professor of Secondary Education at the University of Illinois and Managing Editor of *Educational Administration and Supervision,* pointed to the American middle school and commented:[19]

> It is but a rediscovery of what European nations, in their more intensive cultivation of the restricted and select field of secondary education, have found to be an administratively and pedagogically necessary arrangement. . . . It means that something other than tradition and accident has come to influence our development. It means some sort of uniqueness both in the pedagogy of school subjects new and old and in the spirit of our administration. It means the Americanization of a world tested principle of curriculum building. It means flexibility and therefore science in the manipulation of our total school plants.

An abundance of historical evidence shows that Johnston's enthusiasm for the middle school was shared by many of his immediate contemporaries in public school administration. Standing before an audience of the National Education Association in 1912, J. H. Francis, Superintendent of Schools in Los Angeles, impressed upon his colleagues the following:[20]

18 See the general agreement on this note which was obtained in a survey of the middle school purpose and which is reported in William A. Smith, *The Junior High School* (New York: The Macmillan Company, 1927), pp. 153–204.

19 Charles Hughes Johnston, "The Junior High School," *Educational Administration and Supervision,* Vol. II, 1916, pp. 417 and 423.

20 *Addresses and Proceedings of the National Education Association,* 1912, p. 376. Hereafter cited as *Addresses and Proceedings,* NEA.

The three divisions of the school system are physiologically, psychologically, sociologically, and logically correct. The present organization of eight years in the grades and four years in high school violates the principles of all these sciences.

Such enthusiasm for the middle school unit from foremost figures in public education was bound to be infectious, and indeed the movement did spread rapidly.

By 1914 the North Central Association of Colleges and Secondary Schools had an *ad hoc* committee investigate the extensiveness of the movement in the member states of the Association. Principal Henry E. Brown of New Trier Township High School, Kenilworth, Illinois, reported for the committee. Because certain excerpts of his report are especially germane to an analysis of the middle school organization, they are given here at some length. Principal Brown reported in part:[21]

> Our investigation has led us to conclude that a reorganization of the grade schools, high schools, and colleges should be effected, and that the dividing line between the grades and high school should be made at the sixth grade; that the ideal system would be the 6-3-3 plan, because the pupils of the ages of from twelve to fourteen could then be segregated from those of the three upper years much to the benefit of both groups. First year high school pupils need quite different treatment from those in the upper grades and are more nearly of the same intellectual ability with the seventh and eighth grades than with the tenth, eleventh and twelfth. However, the form of organization should be determined practically by local conditions, due to difference in population and to the financial ability of the community concerned. . . . Of these types of organization and administrative control the 6-3-3 plan seems to be the most successful. Both from Berkeley, California, and Grand Rapids, Michigan, came reports of great satisfaction with the results obtained. Grand Rapids reports that since its organization in 1911 the junior high school has increased in numbers from 430 to 871, and its teaching force from fourteen to thirty-six. The principal of the junior high school reports that the work of the third-year pupils is of a distinctly higher grade than the work of the freshman class in the ordinary four-year school.

From Berkeley, California, comes the report that the loss in the ninth grade under the 6-3-3 plan for the limited period under which they have

---

[21] *Proceedings*, NCA, 1914, pp. 18–26.

been running was 16.7 percent compared with Ayre's study, which showed a loss of 50 percent covering many cities under the old plan.

. . . In the beginning of this movement the subject matter of instruction was substantially the same as it had been before the movement was inaugurated, but gradually, in many of these schools, a change has been effected until now not only is there a difference in organization, but also a change in subject matter. They have gradually become junior high schools.

Even a cursory content analysis of Brown's report reveals some important developmental facts about the early middle school in America. There is in Brown's remarks an implied acknowledgment of the middle school program as *an innovation in educational technology.* Educational technology may be defined as the complex of educational activities through which the school organization renders a professional service for its pupils. It is the process of education. In order to accommodate the innovation in the process of education, the report recommends a three-year organizational unit of grades 7-8-9 to be housed in a separate plant. Where local conditions prohibit a separate plant, other building accommodations might be provided for the unit.

Better service to "direct clients"—pupils—of the public school organization is given as justification for the unit.[22] Maturational and intellectual requirements of early adolescent clients, so Brown's report holds, can best be satisfied in a special school unit apart from the upper high school grades. Brown offered the Grand Rapids experience in support of this proposition.

The report then points to an anomaly. Although the middle school organization was formed to accommodate an innovation in educational technology, some middle schools were still using the traditional technology: Brown's "subject matter of instruction." Gradually, however, as these middle schools innovated the program, their functionally differentiated character became distinctive in the superordinate public school organization.

---

[22] The reference to pupils as "direct clients" of the school organization is Talcott Parsons'. See Talcott Parsons, "Some Ingredients of a General Theory of Formal Organizations," in Halpin (ed.), *Administrative Theory in Education,* p. 56. Hereafter cited as "Some Ingredients of a General Theory."

The status of the pupil in public school organization presents an interesting point for sociological speculation. Is the pupil a "product" of the public school organization, a "client," a "member," or a combination of these? This point will be treated in greater detail in Chapter 2.

Last, there is an inference in Brown's report that pupil retention—holding power—is to be categorized as an important functional value in the public school organization. His specific point of reference is the Berkeley experience.

School administrators of the early 1900's did, indeed, tend to give a heavy weighting to the means value of pupil retention because, more than anything else, the high dropout rate of the period was the most visible symbol of goal failure in the public school organization. Compulsory school-attendance laws, even where they existed, were seldom enforced with any great enthusiasm beyond the fifth grade. Investigation after investigation revealed an appalling loss of pupils from the nation's public schools after the fifth grade.

One such investigation by Leonard P. Ayres in the early 1900's—the Ayres to whom Principal Brown referred—disclosed that in fifty-nine city school systems, only 40 percent of the student body went on to the ninth grade.[23] Strictly by service criteria alone, a public school system which suffered such a heavy client loss could not have been effective as a service organization. For this reason, the functional value of pupil retention was especially esteemed in administrative assessments of the new middle school unit.

A case in point was the experience in Rochester, New York. That city opened a middle school in 1915—Washington Junior High School. After one year of operation, Superintendent Herbert S. Weet stressed the following achievement in his evaluation of the first year:[24]

> Of those who completed the eighth year work last January under the Junior High School organization 94½% have remained for the ninth year work. A year ago in exactly same community but under the grammar school organization only 51% remained for ninth year work. This highly suggests that there were needs among these upper grade pupils that were not being met and that the present Junior High School type of work is meeting these needs.

Little wonder then, given the high administrative esteem that was attached to the value of pupil retention during the early period of the middle school movement, that many should have equated the func-

23 See Leonard P. Ayres, *Laggards in Our Schools* (New York: Russell Sage Foundation, 1909), p. 57. See also Bunker, *Reorganization of the Public School System,* p. 101.
24 Herbert S. Weet, "Rochester's Junior High School: A First Step in Establishing the Six-Three-Three Organization," *Educational Administration and Supervision,* Vol. II, 1916, p. 435.

tional value of pupil retention with the paramount *social value* of the middle school goal. But what precisely is a *functional value?*

The concept of functional, or means, value is especially important when the middle school is analyzed as an organizational unit of a larger system. It is, therefore, necessary at this juncture to define this concept with greater precision in order to distinguish between the *functional value* of operational tasks in a middle school organization and the *social value* of its fulfilled paramount goal. In sum, functional relationships within the following continuum have to be marked: operational tasks in a middle school organization—the paramount goal of a middle school—goals of the superordinate public school system.

These functional relationships, as they are marked discretely for the middle school, also will throw light on certain mechanical and social aspects of public school organization.

2

ASPECTS OF THE SOCIAL SYSTEM

An analysis of a goal-directed organization should begin with a clear-cut statement of the organization's goal. But our subject here is the middle school organization, a unit of a superordinate system: an organization within an organization. No matter, therefore, what the discrete goal of the middle school organization might be, it also has to have functional relevance to the goal, or goals, of the larger public school organization.

But the middle school is more than just an organizational unit of a larger system. It is a *functionally differentiated unit,* an all-important distinction which has to be established at the very outset. For the public school organization is, among other things, a rational structure. It is put together like a machine, a product of man's ingenuity, and rational organizations do not create subsystems by caprice. At least some component of the middle school goal, therefore, has to be unique, else there would be no rational, or administrative, justification for the unit.

In an earlier reference, the functional value of higher pupil retention was singled out for attention. It is now proposed that, within the rationalistic and machinelike structure of public school organization, the paramount goal of the middle school itself must have functional value for goal attainment by the larger system. Again, a functional value, but obviously a value of a higher order. For what is a *functional value* for the superordinate school system is for the middle school organization its *paramount goal, its raison d'être.* It would be risky to treat analytically the goal structure of the middle school before we know precisely what is meant by *functional value.*

In the complex world of values, *functional value* has a special meaning. In philosophical literature such a value is said to be instrumental because it leads to the attainment of a higher-order value; that is, a consummatory object which is esteemed for its own sake—its value is intrinsic. Value, after all, is a judgment; a judgment, or categorization, someone makes of an object—human or non-human—or of an action as useful or desirable, or conversely, as useless or undesirable. But useful for what and desirable to whom?

Clearly, then, before any meaningful discussion of value can take place, a specific frame of reference has to be established. Thus, when the economist speaks of value as the worth of a commodity measured by the amount of other things for which it can be exchanged, his frame of reference is the market place: a phenomenon of economics.

An artist, on the other hand, thinks of color value as the degree of lightness or darkness in a paint with which to produce a response, through visual effects, either within himself or in others. A composer of music thinks of value as the relative duration of a tone, signified by a note, with which to produce a response through audio effects. Therefore, when artists and composers speculate about values in this manner, their frame of reference is aesthetics: a phenomenon of communication.

But the philosopher, in the realm of speculative thought, when he treats values in general, his frame of reference is axiology—what is good? Of course, philosophers from different schools of philosophic thought will treat values differently. Nevertheless, be he a Realist, Idealist, Neo-Thomist, Experimentalist, or Existentialist, when a philosopher engages in an organized and systematic consideration of values, his frame of reference is the axiological question of what is good: a phenomenon of cognition.[1] Our frame of reference will be

[1] For a discussion of values in school administration see Orin B. Graff and Calvin M. Street, "Developing a Value Framework for Educational Administration," in Roald F. Campbell and Russell T. Gregg (eds.), *Administrative Behavior in Education* (New York: Harper and Row, 1957). Also enlightening for a discussion of values in administration is Alfred de Grazia, "The Science and Values of Administration," *Administrative Science Quarterly*, Vol. 5, December 1960.

the formal organization: a phenomenon of the social division of labor. Valuing, then, is a way of categorizing the meaning of objects in some situational context.

A convenient point of departure for a definition of functional value is to recognize in the structure of the public school system a formal organization. Formal organization is a concept which will be enlarged upon in ensuing chapters and structurally scaled in Chapter 10. However, for now, the following will do as a working definition: A formal organization is a mechanism contrived by man as a means of mobilizing human energies and skills which are to be used by some predetermined procedures for the purpose of attaining a goal that is somehow important to some other system and, ultimately, to the universal welfare of society.

There are many such organizations in existence. Indeed, their large number is a hallmark of modern complex society. They are distinguishable one from another by the paramount goals toward which they are oriented in the division of labor in society. In a general classification of formal organizations, they stand out as four general types: business organizations, mutual-benefit organizations, commonweal organizations, and service organizations.[2]

Formal organizations are products of the division of labor in society. Although this theme is introduced now in connection with a discussion of functional value, its enlargement will be given in Chapters 3, 4, and 10. The theme is brought into the discourse now precisely because formal organizations perform specialized, or differentiated, functions in the division of labor in society. The public school organization is one of them.

American society has devised the public school organization as its instrument for fulfilling the social values of universal public education in accordance with certain norms, or rules, which it deems vital for socializing the young. Functionally, therefore, the public school organization renders a special kind of service to direct clients, pupils who come to be educated, and to the families of pupils. From the larger view of society, goal attainment in public school organizations con-

---

[2] An excellent primer for the study of formal organizations is Peter M. Blau and W. Richard Scott, *Formal Organizations* (San Francisco: Chandler Publishing Co., 1962). The classification of formal organizations which is here given is suggested by the authors of *Formal Organizations*. However, other classifications are possible. Talcott Parsons, for one, thinks of organizations that are oriented to economic production as business organizations, political parties as integrative organizations, organs of government as organizations oriented to political goals, and schools as pattern-maintenance organizations.

tributes to maintaining the integrity of the institutionalized value system which defines the structure of the American social system. This is the *differentiated function* of the public school organization in the modern social division of labor.

But just as technological advance has necessitated a division of labor in society through the specialization of formal organizations, so did it in time necessitate an even finer division of labor *within* organizations in the form of secondary differentiations. In this way, what were initially relatively simple structures evolved into complex organizations. The public school organization serves as an illustration.

It began as a simple common school structure. Then educational technology grew in sophistication as more and more was learned from psychological and physiological science about human development. Consequently, as public school organization responded to the service requirements of its pupil clientele at different stages of maturation, it too became differentiated internally. Structurally, secondary differentiation in public school organization is discernible in such units as the kindergarten, elementary school, middle school, high school, and, where it exists, the junior college.[3]

All in all, the formal organization is a mechanistic entity; that is to say, again, it is a product of man's ingenuity. Goal attainment in such an organization is maximized when tasks which are performed by its members are integrated by a set of rational procedures. The task of devising these integrating procedures is one of the major contributions administrators make to goal attainment in the organization.

Skilled administrators, therefore, anticipate certain immediate consequences from system operations. Because the administrative orientation is rationalistic *par excellence,* administrators assess—say value—these consequences as means toward the attainment of organizational goals. They think of them as *means values.* Administrators will measure a *functional,* or *means,* value by its capacity to contribute to goal attainment.

As is to be expected in such a context, not all consequences of action in the organization elicit the same degree of esteem from administra-

[3] The best comprehensive and analytical treatment of this theme is still Emile Durkheim, *The Division of Labor in Society,* translated by George Simpson (New York: The Free Press of Glencoe, 1964), paperback edition. Its origin, of course, is with Adam Smith's economic treatise. See also George Foster, *Traditional Cultures and the Impact of Technological Change* (New York: Harper and Row, 1962); see also Theodore Brameld, *The Cultural Foundations of Education: An Interdisciplinary Exploration* (New York: Harper and Row, 1957).

tors. Indeed, we shall have occasion to note later that the valuation of means activities in an organization assumes a complex classification. But insofar as they do contribute to goal attainment, functional values may be said to exist as two types: *instrumental* and *expressive*. Both types are important for goal attainment in administrative organizations. But because the public school organization is a special type of service organization, expressive values take on a special meaning there. Their meaning, however, can be more sharply defined with the aid of a larger conceptual framework of organization and administration.

The Usefulness of a Conceptual Framework

Actually one building block of a larger conceptual framework has already been set when the public school system was defined as a formal organization, as a mechanistic system. A formal organization, because of its rational orientation toward a goal, is also an administrative organization. Its mission is to attain some goal or goals. The concept of formal organization, even at a very general level of discussion, has led us to a working definition of functional value. But because our purpose is to map a multidimensional view of the middle school organization, more has to be known about those functional values that are of an expressive character and their specific relevance to goal attainment in both the middle school and the larger public school system. It would be foolhardy in the extreme, therefore, to continue in map construction beyond this point without an adequate conceptual framework to guide the task.

The concept of formal organization will serve, then, as one building block of this conceptual framework. It enables us to abstract a view of educative process as a kind of technology which is applied by a body of personnel who perform administratively assigned tasks. In the instance of the middle school, these tasks are performed—whether in a separate school plant or not—in a setting apart from other units of the public school system.

As far as it goes, the concept of formal organization is helpful indeed as an analytical tool. But is it enough? The concept defines the structure of formal organization as it is put together in accordance with dictates of impersonal rationality; that is, as a machine. Roles are defined for members of the organization, tasks are administratively prescribed, a technology is applied, and in the instance of a service organization such as a school clients somehow receive a benefit from it all. This is as it should be when rationality prevails. But does it always prevail?

The concept of formal organization, to be sure, provides a view of the school organization as a mechanistic system, but it shows very little of people in the organization as *human beings*. What it does show suggests that people in the organization are motivated in their behavior to follow the rationalistic blueprint for system operations out of a desire for material gain. But people do not always behave rationally, however strong the motivation of material gain might be. What, then, of people in the organization who fail to conform to the expected behavior in positions they occupy? Even more to the point: what of pupils in the school organization who refuse educational service from teachers, despite all assurances of eventual material gain? The concept of formal organization alone sheds little light upon such organizational problems that turn on human interactions. Although it does indeed provide a useful view of the school organization as a mechanistic system, it fails to show the same school organization as a *social system:* a human system in which psychological motivation is also important and in which intervening cultural variables have to be reckoned with.

The concept of social system will, therefore, serve as another major building block in our conceptual framework. By viewing the school organization at once as a formal system and as a social system, due account is taken of the *human factor* in the *officially prescribed* interactions of people in the organization. Later, in Chapter 4, another major building block will be added to our conceptual framework: a view of the school organization as an institutional, or cultural, system. At that juncture, the public school organization will be seen in a three-dimensional projection as a formal system, as a social system, and as an institutional system.

The conceptual framework we are constructing will be used to treat analytically a host of behavioral phenomena which have been observed in the American middle school over the years. In certain instances, we will find that one building block in the conceptual framework will be more useful than another for getting a fix on the meaning of a specific phenomenon which is under observation. Deep concentration is required for such analytical observations, because the threads of a complex organization are seldom tied conveniently one with another.

One might be tempted to speculate at this point: why bother with anything so involved? Isn't experience at least as dependable for explaining the intricate mechanism of school organization? Experience, to be sure, is valuable. Observations of the school system by those who occupy positions therein have shed valuable clinical light on its organizational problems. But experience alone is not enough when corrective adjustments require analytical light as well.

It is not enough because one's experience is usually acquired within the limits of a specific position in a system. A bias has to be suspected, therefore, in personal experience because the incumbent of a position tends to perceive a selected rather than a random fraction of all school events. Moreover, a value orientation has been institutionalized in each role within the organization and the occupant of a role is likely to reflect the bias of that orientation.

Experience, on the other hand, when it is set within a viable conceptual scheme assumes dimensions of usefulness which it does not have by itself. A concept enables us to assign symboled meaning to an experience; that is, an abstract term with an assigned meaning. It enables us to arrange items of experience into a more powerful system of knowing their essential meaning. A datum of experience, standing by itself, will not tell us all that we ought to know about its meaning. But when it is set against the background of an appropriate theoretical construct, heretofore hidden meanings begin to emerge. It is in this sense that theory is thought of as metaknowledge.

A conceptual framework to be adequate for our purpose here should have the capacity of performing at least two important services for middle school administration. First, it has to enhance the usefulness of our cognitive map so that some experiences of middle school organization can be related with others, even when at first glance there would seem to be no relationship between them. Observations so related assume a greater significance because they are then classifiable in a continuous sequence which together reveal a pattern in the organization. Second, it has to provide a foundation, more substantive than experience alone, from which middle school administrators can with ease identify discrete variables which differentiate the middle school organization as a formal system, as a social system, and as an institutional system.[4]

----

[4] Valuable references for a discussion of the usefulness of concept and theory in educational administration will be found in Daniel E. Griffiths, *Administrative Theory* (New York: Appleton-Century-Crofts, 1959).

Happily, the scientific study of organizations has assumed the position of a major subfield in American sociology. Beginning with Elton Mayo's investigations of the industrial organization in the late 1920's to the present, literally hundreds of important theoretical and empirical studies of organization have been published.[5] However, the man who is today acknowledged by many as a foremost social theorist in American sociology, and one who has contributed these past several decades more than any other to organization theory, is Talcott Parsons. We shall draw from Parsonian theory many conceptual tools for our analysis of the middle school organization. A further word, therefore, about Parsons is in order.

Parsons did his undergraduate work at Amherst College, where he majored in biology. From there, he made his way to Heidelberg University for his doctorate. Across the Atlantic, he became familiar with the elegance of European sociology and the ideas of Emile Durkheim, Georg Simmel, Vilfredo Pareto, Max Weber, and others.

Parsons was especially taken with the theoretical sweep of Max Weber's work. It was Parsons who, in a very real sense, introduced American intellectuals to the ideas of Max Weber, and of these the theory of bureaucracy—a theory which Chapter 10 will expand upon in the more detailed discussion of the middle school as a formal organization—is perhaps best known.

Parsons made his earliest important contribution to sociological scholarship, after his doctoral dissertation, in 1930 with an English translation from the German of Max Weber's *The Protestant Ethic and the Spirit of Capitalism*. That year marked the beginning of prolific scholarship in Parsons' life. But in all of his professional career, Parsons' central preoccupation has been with general theory building.

Indeed, although Parsons has acknowledged more than once the importance of empirical research, he has engaged in it but modestly. His critics find this a convenient target when they are inclined to take

---

[5] The classic study of an empirical *genre* is still the one which Elton Mayo and his associates conducted in the Hawthorne Plant of the Western Electric Co. A comprehensive report of this research will be found in Fritz J. Roethlisberger and William J. Dickson, *Management and the Worker* (Cambridge, Mass.: Harvard University Press, 1939). It is important to note, however, that the dominance of a human relations orientation, which is central in *Management and the Worker*, has since been subjected to questioning criticism. See, for example, Henry A. Landsberger, *Hawthorne Revisited* (Ithaca, N.Y.: Cornell University, 1958); and Mason Haire (ed.), *Organization Theory in Industrial Practice* (New York: John Wiley and Sons, 1962).

him on. But Parsons insists that general theory building is a legitimate specialized field and, in the division of labor in sociological scholarship, he would just as soon leave empirical research to others.[6] But even his severest critics, in one fashion or another, have acknowledged the value of Parsonian theory.

As a comprehensive theory should, Parsonian theory concerns itself with universals. Accordingly, Parsonian theory has wide-ranging utility in analytical studies of society, formal organizations, or for that matter, any other organized action system of society. Its principal components are the three basic elements of structure in all social systems: society, personality, and culture.[7] The building blocks of Parsons' theory of social systems consist of rigorous conceptualizations which are set down in a number of works, but mostly in one which bears the title of *The Social System*. We shall not even pretend here to plumb the depths of Parsonian theory. However, we shall find certain of Parsons' conceptualizations of inestimable value for mapping the middle school organization.

The Social System View

In the light of Parsonian theory, the public school organization is seen as a social system which is action oriented toward the attainment of goals. It is a system within which "interdependent action processes" take place.[8] Parsons distinguishes theoretically between two types of social systems: a total social system and a partial social system.

Only the society is a total social system. As an organized system of action, it alone "meets all the essential functional prerequisites of long-term persistence from within its own resources." All other organized systems of action Parsons calls *partial social systems*. Formal organizations, as partial social systems, are subject in the social division of labor to institutionalized "terms of exchange" which are governed by what Parsons thinks of as a "disposal and procurement" arrangement with

[6] For an exciting intellectual session with Talcott Parsons and his critics see Max Black (ed.), *The Social Theories of Talcott Parsons* (Englewood Cliffs, N.J.: Prentice-Hall, 1962). Copyright 1961. See especially the critical essay by William Foote Whyte, pp. 250–66, and Parsons' response to his critics, pp. 311–63.

[7] It is significant to note that humanistic scholarship also finds these three frames of reference useful in the study of man and his linkages. See, as an illustration, Philip H. Phenix, *Man and His Becoming* (New Brunswick, N.J.: Rutgers University Press, 1964).

[8] Talcott Parsons, *The Social System* (New York: The Free Press, 1963), p. 201. Copyright 1951. Permission of the Free Press of Glencoe.

other systems.[9] These are the consummatory relations of a given system with the environment external of itself. There are many such partial systems in modern society. The formal organization of the public school is but one of them, the one upon which we shall focus our attention.

Because the constituent units of a social system are people, Parsons thinks of them as *actors* who perform in *definable roles*. The social system assigns a status, or position, to each actor and prescribes, through norms—that is to say, rules of the system—the manner of his interaction, his role, with other actors. Here, then, are two aspects: a *positional aspect* which defines an actor's location in the social system in relation to other actors and a *processual aspect* which defines, through rules of the system, what the actor does with other actors in the context of its functional significance for the social system. These rules are so important for optimum role interaction in an administrative organization that they are actually promulgated for all in the organization to know. Such, of course, is the case in a public school organization.

Principal role players in the public school organization are teachers, pupils, counselors, and administrators. Other actors perform in a variety of supporting roles. These people interact, through expected behavior, in order to attain goals of the public school system. Parsons refers to the interaction of actors which is motivated by rules of the system as *cognitive motivation*. The organization expects actors to be "all business," because it is itself *instrumentally oriented* toward the attainment of some goal. This is the evaluative orientation of the organization to actions of its members.

Parsons points out, however, that although it is all well and good for the organization to be instrumentally oriented in pursuit of a goal, actors in the organization, without whom the goal cannot be attained, have to feel the pursuit is worth the cost to *each* of them as human beings. Moreover, unlike another type of a service organization, say a hospital, the public school organization is a *special type* of service organization. When a person enters the hospital organization voluntarily and assumes the patient's role out of a motivation to get well, to a greater or lesser degree his cooperation—interaction with the

[9] *Ibid.*, p. 19. For a discussion of the "disposal and procurement" concept see *ibid.*, pp. 70–73. An illustrative discussion of the concept *terms of exchange* in the context of a school management problem will be found in Dan C. Lortie, "Change and Exchange: Reducing Resistance to Innovation," *Administrator's Notebook,* Vol. XII, February 1964.

hospital staff—can be taken for granted, precisely because the patient wants to establish a specific relation with the doctor as a means of getting well: the relation is for the patient important for its own sake. Not so, however, in the instance of the pupil in a school organization.

His cooperation, even when he enters the school voluntarily, has to be motivated in the strongest possible way by the organization, because here relations between a pupil and teachers serve as means toward ends beyond themselves. Parsons proposes, "There must be a long-standing relation between a pupil and a succession of teachers, and both the structure of the pupil's personality and his future position in the community depend heavily upon the process of education."[10] In the case of a pupil in school, according to Parsons, "the recipient of the service has to be taken into an important kind of *membership* in the technical organization which provides the service."[11] By *the technical organization,* as Chapter 10 will explain, Parsons means in this instance the classroom level of school organization.

Some think of the pupil as a *product* of the school organization. We find Thomas H. Briggs, for example, asserting that schools are "measured in terms of what they did to their product."[12] In a like vein, a member of a public school board of education reported in the *NEA Journal:* "Our plant . . . will turn out another fine batch of first quality products this spring."[13] But Parsons has now provided us with a foundation for conceptualizing the role of the pupil in school organization as that of a *client-member.*[14]

Of course, we must hasten to note that pupil membership in the school organization is of a *special* kind. Although he is a member of the school organization in one sense, the pupil has no *official capacity* for influencing decisions in the school or for determining the technical conditions under which he shall be educated. Nevertheless, the school cannot deal with the pupil-client in the manner of "total institutions"; that is, when the organization dominates the client completely and

---

10 Parsons, "Some Ingredients of a General Theory," p. 51.
11 *Ibid.,* p. 51.
12 *North Central Association Quarterly,* Vol. XIII, October 1938, p. 168.
13 "Annual Stockholders Report," *NEA Journal,* Vol. 51, May 1962, p. 68.
14 There are other service organizations whose clients are also members of the organization. Group Health Plan of St. Paul, Minnesota, by way of an illustration, is a mutual-benefit service organization which renders medical services to a large body of clients. However, one segment of its clientele has, by special arrangement, voting rights. This segment of its clientele elects the board of directors who, in turn, determines policy—except for actual medical activities—for governance of the organization.

prescribes every aspect of his behavior—as for example in a mental hospital or a prison.[15] At the same time, a pupil will often speak of *my school,* whereas a patient seldom speaks of *my hospital* or the welfare client of *my welfare agency.*[16]

Clearly, when a pupil speaks of *my school* he reflects a special kind of emotional, or psychological, identification with the organization which provides him with a service. It has to be so. For the motivation of pupils to cooperate—to interact willingly with other actors in the system—is crucial for success in the educational enterprise. Parsons notes:[17]

> Teaching cannot be effective if the pupil is simply a "customer" to whom the "commodity" of education is "turned over" without any further relation to its purveyor than is required for settlement of the terms of transfer—as in the case of a typical commercial transaction.

Parsons posits this view not as a casual observation but rather as a conceptual means of setting the school organization apart from other types of service organizations. He, therefore, adds: "Teaching presupposes pupils in the school, and therefore settlement of terms on which pupils go to school is a prerequisite for the teaching process."[18] A regard in the relational network of school organization for the *personal price* a youth pays for assuming the pupil role is one of the terms of settlement "on which pupils go to school."

And what precisely is the personal price, say, an early adolescent is asked to pay for the service of the public school organization? He must forego certain immediate gratifications! At this age, he wants to explore constantly. He has become very inquisitive about the world of adults. Many mistake him as *nosey* because of this. At times, he wants to be hypermobile, and at other times he just wants to loaf. Rapid physical growth is sapping his energy. Even more important for him, he wants to be with his buddies; they mean so much for his

---

[15] The sociological concept of "total institution" is the invention of Erving Goffman. For an explication of the concept see Erving Goffman, "The Characteristics of Total Institutions," *Symposium on Preventive and Social Psychiatry* (Washington, D.C.: Walter Reed Institute of Research, 1957).

[16] For an analytical discussion of the pupil's role in the school organization see Richard O. Carlson, "Environmental Constraints and Organizational Consequences: The Public School and Its Clients," in Daniel E. Griffiths (ed.), *Behavioral Science and Educational Administration,* The Sixty-third Yearbook of the National Society for the Study of Education, Part II (Chicago: The University of Chicago Press, 1964), Chapter 12.

[17] Parsons, "Some Ingredients of a General Theory," p. 51.

[18] *Ibid.,* pp. 50–51.

early adolescent existence. They provide comfort and understanding, something that is hard to get from adults at this age. They are the staff of his security at this point of growing up. In interactions with them, they legitimize his otherwise curious behavior at this developmental stage. All of these gratifications, and others, he has to postpone for about six hours each day during the three years of early adolescence.

Although the singular point of reference in the foregoing has been to the pupil, we should be aware that, in Parsons' theoretical construct, the organization demands of *all actors* an appropriate response to its instrumental orientation and, therefore, cognitive motivation. As Parsons has put it, the organization "introduces an element of discipline, the renunciation of certain immediately potential gratifications, including that to be derived from passively 'letting things slide' and awaiting the outcome."[19]   Parsons goes on to point out, however, that although the instrumental orientation of the organization can thus compel an actor's *rational* entry into a role, it does not mean necessarily that he is altogether in the role. He has to enter it *psychologically* as well in order to be completely in the role. Here, following Parsons, is a gratification-discipline dilemma.

Parsons registers this point because he conceives of every actor in the organization as having what he calls a "need-disposition system." An actor's willingness to interact with other actors is affected, therefore, by the manner in which the organization attends to the need-disposition system of an actor.

Components of the need-disposition system, according to Parsons, are of two primary aspects: an *orientational aspect* and a *gratificational aspect*. The orientational aspect is *rational and cultural* in character. It is the mind-set which tells an actor the organization has a purpose and that, by some contractual arrangement, he is expected to help attain that purpose. But the gratificational aspect is *psychological* in character. Despite a rational commitment to a role, it drives an actor to seek personal gratifications even as he is performing in the role. He comes into the organization as a human being, and he will retain his human condition regardless of any organizational constraints. And, Parsons notes, the organization is well served when it provides these gratifications.

He holds that the organization has to motivate an actor both orienta-

19 Parsons, *The Social System,* p. 48.

tionally and psychologically. He refers to such psychological motivation as "cathectic motivation." Effective role interaction, in short, requires a blending of rational and psychological motivation in the actor.

He holds to the latter view out of an awareness that "each individual actor is subject to the exigencies of interaction in a social system."[20] Exigencies produce problems! Problems spell potential conflict in the interaction of actors. Unless means are found for reducing such potential conflict to a minimum, Parsons hypothesizes, actors will experience "difficulty in attaining conformative motivation" in their respective roles.[21]

Members of the organization simply will not conform to organizational expectations. This, of course, would constitute deviant behavior and cause the organization, as a mechanistic system, grave functional problems. In the public school organization, especially, because it exists to render a direct service to pupils, a lack of conformative motivation in pupils can be socially and administratively disastrous. Reflect, for example, what a high truancy rate can mean for a school system.

Parsons suggests that the organization can reduce potential conflict, and, therefore, facilitate role interaction, by taking into official account both the orientational and gratificational aspects of each actor's need-disposition system. It is at this point that management is called upon to make another one of its major contributions to goal attainment in the organization: to facilitate role interaction as a means of enhancing the input of efficiency to the tasks that are performed in the organization; in a word, effective integration.

But the development of patterns for qualitative role interaction demands the most of administrative skill. The impersonal and rationalistic *instrumental orientation* of the organization has to be humanized by what Parsons calls an *expressive orientation:* an orientation which focuses upon members of the organization not alone as a task force, but also as a human group. "Here," according to Parsons, "the primary orientation is not to the attainment of a goal anticipated for the future, but the organization of the 'flow' of gratifications. . . ."[22]

In administrative terms this suggests that if the technical tasks

---

20 *Ibid.,* p. 16.
21 *Ibid.,* p. 35. For an illuminating illustration of the usefulness of this concept as an analytical tool see Max G. Abbott, "Intervening Variables in Organizational Behavior," *Educational Administration Quarterly,* Vol. I, Winter 1965.
22 Parsons, *The Social System,* p. 49.

through which an organization attains its goal is to be performed with human efficiency, as measured by the consumption of an organization's resources, then the "flow of gratifications" cannot be left to chance. These gratifications have to come into existence as direct consequences of administrative strategies to introduce *expressive values*—or, if we will, gratifying *psychological values*—into the organization's climate. Such expressive values are esteemed by administrators because they facilitate an actor's identification with an official role of the organization. They have immediate *utility* for technical tasks and, therefore, also for ultimate goal attainment. In the context of an administrative organization, such values, no matter how they might be judged in another situational context, are *functional values*.

Following Parsons' theoretical frame of reference, we can now think of instrumental orientation, or cognitive motivation, as the organizational posture which generates instrumental values: values that have *primary* relevance for *technical procedures* in the organization. Expressive orientation, or cathectic motivation, on the other hand, we can think of as the organizational posture which generates expressive values: values that have *primary* relevance for *human efficiency* in the organization.

Chester I. Barnard, a onetime President of the New Jersey Bell Telephone Company, and a keen empirical observer of behavior in the administrative organization, anticipated Talcott Parsons' theoretical weighting of instrumental and expressive orientation with the conclusion: Instrumental orientation makes the organization *effective,* expressive orientation makes it *efficient.* Both of these, according to Barnard, are basic components of "an equilibrium between the system and the total situation external to it."[23] To paraphrase Barnard: An organization is "gung ho" when an optimum balance of instrumental and expressive values is effected in the organizational climate.

Therefore, regardless of whether the value of an action in the organization is instrumental or expressive in character, it must also have ultimate value for goal attainment. For when the value of an organizational action is nongoal-related, it likely will be assessed as sterile of functional value. Action in a social system is according to Parsons:[24]

---

[23] Barnard has put down his empirical observations of the formal organization in a book which has become a "must" on all reading lists for those who are preparing for careers in administration. See Chester I. Barnard, *The Functions of the Executive* (Cambridge, Mass.: Harvard University Press, 1947), p. 83.

[24] Talcott Parsons, *Essays in Sociological Theory* (New York: The Free Press, 1963), p. 386. Hereafter cited as *Essays.* Copyright 1954. Permission of the Free Press of Glencoe.

. . . oriented to the attainment of goals, and hence to involve selective processes relative to goals. Seen in their relations to goals, then, all the components of systems of action and of the situations in which action takes place, are subject to the process of evaluation, as desirable or un-desirable, as useful or useless, as gratifying or noxious.

"Functions," as defined by Merton, "are those observed consequences which stem from actions in a goal-oriented organization as "Manifest and Latent Functions."

Functions, as defined by Merton, "are those observed consequences which make for the adaptation or adjustment of a given system; and *dysfunctions,* those observed consequences which lessen the adaptation or adjustment of the system." Then he goes on to make an important conceptual distinction between two types of functions: *manifest functions* and *latent functions.* These he defines as follows:[25]

> *Manifest functions* are those objective consequences contributing to the adjustment or adaptation of the system which are intended and recognized by participants in the system;
> *Latent functions,* correlatively, being those which are neither in-tended nor recognized.

Merton's conceptualization also takes cognizance of *nonfunctional* consequences and of *functional alternatives;* that is, *functional equivalents* or *substitutes.* However, by far, the greater usefulness of Merton's concept for the administrator in action is as conceptual anchorage at periods when substantive changes in the structure and process of the organization become imperative.

Closing the Circle

There is no gainsaying that the valuation of means activities in a middle school organization can be difficult. Nonetheless, if any variable is capable of discriminating between sophistication and artless simplicity in middle school management, it is the skill of effecting, and holding fast to, what for the middle school is a *functionally optimum* balance of instrumental and expressive values in its environment. Warrant for such a claim must, in functional terms, be sought in what Chester I. Barnard has called the "organization purpose," that is to say, the paramount goal of the American middle school.

[25] A full treatment of the concept will be found in Robert K. Merton, *Social Theory and Social Structure* (New York: The Free Press, 1959), Part I, "Manifest and Latent Functions," p. 51. Copyright 1957. Permission of the Free Press of Glencoe.

By putting the matter in this way, we come full circle in the discussion of functional value. It will be recalled that the discussion began with an inference of a higher-level value in the goal of an organization. When the organization was viewed as a machine, all means activities which contribute to technical effectiveness were said to be of instrumental value. However, when the same organization was viewed as a social system, all means activities which contribute to human efficiency were said to be of expressive value. As a guiding principle of administration, such a view of functional values may be taken as having universal application.

But at the level of specificity in middle school management, and when the focus is on the pupil, an especially difficult problem confronts the middle school principal at this juncture. What criterion is there for middle school administrators by which to ascertain when a functional balance of instrumental and expressive value has been attained in the school environment?

Of course, when the goal of an organization is itself specifically expressive in character—as, say, in a country club—then administration which is oriented toward the production of gratifications for the club's members and which are not proscribed by society, is, in Merton's terms, functional for that organization. But the primacy of orientation in public school organization is toward achievement and performance, outputs of universal application. Quite apart then from all other actors in a middle school for whom personal gratifications have to be provided, as in all administrative organizations, at what point is a functional balance attained of instrumental and expressive values for the education of early adolescents? Here we must turn to the paramount goal of middle school organization.

3

THE PARAMOUNT
MIDDLE SCHOOL GOAL

Administrative guidelines for determining what is functional or dysfunctional for goal attainment in any organization have to originate with insight into the institutional purpose society has set for the organization. Cultural clues to institutional purpose are, on the other hand, deeply imbedded in the goal structure of an organization. Therefore, the all-important component of an organization is its goal structure.

The postulate applies to the superordinate system as well as to any of its functionally differentiated suborganizations. For the rational scheme which gives an organization its machinelike attribute mandates that functions of an organization must be determined by the character of its goals. Organizations, especially complex organizations, pursue more than one goal, but one goal is dominant; its *paramount goal*. Powerful rationalistic leverage is exerted, therefore, by the goal structure upon the internal ordering of formal organization. However, this is not all. Even greater power resides in the goal structure of an organization when it is viewed from the larger perspective of society.

For the higher-level social values that repose in the goal structure of an organization link the organization with the institutional network of society. Through such a link, the organization, now no longer a machine alone, is also linked with the *right,* or *legitimation,* to draw from society's resources the required wherewithal for continued existence. Chapter 4 to follow, where the middle school organization is projected as an institutional system, will show that only goals of an organization are capable of being endowed by society with such deep valuation.

Accordingly, and in the context of the foregoing postulate, the following claim may be made for the paramount goal of middle school organization. *The higher-level social value of a middle schools' paramount goal sustains its legitimation as a differentiated organizational unit of the superordinate public school system and, therefore, all occupational roles, resources, and functions which are required to attain that goal are societally warranted.* What follows will lead to a definition of this goal. But first, how was its paramount goal defined at the inception of the American middle school?

The functional value of pupil retention, a thematic thread which provided the transition from Chapter 1 to the discussion in Chapter 2, is useful again at this juncture as thematic linkage. For in point of fact, pupil retention was only *one* among *a larger number* of functional values that schoolmen of the early twentieth century saw in the middle school organization. Verification of this is to be found in any number of early surveys that have been made of so-called "functions of the junior high school." One such survey was conducted, about 1920, by Briggs, a man who represented the best in American pedagogical scholarship for nearly all of the first half of the twentieth century. A survey of sixty-eight established leaders in American education of that period led Briggs to list twenty-five purpose definitions of the American middle school which had come from his respondents.

Briggs' classification included "Provision for Individual Differences," "Departmental Teaching," "Differentiated Curricula," "Combination of Grades 7, 8, 9," and, with still others, "Retention in School."[1] These surveys, moreover, show that respondents tended to confuse goal and function in the middle school organization, a confusion which persisted unchecked in American education until the 1940's.

[1] Thomas H. Briggs, *The Junior High School* (Boston: Houghton Mifflin Company, 1920), p. 49. For still another such classification see Leonard V. Koos, *The Junior High School* (Boston: Ginn and Co., 1927), pp. 17–18.

The matter was righted some in 1940 by William T. Gruhn. He had left the principalship of Simmons Junior High School in Aberdeen, South Dakota, to write a doctor's thesis on the American middle school at the University of North Carolina. In the years that followed, Gruhn was destined to carve for himself an illustrious career in middle school scholarship. A major burden of Gruhn's thesis was to delineate conceptually between the cultural mission of the American middle school and basic functions in its organization which are required to fulfill the mission.[2]

It would seem in retrospect that the utility of pupil retention held a high-order rank among functional values of the early middle school and was mistaken, therefore, by many as its goal, until compulsory school-attendance laws were raised to sixteen years of age and endowed with teeth. After that, it was the high school unit which was expected to increase the holding power of a public school system, mostly because the bulk of sixteen-year-olds were there. Even more significant, however, is the historical fact, as the discussion in Chapter 9 will disclose, that many of those functions which have been mistaken at one time or another as the paramount goal of the middle school—including that of pupil retention—were being performed in the public school organization *before* the middle school came into existence.

The middle school unit was preceded in American public school organization by the six-year high school unit. It was, like the middle school, a consequence of adaptation in the public school system. But unlike the middle school unit, the six-year high school did not introduce any *substantive* innovation in educational technology, only a rearrangement of it. Organizational boundaries of the traditional four-year high school were merely extended downward to include the seventh and eighth grades. Educational technology, however, was left much the same as it had been before the organizational adaptation.

In the six-year high school organization, grades 7, 8, 9 were combined in one unit, ninth-grade subjects were taught by designated departments, and a higher rate of pupil retention was obtained. Nevertheless, public school administrators were soon disenchanted with the organizational value of the six-year high school.

---

[2] William T. Gruhn, "An Investigation of the Relative Frequency of Curriculum and Related Practices Contributing to the Realization of the Basic Functions of the Junior High School." Unpublished Ph.D. dissertation, University of North Carolina, Chapel Hill, 1940. Hereafter cited as "Doctor's Thesis."

A Clue to the Disenchantment

A strong clue to the cause of administrative disenchantment with the six-year high school organization was given by Superintendent W. A. Greeson of Grand Rapids, Michigan. He addressed the 1909 annual meeting of the North Central Association of Colleges and Secondary Schools. In the address, to which he gave the title of "The Six and Six Plan of Organizing Public Schools," he pointed to a major dysfunction in the six-year high school organization.

He said in part:[3]

> Children normally enter the first grade at the close of the sixth year of their existence, and, if promoted regularly, reach the seventh grade at the close of their twelfth year. Many, for one reason or another, have been delayed and are thirteen and fourteen years old; some even older. About this time of life a radical change occurs in the physical, mental and moral nature of a child. The boys are becoming men; the girls are becoming women; and a flood of new impulses, new ideas, new emotions are crowding up in them, making it a very critical and important period of their lives. In the organization of our schools, however, we do not take this into account. Boys and girls of this age are put into one room with one teacher, exactly as the method has been in previous years, and no attempt is made to broaden the curriculum and appeal to the new capabilities and abilities of pupils of this age. Boys of this age naturally crave for organization among themselves. They ought to have their debating clubs, their societies, their athletic games and contests, their baseball teams, their football teams. Competitive games should be indulged in almost without limit. But these things are impossible with the present organization. . . .
>
> The seventh, eighth and ninth grades should be placed in schools separated from the primary grades.

More than lay bare a major dysfunction in the six-year high school, Greeson's remarks hinted strongly at the special cultural purpose of the new educational unit he was proposing for public school organization. His chief point was, clearly, an affective reference to the early adolescent. His indictment of the six-year high school turned on the point that pupils of early adolescent age, to use Parsons' language, had "difficulty in attaining conformative motivation" in the six-year high school organization. The cause of it, in Greeson's judgment, was the dominant universalistic orientation of the school. Educational tech-

[3] *Proceedings,* NCA, 1909, pp. 86, 88.

nology in the unit, the program, was not geared to the "radical change" in pupils at the onset of adolescence. Greeson's words were these: "no attempt is made to broaden the curriculum and appeal to the new capabilities and abilities of pupils of this age."

Had Greeson used Parsonian concepts in 1909, he might have stated the problem as follows:

"The public school is an instrument of socialization. Its cultural mission is to develop in youth commitments to the broad values of society and endow them with capacities which are essential prerequisites of their future role-performance. But at the time when youths reach early adolescence, their motivation to be so developed is difficult to attain in the six-year high school unit. The public school organization, at this point of rendering service, encounters a lack of cooperation from these direct recipients of its service. The highly instrumental environment of the six-year high school unit is too much for early adolescents. It neglects the gratificational aspect of their need-disposition system. Hence, problems which normally stem from official expectations of performance in the pupil role are intensified for them. The settlement of terms under which these pupils are educated will have to be modified."[4]

Here precisely was the rub in Greeson's indictment. Because the early adolescent's unique gratificational orientation was, in fact, at the heart of Greeson's argument, he confronted public school administrators of his day with a difficult functional dilemma.

The six-year high school organization, because it was predominantly universalistic in orientation to pupil achievement and performance, had to have a school climate of affective neutrality. On the other hand, if Greeson's indictment of the unit was valid, it followed that the "radical change . . . in the physical, social, mental and moral nature" of the early adolescent pupil necessitated a substantial affective element of a certain kind in the school environment. But such a condition in the environment of the six-year high school would clash with its universalistic-achievement orientation.

Greeson, therefore, proposed to resolve the dilemma through a new unit in the public school organization—between the elementary and

[4] With due apologies to Talcott Parsons, this might-have-been language of Superintendent Greeson follows language used by Parsons to explain why a special kind of motivation has to be generated in a school organization in order to induce cooperation in the recipients of educational services. See Parsons, "Some Ingredients of a General Theory," pp. 50–52.

high school—in which a special kind of educational program could be *institutionalized;* a program whose diffuseness and affectivity would be normative in the system. Developmental imperatives of the early adolescent, and not immediate scholastic achievement, would be the dominant focus of the unit. Such a unit would functionally accommodate the expressive balancing which was needed to stimulate appropriate *role motivation* in early adolescent pupils. His administrative rationale for proposing the new unit was: "But these things are impossible with the present organization."

Two years following his 1909 North Central address, Greeson did establish such a middle school unit in the public school system of Grand Rapids, Michigan, a year after Bunker opened what some believe to have been the first modern middle schools in the United States. And when Bunker set down his own administrative rationale for recommending the middle school to the Berkeley Board of Education, he wrote:[5]

> While the advent of adolescence brings no greater break than does the change of night into day, yet as night differs from day, imperceptible though the transition from one to the other may be, so the characteristics of the child differ from those of the youth. The school system, in its organic form, and in the articulation of its parts, completely ignores the significant physiological and psychical changes which are ushered in with the advent of adolescence.

These early middle schools were organizational expressions of a *substantive innovation* in educational technology. It was an innovation which necessitated a new type of specialization in the public school organization. The American middle school was established as a *special unit* of public school organization for the education of early adolescents in a protective psychological environment which neither the elementary school nor the high school could provide.

Moreover, the historical evidence is patently clear that the protective intervention of the first American middle schools turned on the human condition at early adolescence. Chapters 12 and 13 will define the conditions in American culture which induced the public school organization to establish in 1910 a new category in its pupil membership. Suffice it to say at this point that, since 1910, the pedagogical validity of the middle school's orientation to early adolescent education

5 Bunker, *Reorganization of the Public School System*, p. 102.

has been reaffirmed many times.   Ellwood P. Cubberley, who held a long tenure at Stanford University as Professor and Dean of the School of Education, reminded public school administrators in 1924 that educative process in the middle school ". . . calls for an understanding of the biological and psychological foundations upon which the modern conception of the school is based."[6]

Almost ten years later, James M. Glass, who had been Principal in 1915 of the first middle school in Rochester, New York, and who subsequently went on to the Pennsylvania State Department of Public Instruction as Director of Junior High Schools, echoed Cubberley when he wrote in 1933: "The philosophy [orientation] of the junior high school movement will be sound in proportion as it is founded upon the psychology of early adolescents."[7]

More recently, Margaret Mead, a cultural anthropologist, reminded Americans in 1963: "The junior high school was set up to protect young adolescents, to provide for their transition, to give them things the elementary school couldn't do in a time when they are too young for the senior high school."[8]

A Warranty of Validity from the Profession

Of all the warranties of validity that had been accorded the differentiated function of the American middle school during its earlier period, none was more special than the one in 1924 from the North Central Association of Colleges and Secondary Schools.   Even before 1924, there had been a number of supportive expressions from the Association for the institutional purpose of the middle school.   These were, in the main, by indirection.   But in 1924, the Association took an overt step to secure the integrity of the middle school's cultural value.   The Association thereby stamped its own seal of endorsement upon middle school legitimation.

Of course, North Central could act only for the school systems of

[6] Ellwood P. Cubberley, "Editor's Introduction," in L. A. Pechstein and A. Laura Mc-Gregor, *Psychology of the Junior High School Pupil* (Boston: Houghton Mifflin Company, 1924), p. viii.

[7] J. M. Glass, "Tested and Accepted Philosophy of the Junior High School Movement," *Junior-Senior High School Clearing House*, Vol. 7, February 1933, p. 334.

[8] Margaret Mead, "The Early Adolescent in Today's American Culture and Implications for Education," *Junior High School Newsletter*, Indiana State College, Terre Haute, Indiana, Vol. I, February 1963, p. 6.   Hereafter cited as, "The Early Adolescent in Today's American Culture."

its region. But such an explicit endorsement from the third oldest voluntary accrediting association in the nation constituted a very special warranty in the larger context of organized professional education.

An earlier reference has been made already to an *ad hoc* committee which was established in 1914 by North Central to investigate the extensiveness of the middle school movement in its area. Then in 1919, on the occasion when the Association undertook a census of secondary schools in its member states, it is altogether significant that three definitive administrative criteria for secondary school units were established for conducting the census. The middle school was one of them. These were as follows:[9]

(a) A Six Year High School is a school in which the entire work above the sixth grade is unsegregated in buildings and is organized and administered by a single staff of officers and teachers.

(b) A Senior High is a school in which the 10th, 11th, and 12th grades are segregated in a building (or portion of a building) by themselves, and are taught by a staff distinct from that which teaches in the grades below.

(c) A Junior High School is a school in which the seventh, eighth and ninth grades are segregated in a building (or portion of a building) by themselves, possess an organization of their own that is distinct from the grades above and the grades below and are taught by a separate corps of teachers.

Unlike the other regional voluntary accrediting associations, North Central had by the early 1920's a permanent Committee on Junior High Schools which, among other things, was exerting a great effort to free the middle school curriculum from high school and college influences. Chapter 12 will explore why this matter should then have been of deep concern in North Central school circles.

The following segment from the 1924 report of North Central's Junior High School Committee is for the time being indicative of the attention this matter received:[10]

In reviewing the progress of the junior high school movement since the last meeting of the Association we find two items of considerable significance. In the first place within the year the number of school systems which have adopted the 6-3-3 plan of organization in North Central territory has increased from 138 to 311. The other significant event is

[9] *Proceedings*, NCA, 1919.
[10] *Ibid.*, 1924, pp. 35–36.

the adoption by the University of Nebraska of a plan whereby colleges and universities were requested to revise their entrance requirements in such a way as to permit students to enter with twelve units of work accomplished in the 10th, 11th, and 12th years of the secondary school. This is the second institution to make this provision. The University of Michigan had adopted this plan of admission more than a year ago. The significance of the action of these two large institutions lies in the fact that the ninth grade is made just as free from college requirements as the grades of the elementary schools are free. In the opinion of this committee it is highly important that the other institutions in North Central territory be urged to take action similar to that already taken by the University of Michigan and by the University of Nebraska. The Committee is firmly convinced that the ninth grade will continue to have its purposes and its methods set by college entrance requirements unless these requirements can be based upon the work of the 10th, 11th, and 12th grades only.

North Central's early interest in the middle school was peaked by an action in 1924 which gave the unit an official status in the Association's affairs. The Association adopted in that year an *official definition* for a "standard junior high school." Through this action, North Central used its legitimate associational authority to pattern prescriptively the structure of a middle school in its member public school systems. By so doing, it institutionalized in its sphere of influence the larger social value of early adolescent education. On the other hand, the Association refrained deliberately from establishing a *rigid standardization* in fear of inhibiting the nascent middle school movement.[11] It was for this reason that North Central established a special category of "recognition" for a "standard junior high school" instead of resorting to its conventional "accreditation."

The following segment from North Central's definition of a "standard junior high school" is a part of the normative framework which the 1924 action set for the structure of middle school organization:[12]

A standard junior high school is a unit of our public school system consisting of grades 7, 8, and 9, organized and administered as a separate unit of the school system, having its own administrative head and corps of teachers and characterized by flexible promotion, provisions for exploration and review of subject matter in the early semesters of

11 See the report of Thomas W. Gosling for the Junior High School Committee of the Commission on Secondary Schools in *ibid.*, 1925, pp. 68–69.
12 *Ibid.*, 1924, p. 27.

the course, and limited choice of elective subjects during the later semester of the course.

(a) *Explanation:* This standard in no wise means that grades 7 and 8 should not be organized on a junior high basis . . . ; nor, that the six year school should not be organized where administrative convenience or necessity demands it. But such schools would not be regarded as standard.

Great esteem was shown by North Central in such actions for the differentiated function of a middle school in the process of socialization. But there was also a latent meaning in the Association's deliberate reluctance to exercise its most powerful instrument of sanction—accreditation—in the middle school.

Scientific knowledge of psychological consequences which stem from the onset of adolescence was relatively recent at that time. Further innovations might be required in the middle school as more became known about early adolescence. By establishing "recognition" instead of "accreditation" as the standard of professional acceptance for the middle school, North Central meant to give the unit an official status within the public school systems of its jurisdiction without "freezing" its potential for further experimentation with curriculum and organization.[13] Altogether, latent in North Central's actions of the early 1920's was an expectation that the middle school will continue to innovate its educative process in a parallel course with the growing scientific knowledge of early adolescent development.

But hidden in North Central's action of 1924 was also a *latent dysfunction* for its middle schools. Chapters 11 and 12 will elaborate in greater detail why it was that by endowing its legitimation of the middle school with a lesser power than that which "accreditation" conveys, North Central middle schools could no more resist external pressures, already at large by the 1920's, to divert the original goal of the American middle school than could those of other regions.

The Middle School Goal Today

Useful as it has been to define the historical goal of the American middle school, there is no telling with confidence what the middle school's goal is in the modern period. Organizations, after all, have

---

[13] See a reference to this very point by J. B. Edmonson on behalf of North Central's Junior High School Committee in *ibid.*, 1923, p. 55.

been known to modify their goals and even to pursue new goals once original goals have been attained. How, then, can the paramount goal of an organization be defined at any point in time? Earlier references to the division of labor in society and to Parsons' theory of social systems will again be useful in coming to grips with this problem.

In the view of social theorists such as Weber, Durkheim, and Parsons, modern society is seen as a complex division of labor in the production of needed goods and services. When society was small, and simple technological processes sufficed for the production of needed goods and services, then so was the pattern in the social division of labor relatively simple. Individuals, or sometimes family groups, cultivated discretely differentiated production processes and exchanged, either through barter or money, products of their labor. But as society grew larger, and more sophisticated technologies were required to satisfy the growing demand for goods and services, new modes of organization for producing these had to be invented.

It was precisely this social imperative for new modes of organization in production that has made the machinelike apparatus of formal organization so attractive for modern society. Formal organizations perform the differentiated functions in the division of labor which formerly were performed by individuals or family groups and, because such organizations do have attributes of the machine, they can be made to perform with great material economy and human efficiency. It is in this context that both Barnard and Parsons think of formal organizations as subsystems of society.

Each organization exists to perform a differentiated function in the social division of labor. It is this *differentiated function* which, from the larger societal view, can be said to be an organization's *paramount goal.*

According to such a functionalist view of society, as each system of organization attains its goal, it produces an *output* which, if it has *input* value for some other system, enables the organization to engage in a process which Parsons conceptualizes as "disposal and procurement." The process of disposal and procurement is itself determined by the *terms of exchange* between systems. Depending upon the type of organizations that are involved in such exchange, the means of disposal and procurement—institutionalized symbolic media which organized systems employ in obtaining control of those objects which are required for their respective goal interests; that is, money, power, influence, commitment to some belief system—may be economic in character, political, psychological, or a combination of these. However, the right to engage in disposal and procurement is for the organization not an absolute.

Society grants this right—or legitimation—to an organization whose output is of social value. The social value of an organization's output is measured primarily by its value as input for some other system of organization or as input to the general welfare of society. Very often, therefore, the index of an organization's success in disposal and procurement is a powerful clue to the character of a society's value system. But whatever the character of a society's value system may be, the network of relations in the social division of labor, according to Durkheim and other functionalists, is a major source of solidarity for the society.

Hence, the following postulate is now proposed in accordance with functional theory: *the differentiated function of an organization in the social division of labor is, from the point of view of society, its specified goal.* At this general level of discussion, it may then be said by way of illustration that the paramount goal of a hospital organization is to make people well, that of a factory organization is to produce some product, and so forth. But for a definition of the American middle school's paramount goal more is required from functional theory; that is, greater specificity.

The need for greater specificity shifts our focus to a still higher order of specialization in modern society: *secondary differentiation* in the division of labor within organizations. The social imperatives for specialization which precipitated the complex pattern in the division of labor through a network of formal organizations have produced, in microcosm, a like effect within organizations. Each organization attains its goal by means of a discrete technology which it has developed for this purpose. Hospital, factory, and school: each employ a specialized technology.

A singular characteristic of a modern society, however, is its dynamism. Its proclivity to change seems to accelerate with the years. But substantive changes in a society tend to proliferate the demand for those goods and services which are required for a stable existence. Society, therefore, depends upon its network of formal organizations to adapt to the changing external environment and proliferate outputs accordingly.

An organization can respond effectively to this expectation of society by enlarging its goal structure. The enlargement of its goal structure will, to be sure, confront an organization with a new set of difficult problems. But, as the discussion in Chapter 4 will elaborate, there is a substantial payoff for the organization which commits itself to responses of this kind. Society esteems the value of such an organization not alone as a machine, but also as an institutional apparatus which helps it survive impacts of change.

Still, an organization, no matter how else it is viewed, is a rationalistic mechanism. Corresponding rational adjustments have to be made, therefore, within the organization whenever its goal structure is enlarged to accommodate a subgoal. Adjustments of this character have forced sophistication upon the structure and process of organizations. These are adaptive rationalizations which have transformed the simple organizations of simple society into the complex, multipurpose, multiunit organizations of modern society. The American public school organization is a case in point.

The American public school organization has turned complex along two principal dimensions in its division of labor. One dimension stands for the process of education—the technology of the organization—and it subsumes teachers performing the technical tasks of education. A teacher in the early period of the public school taught all subjects. The role of teacher was general in the public school of that day, although the role of teacher in the division of labor in society had become discrete. A teacher in a modern public school, on the other hand, is not just *a teacher*. The once diffuse role of teacher has turned discrete through specialization: one speaks now of a mathematics teacher, English teacher, science teacher, industrial arts teacher, and so forth. Here, then, is a secondary differentiation within the public school organization in the form of subspecialists in the relational network of teachers.

A rationalization in kind has also occurred along the second dimension. This dimension stands for the pupils to whom the process of education is applied and it subsumes the known attributes of pupils. Unlike the object to which a technology is applied in the industrial organization, the human attributes of pupils necessitate special conditions under which the process of education is applied to them.

Chapter 2 has already noted Parsons' sharp magnification of this point. "Teaching," Parsons holds, "presupposes pupils in the school, and therefore settlement of terms on which pupils go to school is a prerequisite for the teaching process." By "settlement of terms" Parsons means to suggest that special administrative arrangements are required in the school organization for effective interaction between pupils and teachers who apply the process of education.

A settlement of terms throws light on the differentiations that have occurred along the dimension of pupils in the school. Pupils of a wide range in age came to learn in a public school of the early period. This was one of the conditions in the settlement of terms on which pupils went to school at that time. But this condition no longer exists in the settlement of terms of the modern era.

Pupils now follow a patterned progression of interaction with teachers who apply the process of education to discrete categories of pupils. This patterned progression evolved from developing sophistication in behavioral sciences which illuminate the complexities in the act of learning at different stages of human development. As the finer nuances of early human development became known, conditions in the "settlement of terms on which pupils go to school" had to be modified.

The settlement of terms in the modern era also made necessary unit differention in the public school. Consequently, there are today not only mathematics teachers, English teachers, science teachers, but also a kindergarten, elementary school—upper and lower—middle school and high school, each performing a differentiated function.

But developing rationalization in the form of secondary differentiation along either of these two dimensions did not occur in isolation. Driving cultural influences which constellated along each of these dimensions interacted reciprocally in the environment of a public school. Imperatives which stemmed from this interaction transformed the one-time simple structure of the public school organization into the complex, multiunit system of today.

Obviously, such an involved transformation in structure and process could not have occurred spontaneously. The guiding rationality of appropriate administrative decisions was required to initiate structural changes, and administrative innovation was required to implement them. From these innovations have sprung the subsystems of the modern-day public school organization. One of these subsystems is the middle school. It came into existence about 1910 when, by an administrative decision, early adolescent pupils were designated as a discrete category in the public school's client system. As Chapter 9 will show, the decision to create a middle school unit was linked directly to developing sophistication in American psychological science.

It is altogether important to mark at this juncture that an administrative decision to construct a subsystem in any organization cannot be a product of caprice. For an administrative decision of this magnitude diverts the scarce resources of an organization to a new use. The inherent rationality of an organization will not tolerate capriciousness of this order. Therefore, just as the organization itself performs some differentiated function in the division of labor *in society,* so does each of its subsystems perform some differentiated function in the division of labor *within the organization.* The differentiated function which is assigned to a subsystem by the superordinate organization may be said to be that subsystem's *paramount goal.*

Parsons expresses the foregoing in the following language:[14]

> What from the point of view of the organization in question is its specified goal is, from the point of view of the larger system of which it is a differentiated part or subsystem, a specialized or differentiated function.

Two deductive generalizations can now be formulated, in terms of the social division of labor, about the paramount goal of the American middle school. The goal of the middle school, when it is attained, must implement *some* differentiated educational function in the larger public school system. More, only the social value of this differentiated function can sustain the legitimation of the middle school as an organizational unit of the public school system.

Chapter 13, in which the human condition at early adolescence is treated in the context of contemporary American culture, will spell out the social value of this differentiated function. Now, however, the following is proposed as a definition of this differentiated function and, therefore, also as a defining statement of the American middle school's paramount goal in the modern era:

The differentiated function—hence, the paramount goal—of the American middle school is to intervene protectively in the process of education which was begun in the elementary school, mediate between the human condition at the onset of adolescence and the pressures of

---

14 Talcott Parsons, "Suggestions for a Sociological Approach to the Theory of Organizations," *Administrative Science Quarterly,* Vol. 1, April 1956, p. 68. Hereafter cited as "Sociological Approach."

culture, and continue the general education of early adolescents with a curriculum applied in a psychosocial environment which is functional for learning at this stage of socialization.

There are two major components in this definition of the middle school's goal: one is psychosocial and the other is cognitive. The definition, therefore, is at once *expressive and instrumental* in character. Its evaluative orientation can be said to have elements of the particularistic and the universalistic. However, if a middle school is to fulfill its institutional purpose, then the *guiding influence* in middle school structure and process has to come from the particularistic, or expressive, component.

The cognitive component acknowledges that the middle school must share with all other differentiated subsystems the larger goals of a public school organization. A commitment to the broad values of society has to be internalized and a body of cognitive skills must be learned before pupils can assume future adult roles. This is universalistic. On the other hand, the psychosocial component impels the middle school unit to teach these skills, at this stage of socialization, with appropriate affectivity toward its pupils. A discrete psychosocial environment in the middle school is provided to induce greater learning motivation in early adolescents.

For it cannot be overlooked that the pupil role in a modern-day American public school system is one which society *ascribes and enforces through legal sanctions* up to an age which is determined by local state communities. It is not an achieved role. When social roles are so ascribed and enforced, society must *provide* the necessary institutional structures for expected role performance. Witness, as examples, the social roles of king, prisoner, soldier, the legally-declared insane, and so forth.

Insofar as the latter has relevance for the education of early adolescents, it is altogether necessary to recall again that American society has long since acknowledged both the cruciality and complexity of the pupil role by having made available *differentiated units* in public school organization, at different maturational stages of the pupil, even before the middle school. Up to about 1910, the two major units of public school organization were the elementary school and the high school.

Then, when at the turn of the century psychological science in the United States recognized in early adolescence a discrete maturational sequence on the road to adulthood, the psychosocial significance of an in-between age—from about twelve to fifteen—was discovered. It is an age when childhood is left behind and adolescence is approached. It is a period of transition. But before the transition is completed, there is a period of about three years when youth in modern American culture requires special care. As this new knowledge about human development was assimilated in public education, the agency of a mediating middle school unit was brought into existence to protect early adolescence from the pressures of culture during the period of transition.

That the protective function which the middle school performs in education is still of great social value today was confirmed in 1963 by educational psychologist William W. Wattenberg before a national middle school conference at Cornell University. He told his listeners that early adolescent pupils "are so 'special' that to abandon the idea of separate schools for them would be a mistake."[15] As was stated earlier, Chapter 13 will elaborate on what is so "special" about early adolescents that they require the protective intervention of a special school unit for their socialization.

Implication for Middle School Administration

Perhaps no other unit of public school organization has been so consistently mismanaged as has been the middle school. The most difficult challenge for middle school administration is the *primacy* of the psychosocial, or the particularistic, component in the middle school's goal. Unless its dominant status is shared in a system-wide consensus, it can be, as indeed it has been, a source of debilitating dissonance. A middle school principal performs, after all, in an administrative role of the public school organization which, in evaluative terms, has a decidedly instrumental orientation: an orientation which can be categorized as achievement-centered, universalistic, and affectively neutral. On the other hand, the unit for which he is administratively responsible requires a special type of orientation, one of diffuseness and affectivity, if the unit is to perform the differentiated function for which it was meant. This challenge is of one piece with the question which was put at the close of Chapter 2: What criterion is there for middle school principals by which to ascertain when a functional balance of

15 Quoted in Fred M. Hechlinger, "The Junior Blues," *The New York Times,* July 28, 1963.

instrumental and expressive values has been attained in the school environment?

The administrative skill which is required to effect such a balance in the environment of a middle school is conceptual in character. When the principal of a middle school does not have sharp conceptual perspective of the middle school's differentiated function in the larger public school system, the prospect of mismanagement is distressingly great. How will he define the orientations of its paramount goal for other members of the organization when his own vision of it suffers from myopia? The otherwise technical brilliance of such a principal is no assurance that a functional balance of instrumental and expressive values will pervade structure and process in his school.

For when a principal allows middle school process to become overly expressive at the expense of instrumental values, and cognitive learning is neglected, this is dysfunctional for the goal of the larger public school organization. But when middle school process is allowed to become overly instrumental at the expense of expressive values, and cognitive demands are excessive and strain-producing at a time when nature is already exerting a considerable stress on the young adolescent, this, in turn, is dysfunctional for the middle school. Indeed, such educative process negates the institutional purpose of the unit.

Similar dysfunctions can too easily develop also out of the day-to-day administrative actions of a middle school principal. The delicate expressive-instrumental balance which is required for educative process in a middle school is also required for its general environment. Goal attainment in a middle school requires a psychological environment which is functional for early adolescent education in the classroom as well as in the school. A middle school principal's administrative actions can be, therefore, a powerful regulator of school environment.

It is difficult to determine *a priori* whether the valuation of a given administrative action is as instrumental or expressive. Such a determination has to be made in a discrete action context. *Primacy of relevance to the situation in which an action is viewed must determine which of these two value dimensions is germane.* A middle school principal will require a solid conceptual foundation from which to make such a judgment.

Of course, whether an action in middle school organization has primacy as instrumental or expressive value, it must also have a larger societal reference. Administrators have been known to take as a rule-of-thumb the saying "What is good for the organization is good for the society." We know only too well that such an administrative posture is anathematized by society even when it is perceived in the profit-motivated business organization. In a school organization, such an attitude can be fatal.

Expressive or instrumental elements in a middle school environment are legitimate *only* when they facilitate goal attainment in the organization. When they do not facilitate goal attainment, they are primarily *maintenance values,* and they are, therefore, sterile of any genuine social value.

Subsequent discussion will enlarge the meaning of maintenance value, but for now the following illustration of one aspect of maintenance value will suffice.

Principal Smith wants his middle school teachers to march pupils toward the lunch room in a column formation because this makes for order in the school. But the column formation is for early adolescents a symbol of elementary school discipline, a type of control they had welcomed as children, but now resent wholeheartedly as young adolescents. Nevertheless, it is forced upon them precisely at a time when they have abandoned the childhood self-image and are in search of another. In functional terms, what is the valuational primacy of this action?

It might be claimed that its primacy is as an instrumental value. It results in firmer control and, therefore, the cognitive orientation of the school is strengthened: more solid learning will take place in the school. But will it?

Marching to the lunch room may get for Principal Smith, in this instance, absolute control. However, the drain upon the gratificational element—Parsons' "cathectic motivation"—in the school's environment is likely to be great. Following Parsons, the principal has intensified for the pupil "exigencies of interaction" with other actors in the social system. Because there is no particular relevance in this action to a larger social value, despite its instrumental hue, it should be judged primarily as a maintenance value. The chief beneficiary of this action is actually Principal Smith. He can now boast, "I run a tight ship!"

On the other hand, just as excessive instrumentalism in middle school administration can result in maintenance values, so can excessive expressiveness.

Suppose, to continue the example, Principal Smith resorts to what Merton calls a *functional alternative* as a means of obtaining order on the way to the lunch room. He permits pupils to move to the lunch room with buddies of their choice. In return for an acceptable order on the way, he arranges for some social dancing, checkers, or other low-organized recreation for a part of the lunch period. An administrative action of this kind has been known to result in the following: it serves as an inducement for self-managed order, and it raises the gratificational level of a middle school environment.

Suppose, however, Principal Smith pushes this procedure beyond administrative propriety. In quest of even greater self-induced conformative behavior, he extends the lunch period from thirty minutes— let us exaggerate deliberately for sake of the illustration—to ninety minutes. If a little is good, so he reasons, then a lot must be better. His aim, so Principal Smith rationalizes, is to bolster the expressive element in the school environment. It may very well do so, but consider the cost to his school's cognitive orientation.

Again, because there is no particular relevance in this action either to a larger social value, despite its expressive hue, it too should be judged primarily as a maintenance value. It is not likely that society, or for that matter the larger public school organization, will tolerate for long administrative actions that produce maintenance values to an excess.

Compounding immeasurably the difficult task of middle school administration is the ephemeral nature of the concept of environment. What is environment? It is such an elusive concept. Like mercury, it does have substance, but it is so difficult to grasp. Nonetheless, environment has been established by empirical research as an important component of an organization's effectiveness. Indeed, so important is environment for certain organizations, and the American middle school is one of them, that it takes on the utility of a major tool.

Sociologists have long ago discovered that material objects in the industrial environment are more than just things in themselves. These objects have *socially determined meanings* which, from the perspective of a given actor, can be environmentally either *supportive or threatening* to his role.[16]

More recently, a large-scale study was made of the affect of organiza-

---

[16] See Roethlisberger and Dickson, *Management and the Worker,* as one of many empirical investigations that have led to this discovery.

tional environment in elementary schools. The research identified six distinct environments which were classified on a scale from an "open climate" to a "closed climate." The investigation employed a national sample of elementary schools. Findings of this study indicate that organizational environment in an elementary school is in a significant measure determined by the administrative behavior of its principal and that environment, in turn, affects role interactions in the organization.[17]

Although studies of environment, as it affects the quality of interactions in an organization, have been in vogue for only a short time in empirical research, it has been known for some time, certainly since the Hawthorne studies of the late 1920's, that psychosocial nuances of environment contribute significantly to motivation in the organization.[18] Indeed, so important is environment for the functions of certain service organizations, it is employed directly as a tool in the process of the organization. Such is the case in service organizations wherein maximum benefits can be rendered to clients only as they are made capable of drawing direct comforts from the environment of the organization. More than being supportive of role interaction, environment in such organizations *anticipates and permits* client behavior which, in another setting, would be regarded as deviant. Thus, *milieu therapy* has in the recent past become an important treatment tool in the field of mental health. Apropos of this point, it has been noted, "Psychiatrists have recognized that patients' progress depends upon their total experience in the institution."[19]

[17] Andrew W. Halpin and Don B. Croft, *The Organizational Climate of Schools* (Chicago: University of Chicago Midwest Administration Center, 1963). For still another empirical study of how a leader's behavior affects the environment in which a task-oriented group functions see Robert Freed Bales, *Interaction Process Analysis* (Reading, Mass.: Addison-Wesley Publishing Co., 1951).

[18] See Chapter 2, "Review of Selected Literature," in Eldon James Null, "The Relationships Between the Organizational Climate of a School and Personal Variables of Members of the Teaching Staff." Unpublished Ph.D. dissertation, University of Minnesota, Minneapolis, 1965.

[19] William Foote Whyte, "Parsonian Theory Applied to Organizations," in Max Black (ed.), *The Social Theories of Talcott Parsons: A Critical Examination*, p. 254. © Copyright 1961, by permission of Prentice-Hall, Inc. The environment of all social systems exerts a regulative force on its members. In society at large, it affects the manner in which actors perform ascribed social roles. As an example, the following reference to the painter John Graham is tellingly to the point: "His career as a Russian officer in World War I brought him three awards of the St. George Cross for Valor, and after escaping from the Revolutionary prisons . . . [he] devoted himself to painting—a profession that, Graham wrote, would have been 'unthinkable' in the noble Polish milieu of his birth." See "John Graham, 1881–1961," *Art News*, September 1961, pp. 46 and 51.

In a like manner, the environment of a middle school should be protective of early adolescent pupils, anticipate and legitimize their behavior, be supportive of their "acting-out" of early adolescent tensions at a time when human and cultural conditions beyond their control would make such an acting-out of tensions deviant behavior in other school units. Norms of a middle school environment have to accept the idiosyncratic behavior of early adolescents as their "road map for living" at this age.[20] It will change later. At this stage of human development, they are in greatest need of a school environment which can stand them and understand them.

During early adolescence, when a pupil hides his desperate insecurity by proclaiming to the adult world, "I'm trying to get the best of you so that I can feel big enough to be a person," the middle school unit must continue to instruct him in the commitment and skills which the culture will later require of him as an adult.[21] To be sure, the education of *all youth* is the cultural mission of the macro public school organization, but the education of *early adolescent youth* is the middle school's differentiated function in this mission.

But because the differentiated function of a middle school has become blurred in American public school organization, the unit is hard pressed today to sustain the integrity of its institutional pattern. Consequently, multivaried stresses and strains have induced grave instability in the middle school organization. The American middle school is at a crossroads: a wrong turn now could take it to eventual extinction.

Evidence in support of the crossroads thesis is plentiful. None is more pointed, or perhaps more threatening, than the following statement from *The School Administrator,* official organ of the American Association of School Administrators:[22]

> There is . . . evidence at the present time that the junior high school —its purposes, its program, its functions, its internal and external organization—is becoming a problem of major concern in many communities. In the decade ahead this instructional unit in the organization structure of education will certainly be given more careful scrutiny than it has been given in the past.

[20] C. M. Anderson, "The Self Image: A Theory of the Dynamics of Behavior," in Lester D. and Alice Crow (eds.), *Readings in Child and Adolescent Psychology* (New York: Longmans, Green and Co., 1961), p. 113.
[21] Dorothy Walter Baruch, *New Ways to Discipline* (New York: McGraw-Hill Book Co., 1960), p. 141.
[22] May 1961, p. 7.

The latter statement, coming as it does from the organized body of American school superintendents, conjures up the Biblical vision of handwriting on the wall. For it is the superintendent of schools who ultimately is accountable to the board of education for goal attainment in the public school organization. The albatross of goal failure is no more comfortable around his neck than it is on any other professional administrator. He, moreover, controls decision-making mechanisms in the organization, including the one which determines the allocation of resources and personnel within the organization. Also, it is the superintendent who is directly responsible for administrative recommendations that are brought before a board of education. Therefore, much of the middle school's future fortune will turn on his administrative and institutional assessments of its value for goal attainment in the larger public school organization.

More than mere management, the American middle school organization is now in urgent need of institutional perspective in its leadership. Institutional insight is needed, to be sure, at all levels of public school administration, but the need is desperate at the middle school level. For the American middle school organization will continue to flounder, and perhaps even become extinct, unless its administrators are equipped to assume the posture of institutional leadership. But in order to be capable of assuming such a posture, administrators first have to capture in their intellectual ken the meaning of institution.

It is an aspect of organization which has already been touched upon, albeit peripherally, earlier. Now the theme of institution has to be enlarged in order to explore it more specifically in the structural context of middle school organization.

4

THE INSTITUTIONAL ASPECT

In Chester I. Barnard's catalogue of executive functions in formal organizations, as he knew them from direct experience, control, management, supervision, and administration are singled out as functions which "are exercised not merely by high officials in such organizations but by all those who are in positions of control of whatever degree."[1]

Barnard's insightfulness has been confirmed by other observers of structure and process in organizations. Marshall Edward Dimock, for one, makes much the same point as did Barnard. He writes:[2]

> Irrespective of the nature of the organization, whether it be economic, political, religious, welfare, educational or professional, he who directs and controls it is an executive, and as such is inevitably confronted by certain problems of institutional management which are everywhere the same.

When seen in such a light, the middle school principal is unquestionably an executive. His *vis-à-vis* in an industrial organization would be the plant manager of a complex manufacturing system. Both the

1 Barnard, *The Functions of the Executive*, p. 6.
2 Marshall Edward Dimock, *The Executive in Action* (New York: Harper and Row, 1945), p. 5. Permission of Harper and Row, Publishers, Inc.

principal and the plant manager are middle-management executives, to be sure, but *executives* nonetheless.

Middle school administration gains in quality when a middle school principal is *expected* by organizational norms to function as an executive. The executive role is difficult. It is lonely at times, its high visibility in the organization notwithstanding, and it is unique.[3] There is only one president, one superintendent of schools, one chief of police, one executive director, and one building principal in the respective organizations where these roles exist. But perhaps even more difficult for the executive role is an obligation to internalize an institutional perspective in administrative behavior. When an executive does satisfy this role obligation, he becomes a statesman.

According to Philip Selznick: "The executive becomes a statesman as he makes the transition from administrative management to institutional leadership."[4] Selznick recognized that this is a large order for any executive, because, he says:[5]

> This shift entails a reassessment of his own tasks and of the needs of the enterprise. It is marked by a concern for the evolution of the organization as a whole, including its changing aims and capabilities. In a word, it means viewing the organization as an institution. To understand the nature of institutional leadership, we must have some notion of the meaning and significance of the term "institution" itself.

"Viewing the organization as an institution," following Selznick's lead, calls for insight into the social roots from which its original cultural mission in society had sprung and how, over the years, this mission has been fulfilled. A search for insight into these very facts about the middle school will take us later to the pulls and pushes in American society which led to the revitalization of public school education and, therefore, also to the middle school. But first, as Selznick suggests, some notion is required of what exactly is meant by "institution" in the current instance.

So far the middle school organization has been mapped as a social system in the guise of a formal organization which exists within a larger system. By treating the middle school in functional terms, the

3 For a work which reports an investigation of executive loneliness see Louis Goldstein, "The Social Agency Executive—A Study of Organizational Isolation." Unpublished Ph.D. dissertation, University of Minnesota, Minneapolis, 1960.

4 Philip Selznick, *Leadership in Administration* (Evanston, Ill.: Row, Peterson and Co., 1957), p. 4. Permission of Harper and Row, Publishers, Inc.

5 *Ibid.,* p. 5.

value of its dominant goal for the larger system has been marked and this value was set apart from other functional values. Consequences of action in an organization were said to be of functional value when they are judged to have relevance for goal attainment.

But, the earlier discussion had also dealt, albeit in a general way, with the phenomenon of social value. Social value was said to be a higher-level value. It was stated at the time that the *social value of attained goals* links an organization with the source of its legitimation. This means that the goal of an organization somehow links the organization with the institutional network of society. Therefore, it is precisely this uniqueness of the goal which has to be magnified in the institutional projection of middle school organization. Otherwise, Selznick's institutional reference will elude us.

Most characteristics of administrative organizations are relatively easy to spot on sight once they are captured by the concept of formal organization. Because more or less impersonal rationality governs the structure of a formal organization, such telltale structural characteristics as a table of organization, rules and regulations, and a hierarchy of supervisors are easily discernible in such organizations. However, institutional features are not as easily spotted. One has to reenter the amorphous world of values for this view of the organization. It is a reentry which some middle school principals might wish to avoid, but only at great peril to middle school stability.

The source of the peril stems partly from the location of a middle school in the public school system. The middle school unit, because of location, is vulnerable to a built-in organizational disadvantage. Empirical evidence of a disadvantage, and its meaning, will be presented in Chapter 11, where the middle school unit is treated in the operational context of the larger public school system. For now, let us merely note that because planned organizations are rational, they are judged by the acid test of pragmatism: Do they work as planned? As rational structures, or machines, they are expendable when they fail the pragmatic test. But when a rational organization takes on what Selznick calls a "natural dimension," its status in the society becomes more secure.

Selznick puts the matter in this way:[6]

The term "organization" thus suggests a certain bareness, a lean, nononsense system of consciously co-ordinated activities. It refers to an

[6] *Ibid.*, pp. 5, 21–2.

expendable tool, a rational instrument engineered to do a job. An "institution," on the other hand, is more nearly a natural product of social needs and pressures—a responsive, adaptive organism. . . .

Institutions, whether conceived as groups or practices, may be partly engineered, but they have also a "natural" dimension. They are products of interaction and adaptation; they become receptacles of group idealism. They are less readily expendable.

The natural dimension of which Selznick speaks is the *institutional dimension.* Selznick's thesis has deep meaning for middle school administration. The ensuing discussion of social value is meant to bring out this meaning sharply etched.

The Institutionalization of Values

What has been particularly striking in all of the preceding discussion of values is the many shades of meaning that are encompassed by the concept of value. Now, in the institutional projection of middle school organization, something else is striking: In an institutional projection, *functional value* and *social value* seem to be two qualitative properties of the same entity.

When the value of the middle school's paramount goal was treated earlier in an instrumental context, our specific reference to the goal was in terms of its *functional value.* Now, in an institutional context, our specific reference to the goal is in terms of its *social value.* The following two sociological views of the goal-value nexus suggest the relationship between these two properties. The first is by Talcott Parsons:[7]

In the most general sense the values of the organization legitimize its existence as a system. But more specifically they legitimize the main functional patterns of operation which are necessary to implement the values, in this case the system goal, under typical conditions of the concrete situation. Hence, besides legitimation of the goal-type and its primacy over other interests, there will be legitimation of various categories of relatively specific subgoals and the operative procedures necessary for their attainment.

The other view is that of Amitai Etzioni:[8]

7 Parsons, "Sociological Approach," *Administrative Science Quarterly,* Vol. I, April 1956, p. 68.
8 Amitai Etzioni, "Two Approaches to Organizational Analysis: A Critique and a Suggestion," *Administrative Science Quarterly,* Vol. 5, September 1960, p. 257.

Organizational goals serve many functions. They give organizational activity its orientation by depicting the state of affairs which the organization attempts to realize. They serve as sources of legitimation which justify the organization's activities and its very existence, at least in the eyes of some participants and in those of the general public and sub-publics. They serve as a source for standards by which actors assess the success of their organization.

Both of these views are focused on the value variable in the goal. The goal structure of an organization is seen by Parsons and Etzioni as a receptacle of social values.

Social values may be said to stand for the intrinsic usefulness of those objects for which a society has an affective regard and to which it has given conscious expression through some type of general consensus. A social value in this sense can be thought of as a collective goal of society. Parsons puts it in this way:[9]

> Values generally are patterned conceptions of the qualities of meaning of the objects of human experiences; by virtue of these qualities, the objects are considered desirable for the evaluating persons. Among such objects is the type of society considered to be good, not only in some abstract sense but also for "our kind of people" as members of it.

As collective goals of a society, or as "patterned conceptions" in Parsons' definition, social values somehow acquire a power to prescribe behavior in specific situations through such mechanisms of control as laws, regulations, and social protocols. More than that, patterns which are formed by such values have a power to guide the basic orientation to a society's life style. They are determinants of how man is viewed by society and they condition the societal mind-set toward social action. In short, they define the legitimate structure of a society.

S. I. Hayakawa's description of value orientations to social action in A-town and B-ville, an action which the town fathers in each community had taken in response to an economic depression, illustrates this

[9] Talcott Parsons, "Youth in the Context of American Society," in Henry Borow (ed.), *Man in a World at Work* (Boston: Houghton Mifflin Company, 1964), p. 240. Permission of Houghton Mifflin Co. Copyright © 1964 by the National Vocational Guidance Association, a Division of the American Personnel and Guidance Association.
Parsons' essay of the same title first appeared in *Daedalus*, Journal of the American Academy of Arts and Sciences, Vol. 91, Winter 1962, and subsequently in the book Erik H. Erikson (ed.), *Youth: Change and Challenge* (New York: Basic Books, 1963). Permission of *Daedalus* and Basic Books, Inc. Hereafter cited as "Youth in American Society."

point with dramatic force. Hayakawa's "story with a moral" shows closeup the power of values in basic behavioral orientations.[10]

But by what mystique are the values of a social system—society or organization—endowed with power to prescribe behavior in specific situations and to guide basic orientations when they are not prescribed? More specifically, how are goals of organizations endowed with the extraordinary power which Parsons, Etzioni, and others see there?

Because both society and organizations are generically social systems, Parsons offers the following as a frame of reference for both questions:[11]

> The main point of reference for analyzing the structure of any social system is its value pattern. This defines the basic orientation of the system . . . to the situation in which it operates; hence it guides the activities of participant individuals.

Parsons' meaning of "value pattern" in the foregoing passage will be easier to manage when it is recalled that a Parsonian-defined social system is action-oriented to the attainment of some goal or goals. From the values of a system crystallizes, according to Parsons, a pattern of orientational categories. He holds that it is this evaluative pattern of a social system which defines basic orientations of that system to itself, its universe and, therefore, it also affects the quality of relationships within its relational network. Thus, in his general theory of social systems, Parsons uses the concept of "value pattern" as the foundation of a complex model with which to define analytically value orientations as motivations in conformative or deviant behavior. The model, which he calls "Pattern Variables," consists of "polar alternatives of possible orientation-selection" in the relational network of a given system.[12] "Pattern Variables," although an exceedingly difficult tool to manage in a concrete analytical application, has, nevertheless, been used with telling success to explain dissonance and *causes of conflict* in organized action systems.[13] We have used "Pattern Variables" spar-

---

10 See "A Story with a Moral," in S. I. Hayakawa, *Language in Action* (New York: Harcourt, Brace and Co., 1939), pp. 3–12.

11 Parsons, "Sociological Approach," *Administrative Science Quarterly,* Vol. I, April 1956, p. 67.

12 For a schematic outline of "pattern variables" see Parsons, "The Pattern-Alternatives of Value-Orientation as Definitions of Relational Role-Expectation Patterns," in *The Social System,* pp. 58–88. See also, Talcott Parsons, "Pattern Variables Revisited," *American Sociological Review,* August 1960.

13 See, for example, its application to an analysis of conflict in the "Black Belt" of the South in Thomas F. Pettigrew, "Continuing Barriers to Desegregated Education in the South," *Sociology of Education,* Vol. 38, Winter 1965, p. 102.

ingly in Chapters 2 and 3: references there to universalistic, particularistic, specificity, diffuseness, affectivity, and affective neutrality are
categories of such pattern variables.

At this juncture, however, it is the foundation concept of value pattern that is germane for us. For, as it was stated before in a more
general way, it is the value pattern of a social system which, in Parsons'
view, defines a *desirable general direction of development* for the
system.

Parsons, in this frame of reference, conceptualizes the dominant
American value pattern as one of "instrumental activism." It is a
value pattern whose cultural roots stem from both Puritan traditions
and a history of mastering a harsh frontier environment. It reflects
instrumental activism by means of the Calvinist ethos, an ethos which
conceives of man's role in society—whether the role be that of banker
or of the manual laborer—as one which must be fulfilled and pursued
with zeal for the greater glory of God. These are the values of asceticism, deferred gratification, and achievement which are dominant in
the Calvinist orientation to social organization.[14]

"This system," Parsons stresses, "is in the first instance moral, but
also, at the societal level, it is embodied in legal norms."[15] And Parsons adds:[16]

> It is of great importance that, once institutionalized, the fulfillment of
> such a value pattern need not be motivated by an explicit recognition
> of its religious groundings.

How, then, does the dominant pattern of the American value system
influence basic orientations to societal roles, social action, and social
thought in the American social system? Parsons explains:

> As part of the structure of the society, this value system defines the
> situation of action for its individual members, both as members of the
> society as a whole and as members of various subcollectives within it.
> What are some of its salient features from this point of view?

> First, instrumental activism implies that for cultural reasons the society
> is oriented to mastery of the environment, but it is at the same time

---

14 Here Parsons reflects the Weberian strain in his theoretical system in a pronounced
form. See Max Weber, *The Protestant Ethic and The Spirit of Capitalism,* translated
by Talcott Parsons (London: George Allen and Unwin, 1930).

15 Parsons, "Youth in American Society," p. 240. Permission of Houghton Mifflin Co.,
Copyright © 1964 by the National Vocational Guidance Assoc., a Division of the American Personnel and Guidance Assoc.

16 *Ibid.,* p. 240.

individualistic in a very important sense. The primary obligation of the individual within the framework of his opportunity is to make a maximal contribution to the implementation of the values by helping to make it in the relevant sense *a better society*. The instrumentalism of the society is to be conceived as devoted not to the gratification of the hedonistic wants of its members for their own sake but to facilitating their contributions.

But at the same time the implications are individualistic in that there is no single over-all goal of the society which defines a desirable terminal state. Rather the values sanction a desirable *direction* of development.[17]

One reference in the concept of value pattern is of particular importance for a projection in which the institutional dimension of middle school organization is viewed. It is the Parsonian postulate: "Values, for a given system, large or small, define the broad directions which the system's activities should take. Norms, on the other hand, specify much more narrowly what should be done in particular contexts."[18]

Then Parsons goes on to say:[19]

With all this the normative framework is fundamental. Ours is not an anarchic but an "institutionalized" individualism which lays great stress on certain central freedoms of choice, responsibility and opportunity, and the corresponding limitations on arbitrary control, enforced both through law and through the political and associational system."

Social implications of instrumental activism for early adolescents in contemporary American culture will be treated in Chapter 13. In a like manner, the chapters which follow immediately will deal with the social meaning in Parsons' reference to "institutionalized individualism," as this meaning was defined in the *milieu* from which the American middle school evolved. What is more germane at the moment is Parsons' reference in the foregoing postulate to "norms" and "the normative framework." For it is precisely his reference to a *normative framework* which leads us to the manner in which society obtains conformity to legitimized values in day-to-day relations once a "desirable direction of development" has been defined for society by its value pattern.

Assuming a value pattern of instrumental activism, and all that is

17 *Ibid.*, pp. 240–41.
18 *Ibid.*, p. 247.
19 *Ibid.*, p. 241.

subsumed in an orientation of this kind, how is such an orientation implemented in the structural development of society? A commitment to a body of values might exist in the consciousness of a society as some type of *Volksgeist*—this is ideology—but as Parsons puts it, "The value system does not 'actualize' itself automatically. . . . "[20] Society has to find some way of implementing its values and enforce their positive and negative sanctions in the structure of society.

Society transforms its values from the amorphous state of "existential beliefs"—ideology—into enforceable sanctions by endowing them with the muscle of legitimation. As legitimized values, they materialize laws, rules, and social protocols for their fulfillment. These laws, rules, and ceremonial procedures are the *norms* which prescribe sanctioned behavior in society-at-large and in all of its organized action systems, that is, its subsystems. And how does society endow legitimized values with this power? According to Parsons: "The primary reference point for the linkage of values through legitimation with the structure of the social system is institutionalization."[21]

The manner in which "the linkage of values" occurs is suggested, in part, by Parsons' earlier postulate. This is the postulate which distinguishes between the function of values as existential beliefs and values with endowed power to set norms for their fulfillment. The postulate states, we will recall, "Values, for a given system, large or small, define broad directions which the system's activities should take. Norms, on the other hand, specify much more narrowly what should be done in particular contexts." Norms in this sense, then, may be thought of as prescriptive sanctions, positive and negative, in the conduct of societal affairs.

At this general level of discussion, the founding period of American nationhood serves as an instant example of how legitimized values become linked with the structure of a society by means of institutionalization. The existential values—that is, again, the ideology—which in the minds of the Founding Fathers justified the American Revolution are found in the Declaration of Independence. They had crystallized as a *Volksgeist* during the colonial period and they provided the basic orientation to future development. These values were then legitimized

---

[20] Talcott Parsons, *Structure and Process in Modern Societies* (New York: The Free Press, 1963), p. 173. Hereafter cited as *Structure and Process*. Copyright 1960. Permission of the Free Press of Glencoe.
[21] *Ibid.*, p. 177.

in the Constitution of the United States, where they were endowed with power to materialize laws—norms—for their fulfillment.

But, as we know, social values are not all alike in character. There are economic values, religious values, educational values, political values, and so forth. Norms of orientation that are appropriate for the fulfillment of economic values are inappropriate for the fulfillment of religious values. It is clear, therefore, that norms which constellate about a given value have to be congruent with the character of that value, its object of categorization. So it is!

Differentiated norms evolve in a society in correspondence with the differentiated function of the value they are set to fulfill. Each constellation of norms, as they assume a generalized pattern which is sustained by society over the years, is what has come to be called an *institution*. Constellations of these differentiated patterns, linked one with another, become the institutional network of a society; that is, "the normative framework" which, in Parsons' postulate again, is "fundamental" for the fulfillment of society's value system.

As institutions of society, they incorporate what Parsons calls "value-content" and thereby become invested also with authority, or, as others refer to such authority, "institutionalized power."[22]

However, it is quite obvious that not all institutions have the same type of power with which to set norms of allowed or proscribed behavior. A church, especially in the United States, clearly does not have the same power with which to enforce its institutional patterns as has the government. There are apparently several societal sources which are capable of investing values with some type of legitimate authority. It is necessary, therefore, to ascertain which of these sources has relevance for the institution of public education.

Weber's Three Sources of Legitimate Authority

For centuries before our own day, men have speculated: How is social order, or social cohesion, made possible in a society? Such speculation, as an example, led Thomas Hobbes of the seventeenth century

[22] *Ibid.,* pp. 177 and 196. For an elaboration of authority as institutionalized power see Robert Bierstedt, "The Problem of Authority," in M. Berger, T. Abel, and C. H. Page (eds.), *Freedom and Control in Modern Society* (Princeton, N.J.: Van Nostrand, 1954); also Robert Bierstedt, "An Analysis of Social Power," *American Sociological Review,* Vol. XV, December 1950, which is the same article by this author as in the immediately preceding citation; and Floyd Hunter, *Community Power Structure* (Chapel Hill, North Carolina: University of North Carolina Press, 1953).

to a philosophy of rationalist materialism in which society is viewed as a "war of all against all" and in which a common power, the "Leviathan" of the state, is established by social contract to keep men from destroying or subduing one another. It was also speculation about social order that led Jean-Jacques Rousseau to the view of society which he expressed in his now renowned prize-winning essay of the "Social Contract."

Max Weber, the German social theorist of the late nineteenth and early twentieth century, whose ideas, it will be recalled, exerted a seminal influence upon Talcott Parsons' intellectual development, also speculated about the nature of social order. He identified three sources of *pure types* of legitimate authority in society.

In a cross-cultural investigation of social cohesion, Weber undertook the study of domination systems in both ancient and modern societies. Sociological literature has been enriched manifold by the quality of Weber's scholarship. One work in particular which has had a marked influence on modern-day sociological thought, especially in the field of large-scale organizations, is a book which Weber titled *Wirtschaft und Gesellschaft*. The English translation of Part I of this work is known as *The Theory of Social and Economic Organization*.

Weber concluded:[23]

> There are three pure types of legitimate authority. The validity of their claims to legitimacy may be based on:
>   1. Rational grounds—resting on a belief in the "legality" of patterns of normative rules and the right of those elevated to authority under such rules to issue commands (legal authority);
>   2. Traditional grounds—resting on an established belief in the sanctity of immemorial traditions and the legitimacy of the status of those exercising authority under them (traditional authority); or finally,
>   3. Charismatic grounds—resting on devotion to the specific and exceptional sanctity, heroism or exemplary character of an individual person, and of the normative patterns or order revealed or ordained by him (charismatic authority).

In modern society, legal authority is the most dominant type employed to assure social order. The law is acknowledged as supreme regulator in the conduct of societal affairs. Norms that are deemed

---

[23] Max Weber, *The Theory of Social and Economic Organization*, translated by A. M. Henderson and Talcott Parsons (New York: The Free Press, 1947), p. 328. Hereafter cited as *Social and Economic Organization*. Copyright 1947. Permission of the Free Press of Glencoe.

essential for the general welfare are invested with "the power of the law." Corporate charters, contracts, and constitutions are among the more familiar symbols of legitimation for the rational-legal structures of our society.

Traditional authority is also a source of social order in modern societies, especially in those whose roots have been nurtured by the medieval culture. Tradition, for example, is much more binding in England than it is in the United States. There is much in England's contemporary stratification system which has its origins in medieval society, where the authority of tradition was dominant. But even in the United States, church organizations and a large variety of culture-wide rituals attest to the still prevalent authority of tradition.

Charismatic authority, alone, might strike modern minds as unfamiliar. It is an esoteric reference, to be sure, and one not easy to define. Weber meant this concept to express an authority which comes from a leader whose followers see him as possessed of "the gift of grace," a leader who legitimizes interaction, or a movement, by some power mystique that followers perceive in his person. Biblical literature is full with accounts of charismatic leaders—the prophets serve as examples. In the later historical treatment of the milieu from which sprang the social roots of the American middle school, such concepts as "charismatic leader" and "charisma of office" will be useful. At the moment, however, it has not yet been established how legitimized values are turned into tangible societal assets.

Legitimation and institutionalization alone will not produce these tangible assets. They are, to be sure, necessary first stages to the actual production of tangible assets. Legitimation transforms existential beliefs into values with muscle and institutionalization spells out the norms for fulfilling legitimized values. Parsons thinks of such norms as the three *P's* of society's prescribed, permitted, and prohibited categories of social behavior. But left as institutionalized values, and nothing more, very little of tangible benefit would accrue to the differentiated institutions which incorporate society's values. The action of the North Central Association of Colleges and Secondary Schools in 1924 provides an illustrative footnote to this point.

North Central, it will be recalled from Chapter 3, had stamped its associational legitimation on the middle school by establishing a "Standard Junior High School." The action was then institutionalized through a generalized pattern of norms which prescribed acceptable structure and process in a North Central middle school. But when North Central endowed its associational legitimation with the lesser muscle of "recognition," and not with the more powerful "accreditation," its norms for a "Standard Junior High School" were difficult to enforce in the face of countervailing influences. Chapter 12 deals with this episode in North Central's history at greater length.

Institutions become productive of tangible assets when they are made capable of using the authority which is carried in the values they incorporate. Each institution, we will recall, is differentiated in the institutional network of society by the function of its value-content. Value-content, in turn, consists of societal aspirations for attaining some discrete goal. When the attainment of this goal requires an integrated system of interdependent action processes, the mechanism of an organization is created for the purpose. The goal of fulfilling such values as trial by jury and due process, for example, requires some juridical organization of courts.

The organization is granted permission—legitimated—by society to use the authority of the institution whose value-content it is expected to transform into tangible societal assets. Society sets the mission and mandates the organization to make fulfillment of the mission its *paramount goal.* Society in this way expects the goal structure of organizations to serve as repositories for its esteemed aspirations and ideals—in a word, its values. When an organization does, indeed, fulfill society's expectation, then its goal structure may be said to possess the two qualitative properties of *functional value* and *social value.*

A Return to Selznick's Thesis

To recapitulate: existential beliefs, legitimation, institutionalization, implementation are developmental stages in the transformation of cultural values into tangible societal assets. Existential beliefs are a society's aspirations for *the good life,* however its philosophy or theology defines the good life. Society invokes its existential beliefs to resolve "problems of meaning," to use Weber's expression, and therefore they also provide the broad orientation to the development of society.

Legitimation endows existential beliefs with power to spell out orientations to the good life. Norms prescribe more specifically in social relations categories of expected, allowed, or prohibited individual behavior and interaction. When a generalized pattern of norms crystallizes about a value, as was registered earlier, it is said to be institutionalized. Of course, as was demonstrated in the North Central case before, whether or not institutionalization can be made to stick will depend upon the power of its normative sanctions. In any case, because the value-content of institutions has no way of implementing itself automatically, cultural ingenuity must devise appropriate mechanisms for doing this. Planned organizations are one category of such implementing mechanisms.

A planned organization, in some form of what we shall later define as a *bureaucracy,* is capable of transforming the value-content of institutions into tangible assets with great economy in the consumption of society's limited resources and efficiency in the use of manpower. Planned organizations are classificationally different—business, service, mutual-benefit, and commonweal—because each organization is set in its paramount goal to fulfill value-content in the institution of which it is an implementing apparatus.

Each organization, moreover, devises its own means—technology—for attaining its goals. Waste of resources in the process of goal attainment will incur harsh societal censure for the organization. Instrumental means for goal attainment have to be selected and integrated, therefore, along the rationalistic dictates of economy and efficiency. Out of the value imperatives of economy and efficiency, or means values, have evolved administrative norms in organizations and corresponding administrative roles to enforce them. Society thus entrusts the management of its implementing organizations to incumbents of administrative roles.

Here, precisely, we come to grips with the core of Selznick's thesis. Unless an administrator has "some notion of the meaning and significance" of organization as an implementing arm of some institution, the *means,* or *functional,* value of economy and efficiency can easily become an *end value* in itself: what Merton calls a "terminal value." Selznick's central point is that economy and efficiency are legitimate administrative norms only as a *means* of enhancing an organization's instrumental usefulness in transforming value-content into tangible societal assets. Chapter 11 will reveal how the American middle school organization has been victimized by a kind of administrative myopia which mistook *means values* for *goal values.*

Administrative myopia, on the other hand, cannot be ignored for long by society. Myopia in administrative vision, whatever the cause, can be at once a problem of the organization and a grave hazard for society. Compounding both the problem and the social hazard is the *power* with which administrative roles are invested in organizations.

Planned organizations must have power if they are to be effective. Parsons puts it this way: "The value system *legitimizes* the organization's goal, but it is only through power that its achievement can be made effective."[24] An organization must have power to enforce its administrative norms in system operations. Power is an essential element, but, as will be noted in Chapter 10, by no means the only source from which an organization can draw its integrating solidarities. Therefore, because power is essential for effective goal attainment, and because the organization serves instrumentally institutional interests, it is authorized by society to use institutionalized power for its own purpose. It is this power which administrators are given to use for the enforcement of administrative norms. It is a generalized capacity to obtain from members adherence to their decisions.

Armed with the legitimate power of an organization, administrators are then in a position to enforce administrative norms which they themselves set. But what of an administrator who sets and enforces organizational norms not for the benefit of the organization's larger legitimate purpose, but for his own self-maintenance?

An administrator who is so inclined can easily become imbedded for life in organizational structure and shielded from discovery by superiors by means of a web of obligations in which other members of the organization are ensnared. Once so ensnared by personal obligations, members are less inclined to recognize self-maintenance in organizational norms and in administrative actions; more so when such norms and actions are proclaimed by an administrator to be "for the good of the organization."

Merton refers to such an administrator as a "bureaucratic virtuoso." The bureaucratic virtuoso will master, and use self-servingly, the complex mechanism of an organization. Innovation is discouraged and the power of the organization is used to strike down, or squeeze out, those members who are innovative. But by the evaluative orientation of a self-serving administrator, administrative behavior of this sort seems altogether legitimate. Lacking institutional perspective, the value of self-serving ends blend well in the eyes of the bureaucratic

[24] Parsons, *Structure and Process*, p. 41.

virtuoso with the value of maintaining traditional orientations and procedures in the system, the *status quo,* even when these are out of joint with the times. One is reminded here of Robert Browning's Duke of Ferrara in "My Last Duchess" whose values justified the murder of his Duchess because ". . . she ranked/My gift of a nine-hundred-years old name/With anybody's gift."

In sum, when administrative norms ignore the institutional kinship of an organization, by design or out of administrative myopia, the self-maintenance of the organization is at the expense of society's general welfare—hence, the social hazard.

Conversely, administrative norms are more likely to reflect the larger institutional interest when the organization is regarded as a product of both natural and rational imperatives; that is to say, cultural and organizational imperatives. Accordingly, an executive who is capable of institutional leadership will be sensitive to responsive institutional impulses in the organization. When institutional impulses, in response to social change, strive to effect an adaptation in the organization, the executive, possessed of institutional insight, will provide the necessary leadership for those in the organization who are capable of effecting the adaptation with economy and efficiency. It is this difficult-to-define institutional sensitivity which is, following Selznick's thesis, the discriminating variable in administrative roles between the *executive* and the *executive-statesman.*

In the administrative stewardship of an executive-statesman, an organization effects a successful adaptation to social change when it incorporates in its goal structure emergent *subvalues* which spring from expanding aspirations in society. Institutional value-content increases with expanding aspirations. A changing society brings in its wake social disorganization. It dislocates the established order, exacerbates old problems, generates new ones, and kindles fresh aspirations for stability in the social system. These new aspirations fuse with the value-content of the institutional network and strive to redefine, now for a new milieu, broad orientations to renewed stability in society.

It is at this point that society's stability, and survival of its value system, hinges upon the effectiveness of its organizational network. Society depends on its implementing organizations for the structural and technological innovations which are required for renewed social stability. An inadequate institutional response in the organizational network at this time will sustain the social disorganization and, as history has demonstrated again and again, intensify large-scale alienation from the institutionalized value system: the value system of society is made dangerously vulnerable to infection from alien ideologies.

A society will, therefore, revitalize its institutional network, and thereby reconstruct itself creatively, by infusing it with emergent subvalues which reflect new aspirations. It will insist, accordingly, that implementing organizations of the institutional network enlarge their goal structures, incorporate emergent subvalues, and transform them into tangible assets. An organization which, through institutional leadership, is capable of such responsive action will continue to earn society's support and esteem. One which is incapable of such responsive action will, at best, suffer society's disdain, but it is more likely to be discarded as an obsolete tool and replaced with a more effective organizational mechanism.

The Institution of Public Education

The implications in Selznick's thesis for public school administration are crystal clear. True, the public school organization exists in American society as a "domesticated organization," a reference which means to suggest that society will not discard the public school organization "no matter what."[25] Even so, domesticated organizations have known the harsh consequences of society's disdain. It is a disdain from which the public school organization can be spared by means of institutional leadership.

Selznick's thesis suggests that institutional leadership may be said to exist in public school administration when the goal structure of public school organization is made capable of incorporating emergent educational subvalues. When educational subvalues are so incorporated, and when these subvalues—say subgoals—cannot be transformed into tangible societal assets by means of established structures, institutional leadership will design *differentiated* units for this purpose. The American middle school organization, precisely because it was meant to fulfill a subvalue which had been added to the value-content of the institution of public education, may be offered as an example of institutional leadership from an earlier period.

Organizational units, or subsystems, which are brought into exis-

[25] This is an exceedingly useful conceptualization by Richard O. Carlson in *NSSE Yearbook,* Part II, 1964, p. 264.

tence through institutional leadership are legitimized in the public school system through the educational subvalues their respective differentiated goals are set to attain. In the instance of the middle school, it is the educational subvalue of early adolescent education now incorporated in the goal structure of public school organization. All technical means and occupational roles which are required by the middle school to attain its differentiated goal effectively are in this way also legitimized through a social value. Parsons brings into sharp focus the legitimation of subsystems in an organization in the following:[26]

> When subvalues are institutionalized as such, they, in turn, legitimate subinstitutions which, in turn, are differentiated in relation to the structure and situation of the subsystem in question, and of the requisite categories of roles in it. Thus, we would have variations in mode of legitimation, in the statuses of role-performers within the system, in their situations, and in the institutionalization of sanctions.

The "subsystem in question" in the foregoing may be said to be the organization which has enlarged its goal structure to incorporate subvalues. In Parsonian theory, we will recall, all organizations are regarded as differentiated subsystems of society.

Subvalues, so the history of the United States shows, have been added to the value-content of the institution of public education in parallel development with American society. Soon after the dominant American values had been established in the Constitution by means of legal authority, it became obvious to many in American society that civic competence and literacy were latent imperatives for sustaining the institutional network in which these values were set. Following Merton, these imperatives might be taken as latent functions of free institutions.

James Madison recognized this latent function when he concluded, "Popular government without popular education is a prologue to a farce or a tragedy." In the same vein, Thomas Jefferson wrote in 1816, "If a nation expects to be ignorant and free in a state of civilization, it expects what never was and never will be. . . ." In short, a commitment had to be internalized through the process of education to maintain the integrity of American institutional patterns.

As more and more Americans came to share this view, civic competence and literacy crystallized as societal aspirations; hence, as social values. But because of the Tenth Amendment to the United States

---

[26] Parsons, *Structure and Process*, p. 193.

Constitution these values were legitimized in state constitutions. Specific laws were enacted to serve as a normative framework for the conduct of public education. An organization was then created to give instrumental expression to educational values. The organization was first known as the *common school* and later as the *public school system*.

The structure of the public school, as has been stated earlier, was at first a simple organization. Soon, however, social and economic life in America acquired greater sophistication and complexity. Democratic aspirations, encouraged by sanctioned directions of development in the American social system, had expanded during the Jacksonian era of the common man. After this period, more than mere literacy came to be expected as the end of public school education. The public school was becoming a major repository of the common man's hopes for upward mobility in American society. Entire communities drew strength from it. The public school organization was evolving as an indispensable engine of social democracy.[27]

But substantive cultural changes are always accompanied by strain-producing pushes and pulls in the value system. These pushes and pulls materialize in many forms: dialogue, polemic, pressure group, and, ultimately, the integrating mechanism of the political party. The platform of a political party serves a number of functions, and one of them is to crystallize a consensus in society around emergent sub-values.[28] When a consensus does crystallize, as such consensus emerges

---

[27] For a sociological enlargement of this theme see Ralph H. Turner, "Sponsored and Contest Mobility and the School System," *American Sociological Review*, Vol. 25, December 1960.

Jefferson, Madison, and other Founding Fathers registered their apprehension of illiteracy in elegant expressions, but the unschooled and semiliterate William Manning had apparently sensed the same apprehension. As a "common man," Manning spelled out the utility of universal education for free institutions in a tract which he called *The Key of Liberty* (1798). He wrote: "It is the universal & practis of monorcl & dispotick government to train up their subjects as much in ignorance as they can in matters of government, . . . & to take for truth what ever they say without examining for themselves." William Manning, *The Key of Liberty—Shewing the Causes Why a Free Government has Always Failed, and a Remidy Against it* (Billerica, Massachusetts: The Manning Association, 1922), p. 19. Notes and foreword by Samuel Eliot Morison.

Townsend Harris later also gave eloquent expression to the emerging social orientation in American public education when he urged support of a referendum in 1847 to establish a free public college in New York City with a plea to "Open the doors to all. Let the children of the rich and the poor take their seats together and know of no distinction save that of industry, good conduct and intellect."

[28] For a wide-angled view of the multivariety "political" influences which impinge upon educational values see Roald F. Campbell, Luvern L. Cunningham, and Roderick F. McPhee, *The Organization and Control of American Schools* (Columbus, Ohio: Charles E. Merrill Books, 1965), especially Chapters 2–6.

from a political contest, the subvalues it champions are added to the value-content of some institution.

As a general reference to the manner in which society revitalizes its value system through an infusion of subvalues and through subinstitutions, the foregoing discussion will do. But general references do not disclose specific pulls and pushes which bring a given institution into existence. What were the components of the thrust which propelled into existence the American middle school? It is not enough to declare merely that institutional response in organizations is a reaction to dominant social change and let the institutional definition of the American middle school go at that. What, more precisely, was the character of the change in American society to which the public school organization responded with a middle school? We are constrained at this point to ask of Clio, Muse of History, what are the social roots of the American middle school? It is to these matters of exceeding institutional importance that we now turn our attention.

5

THE CHANGING SOCIETY AND
SOCIAL DARWINISM

From Jamestown in 1607 to the Declaration of Independence in 1776, the history of America's colonial period is replete with accounts of how Europeans were transformed in their view of society by the New World.[1] The values, or existential beliefs, which these Europeans carried in their cultural baggage were of a varied mix. But as has been indicated before, these values were impinged upon by two complementary influences which became dominant in the colonies: the Calvinist ethos and the frontier. Both of these influences placed high value upon deferred gratification and achievement.

Out of this transformation in *Weltanschauung* has evolved in American society the dominant value pattern whose orientation Parsons has categorized as one of instrumental activism. It is a value pattern which esteems achievement in mundane affairs, individualism, and a morality whose roots stem from the Judaic-Christian synthesis of Calvinism.

But legitimate modes of implementing values are also culturally de-

---

[1] See especially Thomas Jefferson Wertenbaker, *The First Americans: 1607–1690* (New York: The Macmillan Co., 1927); and Charles M. Andrews, *The Colonial Period of American History* (New Haven, Conn.: Yale University Press, 1934), 4 vols.

termined. Values, so we have noted, have no automatic means of implementing themselves even when they are institutionalized. Each society, therefore, fashions its own network of instrumental structures for the implementation of its values. Qualitative and quantitative characteristics of implementing structures reflect the stage of development a society has attained at a given period in its history. When, as we know now, implementing structures of a society are incapable, for whatever reason, of transforming its values into tangible societal assets, then the value system is drained of a capacity to set norms for the desired "good life." In brief, society is confronted with a sweeping crisis during such a period.

It is for this reason that a society will reassess during periods of pervasive social change its dominant values and the capacity of its organizational network to implement them. Such a period of pervasive social change confronted American society with the task of reassessing its dominant values, institutions, and implementing organizations during the decades following the Civil War. It was a period calling for social reconstruction.

As is to be expected during such periods of reassessment, Americans looked into history for the origin of their institutions. José Ortega y Gasset, a contemporary Spanish man of letters, had this to say about the utility of history at such a time:[2]

> Here you have the origin of history. Man makes history because, faced with a future which is not in his hands, he finds that the only thing he has, that he possesses, is his past. Of this alone can he make use; this is the small ship in which he sets sail toward the unquiet future that lies ahead.

Our interest in this period of the American past must focus, of course, upon those events and figures which have a particular relevance for the social and educational roots of the American middle school. We shall adhere in this regard to the dictum of Emile Durkheim, who held that society is the source of educational life.

It is a theme to which Durkheim turned again and again in his lectures at the Sorbonne where, for most of the first quarter of the twentieth century, he graced the title of Professor of the Science of Education and Sociology. Nowhere did he score this theme more pointedly

---

[2] José Ortega y Gasset, *Man and Crisis,* translated by Mildred Adams (New York: W. W. Norton and Company, 1958), p. 120.

than in the following passage from the lecture "The Nature and Method of Pedagogy":[3]

> Educational practices are not phenomena that are isolated from one another; rather for a given society, they are bound up in the same system, all parts of which contribute toward the same end: it is the system of education suitable to this country and to this time. Each people has its own, as it has its own moral, religious, economic system, etc.

Following Durkheim, it may be proposed that the American middle school had become "suitable to this country" at a time when the flood waters of reform, in the guise of social reconstruction, were approaching ebb tide. The reform surge was generated by a determination in certain sectors of American society to enhance the viability of the institutionalized value system through necessary adaptations in implementing agencies of society in an age when the country was being transformed rapidly from a predominantly rural-agrarian-commercial culture into one predominantly urban-industrial-commercial. In a comment on this period of reform agitation, Merle Curti wrote, "In the decades between the Civil War and the First World War the ideology of protest and reform became broader in scope and increasingly important in influence."[4]

In order to escape the pitfalls of semantic confusion, let us recognize at once that insofar as so-called "reformers," or "progressives," of that era were determined to retain and reinforce institutionalized values by reshaping the patterns which gave them expression, they actually represented a *conservative* strain in American society. A body of educators, social workers, clergymen, academicians, and other Americans of the post–Civil War period were persuaded that values for which the Founding Fathers of the Republic risked "life, fortune, and honor" were worth taking into the future. As America was being transformed from a folk society into an industrial society, they turned to dominant American values for the guiding orientation with which to regulate the institutional flywheel in a tempo more suited to emerging social conditions. It is in such an historical interpretation of the period that these Americans stand out at once as *reformers* and *conservatives*.

---

3 Emile Durkheim, *Education and Sociology,* translated by Sherwood D. Fox (New York: The Free Press, 1956), p. 95. Copyright 1956. Permission of the Free Press of Glencoe.
4 Merle Curti, *The Growth of American Thought* (New York: Harper and Row, 1943), p. 605. Hereafter cited as *American Thought.* Permission of Harper and Row Publishers, Inc.

Timothy L. Smith, in a passing commentary on those Americans who had relied upon traditional values for an orientation to future development, explains:[5]

> They felt the traditional values of American democracy, the old modes of free competitive enterprise, and their own customary pre-eminence in society threatened from above and below. They resented the immense power which a newly-rich class of oil, steel, and railroad magnates had achieved. They feared even more the organization of militant labor unions, the socialist agitation against property, and the corrupt urban political machines which seemed to feed upon the saloon, the slum, and the immigrant vote. The "progressive" program called for the elimination of corruption in civic affairs, the "Americanization" of the immigrant, the regulation or destruction of business monopolies, and the resolution of conflicts between capital and labor, farmer and businessman, by writing the Golden Rule into law.

That a shift was in progress in the United States, away from Jefferson's dream—an Adamic dream—of an agrarian society toward Hamilton's dream of an industrial society, was discernible even before the Civil War, but it was a relatively slow-paced shift. Nearly 95 percent of the American population was rural in 1790. The United States was then truly a nation of farmers and small farms. It was not until 1840 that the proportion of the urban population exceeded 10 percent of the total. A shift had occurred, to be sure, but Jefferson's dream of an Adamic society was still well preserved.

The theme of an allegorical "Adamic dream" is at once culturally interesting and for us useful. It is useful for our purpose here in that the theme helps us to *feel* as well as *understand* moods in the social environment of Jefferson's agrarian world and the later post–Civil War environment of city and factory.

The Adamic dream is peopled by the figures in American belles-lettres and art before the city had become majestic and grotesque: the dream of an agrarian existence. These are the figures of whom "the good grey poet," Walt Whitman, sang and whom artists like Thomas Doughty and William Sidney Mount loved to paint. These figures were shown to live in a wholesome communion with nature; they were of the earth.

But the people of postbellum America are the figures of the Ash Can

5 Timothy L. Smith, "Progressivism in American Education, 1880–1900," *Harvard Educational Review*, Vol. 31, Spring 1961, p. 169.

painters. They are the figures in John Sloan's "Hairdresser's Window" and George Luks' "The Spielers"; lonely, forlorn in the city, and far removed from Jefferson's idyllic society. These are also the figures in Carl Sandburg's *Chicago Poems.*[6]

The Civil War had put an end to the Adamic dream. The war was a powerful stimulant for industrial development. Northern factories that had grown large by manufacturing the sinews of war found after the war new lucrative markets at home and abroad.[7] The forward push of industrialism and urbanism could no longer be denied after 1865. Factory and city were destined to become the dominant landmarks of the future.

And the future was closer than most Americans had realized. America's industrial potential and ingenuity, once it had been unleashed by the war, materialized within a few postbellum decades in a Gargantuan industrial expansion.

A telescoping of rapid industrial expansion into a few decades, in turn, set off a series of repercussive waves within the American social system. One of these waves came in the form of a powerful urban draw, a pull to the city. Both industrial expansion and urban draw were allowed free play because regulative authority, both in social and economic sectors of society, was inhibited by the classical economic doctrine of laissez-faire.

Little or no planning was done to anticipate the social consequences of a rapidly expanding urban culture. City planning was yet an unknown experience for municipal governments of postbellum America. New cities had sprung up, and established cities grew to metropolitan proportions, without a master plan to guide their development. Like Topsy, they just grew!

Management-labor relations, likewise, were governed by an ethic of

[6] The art works to which reference is made here, as well as representative pieces by Doughty and Mount, will be found at the following locations: Thomas Doughty, 1795–1856, "A Romantic Landscape," 1832, Smith College Museum of Art; William Sidney Mount, 1807–1868, "Eel Spearing at Setauket," 1845, New York State Historical Association, Cooperstown, N. Y.; John Sloan, 1871–1951, "Hairdresser's Window," 1907, Wadsworth Atheneum, Hartford, Conn.; George Luks, 1867–1933, "The Spielers," 1905, Addison Gallery of American Art, Phillips Academy, Andover, Mass. For deeper insight into the "Adamic dream" as well as for reproductions of works by the artists here mentioned, see Oliver W. Larkin, *Art and Life in America* (New York: Holt, Rinehart and Winston, 1949). Also helpful for further insight into this theme is Leo Marx, *The Machine in the Garden: Technology and the Pastoral Ideal in America* (New York: Oxford University Press, 1965).

[7] Joseph Dorfman, *The Economic Mind in American Civilization, 1606–1865* (New York: The Viking Press, 1946), Vol. II, p. 987.

catch-as-catch-can and the devil take the hindmost. Indeed, "the devil take the hindmost" is a fair representation of an ascending mode of behavior in the American social environment as the nineteenth century was drawing to a close.

American cities had been turned into jungles teeming with defenseless human prey in the form of newly arrived immigrants, rural folk, and innocent boys and girls lured from the farm to the city by job opportunities and the glitter of urban life.

Many accounts have been written of the high cost in human resources which an unbridled laissez-faire orientation to the formation of public policy in that period had exacted of American society. As a capsule summary of that cost, none is more dramatic, or revealing, than the one from historians Morison and Commager in the following sketch:[8]

> The continent had been conquered, but the conquest had been attended by an exploitation of soil and forest and water so ruthless that the natural resources of the nation were nearing exhaustion. The agricultural domain had grown beyond the dreams of even a Jefferson, but the farmer was on the verge of peasantry. The industrial revolution had made the United States the greatest of manufacturing nations, but the process had depressed a large element of society and had been accompanied by monstrous perversions in the employment of women and children and in the treatment of the aged, the incompetent, and the infirm. Unemployment and child labor went hand in hand; machinery was marvelously efficient, but no other industrial nation confessed to so many industrial accidents. The nation was fabulously rich but its wealth was gravitating rapidly into the hands of a very small portion of the population, and the power of wealth had already undermined the political integrity of the Republic. In a land of plenty there was never enough food, clothing, and shelter for the underprivileged, and cyclical depressions, apparently unavoidable, plunged millions into actual want. In the great cities the slums grew apace, and from the slums spread corrupting disease, crime, and vice. Science told how to control many of the diseases that plagued mankind but poverty interposed between science and health, and tuberculosis, hookworm, malaria, syphilis, and other diseases of poverty and ignorance took an annual toll that ran

[8] Samuel Eliot Morison and Henry Steele Commager, *The Growth of the American Republic* (New York: Oxford University Press, 1942), Vol. II, pp. 355–56. The reader will find useful the following representative titles for greater insight into this period: Ray Stannard Baker, *American Chronicles* (New York: Charles Scribner's Sons, 1945); John Chamberlain, *Farewell to Reform* (New York: Liveright, Inc., 1932); Thomas C. Cochran and William Miller, *The Age of Enterprise* (New York: The Macmillan Company, 1943).

into the millions. The churches taught the Ten Commandments and philosophers the Golden Rule, but man's inhumanity to man was illustrated in the penal code, in prison conditions, in the treatment of the aged, the poor, the incapacitated, the defective, and the insane, and the attitude toward the criminal and prostitute. The white race was sure of its superiority, but it had forgotten that code of chivalry which placed upon the strong responsibility for the weak, and the callous indifference toward the Indian and the exploitation of the negro [sic] was a blot on American civilization. The educational system was an object of pride, but its benefits were unevenly distributed, and the census of 1900 discovered over six million illiterates. Everyone gave lip service to the principles of democracy, but political corruption cankered the body politic from top to bottom. On all sides thoughtful men feared that the nation which Lincoln had called the "last best hope of earth" would prove instead the world's illusion.

A Deep Social Issue

Many Americans refused to accept pock-marking social and economic ills as fulfillment of American values. These Americans perceived such ills as direct consequences of a *rampant individualism* in private and public sectors of society. Not that they rejected individualism in principle. Individualism, after all, was one of the old values which came out of the natural-law philosophy of the Fathers. Moreover, as Parsons indicates, the dominant American value pattern is one of instrumental activism; a value pattern which has encouraged individualism in American development from the earliest period. Nonetheless, these Americans became convinced that individualism had turned into a cult which could no longer be indulged in postwar society as it had been before. In unbridled individualism, they saw a threat to traditional values. Institutionalized patterns for the exercise of individualism in social and economic behavior would, therefore, have to be adapted to the new conditions of society.

Strong government, anathematized in Jefferson's antebellum Adamic society, came to be seen after the Civil War as the only legitimate power capable of curbing the brand of individualism which some Americans feared was eroding traditional values. It was a view of government that gained greater support in society as American production and marketing technology turned increasingly sophisticated.

A panoramic view of the period suggests the manner in which this came to pass. The Civil War had accelerated the pace of industrial expansion in the United States. The war economy in which this expansion had occurred tolerated an inefficient organization of production procedures because the principal market, a government at war, was guaranteed. Once the war was over, industrial and other business organizations had to compete for markets in private sectors of society and the world. Success in the economic sphere now hinged on cutthroat competition which the successful insisted was sanctioned by the tradition of laissez-faire. Under these conditions, it is altogether understandable why dominant economic groups of that period should have esteemed laissez-faire as a value for all of society.

But there were others who saw in postwar patterns of laissez-faire a threat to societal stability, a drain upon the larger general welfare, and obstacles in the path of future democratic development in society; the only direction of development which, in their scheme, was sanctioned by the American value system. Champions of postwar patterns of laissez-faire, on the other hand, were equally adamant in holding fast to the value of rugged individualism. They insisted that their orientation to American development in the new age was, indeed, sanctioned by the American value system. The issue in time was taken into the political arena where it became the warp and woof of political campaigns for many years.

Against this backdrop, we are now in a position to capture colors and moods of the social environment in which the American middle school was born.

Social Darwinism

Colors and moods of the period were provided by a prolonged contest to modify the status quo. At issue was a demand to curb, through governmental intervention, laissez-faire behavior in social and economic activity. The contest spilled over eventually into every sector of American life. Weapons of the contest varied with the sector of society in which it was engaged. We shall first glance—by necessity a fleeting two-dimensional glance—at the major intellectual weapons of the contest.

Most defenders of the status quo had borrowed their intellectual weapons from Herbert Spencer, an English philosopher-sociologist, who, in the 1860's and after, had developed a system of thought which he called Synthetic Philosophy. Those who turned to Herbert Spencer for scientific support of laissez-faire in public policy are identified by some historians as *social Darwinists*.

Without delving deeply into philosophical social Darwinism, it is enough for our purpose to know that social Darwinism purported to explain the development of societies by principles which Charles Darwin had employed to explain the evolution of the species.

Social Darwinists took as their basic tenet that the evolution of societies is governed by the same natural laws as is the evolution of animal life; namely, that evolutionary progress derives from the struggle for existence and survival of the fittest. Societies evolve to higher stages of development, so social Darwinists held, when the strong are allowed to thrive, through an absence of controls, and the weak are left to fend for themselves the best they can or fall by the wayside.[9]

Not all who had championed laissez-faire patterns turned to social Darwinism for an intellectual defense. Some, like William T. Harris, onetime Superintendent of Schools in St. Louis and later United States Commissioner of Education, defended laissez-faire as a follower of Hegelian philosophy.[10] But it was Herbert Spencer, and not Georg W. F. Hegel, who had provided the more powerful intellectual ammunition for the defense of laissez-faire in social and economic activity.

Defenders of the status quo found in social Darwinism a rationale for a way of life in which dog-eat-dog competition was said to be sanctioned by the authority of natural law. Natural law, they claimed, sanctioned rugged individualism as normative behavior in all of social life and, therefore, unrestrained competition in the economic sphere was altogether justified. Any interference with natural law by curbing laissez-faire patterns, they argued, would weaken the social and economic foundations of society. In addressing himself to this very point, the historian Richard Hofstadter has concluded, "Spencer's was a system conceived in and dedicated to an age of steel and steam engines, competition, exploitation, and struggle."[11]

9 The reader will find a substantial exposition of Spencerian social theory in Herbert Spencer, *The Principles of Sociology* (New York: D. Appleton and Co., 1876–92), 3 vols. For one of the best introductions to social Darwinism as it was employed in defense of laissez-faire in social policy see Richard Hofstadter, *Social Darwinism in American Thought, 1860–1915* (Philadelphia: University of Pennsylvania Press, 1945). Hereafter cited as *Social Darwinism.*

10 For more on Harris as a laissez-faire Hegelian see the chapter "William T. Harris, The Conservator" in Merle Curti, *The Social Ideas of American Educators* (Patterson, N.J.: Littlefield, Adams and Co., 1959). Hereafter cited as *Social Ideas.*

11 Hofstadter, *Social Darwinism,* p. 22.

Illustrative of the fervor with which foremost businessmen of the period had embraced social Darwinism is the following passage from a Sunday-school address by John D. Rockefeller:[12]

> The growth of a large business is merely a survival of the fittest. . . . The American Beauty rose can be produced in the splendor and fragrance which bring cheer to its beholder only by sacrificing the early buds which grow up around it. This is not an evil tendency in business. It is merely the working-out of a law of nature and a law of God.

Impulses which had been set off by Spencer's system were felt everywhere in American intellectual life. Vernon Louis Parrington wrote of this period: "It is probably no exaggeration to say that Spencer laid out the broad highway over which American thought traveled in the later years of the [nineteenth] century."[13] However, of all who have traveled the Spencerian highway, few rivaled the intellectual eminence of William Graham Sumner, an Episcopal rector turned professor at Yale University.

Sumner taught the science of sociology at Yale—despite an abhorrence for the term *sociology,* because he equated sociologists with utopians—with an unconcealed laissez-faire bias. "If we do not like the survival of the fittest," he proclaimed in his lecture hall, "we have only the possible alternative, survival of the unfittest."[14] In a published treatise, in which he took on directly those who would reform the status quo, he wrote:[15]

> Society needs first of all to be free from these meddlers—that is, to be let alone. Here we are, then, once more back at the old doctrine—*laissez-faire.* Let us translate it into blunt English, and it will read Mind your own business. It is nothing but the doctrine of liberty. Let every man be happy in his own way.

So deeply had social Darwinism been impressed upon the American mind that, as late as the 1930's, Robert and Helen Lynd found a considerable residue of it in Middletown. Also, Gunnar Myrdal, at almost mid-point of the twentieth century, felt impelled to polemicize

12 Quoted in William J. Ghent, *Our Benevolent Feudalism* (New York: The Macmillan Company, 1902), p. 29.
13 Vernon Louis Parrington, *Main Currents in American Thought* (New York: Harcourt, Brace and Co., 1930), Vol. 3, p. 198.
14 Henry Steele Commager, *The American Mind* (New Haven, Conn.: Yale University Press, 1959), p. 202.
15 William Graham Sumner, *What Social Classes Owe to Each Other* (New York: Harper and Bros., 1883), p. 120.

against the intellectual social Darwinism of William Graham Sumner.[16]

Not alone was natural law invoked by social Darwinists in defense of the status quo, but also the legal authority of the Federal Constitution. Limits had been fixed upon the powers of government, so it was argued, for intervening in the social and economic affairs of society, and these limits constitute one of the social values which have been legitimized in the Constitution of the United States; an argument which certainly had a ring of legal validity. But in order to preserve its eighteenth-century meaning in the Constitution, defenders of the "limited powers" doctrine insisted that the Constitution was a fixed document, one whose near sacredness would be compromised by a loose construction of it. The following ode to the Constitution by a member of the New York bar is illustrative of the fetish which was built around the Constitution in order to fend off legislated modifications in the institutional network of society:[17]

> Our great and sacred Constitution, serene and inviolable, stretches its beneficent powers over our land—over its lakes and rivers and forests, over every mother's son of us, like the outstretched arm of God himself. . . . Transforming Word! Maker, Monitor, Guardian of Mankind!

For a long time, this defensive strategy worked. Those of that period who were inclined to regard the Constitution as fixed were apparently not troubled by the fact that it had been modified as recently as the Civil War amendments. Ironically, it was the "due process" clause of the Fourteenth Amendment—one of the Civil War amendments—which was most frequently employed to frustrate would-be reformers who resorted to legislative process.

Because the Supreme Court had been persuaded to apply the word *person* in the Fourteenth Amendment to corporations, of the 528 decisions that were rendered by the Court between 1890 and 1910, and which turned on the Fourteenth Amendment, only 19 concerned the Negro, whereas 289 related to corporations.[18] There evolved in time a

16 See the chapter "The Middletown Spirit" in Robert S. Lynd and Helen M. Lynd, *Middletown in Transition: A Study in Cultural Conflict* (New York: Harcourt, Brace and Co., 1937); and Appendix 1 in Gunnar Myrdal, *An American Dilemma* (New York: Harper and Bros., 1944).
17 Quoted in Ralph Henry Gabriel, *The Course of American Democratic Thought* (New York: The Ronald Press Co., 1940), p. 402.
18 C. C. Regier, *The Era of the Muckrakers* (Chapel Hill, North Carolina: University of North Carolina Press, 1932), p. 6.

remarkable affinity between social Darwinism and Supreme Court interpretations of the "due process" clause, so much so that Justice Oliver Wendell Holmes, Jr., was moved to protest that "the fourteenth Amendment does not enact Mr. Herbert Spencer's Social Statics."[19] Let us conclude this quick overview of social Darwinism by noting with Eric F. Goldman:[20]

> The ideas [of social Darwinism], of course, were no deliberate contrivance on the part of evil men. The dominant groups in America had simply done what dominant groups usually do. They had, quite unconsciously, picked from among available theories the ones that best protected their position and had impressed their ideas on the national mind as Truth.

Goldman's "dominant groups" conceptualized a view of man in society which complemented a brand of social and economic behavior that had become fashionable in postbellum America. These groups, moreover, were determined that the direction of American development in the new age of steel, factory, and city would be defined by the values which their view of man crystallized. Such a view of man, they held, was sanctioned by the authority of natural law and the institutionalized American value pattern.

However, there were other Americans of that period who challenged the legitimacy of the direction which dominant groups were setting for society. They saw in this direction a sharp break with the democratic-humanistic orientations of the Declaration and the old values of the Fathers. And because internalized commitments to the older values were still strong, a combination of forces emerged in their defense. Those of that period who so came to the defense of older values have been identified by some historians as *liberal*, or *reform*, *Darwinists*.

In our panoramic view of that period, social Darwinists and liberal

---

19 *Lochner v. New York*, 198 U.S. 45 (1905). The reader will find an excellent source to this facet of American constitutional history in Charles Warren, *The Supreme Court in United States History* (Boston: Little, Brown and Company, 1923), 3 vols. A reference to *Lochner v. New York* will be found in Vol. III, p. 435. The author, Charles Warren, served as Assistant Attorney-General of the United States and is established in American juridical scholarship as a foremost authority. His view of Supreme Court decisions of the late nineteenth and early twentieth century does not, however, correspond with the one of C. C. Regier. The reader would be well served, therefore, to study both of these views. See especially Warren, *The Supreme Court in United States History*, Vol. 3, Chapter 38, "Commerce and the Police Power, 1888–1918."

20 Eric F. Goldman, *Rendezvous with Destiny* (New York: Alfred A. Knopf, 1952), p. 85. Hereafter cited as *Rendezvous*.

Darwinists stand out as the ideological polar groups around whom churned the pattern variables of the Great Debate to decide which value orientations would set the course of American development in an age of pervasive social change, an age which in a number of characteristics was not unlike our own.[21]

---

[21] For a treatment in greater depth of the impact of change on the institutional network see Norman F. Washburne, *Interpreting Social Change in America* (New York: Random House, 1954).

6

THE CHANGING SOCIETY AND
LIBERAL DARWINISM

Champions of the old value orientations had no easy time of it. A mere holding action would not have been enough. Liberal Darwinists, after all, had charged that social Darwinism was alien to the American democratic tradition. Therefore, in order to make their charge stick, liberal Darwinists, at the very least, had to demonstrate by cogent means that the theoretical foundation of social Darwinism was a false foundation. A most formidable undertaking, to be sure!

For the chain of ideas that social Darwinists had commandeered in support of their values was also formidable. After all, as we noted earlier, the Revolution of 1776 was justified in the Declaration of Independence by values which had sprung from natural-law philosophy. There was no denying that the spirit of individualism pervaded the American value system. Liberal Darwinists were compelled, therefore, to attack the citadel of social Darwinism from many directions, a thing which history testifies they did with telling success. They developed what Goldman has called "ideological acids" with which to assault the theoretical foundation of social Darwinism.[1]

---

[1] Goldman, *Rendezvous,* p. 104.

These ideological acids were, for the most part, distillations of a period in American scholarship which saw a coming of age in the social and behavioral sciences. The ideological contest between liberal and social Darwinists had provided a powerful stimulus for the scientific study of man in society. Man's social and psychological behavior became a dominant subject of empirical investigations in American scholarship.

Because Herbert Spencer had set his comprehensive theory of society in a scientific framework, liberal Darwinists were constrained to find the scientific evidence which would expose the false science in social Darwinism. They challenged the scientific validity of the social Darwinist view of man and society. It was, they argued, a *partial view*. Interestingly enough, liberal Darwinists were to compound their most effective ideological acids with ingredients which were also drawn from Charles Darwin's theory of evolution. Liberal Darwinists held that *human behavior* and *social institutions* were also subject to environmental influences. In support of their claim, they turned Darwinian theory on their ideological adversaries.

Is it not a central tenet of Darwinian theory, they asked, that continuous evolution is a consequence of adaptation to environmental change? But social Darwinism, they pointed out, accepts the theory of evolution up to *a certain point in time* and then abandons it. How could any development be regarded as fixed, and independent of environmental influence, once it is acknowledged to be a product of evolution? Therefore, public policy that resists modifications of the status quo by invoking Darwinian principles is untenable.

Lester Frank Ward, one of the early architects of modern American sociology, and William Graham Sumner's ideological polar opposite in academia, exhorted social Darwinists:[2]

> Human institutions are not exempt from this all-pervading spirit of improvement. They, too, are artificial, conceived in the ingenious brain and wrought with mental skill born of inventive genius. The passion for their improvement is of a piece with the impulse to improve the plow or the steam engine.

Lester Ward's liberal Darwinism had a pronounced reform orientation. But not all those whom we put today under the umbrella of liberal Darwinism were reformers. William James, for one, although

[2] Lester F. Ward, *The Psychic Factors of Civilization* (Boston: Ginn and Co., 1893), p. 288.

no reformer himself, is classifiable with liberal Darwinists because he could not accept the fixed truths which social Darwinism promulgated.[3] There were others like James who, out of a repugnance for the ideas of social Darwinism, joined in the intellectual attack on it. But whether by design or not, there is no gainsaying that liberal Darwinists had provided the supportive intellectual climate for the social reconstruction that was to come.

The Liberal Darwinists

A recital of the many-faceted assault on social Darwinism makes for one of the more fascinating chapters in American intellectual history. Here, of course, a recital in depth is out of the question. Nevertheless, it is germane to our institutional projection of the middle school organization that we highlight at least some illustrative aspects of the assault in order to capture the *interrelatedness* of a tangled skein of events which led to the middle school.

We have already identified Lester Ward as a vigorous opponent of social Darwinism. He counterposed Spencer's and Sumner's global theories of society with one of his own. His earliest published work, in which he worked out the theoretical framework for his ideas, appeared in 1883, in two volumes, under the title *Dynamic Sociology*. From the early 1880's, and into the twentieth century, Ward, "the apostle of human progress," pitted his mind and pen against the ideas of the influential William Sumner of Yale.[4]

In the same way as Lester Ward used sociology to strike at ideas of a static society and fixed laws, Frederick Jackson Turner and Charles A. Beard, each in his own fashion, used historical scholarship as a club against the "germ theory" of history and the cult which had been built around the Constitution.

Turner had taken his doctor's degree from Johns Hopkins, where Herbert B. Adams had directed his thesis. He graduated from the

---

3 See the chapter "William James, Individualist," in Curti, *Social Ideas.*

4 Sumner's most enduring work is *Folkways.* It was first published in 1906 and brought out again in 1940. In *Folkways,* Sumner analyzed the manner in which customs and mores become one with the channeled behavior of society. See William Graham Sumner, *Folkways* (Boston: Ginn and Co., 1940).

Lester Ward has been singled out in the discussion as *representative* of a group. Indeed, this holds for the other liberal Darwinists who have been singled out. There were other sociologists, contemporaries of Ward, who also leveled telling blows at social Darwinism; Edward A. Ross (*Sin and Society*) was one, Charles H. Cooley (*Human Nature and the Social Order*), another.

University of Wisconsin, and he obtained the master's degree from the same institution in 1888. His master's thesis dealt with the fur trade in Wisconsin.

Turner's interest in frontier history inclined him as a graduate student, and later as a mature scholar and professor of history at the University of Wisconsin, to be identified with what has come to be known as "historical realism." As a historical realist, Turner rejected the theory of history which was held by his onetime professor Herbert Adams.

Adams belonged to a school of history which conceived of American democratic institutions as having flowered from the development of European society. Society, this school held, is an organism which, following Darwin, has developed along an evolutionary pattern. Therefore, a systematic study of American democratic institutions had to begin with Old World civilization.

Some social Darwinists had turned to this theory of history in order to bolster an ethnocentric claim for Anglo-Saxon superiority, a claim which rested on a belief in the existence of an Anglo-Saxon race. Anglo-Saxons, so the claim went, were born with an innate bent for liberty which they had brought out with them from the primitive Black Forests of Germany. East European and African stocks were denied this trait by nature and could, therefore, never acquire it. Because a fierce love of freedom was indispensable to democratic institutions, only those in American society of Anglo-Saxon antecedents were fit keepers of such institutions.

Turner the historian, like James the psychologist, was not a reformer, but such a view of American development cut against the grain of his own historical scholarship. Working quietly in the archives of the University of Wisconsin, he proceeded to debunk, and with pulverizing effect, the extravagant claim of Anglo-Saxon theorists. In a paper which he read before the Wisconsin Historical Association in 1893, he gave to historical scholarship his now famous "Turner thesis" on the significance of the frontier in American history.

Turner's central thesis is contained in the following two passages from his memorable paper. In the first of these, Turner established the dialectical relationship of American social development and the frontier environment:[5]

[5] Frederick Jackson Turner, "The Significance of the Frontier in American History," *Proceedings of the State Historical Society of Wisconsin*, 1893, p. 80. Later, Franz Boas was to challenge Anglo-Saxon racial theorists with anthropological evidence.

American social development has been continually beginning over again on the frontier. This perennial rebirth, this fluidity of American life, this expansion westward with its new opportunities, its continuous touch with the simplicity of primitive society, furnish the forces dominating American character. The true point of view in the history of this nation is not the Atlantic coast, it is the Great West.

The second passage took on Germanic claimants of American democratic institutions:[6]

In the settlement of America we have to observe how European life entered the continent, and how America modified and developed that life, and reacted on Europe. Our early history is the study of European germs developing in an American environment. Too exclusive attention has been paid by institutional students to the Germanic origins, too little to the American factors. Now, the frontier is the line of most rapid and effective Americanization. The wilderness masters the colonist. It finds him a European in dress, industries, look, modes of travel, and thought. It takes him from the railroad car and puts him in the birch canoe. It strips off the garments of civilization and arrays him in the hunting shirt and the moccasin. It puts him in the log cabin of the Cherokee and Iroquois, and runs an Indian palisade around him. Before long he has gone to planting Indian corn and plowing with a sharp stick; he shouts the war cry and takes the scalp in orthodox Indian fashion. In short, at the frontier the environment is at first too strong for the man. He must accept the conditions which it furnishes, or perish, and so he fits himself into the Indian clearings and follows the Indian trails. Little by little he transforms the wilderness, but the outcome is not the old Europe, not simply the development of Germanic germs, any more than the first phenomenon was a case of reversion to the Germanic mark. The fact is, that here is a new product that is American.

Turner's fame and scholarly influence spread with mercurial swiftness after 1893. Literally dozens of doctoral dissertations in history have been inspired by his frontier thesis. By now, a host of scholarly works have been published either in defense or in refutation of the Turner thesis. But whatever the status of the Turner thesis may be in modern-day historical scholarship, there is no gainsaying the fact that Turner, although himself not a social reformer, had provided historical ammunition which social reformers at the turn of the century were to use against Anglo-Saxon supremicists. After Turner, few would claim

[6] *Ibid.*, pp. 81–82.

the Black Forest of Germany as the source of the American value system, anymore than Olympian idealism would be claimed as the source of inspiration for the Federal Constitution after Charles A. Beard had published his *An Economic Interpretation of the Constitution of the United States.*

By the time Beard published his *An Economic Interpretation of the Constitution of the United States* in 1913, successive waves of liberal Darwinists, from Henry George (*Progress and Poverty,* 1879) to J. Allen Smith (*The Spirit of American Government,* 1907), had already attempted to demonstrate the force of economic influences in human affairs. Even so, it was quite daring of Beard to subject the most revered document in American society to the realism of an economic interpretation.

The claim that economic influences had a hand in shaping the United States Constitution was, in fact, not new with Beard.[7] But unlike earlier writers, Beard went into the archives of the Treasury Department for the historical research with which to validate his claim.

It was never Beard's intention to denigrate the dignity of the Constitution or otherwise to assault its moral integrity. Indeed, it is no accident that the book bears in its title the indefinite "An Economic Interpretation" rather than the definite "The Economic Interpretation," for Beard had not meant to suggest that the Constitution was the product of economic determinism alone. He had merely used painstaking historical scholarship to reveal the economic sources of the Constitution, and with this weapon against constitutional cultists he meant to save the Constitution of the United States from the dangers of ancestor worship.

With his canny Hoosier foresight, Beard then presented to the world his economic study of the Constitution as staid scholarship. Without polemics, and without resort to a flashy writing style—even though, as Goldman has observed, Beard "could write with either shillelagh or stiletto"—he gave his most important conclusions in what appears to be singularly uninspired prose.[8]

Beard wrote:

At the close of this long and arid survey—partaking of the nature of catalogue—it seems worthwhile to bring together the important con-

---

[7] See, for example, A. M. Simons, *Social Forces in American History* (New York: The Macmillan Company, 1911), especially Chapters 7 through 10.

[8] Goldman, *Rendezvous,* p. 153.

clusions for political science which the data presented appear to warrant.

The movement for the Constitution of the United States was originated and carried through principally by four groups of personality interests which had been been adversely affected under the Articles of Confederation: money, public securities, manufacturers, and trade and shipping.

The first firm steps toward the formation of the Constitution were taken by a small and active group of men immediately interested through their personal possessions in the outcome of their labors.

More:[9]

The Constitution was not created by "the whole people" as the jurists have said; neither was it created by "the states" as Southern nullifiers long contended; but it was the work of a consolidated group whose interests knew no state boundaries and were truly national in their scope.

Reactions to the book came quickly. By the personal bias of the reader, it was either vehemently condemned or praised. Beard's own account of the reaction reports:[10]

Some members of the New York Bar Association became so alarmed by the book that they formed a committee and summoned me to appear before it; and, when I declined on the ground that I was not engaged in legal politics or political politics, they treated my reply as a kind of contempt of court. Few took the position occupied by Justice Oliver Wendell Holmes, who once remarked to me that he had not got excited about the book, like some of his colleagues, but had supposed that it was intended to throw light on the nature of the Constitution, and, in his opinion, did so in fact.

Even as Beard had used history to free the Constitution from ancestor worship, so did Louis D. Brandeis, about five years before Beard's book appeared, strike a mighty blow to free it from the grip of dead legal precedent. His weapon was the "Brandeis Brief."

When Brandeis came before the Supreme Court of the United States in 1908 to argue, in behalf of the State of Oregon, in the case of

[9] Charles A. Beard, *An Economic Interpretation of the Constitution of the United States* (New York: The Macmillan Company, 1946), pp. 324–25. Copyright 1935. Permission of the Macmillan Co.
[10] See Beard's "Introduction to the 1935 Edition" in *ibid.*, pp. viii–ix.

Muller v. Oregon, he followed Oliver Wendell Holmes, Jr., and Roscoe Pound in urging upon the legal profession the concept of "the living law." As early as 1881, Holmes had written: "The life of the law has not been logic: it has been experience."[11] But it was the Brandeis victory in the case of *Muller v. Oregon* that gave "the living law" concept judicial acceptance in the federal courts.

Brandeis was a successful and wealthy corporation lawyer at the time he was engaged by the State of Oregon to plead its case. Why, then, did he agree to argue in defense of a state statute which would limit the hours of labor for women in industry? His biographer suggests the answer:[12]

> . . . Brandeis noted with much concern the waning public respect for law, for lawyers, and for judges. This happened many times before in history. The lawyer's failure to keep up with social and economic progress, Brandeis said, was as old as the profession itself—it was inherent in the very process of erecting a working law for today upon the precedents of yesterday and the day before. . . .
>
> Brandeis saw this divorce of law from life as peculiarly dangerous in America, where constitutional limitations were invoked "to stop the natural vent of legislation. Where statutes giving expression to the new social spirit were clearly constitutional, *judges imbued with the restless spirit of individualism,* often construed them away." [*Italics added.*]

Brandeis appeared before the highest tribunal of the land in the case of *Muller v. Oregon* with a brief which contained only *two pages* of legal argumentation and over a *hundred pages* of social statistics. He had drawn upon social experience and industrial conditions in Europe —mainly from Germany and the Scandinavian countries—and the United States to persuade the Court that the statutory regulation of working conditions for women and children in industry does raise the level of public health and morals in society.

Brandeis had gambled on sociological jurisprudence to carry the day for him in *Muller v. Oregon,* because he had noted that "in all the cases in which social legislation had been set aside, the judges, by recourse to abstract logic, had confidently denied any 'reasonable' relation be-

---

11 Oliver Wendell Holmes, Jr., *The Common Law* (Boston: Little, Brown and Company, 1881), p. 10.
12 Alpheus Thomas Mason, *Brandeis: A Free Man's Life* (New York: The Viking Press, 1946), p. 246.

tween the legislation and the stated objective of improved public health."[13]

Brandeis won his gamble. The Supreme Court of the United States, in *Muller v. Oregon,* for the first time sustained an hours-of-labor statute of a state legislature; theretofore, it had declared such laws as unconstitutional. The case of the New York bakers in *Lochner v. New York* is a prominent case in point. By deciding for Oregon in the Muller case, the Court had taken judicial notice of sociological jurisprudence. But more than that, in the contest of sanctions between social and liberal Darwinism for orientational hegemony in public policy, the Court's decision had put a new powerful weapon into the hands of social reformers in the form of a "Brandeis Brief." Through the legal authority of the Court to interpret the Constitution, eighteenth-century values were endowed with new patterns of expression and, therefore, with a capacity to prescribe *norms of behavior* toward women in twentieth-century factories:[14]

> For the first time, argument in a Supreme Court case was based not on dead legal precedents, but on the living facts of industrial America. Brandeis brought law and life together. Fitting eighteenth-century concepts to twentieth-century conditions, he made the law grow a hundred years in a day.

After the Muller case, variations of a "Brandeis Brief" were to be used many times in defense of social legislation. Court decisions of the type that had come out of the Muller case have influenced deeply the course of American social policy. In sum, acceptance by the Court of a "Brandeis Brief" trumpeted the decline of historical jurisprudence in American society and the ascendance of sociological jurisprudence.

Reformers, Popular Writers, and Muckrakers

Insofar as the tug-of-war over sanctioned value orientations between social and liberal Darwinists has relevance for the middle school, it is the inescapable conclusion that out of the contest had come an enlargement of social vision in the United States. What today we call *the helping professions* began to assume a bolder posture in the day-to-day

---

[13] *Ibid.,* p. 248. It is relevant for the later discussion in Chapter 8 to note here that Florence Kelley, Chief Factory Inspector of Illinois, and the one who also opened young Charles Beard's eyes to the squalid conditions in Chicago factories, had a direct hand in engaging Brandeis for the Oregon case.

[14] *Ibid.,* p. 245.

affairs of city life. Especially social workers, educators, and churchmen —incumbents of social roles in organizations whose function it is to maintain the integrity of the institutionalized value system—were no longer content to be mere observers of the passing scene. Indeed, many church and synagogue social-action programs of our own time trace their initial impetus to the revitalizing drive of such clergymen as John Haynes Holmes, Walter Rauschenbusch, Rabbi Stephen S. Wise, and Father John Augustine Ryan.

More and more, members of the helping professions came to see themselves as agents of institutional change. Social Darwinism was for them more than a theoretical abstraction. Each day brought them a close-up look at its social and economic consequences in the tenements and sweatshops of the city. These, and other Americans, refused to accept squalor-bred human degradation as the heritage of 1776. They were conservative about maintaining the integrity of the values in the heritage of 1776, but at the same time they acknowledged an obligation to make the heritage viable, through adaptations in the structure of institutions, for life in the new age. A steadfast commitment to the old values of social democracy sharpened their zeal for social reconstruction.

But their zeal might well have been blunted against the granite surface of an indifferent public opinion had it not been for the work of journalists, novelists, and a host of popular magazine writers. These writers flooded the country with a vast assortment of popular literature which carried criticisms of social and economic abuse. They thereby made receptive the broad base of American society to so-called reform programs.

Popular opinion, for the most part, had been little affected by intellectual exchanges between social and liberal Darwinists in the halls of academia and in scholarly journals. The scholarly books of Ward, Turner, Sumner, and other liberal and social Darwinists were of no direct interest to the populace of countryside and city. The great impact of such books was upon small circles of intellectuals in the professions, the business community, and politics. Novels and magazines, on the other hand, were eagerly consumed by large audiences in town and country.

Because the mix of social experience is a product of many discrete events, we should be aware that while social experience can indeed be explained as a body of separate events which, in recital, seem to have occurred at random, they have little cognitive value for the social sciences unless they are perceived in the cultural matrix in which they have occurred. We have to follow, therefore, with our "mind's-eye," the *simultaneous* influence on the social climate of liberal Darwinists in college classrooms, popular writers, and the work of would-be reformers. In the live context of their age, they reinforced each other. Liberal Darwinists provided the ideological rationale for legislated change, reform-minded pressure groups petitioned government for the change, and popular magazines at the same time turned a political identification with reform programs into a political asset. And because popular writers and popular magazines *did exert* a powerful influence in molding supportive public opinion for social reconstruction, they merit at least a passing reference in our historical sketch of the period in which the middle school first appeared.

At the same time that scholars attacked social Darwinism in academic language, popular writers exposed the social and economic consequences of social Darwinism in language that irritated popular feeling and drove it to protest. Henry Demarest Lloyd's *Wealth Against Commonwealth,* published in 1884, was one of the earliest contributions to such an emerging literature of exposure. Lloyd's book exposed the nefarious behavior of a great corporation. It had a wide circulation and it served as a model for Ida Tarbell's later history of the Standard Oil Company. Lloyd's book to this day stands as a marker in the annals of protest literature.

Lloyd denounced with great eloquence the practices of big business. His pen, like a sharp knife, cut deep into the value symbolism of social Darwinism. "Survival of the fittest" was a thorn he especially could not endure: He wrote:[15]

> There is no hope for any of us, but the weak must go first in the golden rule of business. There is no other field of human associations in which any such rule of action is allowed. The man who should apply in his family or in his citizenship this "survival of the fittest" theory as it is practically professed and operated in business would be a monster and would speedily be made extinct.

Another writer who expressed great indignation at social abuses was David Graham Phillips. His *Treason of the Senate* told of senators who were loyal to their business masters but traitors to their constitu-

[15] Henry Demarest Lloyd, *Wealth Against Commonwealth* (New York: Harper and Bros., 1884), pp. 494–95.

ents. Together with Anna Spencer, who wrote *Women's Share in Social Culture,* Phillips had interested himself in the social and economic problems of women. Perhaps his best work on this subject is the novel *Susan Lenox: Her Fall and Rise,* a story of the vicissitudes in a woman's life as it was affected by the social environment. Phillips also contributed many reform articles to the magazines of his day—usually bold articles which were read widely.

Unique among writers during this period were the Van Vorst sisters. They had written a series of articles for *Everybody's Magazine* in 1902 under the title "The Woman Who Toils, Being the Experience of Two Ladies as Factory Girls." The content of their story was drawn from personal experience. The ladies had worked in a Pittsburgh pickle factory, a clothing mill in New York, a shoe factory in Massachusetts, and a cotton mill in the South. They told of how women workers were subjected to shameful treatment in factories. These articles contained in a somewhat underdeveloped form the journalistic realism which was later to stamp muckrake literature.

Before 1900, the novel of rococo romance and local color held sway in America, and the novel which dealt with social problems was the exception. After 1900 the trend was reversed. The vast majority of the novels which came from the presses during the ten-year period 1900 to 1910 were concerned chiefly with social problems of one kind or another. Two explanations for the turn in book publishing were the appearance of low-cost, mass-circulation magazines and the advent of a new style of journalism. It was a style of journalistic reporting which President Theodore Roosevelt, in a moment of pique, called "muckraking." The intervention of these two elements stimulated the national appetite for a type of literature which was to alter the character of American belles-lettres.

Criticism of social abuse in the literature of the late 1800's had been couched in general terms, and seldom had it specified persons or corporations. Muckrake literature, on the other hand, was specific and sometimes deliberately personal. For a period of about ten years, muckrake writing laid bare for Americans the worst of social and economic conditions in their midst. Muckrake writers were essentially journalists and not reformers. However, because circulation-hungry magazines paid well for muckrake copy, the more talented journalists of the period turned to muckraking. They were reporters of the passing American scene.

Before 1880 there were four important magazines publishing in the United States: *Harper's, Century, Atlantic,* and *Scribner's.* These magazines appealed primarily for the patronage of cultivated America. They were sedate and exclusive, they sold for thirty-five cents, and they had no competitors.

But by 1890 three new magazines had appeared: *Ladies Home Journal, Munsey's,* and *Cosmopolitan.* These newcomers were bidding for larger audiences through a no-holds-barred competition which, among others, included a search for means of selling at the corner stand for less than twenty-five cents.

It was at this time that Samuel Sidney McClure entered the magazine field. The story of McClure's entry into the magazine business is in itself a Horatio Alger story.[16] The success of the English low-priced magazine had convinced McClure that such a magazine could also be successful in the United States. On June 1, 1893, accordingly, American newsstands saw for the first time a magazine called *McClure's,* which sold for fifteen cents a copy. That first issue sold 8,000 copies, and McClure was convinced he was on the right track. The low-priced magazine had arrived in the United States, and with the exception of *Munsey's, McClure's* circulation by 1900 had out-distanced all other magazines.[17]

McClure rejected a notion, which some editors of his day held, that "this or that was very good but it wouldn't interest the people of the Middle West or the people in the little towns."[18] He insisted that these people would respond to whatever was interesting just as would readers in New York or Boston. So it was that McClure came to publish lively articles on rather complex subjects. He engaged a permanent staff of trained writers, a staff that was to serve him well in making *McClure's* the foremost publication among popular magazines.

Because McClure aimed at a mass public, he put the reader's interest above everything else. His formula for getting the important stories for the magazine were to pay the writer well, make the expense money generous, and give the writer all the time he needed to prepare an article.

Among the many notable authors who have contributed to *Mc-*

---

16 For an insider's account of how muckraking and competition for magazine circulation became linked soon after the turn of 1900 see Samuel Sidney McClure, *My Autobiography* (New York: Frederick A. Stokes Co., 1913).

17 *Ibid.,* p. 222.

18 *Ibid.,* pp. 130–31.

Clure's, three especially stand out because of their journalistic brilliance: Ida Tarbell, Ray Stannard Baker, and Lincoln Steffens. These three were permanent members of *McClure's* editorial staff.

Early in the 1900's McClure had assigned each of them to prepare articles on three *different* subjects. Tarbell was to do a story on the Standard Oil Company, Baker was assigned to do a story on trade unionism, and Steffens was to travel in the United States and write about American cities. Each of these writers had a story ready for the issue of January 1903. Steffens had an article on American cities, "The Shame of Minneapolis," Tarbell was ready with a third installment on the Standard Oil Company, and Baker had prepared a story on the anthracite coal strike of 1902.

Not until the magazine was in dummy form did it occur to McClure that the three articles, although written by *different* authors on three *different* subjects, bore a remarkable resemblance to one another in that they were actually treating *the same general subject.*

McClure's keen editorial sense told him that he was on to something of importance. Before him was not just another issue of *McClure's* magazine. In dramatic fashion, he proceeded to insert, at the last moment, on the last page of the January 1903 number an unusual semieditorial. The editorial—one of the most significant in American magazine history—called the reader's attention to the three articles by asking:[19]

> How many of those who have read through this number of the magazine noticed that it contains three articles on one subject? We did not plan it so; it is a coincidence that the January McClure's is such an arraignment of American character as should make every one of us stop and think. How many noticed that?
>
> The leading article, "The Shame of Minneapolis," might have been called, "The American Contempt of Law." That title could well have served for the current chapter of Miss Tarbell's "History of Standard Oil." And it would have fitted perfectly Mr. Baker's "The Right to Work." All together, these articles come pretty near showing how universal is this dangerous trait of ours. Miss Tarbell has our capitalists conspiring among themselves, deliberately, shrewdly, upon legal advice, to break the law so far as it restrained them, and to misuse it to restrain others who were in their way. Mr. Baker shows labor, the ancient enemy of capital, and the chief complaint of the trusts' unlawful acts, itself committing and excusing crimes. And in "The Shame of Min-

[19] S. S. McClure, "Editorial," *McClure's,* Vol. XX, January 1903.

neapolis" we see the administration of a city employing crimes for the profit of the elected officials, while the citizens—Americans of good stock and more than average culture, and honest, healthy Scandinavians—stood by complacent and not alarmed.

. . . We all are doing our worst and making the public pay. The public is the people. We forget that we all are the people; that while each of us in his group can shove off on the rest the bill of today, the debt is only postponed. The rest are passing it on back to us. We have to pay in the end, every one of us. And in the end the sum total of the debt will be our liberty.

With this issue of *McClure's*, exposure became the fixed policy of the magazine, a policy which established muckraking in the annals of magazine history. It was not yet called muckraking; this came later, when President Theodore Roosevelt gave it the name in 1906.

Partly by chance and partly by a new technique of reporting, muck-rake writers exposed the sores of American society. No reformers themselves, they nevertheless buttressed the reform climate at one level of society just as liberal Darwinist scholarship did at another. What muckrake writers did was to look at their world with an unvarnished realism. They reported honestly, fully, and above all interestingly what they had found. The public, now anxious and indignant, eagerly read the long and sometimes complicated and serious articles which they wrote. These writers turned the white glare of publicity on areas of social abuse. As one leading muckrake writer had put it, "This was a moral, dramatic, factual and interesting writing down of American ways, institutions, and leaders."[20]

A Watershed of Reform

What began soon after Appomattox as a relatively mild discontent with emerging orientations in social behavior had by the late 1800's become a loud chorus of protest. Strong voices began to challenge the legitimacy of these new directions. These voices blended eventually with calls for change in the institutional patterns of the American social system.

Happily, political mechanisms in the United States allowed for institutional change without a resort to armed violence. Consequently, a host of institutional modifications, in private and public sectors of

[20] Ray Stannard Baker, *American Chronicles* (New York: Charles Scribner's Sons, 1945), p. 169. By permission of Charles Scribner's Sons Company.

America, eventually reconstructed American society into the familiar image of the World War I period.

But before World War I distracted American minds from social reconstruction, the need for a tightening of controls on laissez-faire had become established social policy. State and federal regulatory commissions were created to intervene in the operations of factory and market place. Spurred on by institutional leadership, established social service organizations enlarged their goals and broadened their sphere of activities. Where the exigencies of social life demanded it, new organizations were brought into existence to perform functions that were beyond the scope of established organizations.

Such changes in the institutional network of American society were visible manifestations of a renewed and dynamic social outlook which had swept over the country. Historian Harold Underwood Faulkner has interpreted this episode in the American past as "the quest for social justice."[21]

Even a passing reference to just a few of the *new* "helping" organizations that appeared between 1865 and 1914 leaves a lasting impression. The Salvation Army, a product of English urban life, took hold in the American city when, in 1880, seven Army lassies, led by Commissioner George Scott Hamilton, crossed the Atlantic to "open fire" in America.

Another import—cultural borrowing—from English city life during this period was the settlement house. London's Toynbee Hall stood as the ancestral model for Hull House in Chicago, Henry Street Settlement in New York, and Andover House in Boston. Among reformers who had come from the ranks of the helping professions, the names of Jane Addams, William Wald, Robert A. Wood, Mary Simkhovitch, and other pioneering social workers had by 1914 become inseparably identified with social reconstruction.

Juvenile courts, probation departments, private philanthropic associations, the Visiting Nurses Association, and baby-get-well clinics are some of the other public and private service organizations that were established to give expression to an aroused concern for man and his social environment.

No sphere of American life escaped the many-faceted quest for social justice which the new humanitarianism exuded. When the twentieth

21 See Harold Underwood Faulkner, *The Quest for Social Justice, 1898–1914* (New York: The Macmillan Company, 1931). Hereafter cited as *Social Justice*. Copyright 1931. Permission of the Macmillan Company.

century was still very young, there was much in American society to suggest that those value orientations to future development which more faithfully expressed the democratic ideal were in the ascendancy.

Evidence of this in the sector of public education was to be seen in transformations that had been wrought in what began soon after the Civil War as "the new education." The new education was a product of the same dynamic that was reconstructing the institutional patterns of American society. Public education, like other institutions of the period, responded adaptively to a vigorous reassertion of American ideals which lay imbedded in the old values. Altogether, we see here the verity of Durkheim's dictum that society is, indeed, the source of educational life.

In the chapters to follow, we shall observe how remarkably close developments in public education paralleled events in the general society. The social matrix, we shall find, impressed its shape deeply upon the public school organization of the new era.[22]

---

[22] For deeper insight into the relationship between ideals and values of a society see Emile Durkheim, *Sociology and Philosophy,* translated by D. F. Pocock and J. G. Peristiani (New York: The Free Press, 1953), especially pp. 80–97.

7

THE CHANGING SOCIETY AND
PUBLIC EDUCATION

Because the contest in which social and liberal Darwinists were protagonists had spilled over into the sector of public education, we shall find that American education had its own assortment of social Darwinists, liberal Darwinists, reformers, and even a muckraker here and there.

Events that led to the middle school in 1910 came closely bunched, paralleling the industrialization and urbanization of the latter half of the nineteenth century. Event followed event at such a fast pace that it is altogether easy to overlook today that the American middle school represents a *reform of a still earlier reform* in American secondary education. How did this come about?

The end of the Civil War found American education woefully backward. Neither private nor public education was prepared for the aggressive urban and industrial growth which lay ahead. College education was at low ebb in the United States, and formal postgraduate study was rare. Most American scholars of that period traveled to German universities for their doctorates.

Underneath it all, however, ran the American faith in education.[1] True, the war, and later the Panic of 1873, did distract Americans from the public school, whose place in society had been secured firmly before the war by educational statesmen such as Horace Mann and Henry Barnard. But following the 1870's, when the backwardness of American education was pressed home by European contrasts, Americans again turned their attention on the schoolhouse.

Just how backward education was in the United States came to Americans under embarrassing circumstances. The year 1876 was a time for great national celebration. It was the centennial of the Republic! What could have been more pleasing to national pride than a mammoth world exhibition of the noblest and best that had come from the American people? So on May 10, 1876, a Centennial Exposition was opened in Fairmount Park, Philadelphia.

There was much in the Centennial Exposition to put a glow on American national pride. Americans were especially pleased with achievements of their manufacturing industries, the progress of their science and technology, and with their diversified agriculture. But their pleasure subsided some as they studied the many educational exhibits at the Exposition.

The place of education in society was prominent in the theme of the Centennial Exposition, and there were many exhibits of school life in the United States and Europe. Thanks to eloquent lifelike models, millions of Americans for the first time became exposed to facets of European pedagogy. Especially impressive was what Americans saw of European technical education.[2] But even more significant for the American middle school of the future was what they saw of European childhood education.

Two entire buildings were given over to exhibits of childhood education in Germany, Belgium, and Switzerland. Childhood education in America was shown up, on comparison, as far behind these countries.

---

[1] In a retrospective reflection upon the evolution of American society, Herbert Croly noted in 1909: "The American faith in education has been characterized as a superstition. . . . " See Herbert Croly, *The Promise of American Life* (New York: The Macmillan Company, 1918), p. 400. Copyright 1909. Permission of the Macmillan Company.

[2] For an illustrative reference to the American reaction see *Proceedings of the First Annual Convention of the College Association of the Middle States and Maryland, 1889,* p. 4. When forty-four preparatory schools were admitted to membership in 1892, the Association changed its name to the "Association of Colleges and Preparatory Schools of the Middle States and Maryland." Hereafter cited as *Proceedings,* Association of Middle States.

Americans must have been taken with what they had seen, for, within two decades following the Exposition, there was a "catching up" in the kindergarten and elementary school. Elementary school programs —not all of them, to be sure—took on the diffuseness of a child-centered orientation, and private and public kindergartens increased in the United States from less than two hundred in 1878 to nearly three thousand by 1898.[3]

Seen in retrospect, what the exhibits of European education did was to stimulate popular enthusiasm in America for the pedagogical practices of European countries in which the ideas of Rousseau, Pestalozzi, and Froebel were dominant. As strains of their pedagogical thought crossed the Atlantic, reforms—some more profound than others—in the elementary school curriculum and in methods of instruction became more frequent. Indeed, much of what came with educational reform in the elementary school had sprung from the seedbed of their ideas.

The arrival of the twentieth century found much in the elementary school of the United States that was still shoddy and outmoded. But by then, thanks to Francis Wayland Parker and others of his pedagogical mien, it was no longer because America lacked for native models of superior elementary school programs.[4]

Indeed, Nicholas Murray Butler, who at the time was on the faculty of Columbia College, and later became President of Columbia University, observed in 1895, "No secondary school or college in America can show teaching to compare . . . with the best teaching to be seen in many of the public elementary schools. . . ."[5]

Many today will probably find it difficult to fathom a qualitative gap between elementary and secondary school teaching of the magnitude suggested in Butler's statement. But at the time of Butler's statement, in the 1890's, there was only the barest operational integration in American school systems between elementary and secondary school units. Elementary and secondary school units functioned at the time almost as independent organizational structures. The elementary school was primarily a school for children of the masses. For an overwhelming majority of these children, elementary school education was terminal. However, because the most frequent point of contact with

---

[3] Arthur Meier Schlesinger, *The Rise of the City, 1878–1898* (New York: The Macmillan Company, 1933), p. 162.
[4] See the chapter "Francis Wayland Parker, Democrat," in Merle Curti, *Social Ideas.*
[5] *Proceedings,* Association of Middle States, 1895, p. 102.

the school system was in the elementary school, the latter school unit was closest to the people and, therefore, was most susceptible to societal pressures for change.

The American public high school, on the other hand, was tied to the college. It was a school for that small fraction of the public school population which went on to college. Although tax-supported *like* the elementary school, the high school, *unlike* the elementary school, stood aloof from emerging aspirations at the mass base of society. There was little in the American public high school of the period with which the common man could identify. Its structure, process, and institutional mien was college-oriented. Largely because of this, secondary education in America was, in effect, a prisoner of the colleges.

Because the high school was bound by tradition to such a relationship with the college, and because schools, as pattern-maintenance organizations, are inherently conservative, there was *no leverage point* at which *change* in secondary education could be initiated by an *internal change agent.* Any change in the character of the public high school had to be sanctioned by the colleges, or else the high school risked a loss of prestige as a college preparatory school. However, the temper of the period was running against the colleges and they were constrained by emerging conditions in society to assume the role of *external change agent* in American secondary education.

Even as the colleges were holding the high school to an academic tradition no longer functional for American society, they too had become prisoners of the past.[6] The same dynamics of economic and social change that had made obsolete American secondary education had also stamped the mark of obsolescence upon American higher education. Both were out of joint with the time. But so long as the authority of tradition kept the high school in a subordinate relationship to the college, the incentive for change in the high school had to come from the college.

And higher education at last did provide that incentive. A strategy

---

[6] The entrance requirements to Yale in 1894 were as follows: (1) Latin grammar; (2) Caesar, *Gallic War* (books I–IV); (3) Cicero, *Orations;* (4) Virgil, *Bucolics* and six books of *Æneid;* (5) Ovid, *Metamorphoses,* translated at sight; (6) translation at sight of passages from Latin; (7) translation into Latin of connected passages of English prose; (8) Roman history; (9) Greek grammar; (10) Xenophon, *Anabasis,* four books; (11) Homer, *Iliad,* three books; (12) translation of Greek into English at sight; (13) translation of connected passages of Greek into English; (14) Greek history; (15) higher arithmetic; (16) algebra; (7) plane geometry; (18) French or German; (19) English literature. See in *ibid.,* 1894, pp. 96–97.

was devised to maintain the high school in its traditional role as a college preparatory school and at the same time rescue the college from its own predicament by shifting certain courses in the college curriculum down to the high school. The chief architect of the strategy was Charles William Eliot, President of Harvard University from 1869 to 1909.

President Eliot's stratagem was at once innovative and bold, but then, innovative boldness was an Eliot hallmark. His reputation as a superb college administrator, the prestige of Harvard University, and his own strong personality combined to gain wide currency for the Eliot stratagem. Eliot, alas, had been stamped in the mold of the *charismatic leader*.

Unless we pause at this juncture to look closer at the concept of *charismatic leader*, it would be difficult to fathom the immense influence that Eliot exerted on American secondary education and why he was able to exert such an influence.

It will be recalled from the earlier discussion of authority that Max Weber identified three pure types of legitimate authority in a society. One of these was *charismatic authority*. Such authority, it was stated, is acknowledged by followers of a leader in whom they recognize "the gift of grace." Followers of the charismatic leader commit themselves to an organized action by the authority of some mystique which they claim resides in the person of their leader.

However, action which is legitimized—or, if we will, sanctioned—by charismatic authority constitutes a *break* with tradition to a greater or lesser degree. Therefore, if a movement which is sanctioned by charismatic authority is to assume permanence, there has to occur what Weber refers to as "the routinization of charisma."[7] Structures emerge in which the movement is routinized through formal procedures. These structures, if they survive the clash with traditional authority, themselves in time become traditional.

Not only was Charles Eliot of a charismatic cut, but, as President of Harvard University, he was regarded as one who spoke with *special authority* on matters in education. For alongside Eliot's own charismatic personality was the *charisma of his office*.

Charisma of office, like charisma itself, is difficult to define. It is essentially an emotional, or affective, response to an office. Perhaps

[7] Max Weber's discourse on "routinization of charisma" will be found in Weber, *Social and Economic Organization*, pp. 363–86.

the following illustration, which the political reporter Stewart Alsop has used to illuminate a special political asset which an incumbent of the office of President of the United States enjoys, will serve even better than a definition. Of the many political assets in this office, Alsop writes,[8]

> . . . is the mystique which surrounds the presidential office. . . . A mere senator, a human being like the rest of us, cannot compete against the Great Seal; or the band playing *Hail to the Chief;* or that swelling murmur in the crowd: "Look, look, it's the President."

Eliot, the charismatic leader, had by the 1880's crystallized a plan for the reorganization of secondary education in the United States. But Eliot had not reckoned with the latent consequences of an action which weakens the authority of tradition.

History has demonstrated many times over that a tampering with tradition is fraught with grave latent consequences for tradition-secured interests. The French Revolution stands as a classic example of this phenomenon.

It was Chateaubriand who wrote, "The patricians began the Revolution, the plebeians finished it."[9] French aristocracy had attempted to strengthen itself during a period of national crisis at the expense of the monarchy by tampering with traditional political structures. How could they have anticipated the latent consequences of their radical action, any more than the barons of England could have anticipated the democratic uses to which Magna Carta would be put after they had wrested it from King John at Runnymede in 1215?

Perhaps it is stretching similitude too far, but as we move still closer to the events that led to the middle school, it is difficult to resist the temptation of giving a transposed application to the sense of Chateaubriand's comment by suggesting this: Patricians in higher education

---

[8] Stewart Alsop, "Presidents Don't Lose," *The Saturday Evening Post,* November 2, 1963.

[9] Quoted in Georges Lefebvre, *The Coming of the French Revolution,* translated by R. R. Palmer (Princeton, N.J.: Princeton University Press, 1947), p. 3. In an assenting comment on Chateaubriand's statement, Georges Lefebvre, acknowledged as a foremost authority on the French Revolution, wrote the following: "The first act of the Revolution, in 1788, consisted in a triumph of the aristocracy, which, taking advantage of the government crisis, hoped to reassert itself and win back the political authority of which the Capetian dynasty had despoiled it. But, after having paralyzed the royal power which upheld its own social preeminence, the aristocracy opened the way to the bourgeois revolution, then to the popular revolution in the cities and finally to the revolution of the peasants. . . . " (P. 3.)

began the reorganization of American secondary education, plebeians in the public schools finished it.

The Era of Charles W. Eliot

Eliot's intervention in the sector of public education was supported by his excellent credentials as an educational innovator. He had come to the presidency of Harvard at a time when higher education in the United States was struggling to escape from its low intellectual estate and when Harvard was a "poverty-stricken college, with vague relations to learning and research. . . ."[10]

Eliot was no stranger to Harvard. He had graduated from there at the age of nineteen. Following a period of service with the Union forces during the Civil War, where he attained the rank of Captain, he returned to Harvard as an Assistant Professor of Chemistry. He distinguished himself neither as a teacher nor as a research scholar while in this rank, but he did show a pronounced talent for administration which was recognized and used by the central administration of Harvard.[11]

When he was bypassed in an appointment to a chair in chemistry, Eliot left Harvard for travel in Europe. There he set himself to studying educational systems of Western Europe.

His observations of European collegiate education led to the publication in 1868 of two articles in the *Atlantic Monthly* under the title "The New Education." Eliot spelled out in these articles his notion on how American universities ought to be developing. His model was the German university. Eliot's ideas apparently had made a deep impression upon some of the trustees at Harvard, because when the President's office became vacant he emerged as a strong contender for the post. After overcoming some resistance on the part of the Harvard faculty, Eliot received the appointment and he embarked in 1869 upon a long and illustrious career as President of Harvard.

Samuel Eliot Morison, official historian of Harvard, reports that when Eliot was inaugurated in 1869:[12]

---

10 Allan Nevins, *The Emergence of Modern America, 1865–1878* (New York: The Macmillan Company, 1927), p. 264. Hereafter cited as *Modern America*. Copyright 1927. Permission of the Macmillan Company.
11 Samuel Eliot Morison, *Three Centuries of Harvard, 1636–1936* (Cambridge, Mass.: Harvard University Press, 1936), p. 325. Hereafter cited as *Three Centuries at Harvard*.
12 *Ibid.*, p. 323.

. . . America was in the midst of the most roaring spectacular material development that she had ever known. Exploitation and expansion were the order of the day. . . . Everyone was making money and expecting to make more; the inevitable post-war depression was not even suspected; the clank of machinery and the clink of dollars silenced religion, letters, and the arts.

Eliot's inauguration, therefore, should be seen in historical perspective as a welcome event in American higher education. Up to that time, American colleges were for the most part led by theologians. There was little dialogue between the college and the high school. Now, a new kind of educational leadership was needed in higher education; a leadership which was sensitive to the sweeping changes that had come in the aftermath of war. The trustees of Harvard saw in Eliot a potential for institutional leadership.

Harvard's confidence in its young president proved well placed. Eliot transformed "Harvard from a small undergraduate institution with a few loosely affiliated schools into a great modern university."[13] But because of its later significance for the revitalization of American secondary education, we should note that other institutions of higher learning had also appointed men to the top position who personified the new leadership. Among Eliot's immediate contemporaries by 1900 were such illustrious college presidents as Andrew D. White of Cornell, James McCosh of Princeton, Noah Porter of Yale, James B. Angell of Michigan, Daniel C. Gilman of Johns Hopkins, and William Rainey Harper of Chicago. These men collectively revitalized higher education in the United States and, in order to secure its success, they precipitated also the revitalization of secondary education.

Eliot proceeded upon assuming administrative stewardship of Harvard to revitalize that institution in the image of the new education which he had proposed in the *Atlantic Monthly* articles. No part of Harvard escaped his reform-bent determination: organization, curriculum, student life, and educational objectives were subjected to *radical* change. Entrance requirements were stiffened, the curriculum was enlarged to accommodate new advances in science and scholarship, a greater maturity in student life was encouraged, professional training in law, engineering, and medicine was raised to a postgraduate status, and, perhaps the boldest innovation of all, Eliot committed Harvard, all out, to the elective system. So strong was the commitment to the elective system that, by 1875, Harvard juniors had but three prescribed

13 Curti, *American Thought,* p. 515.

courses and seniors only one.[14] Harvard was, in fact, telling Americans through its elective system that the demands of the new age upon collegiate education precluded a student from taking all the offered courses at Harvard in four years. In brief, the dominant orientation of a Harvard education was no longer toward the quality of commitments to the institutionalized values alone, but also toward the universalistic-achievement imperatives of a rapidly developing industrial society. Harvard education, in an important sense, was transformed by Eliot into an object of utility.

Eliot's innovations at Harvard were before long emulated by presidents at other schools. Influential alumni gave enthusiastic endorsement for more advanced study in what is popularly called the "practical subjects." Moreover, the land-grant colleges that had been established under the Morrill Act of 1862, and which unlike the older private colleges were not bound by tradition, already had built-in incentives for infusing the college program with greater *practical* usefulness. So it was that within a span of several decades following the Civil War, American higher education was as one with the new age.

A group of bold and far-sighted college presidents had raised the intellectual level of the American college. They had at the same time turned an outmoded educational organization into a functional mechanism of the developing industrial culture. Because of such magnificent achievements in executive statesmanship, these college presidents became in time the undisputed leaders—the baronial figures—of all American education. Their collective prestige, influence, and power were without equal in the educational community.

And in the center of this prestigious group of college presidents stood the figure of Charles W. Eliot. He had been the pace-setter in the modernization of the American college, and by the 1880's, he was undeniably the *primus inter pares* of the group. A brilliant administrator, he had first put his own organization right. He expanded the organizational goals for Harvard, goals which were more in keeping with new cultural needs than the old had been, and he had made them stick.

But his sharp administrator's sense told him that in order to reap the full benefits of a modernized Harvard, attention would have to be given to the matter of *student input*. More than anything else, it was this concern with student input that took Eliot and other college presidents into the sector of secondary education with seven-league boots.

[14] Nevins, *Modern America*, pp. 265, 269–70.

A number of things about student input were troublesome for the colleges. First, there was the vexatious problem of college entrance requirements. No procedural coordination of any consequence governed student transition from high school to college. Secondary education, like higher education, was in a state of confusion during the decades following the Civil War. The curriculum was fragmented by a profusion of courses which seemed to lack purpose, and there was no such thing as clearly recognized standards anywhere in the country.[15] Both college and public school administrators were driven to distraction by a lack of uniform requirements governing college entrance.

Coupled to the problem of high school–college transition were two characteristics of incoming college students which were especially serious impediments to the upgrading of both liberal arts education and professional programs. High schools were graduating students late in life and lacking the scholastic skills which the college of the broadened curriculum, and of the elective system, demanded of them. Students came from high schools which were still geared for the most part to the classical tradition and where the elective system was yet unknown. Eliot had complained as late as 1896, "In Massachusetts, out of about two hundred and forty high schools in the state, there are not more than twenty-five capable of sending pupils regularly to Harvard College."[16]

The following reference in 1889 to the matter of student input, by a spokesman for the colleges, provides a sharply delineated statement of the problem:[17]

What has sometimes been called the chaotic condition of our educational processes makes it very late before a student can complete the ordinary college and professional course of study. The average student of Harvard, for example, will be twenty-six years of age before he is ready to go into an office as lawyer's clerk. He will generally be regarded as fortunate if from that time on he can earn his own support. If dependent on himself, he will be in no condition to marry before he is thirty.

Compounding the problem of prolonged collegiate and professional education was the growing protest from students and parents. College

[15] Edgar W. Knight, "The Southern Association: Retrospect and Prospect," *The Georgia Review,* Vol. 1, Spring 1947, p. 2.
[16] *Proceedings,* Association of Middle States, 1896, p. 80.
[17] *Ibid.,* 1889, p. 5.

was no longer exclusively for a genteel, home-supported student population. New social and economic conditions in America had made of higher education a passable road for upwardly striving Americans. For these Americans, impatient to pass on this road, time was of the essence!

Formation of Regional Accrediting Associations

Of the interlocking difficulties which affected the characteristics of student input, the colleges first attacked in concert the diversity of college entrance requirements. Out of this effort have emerged today's influential regional accrediting associations. Entirely under college auspices and control at first, these associations became eventually centers of formal and informal interaction between college presidents and public school administrators. Moreover, it was in these regional accrediting associations where some of the hard battles were fought in behalf of the comprehensive American high school and, later, for the middle school.

The earliest of these voluntary associations appeared in 1885, with the formation of the New England Association of Colleges and Preparatory Schools. The event was an outcome of a series of conferences which were begun in 1879 at Trinity College, Connecticut. Here was the first regional association in the United States which was formed for the purpose of standardizing college entrance requirements.

By 1889 the College Association of the Middle States and Maryland, the second regional association, held its first annual meeting. The Association was an expansion of the College Association of Pennsylvania, which was organized in 1887, and it was 1892 before secondary schools were admitted to membership. Its name was then changed to the Association of Colleges and Preparatory Schools of the Middle States and Maryland. It too was organized for the purpose of standardizing college entrance requirements.

As is to be expected, Charles Eliot's influence was felt everywhere in the Middle States and Maryland Association. In 1900 the Association of the Middle States and Maryland established the College Entrance Examination Board, whose examination became immediately, as it is to this day, a powerful regulator of college admission in America.[18]

[18] Charles W. Eliot, "What Has Been Gained in Uniformity of College Admission Requirements in the Past Twenty Years?" *The School Review,* Vol. XII, December 1904, p. 767.

Unlike its sister associations, the North Central Association of Colleges and Secondary Schools was from its inception a collaborative enterprise of colleges and secondary schools. It was no accident that "secondary schools" rather than "preparatory schools" had been taken for the North Central name. Much more democratic in institutional mien than were the older eastern universities, the midwestern universities had cultivated an open relationship between themselves and the secondary schools of their region.

In point of fact, the initial impetus for a North Central Association had come from secondary school circles. Principal W. H. Butts of the Michigan Academy had learned first hand about the New England Association upon the occasion of a visit to New England. After his return home, Butts introduced a resolution, in 1894, before the Michigan Schoolmaster's Club to the effect "that the presidents of the University of Michigan, the University of Wisconsin, the Northwestern University, and the University of Chicago, be asked to unite with a committee of the Club in issuing a call for a meeting to form an association of schools and colleges in the North Central States."[19] The motion prevailed, and in 1895 the North Central Association of Colleges and Secondary Schools was established with President J. B. Angell of Michigan University as its first head.

Simultaneously with the formation of the North Central Association came the Association of Colleges and Preparatory Schools of the Southern States. Its chief architect was Chancellor James H. Kirkland of Vanderbilt University. Charter members at its inception in 1895, as was the case with its sister associations of the New England and the Middle States regions, were all institutions of higher learning.

Much later, in 1918, the Northwest Association of Secondary and Higher Schools held its first annual meeting at Spokane, Washington. It too was concerned with orderly college entrance requirements in its region. However, because it was the last of the regional associations to be organized, and because college entrance was no longer the problem it had been earlier, the Northwest Association was able to accredit at its first annual meeting twenty-five secondary schools and eight "higher schools."[20]

As normalizing mechanisms in consummatory high school–college relations, these regional associations were an unqualified success. Mostly

---

[19] *Proceedings*, NCA, 1895, p. 5; 1915, p. 6.
[20] *North Central Association Quarterly*, Vol. 1, 1926, p. 103. Hereafter cited as NCA *Quarterly*.

through the urging of the eastern associations, the Carnegie Foundation for the Advancement of Teaching was persuaded to turn its vast resources upon the problem of college admission procedures. Out of this has come the now familiar Carnegie Unit, a device which is in fact the modified form of a *unit system* of college admission which was in use experimentally by 1896 at the University of Chicago.[21] Altogether, as these regional accrediting associations gained in influence, their effectiveness as interpreters of norms increased. Indeed, the standardization of college admission had made such good progress by 1912 that the Carnegie Unit was even then attacked as too restrictive. Defensively, the Carnegie Foundation felt constrained to declare in its report for 1912:[22]

> These units have now served their main purpose. They were never intended to constitute a rigid form of college admission, but merely a means of comparing high schools. Already the progress in this matter has been so satisfactory that the general conception of college admission no longer contemplates a certain number of units, but the completion of a satisfactory four-year high school course.

But the formation of regional accrediting associations reflected also the growing sophistication of educative process during that period. Educational technology in America was moving in a parallel direction of development with *all other technologies* in the culture. As is the case when *any technology* turns complex and, therefore, more specialized, a sharper definition of norms became necessary in the educational division of labor between the high school and the college. Because there was no legal authority extant to set and enforce these norms across state lines, college and secondary school administrators had to resort to voluntary associations.

With the exception of North Central, leadership and control of these associations had been before World War I in the hands of college

---

[21] *Proceedings*, Association of Middle States, 1896, pp. 130–31.

[22] Quoted in *Ibid.*, 1915, p. 33. The history of the Carnegie Unit illustrates with singular clarity the deleterious effects of the fetish of routine to which both American college and public school administration are addicted. Despite its long-outlived usefulness for regulating college entrance procedures, it was reported in 1953 that about 60 percent of the nation's colleges and about 63 percent of its high schools were still resorting to the Carnegie Unit for measuring achievement in the high school. For an extensive historical treatment of the Carnegie Unit, as well as for an objective assessment of its strengths and weaknesses, see Ellsworth Tompkins and Walter Gaumnitz, "The Carnegie Unit: Its Origin, Status, and Trends," *The Bulletin of the National Association of Secondary-School Principals*, Vol. 48, January 1964. Hereafter cited as *The Bulletin*, NASSP.

people whose thinking inclined toward a social Darwinist bent. Charles Eliot and Nicholas Murray Butler, for example, gave to a fund for the reprinting of a collection of Spencer's essays at a time when the latter's influence in America had already waned considerably.[23] Enoch Perrine, Professor at Bucknell University, and a member of the Executive Committee of the College Association of Pennsylvania—the Association which was to reorganize as the College Association of the Middle States and Maryland—has left us a candid statement of their social Darwinist inclinations. He said in 1888:[24]

> Huxley truly says that everybody recognizes that in the struggle for existence the successful man uses more knowledge, skill, and industry than his competitor; and our task is to show that the college . . . will not take these qualities away from a man, but help him to develop them. I will speak, then, of a college education not as being beneficial to the state, but to the individual; and not to the individual as a refining influence or a restful vocation, but as a means for conquering the battle for life.

However, as more and more public secondary schools were admitted to membership through accreditation, leadership roles in these associations came to be shared on more equal terms between representatives of colleges and high schools. With a shift of control and in leadership, the associations in time became forums for those voices which called for an American high school structured closer to the democratizing attributes of the American value system. It is altogether significant in this context that, in 1920, the Middle States and Maryland Association established a Commission on Secondary Schools and that, in 1926, "secondary schools" was substituted for "preparatory schools" in the name of the Association.[25]

Eliot Addresses the Superintendents

Successful as the regional accrediting associations had been in normalizing high school–college relations, it was not enough. Once the

23 Hofstadter, *Social Darwinism*, pp. 35–36.
24 *Proceedings of the Second Annual Convention of the College Association of Pennsylvania,* 1888, p. 7. See also the debate on the resolution to lower college entrance requirements in the Middle States and Maryland region in *Proceedings,* Association of Middle States, 1896, pp. 130–204.
25 See also the attack on social Darwinism by Professor Carl Kelsey of the University of Pennsylvania during the 1918 annual meeting of the Middle States and Maryland Association in *ibid.,* 1919, p. 22.

colleges had formed regional accrediting associations, it was relatively easy for them to establish, and compel adherence to, uniform college entrance requirements. These were made the new terms of exchange in consummatory relations between public school and college systems. The influence of colleges in high school–college consummatory relations is indeed a powerful leverage for colleges. By accepting large numbers of high school graduates, they warrant the norms of public school education. And public school patrons, recipients of what economists call "third-party benefits," thus become more inclined to support public school systems. It was an *external control* public school systems could not resist. However, the curriculum of the high school unit continued unchanged, a condition which was most disconcerting to Charles Eliot.

Eliot had been looking critically at the public high school curriculum for some time. He saw in it a threat to the elective system as well as to other college reforms. His eyes were fixed especially on that segment of the secondary school population which went on to college. The college of the new education required a more sophisticated high school graduate, one capable of successful achievement in an advanced college curriculum without prolonging his college years.

Eliot hammered persistently at this theme from the early 1870's, when he first called attention in the *Harvard Reports* to the advanced age of entering freshmen, to the time, in 1888, when he was invited to address the Department of Superintendence of the National Education Association.

Eliot now made the most of his opportunity. He was to address the organized body of the nation's chief school administrators. In a speech bearing the teasing title "Can School Programs Be Shortened and Enriched?" he shook the very foundation of traditional public school organization.

Eliot made no attempt to conceal his bias. On the contrary, in the very first paragraph of his text there was a candid statement of special pleading on behalf of the colleges. He was after still better exchange conditions in the inescapable consummatory relations between systems of public school education and of higher education. It was, seen in retrospect, an altogether correct, role-motivated expectation. Eliot wanted benefits for the colleges through reforms he would recommend for the public high schools. He said:[26]

[26] Charles William Eliot, *Educational Reform* (New York: The Century Company, 1901), p. 151.

In the process of improving secondary schools, colleges and professional schools of the United States—a process which has been carried out with remarkable energy since the Civil War—certain new difficulties have been created for the higher education in general, and particularly for colleges. These difficulties have to do with the ages at which young men can get prepared for college, and therefore with the ages at which boys pass the successive stages of their earlier education. The average age of admission to Harvard College has been rising for sixty years past, and has now reached the extravagant limit of eighteen years and ten months. Harvard College is not at all peculiar in this respect; indeed, many of the country [sic] colleges find their young men older still at entrance. The average college student is undoubtedly nearly twenty-three years old at graduation; and when he has obtained his A.B. he must nowadays allow at least three years for his professional education. . . .

The problem, Eliot told his audience, was with the traditional public school organization and curriculum. Both were outdated and he questioned their viability in the new milieu. He indicted the public elementary schools of the nation for wasting precious years in tedious drill and in inferior instruction. Then he urged upon his listeners to shorten the curriculum of the elementary school and enrich it by introducing in its upper grades such secondary school subjects as modern languages, science, and more advanced mathematics. An enrichment of this sort would allow for a careful pruning of the high school curriculum: certain subjects could be dropped entirely and others shortened. By such means, he urged, the average age for admission to college could be lowered to eighteen without deteriorating admission standards.

Here, now, was the charismatic figure of Charles Eliot, the most prestigious college president of his day, advocating bold and revolutionary ideas for the revitalization of public education in America. In an age when the authority of tradition demanded that a pupil repeat over and over a course which had been failed, Eliot advocated the radical notion of *age-grade placement*. He told the nation's school superintendents:[27]

---

[27] *Ibid.*, p. 169. Eliot's educational reforms at Harvard were so revolutionary that nearly thirty years after his death, the historian Samuel Eliot Morison, an admirer of Eliot, was, nevertheless, moved to write: "It is hard saying, but Mr. Eliot, more than any other man, is responsible for the greatest educational crime of the century against American youth—depriving him of his classical heritage." Morison, *Three Centuries of Harvard*, pp. 389–90.

The great body of children ought to pass regularly from one grade to another, without delay, at the ages set down on the programme; and any method of examination which interferes with this regular progress does more harm than good.

Deep soul-searching, and agitated discussions, in public school circles followed Eliot's momentous address of 1888. Eliot in the meantime kept on pressing his position by restating the theme of his address in articles and in subsequent talks.[28]

American public school administration was in a bind. There was no gainsaying Eliot's indictment of the public school, but at the same time school administrators had no guiding precedent for taking the bold steps Eliot urged. Eliot sanctioned a break with tradition, but how, precisely, was this to be done?

When Eliot again addressed school administrators in 1892, college-generated pressures for the revitalization of secondary education could no longer be resisted. Upon the recommendation of the National Council of Education, the National Education Association brought the matter to a head by appointing a Committee of Ten on Secondary School Studies, or just the Committee of Ten, as it is now popularly known. It is altogether significant that Charles Eliot was asked by the NEA leadership to head the Committee of Ten.

Eliot had opened the floodgates of reform in American public school education. Now, as Chairman of the Committee of Ten, he was strategically placed to also set the direction which this reform would take, an opportunity Eliot did not fail to exploit. But because Eliot's direction for the revitalization of secondary education was not in step with the already ascending humanistic orientations that had crystallized in the new age, intervening thrusts were to divert the direction of educational reform in America from the course Charles Eliot had set for it.

---

[28] See, for example, Eliot's article, "The Gap Between Common Schools and Colleges," in Eliot, *Educational Reform,* pp. 197–219. See also his talk before the National Education Association on Feb. 16, 1892, "Shortening and Enriching the Grammar-School Course," in *ibid.,* pp. 253–69.

8

COMMITTEES AND
MORE COMMITTEES

The Committee of Ten on Secondary School Studies was the first of many committees through which Eliot's proposed break with tradition was to be routinized. None, however, was to rival in historical, or for that matter in educational, importance the Committee of Ten. Indeed, many of that period regarded the report of this Committee as "the most important educational document ever issued in the United States."[1]

Moreover, it would seem in retrospect that the Committee of Ten represented a personal triumph for Charles Eliot. Its formation was after all a sanction from the largest organized body in American education to subject the traditional high school curriculum to a critical scrutiny. The report of the Committee of Ten, therefore, was to be the first comprehensive assessment of the high school curriculum in the

---

[1] N. A. Calkins, "Prefatory Note," *Report of the Committee of Ten on Secondary School Studies: With the Reports of the Conferences Arranged by the Committee* (New York: The American Book Company, 1894), p. iii. Hereafter cited as *Report, Committee of Ten.* N. A. Calkins was at the time Chairman of the Board of Trustees of the National Educational [sic] Association.

United States. Unwittingly, it also prepared the way for the middle school.

The Committee of Ten was numerically college-dominated. Five college presidents and one college professor were matched by two private school headmasters, one public high school principal, and William T. Harris, U.S. Commissioner of Education. Its charge from the NEA leadership was to look at "each principal subject which enters into the programmes of secondary schools in the United States and into the requirements for admission to colleges. . . . "[2]

Beyond this, the Committee was empowered to convene a conference of college and high school personnel for each of the principal subjects in the high school curriculum. Nine such conferences were convened. Forty-seven of the conferees were from colleges, forty-two were from secondary schools—private and public—and one was from government.[3]

The Committee did its work in quick time. A final report, filed in 1893, recommended changes in high school structure which, in the words of the Chairman of the Board of Trustees of the NEA, were of "a radical nature."[4] But, despite the *"radical character"* of the recommended changes, their driving purpose was to retain the American high school as a *college preparatory institution*—something which would serve college interests but which could not have been realized without a reorganization of the traditional secondary school curriculum. And this, precisely, had been all along at the center of Eliot's program. For Eliot was convinced that the bulk of future college enrollments would come from "the public high school supported by taxation."[5] The ensuing years were to prove his conviction true.

In 1891, by way of an illustration, public high schools had sent 128 students to Harvard and 212 in 1900, an increase of better than 65 percent. Private high schools during the same period had sent 147 students in 1891 and only 105 in 1900, a decrease of over 28 percent.[6] It was, therefore, imperative in Eliot's strategy that the burgeoning public high schools should retain much of the character of a college preparatory school. In part, this helps to explain Eliot's steadfast opposition to curriculum differentiation in the high school.

2 *Ibid.*, p. 3.
3 *Ibid.*, p. 11. Such dignitaries as the historian A. B. Hart and the then future President of the United States Woodrow Wilson were among the conferees.
4 *Ibid.*, p. 13.
5 *Proceedings*, Association of Middle States, 1896, p. 97.
6 *Addresses and Proceedings*, NEA, 1907, p. 577.

He had expressed his opposition to curriculum differentiation before an annual meeting of the Middle States and Maryland Association in the following language:[7]

> I do not believe for a moment in this supposed necessity for separating before eighteen these two classes of high school persons, just because their destinations are different after eighteen. What is best for one up to eighteen is best for the other. Up to that age the problem for the two is the same—how to inspire the love of learning, and to develop the capacity for acquiring exact knowledge. Can we say which needs this capacity the most?

Accordingly, it is no accident that the Report of the Committee of Ten discouraged curriculum differentiation in the high school "no matter what the probable destination of the pupil may be, or at what point his education is to cease."[8]

But it was another of the recommendations of the Committee of Ten that was to have *paramount significance* for the future middle school. Again, this recommendation also attests loudly Eliot's influence on the Committee. For the language of the recommendation was almost identical with passages in Eliot's addresses of 1888 and 1892. The intent of this recommendation was to assure for the colleges a student input which would be capable of relating with the new education of American colleges.

The Committee of Ten had modified sharply secondary school programs in classical and modern languages, history, English, and mathematics. However, because they were aware that the traditional four-year high school organization could not accommodate these changes, they recommended the following two modifications in the traditional structure as viable alternatives:[9]

> In preparing these programmes, the Committee were perfectly aware that it is impossible to make a satisfactory secondary school programme, limited to a period of four years, and founded on the present elementary school subjects and methods. In the opinion of the Committee, several subjects now reserved for high schools—such as algebra, geometry, natural science, and foreign languages—should be begun earlier than now and therefore within the schools classified as elementary; or, as an alternative, the secondary school period should be made to begin two years earlier than at present, leaving six years in-

[7] *Proceedings,* Association of Middle States, 1896, p. 87.
[8] *Report, Committee of Ten,* p. 17.
[9] *Ibid.,* p. 45.

stead of eight for the elementary school period. Under the present organizaiton, elementary subjects and elementary methods are, in the judgment of the Committee, kept in use too long.

It would be difficult to exaggerate the impact of the Report of the Committee of Ten upon American secondary education. It became immediately "the *sine qua non* of every discussion in the field of secondary school administration."[10] Why not? The personnel of the Committee were of high rank, its sponsorship was respectable, and, especially after the United States Bureau of Education—today's U.S. Office of Education—published and distributed its final report, there was no questioning the legitimacy of its recommendations.

College people regarded the report "as a legislative act."[11] Again, and why not? The Report of the Committee of Ten had rescued the colleges from a tangled high school curriculum by formulating a "definition of the various subjects included in the college requirements with reference both to quality and quantity . . . to be covered."[12] The elective system, moreover, had been secured and Eliot's grand design for the future of American secondary education was advanced substantially by the Committee of Ten. It was now up to public school administrators to implement the grand design and all would be well with American higher education.

Public school administrators, on the other hand, responded to the recommendations of the Committee of Ten with considerably less enthusiasm.[13] Some school systems did yield to a bandwagon effect and instituted immediately some curriculum changes in the spirit of the Committee of Ten. Some departmentalized subjects of the upper grades in the elementary school, others brought down from the high school into the seventh and eighth grades such subjects as science, geometry, and modern languages. These modifications, however, were transitory and did not reflect any significant shift from the traditional pattern.

It would seem that while general school administrators had agreed with Eliot in principle that secondary school education needed an overhauling, they were not willing, at least not in the early 1890's, to give up the traditional eight-year elementary school organization in order to effect it. The Committee of Ten, we will recall, had urged as an

10 Edwin C. Dexter, "Ten Years' Influence of the Report of the Committee of Ten," *The School Review*, Vol. XIV, March 1906, p. 254. Hereafter cited as "Ten Years' Influence."
11 *Proceedings*, Association of Middle States, 1895, p. 70.
12 *Ibid.*, 1915, p. 28.
13 Dexter, "Ten Years' Influence," *passim*.

alternative to bringing down several high school subjects into the elementary school that "the secondary school period should be made to begin two years earlier . . . , leaving six years instead of eight for the elementary school period." School superintendents were not ready apparently to regard this as a viable alternative. They were, after all, administrators of a pattern—maintenance organization in the social division of labor.

Even before the Committee of Ten had rendered its report, the Department of Superintendence—now the American Association of School Administrators—established its own committee "to investigate the organization of school systems, the coordination of studies in primary and grammar schools, and the training of teachers."[14] Superintendent William H. Maxwell—a figure in public education of that period whom we shall encounter again in Chapter 9—was appointed chairman and the committee was to become known as the Committee of Fifteen.

The Committee of Fifteen was comprised of thirteen school superintendents, one college president, and United States Commissioner of Education, William T. Harris, who also had served on the Committee of Ten. Operational procedures of the Committee of Fifteen followed closely those of the Committee of Ten, in that, like the Committee of Ten, the Committee of Fifteen was empowered "to organize subconferences on such subdivision . . . as may seem appropriate. . . ."[15] A report from the Committee of Fifteen was ready in 1895.

The Report of the Committee of Fifteen rejected the notion of a six-year elementary school, although it did acknowledge the desirability of a smoother transition from elementary school to high school:[16]

> Your Committee is agreed that the time devoted to the elementary school work should not be reduced from eight years, but they have recommended . . . that in the seventh and eighth years a modified form of algebra be introduced in place of advanced arithmetic, and that in the eighth year English grammar yield place to Latin. This makes . . . a proper transition to the studies of the secondary school and is calculated to assist the pupil materially in his preparation for that work. Hitherto, the change from the work of the elementary school has been too abrupt. . . .

---

14 *Report of the Committee of Fifteen on Elementary Education; with the Reports of the Sub-Committees: On the Training of Teachers; On the Correlation of Studies in Elementary Education; On the Organization of City School Systems* (New York: The American Book Company, 1895), p. 7. Hereafter cited as *Report, Committee of Fifteen.*
15 *Ibid.,* p. 7.
16 *Ibid.,* p. 95.

Reduced to essentials, it would seem in retrospect that while school superintendents of the early 1890's could agree with college people that a modification of the secondary school curriculum would be timely, they would not have the modification at the expense of the traditional elementary school organization.

Altogether, neither the Committee of Ten nor the Committee of Fifteen had effected the immediate reorganization of secondary education in America. The contest of committee reports was a standoff. However, both of these committees had made significant contributions to an eventual crystallization of the middle school idea.

The prestigious Committee of Ten had first broached the notion of a 6-6 public school system, thereby weakening the authority of tradition over the structure of public school systems. Then the Committee of Fifteen, although they rejected the idea of a six-year elementary school, nevertheless forced to the forefront of public school consciousness the imperative of curricula articulation. *Articulation* was thereafter to become an often-used expression in pedagogical literature. In structural-functional terms, *articulation,* we recognize today, turns on the problem of continuity among the organizational units of a public school system, a problem which at the turn of the century emerged as a concomitant of growing sophistication in educational technology. The problem of articulation, we shall later find, was but one of several functional problems that would ultimately lead public school administrators to the middle school.

But although the contest of committees was a standoff, it would not have been *politic* for the stewards of public education to let the matter of educational revitalization rest. Eliot, after all, had nailed some serious indictments to the door of the American public school. Had not Eliot thrown down the gauntlet before public school administrators in his 1888 address "Can School Programmes Be Shortened and Enriched?" Therefore, it was the Department of Secondary Education of the NEA—now the National Association of Secondary School Principals—that took the matter in hand.

The Onward Stride of Reform

A committee was established by the latter body in 1895 and was given the name of the Committee on College-Entrance Requirements. A. F. Nightingale of Chicago was appointed chairman. The personnel of the Committee consisted, in an equal number, of members from the Department of Secondary Education and the Department of Higher Education. In the course of their deliberations, the Committee consulted with representatives of all the regional accrediting associations then extant and with such learned societies as the American Historical Association and the American Mathematical Association. A report was presented publicly at the 1899 annual meeting of the NEA.

The Report of the Committee on College-Entrance Requirements was given a positive disposition. The Committee adopted a number of resolutions "to put in concrete form the leading principles that guided the committee itself in its consideration of the special reports, and which in its judgment are to be considered as first principles in the adjustment of relations between secondary and higher schools."[17]

One of the resolutions—the fourth—had a singular significance for the future middle school. It stated: ". . . we favor a unified six-year high-school course of study beginning with the seventh grade."[18] In support of their recommendation of a 6-6 public school organization, the Committee on College-Entrance Requirements offered the following:[19]

> The most necessary and far-reaching reforms in secondary education must begin in the seventh and eighth grades of our schools. . . . These reforms require the highest pedagogic knowledge and the most efficient supervision. . . . The seventh grade, rather than the ninth, is the natural turning-point in the pupil's life, as the age of adolescence demands new methods and wiser direction. Six elementary grades and six high school . . . grades form symmetrical units. The transition from the elementary to the secondary period may be made natural and easy by changing gradually from the one-teacher regimen to the system of special teachers, thus avoiding the violent shock now commonly felt upon entering the high school.

An analysis of the Report of the Committee on College-Entrance Requirements shows that the Committee succeeded in a remarkable feat. By recommending a 6-6 reorganization, they almost imperceptibly diverted the direction of public school modernization from the course which had been set by Charles Eliot and the colleges. True, the Report of the Committee of Ten had also suggested the alternative of a

[17] *Addresses and Proceedings,* NEA, 1899, p. 655.
[18] *Ibid.,* 1899, p. 659.
[19] *Ibid.,* 1899, p. 659.

six-year high school, but the intent of the suggestion, despite pious pro-
testations to the contrary, was to serve the goal interests of the college
organization.

The Report of the Committee of Fifteen, on the other hand, was a
defensive report. It insisted that curriculum rearrangement could be
accommodated in the traditional public school organization. "I cannot
see any reason for reducing the elementary course to six years," wrote
one administrator-respondent in reply to a survey by one of the sub-
committees of the Committee of Fifteen, "I think, however, that such
a reduction is to be inferred from the recommendations of the Committee of Ten."[20] The focus of the Committee of Fifteen was clearly
upon the universalistic character of the curriculum and not upon the
particularistic requisites of pupils as human beings.

But the Committee on College-Entrance Requirements took a position in between that of the Committee of Ten and the Committee of
Fifteen by focusing on the pupil, the direct client of the public school
organization. Secondary school members of the Committee were aware
that a reaction was setting in against excessive college intrusions into
secondary school affairs. For in the external integration of public
school systems with consumers of their output, there were now other
sectors of society that had to be considered. More and more high
school graduates were entering organizations in the world of work, although the college organization was still a principal consumer of high
school output. One public high school principal was later to express
the emerging reaction thus:[21]

> Changes in courses and plans for equipment ought to originate, and
> reach the practical stage, thru [sic] the co-ordinating agency of councils
> of principals and teachers of such schools. To be directed most wisely,
> the affairs of secondary schools must be ordered from within rather
> than without. The college professor can regulate most wisely the higher
> education of the country, but he is not sufficiently acquainted with the
> conditions of secondary-school work to legislate for the secondary
> schools.

On the other hand, college members of the Committee were not
about to surrender the advantage which the recommendations of the
Committee of Ten had secured for college interests.

[20] *Report, Committee of Fifteen*, p. 165.
[21] *Addresses and Proceedings*, NEA, 1903, p. 477.

Following four years of intensive deliberation, and many consultations with other groups within professional education, the Committee on College-Entrance Requirements succeeded in effecting a compromise between the two earlier committee reports. With proper obeisance to the Committee of Ten, the Committee on College-Entrance Requirements endorsed the procedural recommendations of Eliot's Committee. But whereas the Committee of Ten had suggested the six-year high school as an alternative course to "a satisfactory secondary school programme," the Committee on College-Entrance Requirements now endorsed a 6-6 reorganization of the public school system because "The seventh grade, rather than the ninth, is the natural turning-point in the pupil's life. . . . " By focusing upon the diffuseness of "the pupil's life" in the rationale for a six-year high school, the Committee on College-Entrance Requirements had, in point of fact, introduced an affective element in proposals for secondary school reorganization.

After the Committee on College-Entrance Requirements had filed a report in 1899, a 6-6 reorganization of the public school system was to become a viable point of convergence for both child-oriented and subject-oriented educational reformers. As a foremost spokesman for the former group, John Dewey assured an audience of the Annual University of Chicago Conference: "The proper aim of the elementary tuition is to organize the instincts of children into working interests and tools. . . . Six years ought to be enough to accomplish this task."[22]

Subject-oriented educators were assured at the same time that a shortened period of elementary schooling need not result in a learning loss. Superintendent of Schools James M. Greenwood of Kansas City told his fellow superintendents, in 1903, about the experience in Kansas City, where, since 1867, seven-year elementary schools had been in operation. Greenwood's report had posited the question "Can children of average intellectual ability complete a substantial ward-school course of study in seven years?" Then, with supporting statistical data, Greenwood proceeded to answer the question "in the affirmative, without any reservation whatsoever."[23]

Greenwood was destined thereafter to recite the Kansas City experience many times on platforms provided by important educational organizations. In time, other school superintendents stepped forward to confirm the advantages that were being claimed for a shortened ele-

22 See John Dewey's "Discussion" in *The School Review*, Vol. XI, January 1903, p. 18.
23 *Addresses and Proceedings*, NEA, 1903, p. 248.

mentary school. Superintendent J. H. Phillips of Birmingham, Alabama, for example, not only confirmed all of Greenwood's claims for the seven-year elementary school but then went on to add, based upon Birmingham's experience, "The most manifest benefit of this plan is the large increase of pupils entering the high school."[24]

Diverting Thrusts on Eliot's Course

As committee after committee was established to routinize proposed modifications in public education, and as report was piled upon report, it became manifestly clear that thrusts other than Eliot's revolutionary proposals had impinged upon traditional value orientations in the public school organization. By 1900, the central focus of secondary school revitalization was no longer on the college-bound segment of the public high school, as the colleges would have had it at first, but on *all pupils* in the high school. The shift in focus was of a piece with the general resistance to the social Darwinist orientation in social policy. As in the society at large, resistance in the sector of public education was to be seen at different fronts.

At the philosophical front stood the influential and nonpareil figure of John Dewey. His weapon was a philosophical system now generally known as Instrumentalism, or Pragmatism.

When Darwinian evolution began to eclipse Transcendentalism as the favored philosophy of Americans, and as Herbert Spencer's *Social Statics* acquired favor with dominant groups, those who had no taste for social Darwinism turned to other systems of philosophy. William T. Harris, for example, found Hegelian idealism attractive. But by using Hegelian idealism as his vehicle for escaping the materialism of social Darwinism, Harris had overlooked the impact of science on social life. Spencer's system, after all, justified a mode of social organization and conduct in accordance with what was purported to be scientific law. It was precisely this ingredient in Spencer's *Social Statics* which appealed so much to defenders of laissez-faire in public policy. What was needed as a viable philosophical alternative to social Darwinism was a philosophy which was capable of being comfortable with science and humanistic values at the same time. Such a philosophy was Pragmatism.

The foundation of American philosophical pragmatism was laid by Charles Pierce. William James borrowed from Pragmatism to define

24 *Ibid.,* 1907, p. 294.

his own theory of knowledge and to explain his philosophical empiricism. John Dewey then gave Pragmatism another philosophical convolution and it became Instrumentalism.

Dewey's Instrumentalism held truth to be evolutionary, not as something fixed for all time. Human thought, Dewey held, was an instrument for solving social and psychological problems. As problems change, so does human thought and, therefore, activity. His Instrumentalism rejected authoritarianism and rote in education and pleaded for learning experiences motivated by student maturational needs.

It seems almost inevitable that intellectual disciples of Charles Pierce should have become reformers in different fields of human endeavor. The influence of Pragmatism was clearly discernible in the thinking of Jane Addams, in the sociological jurisprudence of Roscoe Pound and Louis Brandeis, and in the works of other liberal Darwinists. But of them all, the most active social and, more especially, educational reformer among exponents of Pragmatism was John Dewey. Charles Beard in an interview one day said of his close friend John Dewey, "He's the quiet one, my friend, who looks like your milquetoast uncle and who is undermining the whole world of the nineteenth century with his pragmatism."[25]

At this distance in time, John Dewey stands out as an aurora borealis shining in the intellectual sky of his period. His intellectual interests were catholic: they ranged the broad spectrum of human affairs. At the age of thirty-four, he was already established in the academic world as head of the philosophy department at the University of Chicago. But his special interest was, and remained so to the end of his days, the education of youth. At the University of Chicago, he organized a department of pedagogy and attached to it an elementary school for demonstration and experimentation purposes—the now renowned Dewey School.

Dewey was an implacable foe of social Darwinism to the end. He fought social Darwinism in the philosopher's classroom and in the hurly-burly world of affairs. Toward the twilight years of his life, he wrote, "Anything that obscures the fundamentally moral nature of the social problem is harmful, no matter whether it proceeds from the side of physical or of psychological theory."[26]

This was Dewey's credo. It had been buttressed by an evolutionary

[25] Quoted in Goldman, *Rendezvous*, p. 155.
[26] John Dewey, *Freedom and Culture* (New York: G. P. Putnam's Sons, 1939), p. 172.

doctrine which rejected a conception of human nature as fixed.[27]   Human nature, in Dewey's philosophical system, was capable of modification as a consequence of cultural change.   And education was for Dewey a *decisive component* of culture.   Therefore, it was neither accident nor caprice that "one of America's leading philosophers devoted his chief efforts and interests to the field of education. . . ."[28]

Dewey's educational values had crystallized in his system of Instrumentalism, which, as a system of philosophy, complements the Parsonian definition of the American value pattern.   And Dewey was not one to rest his value commitments in any ivory tower.   He was in constant demand for programs of the NEA and its constituent departments, of regional accrediting associations, and of such perennial educational conferences as the Annual Conference of the University of Chicago.   On the occasion of such public appearances, and in numerous popular and scholarly articles, Dewey used his philosophical constructs as ramparts from which to strike at social Darwinism in education and as defenses for his own values.   And the strength of his influence was as the strength of ten.

His deep interest in public education and his steadfast commitment to democratic-humanistic values were of one piece.   Therefore, his central focus in educational matters was at all times upon the pupil.   It was for this reason that Dewey lent his support to the idea of a six-year elementary school and a six-year high school.   "The wider high school," Dewey was persuaded, "relieves many of the difficulties in the adequate treatment of the individual as an individual."[29]

Both friend and foe have acknowledged John Dewey as the architect of the philosophical orientation that has shaped the course and character of public education in twentieth-century America.   But even the influence of one so eminent as John Dewey might not have been enough to deflect future educational development from the direction set for it by Charles Eliot, had it not been for the disclosure of gross inequities in public education.   Here, then, was another diverting thrust on Eliot's course in the guise of exposure.   In the public sector

[27] See Chapter 3, "Culture and Human Nature," in *Freedom and Culture* for an illustrative expression of Dewey's view of human nature.
[28] Faulkner, *Social Justice*, p. 190.   For an excellent reference to the reform of American education during this period, and to Dewey's considerable role in it see Lawrence A. Cremin, *The Transformation of the School* (New York: Alfred A. Knopf, 1961).   See also the chapter "John Dewey" in Curti, *Social Ideas*.
[29] Quoted in *Addresses and Proceedings*, NEA, 1908, p. 611.

of society, those who engaged in such exposure activities, we will recall, were labeled muckrakers.

Exposures in the Schoolhouse

Disclosures of inequities in public education were made for the most part by people within professional education. These educators engaged in exposure activities out of a motive other than the one which had induced journalistic muckrakers. The latter—Lincoln Steffens, Ida Tarbell, and others—cultivated muckraking because it was profitable to them as journalists and writers: in the parlance of journalism, it produced "hot copy." While journalistic muckraking did indeed buttress social reform, the buttressing was incidental to immediate journalistic gains. But those who had set out to expose defects in American public education did so not for direct gain, but to effect immediate reforms. The writer J. M. Rice, however, was a singular exception.

Rice was engaged, in 1892, by *The Forum* magazine to write a series of articles about American public schools. After having visited thirty-six cities, Rice found "the schools of different localities . . . very unequal, so much so that while those of some cities had already advanced considerably, those of others were still far behind the age."[30]

Rice then proceeded to report deficiencies in school systems that were so glaring that even he, a casual observer who had traveled to thirty-six cities within a short period of five months, could not miss them. But the more pernicious social consequences of schools "still far behind the age" had escaped Rice. These were to be uncovered within the profession by its members.

Extensive exposure in the schoolhouse was a direct consequence of a critical self-examination within the profession which had followed Eliot's call for reform. Eliot, we will recall, opened the door to reform by questioning the functional value of a traditional four-year high school structure. Later, the Committee of Ten struck another blow at traditional high school structure. However, had Eliot's direction for educational development been allowed to run its course, it would have led to a modernized model of the college preparatory high school. School administrators, we know, agreed with Eliot that the American

---

[30] J. M. Rice, "Our Public-School System: Schools of Buffalo and Cincinnati," *The Forum*, Vol. XIV, November 1892, p. 293.

secondary school curriculum needed changes, but once the reform impetus had been unleashed, many of them began to insist that changes be made compatible with new social aspirations.

Accordingly, as the nineteenth century was drawing to a close, the tenor of educational meetings and conferences was taking on a pronounced pupil-centered character. John Dewey magnified for leaders in public education their institutional obligation in the conduct of *practical affairs*. At the same time, school administrators discovered how incongruent certain *practical affairs* of the schoolhouse were with crystallizing social aspirations in the larger society.

They had come upon this unpleasant verity about school life, in large part, through investigations which were reported before professional meetings. Typical of such reports was the one by Lucia Stickney of Hughes High School in Cincinnati, Ohio, which she gave before the National Council of Education in 1899. She prefaced her report with the following remarks:[31]

> I desire to present to the Council . . . a picture of the home life of the greater part of the down-town people whose children are in the public schools. It is not a picture of the submerged tenth with whom the police and slum sisters of the Salvation Army have to do, but, perhaps, of a third of the other nine-tenths, better known to the truant officer, the settlement worker, and the kindergarten teacher.

Those administrators who had departed from Eliot's course discovered that American public education which had been represented to the world as a noble institutional expression of the democratic ideal was, in fact, a fiction. Large numbers of students were being squeezed out from the supposedly democratic public school system by harsh curricular practices, sterile methods of teaching, and haughty teacher attitudes.

In the America of which Walt Whitman had sung: "O America, because you build for mankind, I build for you," Superintendent Edward Brooks of Philadelphia discovered that "less than three and one-half percent" of his elementary school enrollment entered high school.[32]

The principal of St. Louis High School, Missouri, was shocked to find the following condition in his school:

---

[31] See Lucia Stickney, "The Homes of Our Down-Town Children," in *Addresses and Proceedings*, NEA, 1899, p. 388.
[32] *Proceedings*, Association of Middle States, 1896, p. 75.

330	boys	entered	in	1895	and 81	were	left	in	1896
353	"	"	"	1896	" 89	"	"	"	1897
348	"	"	"	1897	" 79	"	"	"	1898
379	"	"	"	1898	" 97	"	"	"	1899
326	"	"	"	1899	" 69	"	"	"	1900

He found, moreover, that the dropout rate for girls was not much better.[33]

Once the high rate of school dropouts had been recognized as incompatible with democratic orientations of American society, it became a frequently discussed subject at educational meetings. It became quite the vogue during the middle nineties, and thereafter, for principals and superintendents to conduct local holding-power studies. Interest in pupil retention was stimulated further by a report from the United States Commissioner of Education to the effect that during the school year 1905–06, less than 4 percent of an estimated school population of 24 million were enrolled in public secondary schools.[34]

But the more conclusive statement of the problem, one that was confirmed by later studies of Leonard Ayres and George Strayer, was given by Edward L. Thorndike in 1907. Thorndike had undertaken a study of pupil retention in twenty-three cities. In his report of the study, *The Elimination of Pupils from School,* Thorndike showed that of all pupils who had entered high school in the twenty-three cities, 37 percent dropped out before the second year, 29.4 percent of the second year did not enter the third, and 33.3 percent of the third year failed to enter the fourth year. Thorndike concluded from these statistics:[35]

> The fact that the elimination is so great in the first year of the high school gives evidence that a large share of the fault lies with the kind of education given in the high schools. One can hardly suppose that very many of the parents who send children on to the high school do so with no expectation of keeping them there over a year, or that a large number of pupils who complete the elementary-school course and make a trial of the high school are so stupid or uninterested in being educated that they had better be got rid of in the first years.

33 *Addresses and Proceedings,* NEA, 1902, p. 24.
34 *Ibid.,* 1908, p. 606.
35 Quoted in *ibid.,* 1908, p. 609. For the full impact of the dropout rate early in the twentieth century, the following trilogy of reports is by far the best source: E. L. Thorndike, *The Elimination of Pupils from School,* Bulletin No. 4, U.S. Department of the Interior, Bureau of Education, 1907; Leonard P. Ayres, *Laggards in Our Schools* (New York: Russell Sage Foundation, 1909); George D. Strayer, *Age and Grade Census of Schools and Colleges,* Bulletin No. 5, U.S. Department of the Interior, Bureau of Education, 1911.

Just as Lincoln Steffens had exposed the corruption of public officials by respectable middle-class citizens as "The Shame of the Cities," so did members of the profession expose high dropout rates and the undemocratic character of American secondary education as *The Shame of the American High School.* "It is an appalling fact," Boys' High School Principal Reuben Post Halleck of Louisville, Kentucky, told his colleagues at the 1905 Annual Meeting of the Department of Secondary Education, "if fifty percent of the school children of a republic whose watchword is 'education' do not get beyond the fourth grade. This whole nation," he continued, "ought to rise and discover the reason for this condition."[36]

When public school administrators at last did "rise and discover the reason for this condition," they found, among other things, that many secondary school teachers were woefully unprepared for teaching in a public high school. The following lament by one high school principal is eloquently typical of the many that were addressed to this problem. At the meeting of the Department of Secondary Education in 1908, Principal Gilbert B. Morrison of McKinley High School, St. Louis, Missouri, complained:[37]

> While good teaching may be found in certain places, we have an army of teachers, many of them college graduates, drawing a moderate salary, going through with the purely conventional processes of assigning lessons, learning [sic] them, giving examinations, and measuring their standards by the number of pupils they fail to pass; teachers who are giving much attention to their subjects and little attention to their pupils.

The payoff, concluded Principal Morrison, was a high dropout rate.

Another prominent schoolman, General Francis A. Walker, a leader in the emerging vocational education field, reinforced a growing discontent with dominant orientations in the American high school through talks and articles about the "neglected half" and the "danger period" of high school years. He pleaded feelingly for those pupils who were being driven out of high school by a rigid grading system whose paramount valuation was upon rote learning. These pupils, he charged, are denied their rightful entitlement to educational opportu-

---

[36] Reuben Post Halleck, "Why Do So Many Pupils Leave the Public High School During the First Year," *School Review*, Vol. XIII, September 1905, p. 551.
[37] *Addresses and Proceedings*, NEA, 1908, p. 580.

nity because of a lack of differentiation in the high school curriculum. Walker cried out poignantly:[38]

> There is no place, or only a most uncomfortable one, for those boys who are strong in perception, apt in manipulation, and correct in the interpretation of phenomena, but who are not good at memorizing, or rehearsing the opinions and statements of others; or who, by their indifference or slowness of speech are unfitted for ordinary intellectual gymnastics. These boys are quite as numerous as the other sort, and are quite as deserving of sympathy and respect, besides being rather better qualified to become of use in the industrial and social order. And yet for this class of boys the school offers almost nothing upon which they can apply their priceless powers.

While the twentieth century was still very young, there was no longer any doubt but that the routinization of Eliot's revolutionary proposals had taken on pronouncedly democratic-humanistic hues. The annual meetings of the NEA, the very organization whose leadership had set up the Committee of Ten in the early 1890's, now resounded with addresses in defense of educational goals which John Dewey, and others of his mien, championed. Superintendent M. G. Brumbaugh of Philadelphia addressed one general session of the 1908 NEA meeting and pleaded for child-labor laws and compulsory school attendance by saying, "We must, as educators, take our stand with those that oppose the coining of the blood of childhood into the currency of the market place."[39]

Indeed, it is altogether significant, in the context of our social Darwinism–liberal Darwinism thesis, that some of the very people Superintendent Brumbaugh would have educators join in the battle against child exploitation were also on the NEA program of 1908. Helen MacMurchy, active in programs for feeble-minded children, reminded her audience of educators of how Lillian Wald had begun, in 1902, the school nurse program in New York City public schools by sending, as an experiment, a Henry Street Settlement House nurse to a public school.

Jane Addams of Hull House, Robert W. Bruce, Secretary of the New York Committee on the Physical Welfare of School Children, and General Secretary Florence Kelley of the National Consumers' League, the same Florence Kelley who had opened young Charles Beard's eyes

---

[38] Quoted in *ibid.*, 1910, pp. 10–11.
[39] *Ibid.*, 1908, p. 83.

to factory conditions in Cook County during the 1890's, and who had been instrumental in obtaining wealthy corporation lawyer Louis Brandeis to plead before the Supreme Court of the United States in *Muller v. Oregon,* also addressed segments of the 1908 NEA meeting.[40]

So it was that in the sector of public education, just as in the larger society, liberal Darwinists and reformers reinforced one another in efforts to adapt the institution of public education to the new urban-industrial milieu. Out of these efforts was to come, among other things, the American middle school.

[40] *Ibid.,* 1908, pp. 926, 1113, 1222. See also Franklin Parker, "A Golden Age in American Education: Chicago in the 1890's," *School and Society,* Vol. 89, March 25, 1961.

9

A REFORM WITHIN A REFORM

No longer shielded by tradition, exposed as a school out of joint with social aspirations in a changing culture, the four-year high school structure was losing its hold on secondary education by the turn of the century. Its *deinstitutionalization* was under way. Charles Eliot's call for the reform of secondary education had been answered. At issue by the turn of the century was no longer whether secondary education would be reformed, but rather the categories of valuation around which the reform would be routinized. The search for a resolution of this issue was now the larger collective mission of *ad hoc* committees which were appointed by professional organizations in education.

As these committees pursued the mission, they became focal points of debate between those who subscribed to conflicting orientations in education. Chairman A. F. Nightingale, who gave the report of the Committee on College-Entrance Requirements in 1899, had the record show, as a case in point, that his committee "found it difficult to keep pace with the evolution of educational opinion."[1]

Nightingale's Committee on College-Entrance Requirements, we will recall, had endorsed in principle the six-year high school. What remained to be settled were the procedural steps for bringing about the

[1] *Addresses and Proceedings,* NEA, 1899, p. 625.

new high school unit. To formulate these procedures, the Department of Secondary Education appointed still another committee in 1905 and named it "The Committee on an Equal Division of the Twelve Years in the Public Schools Between the District and High Schools." Informally, however, the Committee soon took the name of the "Committee on Six-Year Courses."

Several reports were filed by the Committee on Six-Year Courses between 1907 and 1909. Each of them was strongly supportive of the 6-6 plan of organization. The report of 1907 is particularly germane because it spelled out the functional values that could be expected of a six-year high school. Those who are familiar with middle school literature will recognize here functional values which were later mistaken as goals of the middle school organization. Functional expectations that the Committee on Six-Year Courses had set for the six-year high school were as follows:

1. This plan would give pupils the advantage of being taught by teachers especially trained for the different branches, such as English, mathematics, science, history, and geography.

2. The departmental plan would give the children the advantages of daily contact with several personalities instead of that all-day association with one teacher which often breeds an artificial psychic atmosphere that savors of the abnormal.

3. In the high school, the pupils would have the advantages of laboratories in which elementary science might be advantageously begun much earlier than is at present.

4. If in the high school, the manual-training shops could be modified, enlarged, and employed to start the pupil in this work without sending him off to another school in another part of the city. . . .

5. The work in modern languages could be begun earlier and continued longer than at present, thereby making it possible to learn the language naturally by means of conversation and primary reading before making the study of grammar and construction such laborious and strenuous affairs.

6. The downward extension of secondary school work would mitigate the present abruptness of the transition from the district school.

7. *In the opinion of the Committee the six years division would cause more pupils to enter the ninth year than do under the present plan.*

8. An equal division of the twelve years would make the system more nearly self-consistent.

9. The downward extension of the high-school course would give the pupil time to prepare for college.

10. The lengthening of the high-school course to six years would help to solve the problem of the outward extension of the course of study and the crowded curriculum.[2]

The six-year high school organization, once it became operational, was the routinization of a break with traditional public school structure which Charles Eliot had precipitated. To be sure, the college-preparatory goal of the American high school had been enlarged in the new school by the intervention of emergent social aspirations. Witness, for example, the expectation of greater holding power in the six-year high school. Nevertheless, the larger goal orientation of the six-year high school was still toward the college. It was still meant to be a subject-centered school. Precisely because such was the case, college educators, including Charles Eliot, could endorse it.

Eliot's endorsement was transmitted to the Committee on Six-Year Courses in a communication which read:[3]

> The proposed equal division of the twelve years in the public schools between the district and high schools has an important bearing on the work of the University because of the better training which such a training would afford. The lengthening of the high-school course at the lower end would tend to the earlier introduction of certain subjects now deferred to the pupil's disadvantage, and it would at the same time admit the pupil sooner to the departmental system of instruction in these and other subjects—a system which more and more high schools can afford, but which is often beyond the means of the district school.

By 1910 the six-year high school was a *fait accompli*. The Committee on Six-Year Courses noted in its report of 1909, "In some cities six-year courses in the high school have been in vogue for several years."[4] School systems that turned to a six-year high school did so out of a conviction that it was the appropriate high school organization in the twentieth century just as its predecessor four-year organization had been in the nineteenth century. But before long, certain of the more institutional-minded school superintendents began to question the functional adequacy of the newer model high school. Doubt led to a critical scrutiny of educative process in the six-year high school unit,

[2] *Ibid.,* 1907, pp. 705–08.
[3] *Ibid.,* 1907, p. 709.
[4] *Ibid.,* 1909, p. 499.

and as we already know, some, like Superintendent W. A. Greeson of Grand Rapids, Michigan, decided against the six-year high school on functional grounds.

The Child-Study Movement

What caused school administrators to question the functional adequacy of the six-year high school unit was the aggressive intervention of psychological science in educational affairs. The emergence of the Department of Child-Study in 1893, and of the middle school nearly twenty years later, may be taken as evidence of how influential that intervention had been.

Even while the agitation for a six-year high school was in progress, there was already evidence that the developing science of psychology was influencing pedagogical decisions. The following argument for the six-year high school by Principal E. W. Coy of Hughes High School, Cincinnati, Ohio, is revealing of the trend. Principal Coy said in 1903:[5]

> The method of the elementary school differs from the method of the secondary school just as the method of the secondary school differs from the method of the university. This difference in method is founded upon a difference in the state of mental development of the pupil. To use the secondary-school method in the elementary stage is to offer a stone when asked for bread; to continue to use the elementary method in the secondary stage is to feed a boy with gruel when he is crying lustily for a substantial diet. We have continued to use the elementary method too far and too long, and in the upper grades of the lower schools we have been feeding gruel until there have often resulted mental anemia, arrested development, and general intellectual flabbiness. The interest of the child demands that this transition be made earlier and less abruptly than we are now doing. If the boys and girls at the end of the sixth year of their course can be admitted to the school in which they are to complete their public-school education, a course of six years can be arranged for the high school by which they can with less friction and greater success be carried forward farther than they are under our present system. Then the change can be made from the elementary to the secondary method gradually and naturally, without jar or jolt, instead of making it in a day, as we do under our present system.

[5] E. W. Coy, "A Readjustment of the High School Curriculum," in *ibid.*, 1903, pp. 180–81.

At the same time that the reorganization of the American high school was in progress, the human sciences reflected the period's accelerated interest in man and his environment—an interest which was fanned by social Darwinist–liberal Darwinist polemics—by moving rapidly toward maturity. Evidence of this is to be seen in the learned societies that were founded during that period: among which were professional associations in history (1884), economics (1885), psychology (1892), and sociology (1906).[6]

Psychology, especially, was well started by the 1890's on the road to its modern-day sophistication. Among American psychologists who were active around the turn of the century were such luminaries as John Dewey, G. Stanley Hall, Morton Prince, G. H. Mead, Boris Sidis, Edward L. Thorndike, James Cattell, and William James.[7]

William James had not been involved as closely with professional education as was John Dewey. Nevertheless, one estimate has it that, between 1890 and 1910, 90 percent of America's teachers who studied any psychology at all had read William James.[8] Moreover, at about 1892, James began a series of lectures to teachers—the now renowned "Talks to Teachers"—which intensified the sensitivity of teachers "to the purposes and methods of education."[9] There are those who hold to the belief that William James, together with John Dewey, laid the scientific foundation of modern-day educational psychology.

It was no accident, therefore, that the beginning of a child-study movement in the United States should have coincided with the advent of modern psychology as an influence in American education. And G. Stanley Hall was the undisputed leader in the child-study movement.

Hall stands out as an enigmatic figure in American education. Even before his passing in 1924, his major contributions to psychological theory had been for the most part discredited. But at the zenith of his professional career, which was at the turn of the century, his influence was great in American pedagogy.

At Johns Hopkins, Hall was the second professor of education in an American university. He was a prolific contributor to both popular

---

[6] Also significant in this regard was the appearance at the University of Chicago in 1892 of the first Department of Sociology in an American university. This department, under the headship of Albion Woodbury Small, from the first set a fast pace in sociological scholarship. Later, in the 1930's, Chicago's Department of Sociology stood foremost in the nation because of its brilliant ventures in empirical sociology.

[7] See the Sherwood D. Fox introduction to Durkheim's *Education and Sociology*.

[8] Curti, *Social Ideas,* p. 443.

[9] Fox, in Durkheim's *Education and Sociology,* p. 14.

and educational journals. It is estimated that he had delivered during his active period some 2,500 lectures, outside the classroom, in forty states.[10] In the annals of American education, Hall is the acknowledged founder of the child-study movement in the United States, a movement that was to help shift the central focus of process in the public school organization from subject matter to the pupil.

That such a shift was in progress, indeed, could be seen in the organization of the Department of Child-Study. The latter held its first meeting in 1893 as an affiliate of the National Education Association. In the years that followed, the field of child study expanded at a fast rate, and able talents from the fields of psychology and physiology were attracted to its activities. Its singular purpose was "to study the child's psycho-physic organism objectively and scientifically under varying conditions just as one would study any other organism."[11] The growing influence of the child-study movement in American education led G. Stanley Hall, by then President of Clark University, to say publicly in 1908 that "child-study in its larger ranges occupies today the very center of the stage in both the theory and practice of education."[12]

In dramatic language, pregnant with deep implications for the process of education, Hall made it known to American educators:[13]

> Like the revolution of Copernicus, from a geocentric to a heliocentric view of the world, so child-study has made men realize, as it had sadly come to need to realize, that the school is for the child and not the child for the school, and that everything from kindergarten to university must be plastic and subordinated to the nature and needs of childhood and youth.

The works of G. Stanley Hall and C. W. Crampton are the best-known products of the early child-study movement. These two provided a powerful scientific thrust to the coming of the middle school. They worked independently, but the study of "the child's psycho-physic organism objectively and scientifically" was a goal interest they shared in common. Results of their respective studies fed the apprehensions of those administrators who felt that, for physiological and psychologi-

[10] See the chapter "G. Stanley Hall, Evolutionist" in Curti, *Social Ideas,* pp. 425–26; see also Robert E. Grinder and Charles E. Strickland, "G. Stanley Hall and the Social Significance of Adolescence," *Teachers College Record,* Vol. 64, February 1963.
[11] From "President's Address," Department of Child-Study, *Addresses and Proceedings,* NEA, 1908, p. 908.
[12] *Ibid.,* 1908, p. 248.
[13] G. Stanley Hall, "Recent Advances in Child-Study," in *ibid.,* 1908, p. 948.

cal reasons, the revitalization of secondary education should not end with the six-year school unit.

Crampton was a medical doctor who directed the physical training program for the New York City Public Schools. He began a scientific investigation in 1901 of the physical characteristics of 4,800 New York City high school boys between the ages of 12.5 and 18.0. His direct observations of these boys led him to classify them under three categories of physiological development. Those who were *prepubescent* were classified as immature, those who were *pubescent* were classified as maturing, and those who were *postpubescent* were classified as mature. The results of this investigation took Crampton to the concept of "physiological age"; a concept which was destined to be in vogue for many years in American education.

By isolating puberty as the variable for determining physiological age, Crampton discovered two significant characteristics for the group of boys in his study. First, as the following table shows, he found, with empirical support, that the boys in his sample moved at an uneven rate through the pubic interval.

C. Ward Crampton's Sample[14]

	Physiological Age Groups		
Age in Years	*Immature*	*Maturing*	*Mature*
12.50–13.00	69%	25%	6%
13.00–13.50	55	26	18*
13.50–14.00	41	28	31
14.00–14.50	26	28	46
14.50–15.00	16	24	60
15.00–15.50	9	20	70*
15.50–16.00	5	10	85
16.00–16.50	2	4	93*
16.50–17.00	1	4	95
17.00–17.50	0	2	98
17.50–18.00	0	0	100

But of even greater significance was Crampton's discovery of marked physical changes that accompanied pubescent change. He found that the mature were more than 33 percent heavier, 10 percent taller, and 33 percent stronger than the immature.

[14] *Ibid.*, 1908, p. 926. Rows marked by an asterisk do not report for the total sample. A detailed report of this study is to be found in C. W. Crampton, "Physiological Age," *American Physical Education Review*, March–June, 1908.

Crampton's was a pioneering investigation. His general conclusions were confirmed later by B. T. Baldwin, who, at the State University of Iowa, replicated phases of Crampton's investigation and broadened its scope by including girls.

Crampton's findings were given wide circulation in educational circles. They were cited from platforms of regional meetings and national conferences. It was at the 1908 meeting of the Department of Child-Study that G. Stanley Hall rose to say, "I have very high regard for Dr. Crampton's work, but in none of his studies has he touched upon the very important question of psychological age."[15]

If G. Stanley Hall seemed exercised over Crampton's omission of psychological age, there was some justification on his side. Hall, after all, had given many years to the psychological study of children. Even after he had become the first President of Clark University, Hall maintained an active interest in the psychology of children. Indeed, some have been inclined to date the child-study movement in the United States from 1894, when Hall published *The Contents of Children's Minds on Entering School*. Moreover, G. Stanley Hall, apart from being a prestigious figure in academic circles and possessor of the first American doctoral degree in psychology, had popularized in professional education the concept of "psychological age."

But Hall need not have been exercised over Crampton's omission. Crampton was not a psychologist. His interest in physical education led him to focus upon the physical characteristics of youth at the threshold of adolescence and beyond it. Hall, on the other hand, was a psychologist. His driving interest in children had alerted him to what Crampton overlooked. Together, however, they had discovered the physiological and psychological attributes of early adolescence, an event of great moment for the early adolescent in the American public school.

G. Stanley Hall's *magnum opus* on adolescence was published in 1905. It appeared in two volumes bearing the imposing title *Adolescence: Its Psychology and Its Relations to Physiology, Anthropology, Sociology, Sex, Crime, Religion, and Education*. An imposing work it was, indeed. Even by standards of modern scholarship, it leaves a lasting impression on those who read it. Hall must have culled all extant literature on adolescence from antiquity to his own day. No reference to adolescence in biblical, secular, or scientific literature

15 *Addresses and Proceedings*, NEA, 1908, p. 930.

seems to have escaped his searching eyes. Even so, Hall told his readers, his work was but a beginning.

However, we know now that Hall's attraction to Herbert Spencer's theory of society led him to commit a fatal theoretical error. Hall set his empirical data on adolescence in an untenable framework. He had borrowed the theory of embryonic germ layers from Karl Ernst von Baer, an Estonian biologist, to explain adolescent phenomena. Some refer to Hall's theoretical construct as the "culture-epoch theory," others as simply "recapitulation theory."

Reduced to simple explication, Hall's culture-epoch theory postulated that in his social development from infancy to adulthood, individual man recapitulates in microcosm mankind's social evolution in civilization. The behavior pattern of the infant, child, adolescent, young adult, and mature man reflects, according to Hall's theory, a discrete period in the social evolution of humankind which the individual is reliving at a corresponding stage of development.

With a touch of exquisite eloquence, Hall gave the basic matter of his conceptualization the following exposition in an address of 1908 before the Department of Child-Study. He began by asking:[16]

> . . . "What is a Child?" We know that he is neither the congenitally depraved being Calvin thought, nor a Wordsworthian little deity trailing clouds of glory direct from heaven, all pure and good. We know that children are not so desirable as to be wanted in unlimited numbers, especially if they be the spawn of families like the Jukes; nor are they to be especially prevented by mothers who prefer society to the nursery. The child is first of all a bunch of keys, large and small, capable of unlocking most of the secrets of the entire history of life; a few keys are lost, some distorted, some locks are rusty or not yet found; but for science, the child is geologic ages older than the man. Adult traits of body and soul are novelties lately added, new and less substantial stories built on ancient foundations. Hence the child is not so much the father of man as is every remote, primitive ancestor. The human infant is a very unique specimen in human nature, a relic or memento of a past vastly older than recorded history. Under the guidance of Mother Nature, he is climbing daily, at first with almost breakneck speed, up the uncounted rungs of the evolutionary ladder, the bottom of which rests deep in the protoplasm of the primitive sea, while its top touches the superman that is to be so much nobler than we are

[16] *Ibid.*, 1908, pp. 950–52.

today. Thus science looks with new awe and reverence upon this candidate for humanity. The infant inherits not only scores of organs but as many instincts and feelings from a past older than man. It does or tries to do a little of about everything that all the creatures in its lines of descent did.

. . . The child is not a man or woman of reduced dimensions of body and soul, but is as a grub is to a butterfly, or an egg to a bird. Their prime need is to develop to the uttermost each of the stages through which they pass, and to be retarded more than accelerated; to linger in the paradise of the recapitulatory stages is the new ideal of liberal humanistic culture, which is that each should experience all the essentials that the race has experienced in its long pilgrimage upward.

Of all the stages in human growth and social development, Hall held the period of adolescence to be the most critical for the future of man. He spoke of the onset of adolescence as "a new birth," a stage "suggestive of some ancient period of storm and stress." Hall then went on to note that even primitive societies mark the advent of puberty with elaborate ceremonial rites and that religious rituals, as the Hebrew Bar Mitzvah, have their origins as pubescent customs.[17]

Although it is true that no psychologist of any consequence subscribes now to Hall's culture-epoch theory, there is no gainsaying the seminal service of his pioneering work. Before G. Stanley Hall, educators generally held that, in the maturation cycle, the human organism moved from childhood to adolescence and little, or no, attention was paid to the stressful in-between period. Let us recall, as an example, Principal E. W. Coy's argument of 1903 in support of a six-year high school. Hall changed all that by focusing upon the years which separate early adolescence from later adolescence.

Too bad, for sure, that he had selected an inappropriate theory with which to explain his empirical observations of early adolescent traits, but his observations have been confirmed, nonetheless, by modern-day psychologists. To illustrate: when Fritz Redl speaks today of "organismic disorganization" to explain early adolescent behavior and Erik H. Erikson speaks of "ego diffusion" to explain the same phenomenon, are they not seeing those very manifestations of early adolescence that moved G. Stanley Hall to speak of the adolescent onset as "a new birth?"

[17] See G. Stanley Hall, *Adolescence* (New York: D. Appleton-Century Co., 1905), Vol. I, *passim*.

The Turn to the Middle School

Insofar as it concerns the middle school *after* it had appeared as a functionally differentiated unit of the public school organization, the work of psychologists such as Edward Lee Thorndike and Lewis Madison Terman—pioneers in mental measurement and differential psychology—provided much greater staying support to the middle school idea than did Hall's culture-epoch theory.

Terman had put to extensive empirical use his Stanford Revision of the Binet-Simon Intelligence Tests, and in a study in 1919 of mental ages in a typical public school system, he found that, on a Stanford-Binet scale, the upper distributions of the first and fifth grades overlapped respectively the lower distributions of the fifth and ninth grades.[18] But more to the point, as differential psychology discovered the deeper complexities about individual differences, it was found that the widest spread of differences existed in groups of 12–15 year-olds, the age which the human sciences of the period had defined for early adolescence.

But for historical accuracy, it is important to note that differential psychology had made its great impact upon professional education *after* the appearance of the middle school. L. M. Terman, L. M. Thurstone, M. A. Merrill, and other prominent contributors to the literature of differential psychology published their major works *following* World War I, when the middle school was already on the scene. Moreover, once the significance of individual differences had impressed itself upon educative process, the event was reflected at all levels of the public school organization.

To claim, as some do, that the original goal of the American middle school was to provide for individual differences is to suggest, inferentially at least, that the elementary school and high school had ignored the emerging awareness of individual differences. In point of fact, to this day, educational experiences from kindergarten and up take into careful account individual differences in student groups as well as the differences of traits within individual students.

Nor is it tenable from an historical perspective to hold that "the junior high school is nothing more than the institutional recognition

---

18 Lewis M. Terman, *The Intelligence of School Children* (Boston: Houghton Mifflin Company, 1919), p. 26.

of the fact that subjects which used to belong to the high school can be taught at a point earlier than was formerly the case."[19] It is clear from the several reports of the Committee on Six-Year Courses, as well as from other historical evidence, that the six-year high school unit was created to allow for—in the language of the Committee on Six-Year Courses—precisely "the downward extension of the high school course."

Seen in historical retrospect, and as was noted earlier in the discussion, the six-year high school organization stands out as a fusion of two orientations to the categorization of goal objects in secondary school education. Eliot could accept the six-year high school because it in fact routinized the reform of secondary education which he had been advocating through a downward extension of high school subjects. Public school administrators, on the other hand, bedeviled by high dropout rates on one side and pressure from the colleges on the other, could accept the six-year high school because they saw in it a means for coming to terms with educational imperatives of the new age.

But the fusion was short-lived. For one thing, there were school administrators who felt that Eliot's type of six-year high school, like the four-year high school before it, was still out of step with new social aspirations. A case in point was the experience in St. Paul, Minnesota.

Glenn F. Varner, who for near a half-century served in the St. Paul system as high school teacher, guidance counselor, and Assistant Superintendent of Secondary Education, recalled:[20]

> We had the six-year high school in St. Paul, but we abandoned it. We gave up on the 6-6 organization because the six-year high school didn't give us the holding power we felt a democratic high school ought to have.
>
> The six-year high school did lower the dropout rate some, if for no other reason than that pupils were trapped in the same building as they went from the eighth grade into the ninth. But once they had passed the compulsory school-attendance age, many pupils still dropped out because the curriculum of the six-year high school was essentially college oriented. Work-bound pupils, or academically low-ability pupils, found little purpose in staying beyond the sixteenth birthday.

Disenchantment with the six-year high school organization moved some public school administrators to reconsider the terms on which the

[19] Charles H. Judd, "Fundamental Educational Reforms," *Elementary School Journal,* Vol. XIII, January 1923, p. 239. By permission of the University of Chicago Press.
[20] Interview with Glenn F. Varner, Dec. 18, 1963. Verified by Varner.

reorganized secondary school curriculum had been settled. Then, when psychological science discovered the qualitative significance of early adolescence in American culture, certain school superintendents were persuaded that no mere *reorganization* of the secondary school curriculum would do, which the six-year high school represented, but that a *dynamic adaptation* would have to be effected in the process of socialization at early adolescence. The terms under which early adolescents come to school—in a Parsonian reference, the terms of exchange between early adolescent pupils and the public school organization—would have to be changed.

These public school administrators were now at the cutting edge of institutional leadership. For now the goal structure of the macro public school organization had to be enlarged in order to incorporate the new educational subvalue which had emerged in society. Educational services would in the future have to take *special cognizance* of early adolescent education. But we will recall Superintendent W. A. Greeson had told his colleagues of the 1909 North Central Association meeting that neither the elementary school unit nor the six-year high school unit was functionally equipped to provide this new educational service. An administrative imperative of institutional leadership, generated by cultural conditions in American society, had necessitated a *functionally differentiated* unit in the public school organization.

By fixing our attention on Superintendent William H. Maxwell of New York City, we can observe with remarkable clarity how the influence of psychological science wrought a transformation in the administrative perspective of the early 1900's and which led to the middle school.

Maxwell, we will recall, had been the chairman of the Committee of Fifteen, the Committee which, in 1895, resisted encroachments on the traditional eight-year structure of the elementary school. There are those who have branded hidebound the Report of the Committee of Fifteen precisely because it had ignored psychological influences on educative process and was, therefore, subject-matter-centered. Nothing in the Report of the Committee of Fifteen suggests that Maxwell had dissociated himself from any part of that document. But there is reasonable cause for doubting whether such would have been the case some ten years later.

Maxwell addressed the meeting in 1903 of the Middle States and Maryland Association, and he used the occasion to deliver himself of some solid educational sociology, coupled with huge doses of G. Stanley Hall's psychology. He said in part:[21]

> The school is that institution which society has created to bring about this adjustment between the personality of the human being and his environment in the most perfect and economic manner. The secondary school has a distinct work to perform in this process. It deals with the adolescent, receiving him just after he has experienced the "new birth" incident to this stage of his development.
>
> The secondary school of the United States may thus be said to be that part of the great social institution called the school which deals with the early adolescent, and its function may be stated as that adaptation of the adolescent to his environment which will enable him to comprehend and appreciate it most intelligently and to control it most effectively.
>
> Those facts and principles involved in the performance of this function which have a direct bearing on the administration of the program of studies may be grouped for purposes of analysis under four heads.
>
> First, the relation of the secondary school in society, and its peculiar relation to the society of a democracy. A school is a social institution created by society to satisfy its needs. Its first function, then, is to minister to those needs. The needs of a democracy are individual needs.
>
> . . . Second, the individual, the first factor in the educational process. The individual of the secondary school is in that stage of his development termed the early adolescent. From the study of genetic psychology we learn that while in the common school each child has his own individual characteristics, at the beginning of the adolescence their natures become more divergent. Each at this time becomes surcharged with an overabundance of nervous activity that must have an outlet. There has just been opened up to him an entirely new world, the life of the race, and so he seeks to relieve this overpressure of nervous force by endeavoring with almost uncontrollable eagerness to explore it. As yet, however, he has not had any experiences which will guide him in making his exploration. He is at a loss to know which way to turn, and so, plunges ahead in confusion. His interests are wide ranged, and they are apt to be fitful and irregular. His likes and dislikes are usually strong, sometimes continuous and sometimes short-lived. The program of studies and its administration must be so shaped as to conserve those qualities that should be strengthened and to prevent the development of those traits that are injurious.

[21] *Proceedings,* Association of Middle States, 1904, pp. 15–16.

When developing pupil-centered consciousness in administrative minds, which Maxwell reflected so distinctively in 1903, was transformed into administrative decisions, one of the outcomes, among others, was the middle school. A functionally differentiated school unit came into existence whose paramount purpose was to provide educational services for early adolescents by means of a process predominantly oriented toward this goal. When, moreover, it was discovered that the new middle school organization is better equipped to produce the functional values which had been expected of the six-year high school unit, an early demise of the latter was inevitable. But, as has been registered in Chapter 3, there is no institutional doubt that the *paramount goal* of the early American middle school was to intervene protectively in the process of education, mediate between the human condition at the onset of adolescence and the pressures of culture, and continue the general education of early adolescents with a curriculum applied in a psychosocial environment which is functional for learning at this stage of socialization. In the words of Superintendent Frank F. Bunker again, who, it will be recalled, is credited as the architect of the first middle schools in the United States:[22]

> The Hall school of child study has made clear the existence of at least two significant periods in the development of our children—the adolescent and the preadolescent periods. Each of these is shown to have differentiating and distinguishing characteristics, both physical and mental. . . . [Moreover] the six-three-three arrangement of grades is one which recognizes these stages in child development and . . . it is an arrangement of school machinery making it easy for school officials to plan and carry their work into effect in conformity to the differing characteristics of these periods. In the selection of the content of a course of study and in the arrangement of the details in an orderly and progressive whole, due regard must be paid to the matter of stages in child growth.

It is a coincidence of history that Charles Eliot retired as President of Harvard with the advent of the American middle school, a unit of public school organization which his break with tradition had indirectly precipitated. He retired in 1909, and the first middle schools appeared at about the same time. But there is still other historical and educational significance in these two juxtaposed events. Eliot's retirement marked the end of one period in American secondary education and the coming of the middle school heralded the beginning of another.

22 Bunker, *Reorganization of the Public School System,* p. 117.

Secondary education of the Eliot era had been college-oriented and for the most part was unresponsive to aspirations for an enlargement of educational opportunities at the mass base of American society. Had Eliot's course for the reform of secondary education prevailed, its institutional mien and corresponding orientation would very likely have remained much the same. But Eliot's course did not prevail.

It was caught up in a tidal wave of social reconstruction which wanted a more hospitable climate for aspirations of the common man and which resisted the accelerated rationalization of American society at the cost of humanistic values. As we look back for the last time to the period from which the American middle school had sprung, we behold a kaleidoscopic fusion of men and events asserting the importance of human values in the cultural development of society.

Inherent orientations of the institutionalized value system provided the leverage to reconstruct the new America of factories and cities. All sectors of the institutional network were pressed into the task of social reconstruction. All of the American social system was confronted with exigencies of adaptation to substantive cultural change. In the sector of public education, the so-called "democratic revolution" in secondary education transformed the American high school into a multipurpose organization.[23] Its onetime singular goal of preparing youth for college was linked by the time of World War I with other educational goals. To be sure, the preparation of youth for college was still a goal of the American high school, but it had also taken on other goals in behalf of society.

Public school organization was now turned in its consummatory relations toward the whole of American society. The base of educational opportunity in America had been widened, and the coming of the middle school was, among others, but one manifestation of the event. But, alas, the new middle school unit of public school organization was but a bare few years in operation when it fell victim to what Victor A. Thompson has called "bureaupathology." It is a condition which by and large, as we shall see in Chapter 11, has remained unchecked to this day.[24]

[23] This theme has been enlarged in any number of works. For a more recent investigation of secondary education in America during the period under discussion here see Moses Stambler, "The Democratic Revolution in the Public High Schools of New York City." Unpublished Ph.D. dissertation, New York University, New York City, 1964.

[24] Thompson uses "bureaupathology" as a reference to undesirable behavior in organizations which results from the character of bureaucratic structure. See Victor A. Thompson, *Modern Organization: A General Theory* (New York: Alfred A. Knopf, 1961).

10

ASPECTS OF THE FORMAL ORGANIZATION

A reference to bureaupathology is one way of calling attention to the fact that the mechanism of formal organization can malfunction. Causes of malfunction may be either rational or psychological in character. Most often, however, malfunction is due to a confrontation between countervailing rational and psychological influences within the organizational structure. But whatever the cause of malfunction, modern society is in trouble when it is allowed to become a widespread condition in its formal organizations. For the formality of organizations is the social cost of complex and large-scale society.

It is the price modern society pays for the benefits of rationalization which governs the production of its essential goods and services. Large-scale organizations of government, business, education, defense, and so forth, which perform the differentiated functions in the social division of labor, and which are required for stability in the modern age, would become ineffectual overnight were they to abandon their so-called bureaucratic characteristics. There is no escaping it, the planned efficiency of bureaucracy is an indispensable condition of modern social process. Bureaucracy is one of the brilliant inventions of man. But in the hands of an unskilled or self-serving administrator, the bureaucratic mechanism can easily become a social hazard.

And the social cost of bureaucracy comes high in modern society even under the best of conditions. Unchecked by the larger values which give meaning to man's existence, the bureaucratic mechanism is capable of draining society of its humanistic characteristics and turn it into some monstrous machine. For the invention of bureaucracy epitomizes the rationalization of society.

The social dangers of excessive rationalization in the structure of society were already anticipated in the biblical world. It was the prophet Isaiah who cautioned, "Woe unto them that join house to house, that lay field to field, till there be no room, and ye be made to dwell alone in the midst of the land." Not until the modern era, however, was Isaiah's caution taken seriously. A turning point was the displacement of animal power by the mechanical power of steam.

The rate of industrialization and urbanization in post–Civil War America was cultural evidence that accelerated rationalization had overtaken both technological processes and social relations in the United States. Rising bureaucratization in the new culture of factories and cities dispelled forever the Adamic dream of Jefferson and Whitman. Americans became aware for the first time of the social consequences when house is jointed to house "till there be no room."

It was precisely this awareness which the ideology of liberal Darwinism impressed upon the national consciousness. The direction of development which social Darwinists wanted for post–Civil War society esteemed the instrumentalism of rational values above all else. They were willing to break with humanistic traditions of the past in order to establish the rational values of universalistic-achievement as the dominant force in the new society. Liberal Darwinists resisted such an orientation to future development with a program of institutional reforms which would reconstruct American society through a compatible synthesis of human and societal interests. Essentially, at the heart of the ideological contest beween social Darwinism and liberal Darwinism was the conflict between the demands of industrial society and individual human or, if we will, social needs.

State legislatures, the Congress, public education, the Supreme Court, and other institutional systems have performed, as we know, critical reconstructive functions in the period following Appomattox. But social reconstruction, it seems, is hard pressed to keep apace of continuing rationalization in society. "Promoting individualism without losing community" is still seen as the central social issue of our own day.[1] William H. Whyte, Jr., in *The Organization Man,* Norbert Wiener, in *The Human Use of Human Beings,* Robert Presthus, in *The Organizational Society,* and others have come to grips with this problem in the modern period. But it was Ferdinand Toennies, a German sociologist of the later nineteenth century, who first conceptualized this problem as a conflict of man's social needs and the rationalistic imperatives of modern society.

Toennies published in 1887 under the title of *Gemeinschaft und Gesellschaft.* The problem which Toennies defined in this book is the social condition of man in industrial society. It is a problem that has not yet been resolved to this day.

The social problem which Toennies had perceived in the developing industrial *milieu* of the late nineteenth century is essentially this: How can large-scale society save man from threatening social anonymity when his involvement in primary group associations is weakened, and even severed, by the conflicting demands of "society" and "community?" What is at stake in this problem is the organic solidarity of modern society.

Toennies conceptualized this problem in terms of paired contrasts which, with the paired comparison, has since then been used widely in modern sociology. Paired contrasts, especially, came into wide use when sociologists began to analyze consequences of interaction between two countervailing, but legitimate, forces in society. The dichotomy of formal-informal organization, which is central to the discourse of this chapter, is one such set of contrasts. Parsonian pattern variables are constructed precisely with such paired contrasts.

As was stated before, Toennies' central thesis in *Gemeinschaft und Gesellschaft* is the conflict of values that arises from man's rational pursuit of self-interest—this is *Gesellschaft*—and the social imperative for maintaining one's primary group relationships—this is *Gemeinschaft.*

Gemeinschaft defines a type of random behavior one sees in a primary group which the sociologist Charles Horton Cooley has defined as an "intimate face to face association." It is personal and informal, and it is, more often than not, motivated by sentiment, emotion, and feelings of the moment; in a word, it is expressive behavior. Ideal set-

[1] Robert Beck, "Perception of Individualism in American Culture and Education," *Educational Theory,* Vol. XI, July 1961, p. 129.

tings for observing this type of social behavior are kinship and friendship groups or the rural village.

Gesellschaft, on the other hand, is a type of rational behavior one sees in a secondary group. It is impersonal and formal, and it is calculated; in a word, it is instrumental behavior. Ideal settings for observing this type of social behavior is a market, industrial factory, business office, or the large city.[2]

Altogether, it is patently clear from the social history of industrial-urban societies that the continuing rationalization of society has compounded manifold the social problem which Toennies first defined in 1887. One has *to work* at maintaining primary group relationships in the modern-day social climate, whereas one cannot escape almost daily involvement in some secondary group. In terms of Toennies' conceptualization, then, the loss of *Gemeinschaft* values in social relationships, and the dominance of *Gesellschaft* values, is part of the social cost of bureaucracy in modern society. For no other secondary group in modern society exerts a more commanding influence upon social relations than does the bureaucratic organization. It follows, therefore, that a deeply significant correlation exists between the quality of social relations in modern society and the quality of management in bureaucratic organizations. It is a correlation which is also latent in a reference to bureaupathology.

But since modern society must resort to some form of bureaucracy in order to maintain a stable state, it can reduce the social hazards of bureaucracy by entrusting the management of its formal organizations in the hands of those who know "the nature of the beast" and who, at the same time, have internalized institutional commitments. The alternative is to suffer increasing bureaupathologies in society.

But institutional commitment alone, as this is characterized by social idealism, is not enough. The two qualifying conditions upon which society must insist, knowing the structure of bureaucratic organizations and institutional commitment, are inseparable. Institutional innovations have been known to flounder, and even face extinction, precisely because they were not implemented by effectively managed organizations. The history of the American middle school provides us with a remarkable case in point.

---

2 For more on *Gemeinschaft und Gesellschaft* see Ferdinand Toennies, *Community and Society*, translated by Charles P. Loomis (East Lansing, Mich.: Michigan State University Press, 1957).

From every indication at hand, it would seem that what has gone wrong with the American middle school is not its institutional purpose, as this purpose was defined by its founders, but the administration of its organizational structure. The middle school organization was from the first meant to implement early adolescent education, once the latter was incorporated as an educational subvalue in the goal structure of public school organization. Here, and this bears repeating, was a case of institutional leadership in public school administration. Administrative leadership facilitated in this instance an institutional change in the organization of public education as a means of satisfying a new social need. Administrative rationality guided the course of a natural response in the institution of public education.

That institutional leadership of the 1910 period had exercised sound administrative judgment in providing a separate organizational unit for early adolescent education is confirmed in our own day by three recent studies which were conducted by the Research Division of the National Education Association.

A study in 1961 reported that in predominantly urban America, the middle school "is found in 53 percent of the urban school systems." Moreover, during the 1950's, school districts with *separate* middle schools had increased from 40.1 percent to 53.3 percent.[3]

Another study by the NEA Research Division put the following question to a representative sample of the nation's teachers:

In your opinion which of the following methods of organizing elementary and secondary school is best for the all-round development of pupils, considering all age groups?

An overwhelming 70 percent of respondents endorsed a separate middle school "as the best pattern for the all-round development of pupils."[4]

Still another study which was conducted by the NEA Research Division asked the following question of a representative sample of the nation's elementary school principals:

Considering their all-round personal and educational development, which, in your opinion, is the best organization for educating pupils in grades 7 or 8?

[3] National Education Association, Research Division, "The Junior High School Today," *NEA Research Bulletin*, Vol. 39, May 1961, pp. 47–50. The U.S. Bureau of the Census definition of an urban community was used in the study; thus only districts with a population of 2,500 and over were treated.
[4] Reported in *NEA Journal*, Vol. 40, February 1962, p. 43.

An analysis of the responses is as follows: 18.3 percent favored the eight-grade elementary school; 51.0 percent favored a three-year middle school of grades 7–8–9; 23.1 percent favored a two-year middle school of grades 7–8; while only 2.5 percent favored a six-year high school of grades 7–12. Altogether, 74.1 percent of the elementary school principals in this survey regarded a separate middle school as "the best organization for educating pupils" of early adolescent age.[5] The contrast presented by modern-day professional endorsements of the middle school's original institutional purpose and the erratic course of its fulfillment since 1910 may be taken as pointed clinical evidence of an enduring malfunction in the middle school organization—a very bad case of bureaupathology indeed.

The chapter to follow will pinpoint the sources of malfunction in the middle school organization. First, however, a more detailed definition of the middle school as a formal organization has to be given. Threads of such a definition have already been introduced in the early chapters. Indeed, our first view of the middle school was as a formal organization. These threads are now pulled together within an enlarged projection of formal organization.

The Source of Rationalistic Orientations

Thematic references to the concept of organization in earlier chapters have already established that all bureaucratically structured organizations, because they are rational systems, are subject to imperatives of effectiveness and efficiency in the performance of organizational tasks. It does not matter whether the system in mind is the macro organization or one of its micro units, as, say, the middle school in a system of public education. So long as it is a rationalistically structured system in the care of an administrative staff these imperatives will prevail.

The concept of rational structure, of course, takes as "a given" some kind of planned order. A public school organization, as we already know, has such a planned order. It has goals which are attained by

5 National Education Association, Research Division, "Principals' Opinions," *NEA Research Bulletin,* Vol. 40, May 1962, p. 61. An infinitesimal 0.8 percent thought the type of organization made "little or no difference," and 4.3 percent responded as "undecided." The following sampling technique was employed for this survey: "Using its newly developed small-sample techniques, the Research Division selected principals [N-721] to represent school districts of all sizes, which had been grouped according to the number of teachers employed: fewer than 50, 50 to 1,000, and 1,000 or more." *Ibid.,* p. 61.

means of patterns of operation that are performed by a corps of skilled personnel recruited for this purpose. Each person who enters the system of public school organization in an official capacity is assigned a role and is expected to perform the role in accordance with regulations, or norms, which have been prescribed.

Beyond prescribing what the public school organization regards as normative role behavior, these regulations serve other useful functions. For one thing, rules and regulations obviate the necessity of having to parade constantly authority symbols before members of the organization; that is to say, administrators do not have to resort to what Peter M. Blau calls "specific sanctions" in order to get tasks done. For another, and this is a latent function of rules and regulations, administrators can with discretion apply them in a manner that will induce greater voluntary cooperation in members of the organization. Blau conceptualizes such administrative strategy as "strategic leniency," and Alvin W. Gouldner thinks of it as an "indulgency pattern."[6]

But, of course, no matter how softly regulations are used in a public school organization, they are still expressions of power, power which has been legitimized by some legal authority. The public school organization employs this power to enforce rational procedures that have been established for system operations. The public school organization is, therefore, at once a rational system and a domination system. It is classifiable in a typology of organizations as a rational-legal system.

According to Max Weber, when a rational-legal system requires an administrative staff to plan and integrate its operations, it will assume the form of a bureaucratic organization. The general and special literature in the field of administration is replete with references to the concept of bureaucratic structure. Expressions such as *planned organization, administrative organization, formal organization, instrumental organization, goal-directed organization, complex organization,* and others, have a direct bearing on the concept of bureaucracy.

6 Peter M. Blau, *Bureaucracy in Modern Society* (New York: Random House, 1956), pp. 69–83. The reader will find models by Alvin W. Gouldner, Philip Selznick, and Robert K. Merton which suggest means of reducing the visibility of authority relations in bureaucratic organizations, and of inducing greater cooperation in members, in James G. March and Herbert A. Simon, *Organizations* (New York: John Wiley and Sons, 1958), 34–82. For a demonstration of how the Gouldner model can be used to explain intended and unintended consequences of rules and regulations see Daniel E. Griffiths, "The Social Sciences and Administration: A Rational Response," in Lawrence W. Downey and Frederick Enns (eds.), *The Social Sciences and Educational Administration* (Edmonton, Alberta: The University of Alberta and The University Council For Educational Administration, 1963), pp. 16–18.

Bureaucracy received its most disciplined definition from Max Weber. We will recall from Chapter 4 that Weber's interest in the phenomenon of social order led him to the study of domination systems in ancient and modern societies. His sharp sociological insights recognized order in society as a product of power which stems from three sources of legitimate authority: legal, traditional, and charismatic. But, we must hasten to note, Weber's scholarly interest did not extend to the *internal* mechanisms of bureaucratic organization. His central preoccupation was the study of social cohesion in the larger society.

Power, in Weber's sense, means domination; power with which to impose one's will upon the behavior of others and which the "others" acknowledge as a *legitimate* use of power and, therefore, submit to it. The most prevalent type of domination system of modern times is what Weber has called a bureaucracy.

Blau's compact definition of bureaucracy states, "The type of organization designed to accomplish large-scale administrative tasks by systematically coordinating the work of many individuals is called a bureaucracy."[7] As a mechanism for obtaining ordered integration in a complex division of labor, Weber held up the bureaucratic organization as the technical superior of all other types. Indeed, basic to the ordered efficiency of modern society, according to Weber, is the patterned form of bureaucracy.

Weber's conceptualization of bureaucratic organization had as its model an ideal type. Some believe that it was the Prussian civil service which served as Weber's model. But however the case may have been, Weber abstracted those characteristics of bureaucracy which he saw as *generic* to all types. He then formulated an elaborate statement of principles which for him seemed to explain the instrumental efficiency of bureaucratic organizations.

Some of the more major administrative, or bureaucratic, characteris-

[7] Blau, *Bureaucracy in Modern Society*, p. 14. The literature on bureaucracy is voluminous. Several titles have already been cited in earlier footnotes. As has been noted in an earlier reference, Max Weber's own exposition of domination systems, including bureaucracy, is contained in a study, interrupted by death, entitled *Wirtschaft und Gesellschaft*, Part I, which in English is available as Max Weber, *The Theory of Social and Economic Organization*. See also Robert K. Merton, Ailsa P. Gray, Barbara Hockey, and Hanan C. Selvin (eds.), *Reader in Bureaucracy* (New York: The Free Press, 1953); Reinhard Bendix, *Max Weber: An Intellectual Portrait* (New York: Doubleday and Co., 1960), especially Chapters 9–13; H. H. Gerth and C. Wright Mills (eds.), *From Max Weber: Essays in Sociology*, translated by the editors (New York: Oxford University Press, 1946); and Chester I. Barnard, *The Functions of the Executive*, especially Parts II–III, which has been cited in an earlier footnote.

tics of an ideal type of bureaucracy are in Weber's classification as follows:

1. A clear-cut division of labor governs the tasks of members in the organization.

2. A hierarchy of offices defines authority relationships in the organization; that is, a subordinate–superordinate network is established in which incumbents of higher offices are held responsible for the performance of those below them.

3. A system of rules and regulations is promulgated to set standards for the performance of official tasks, to facilitate coordination, and to otherwise regulate the behavior of members in the organization.

4. Officials of the organization perform administrative duties with detachment and standards of economy and efficiency alone guide their judgments.

5. Employment or promotion is governed impartially by criteria of competence and seniority in the organization.

6. Records are kept in order to develop production norms which, in turn, are used as means for predicting future performance by members of the organization.[8]

Weber's model of the bureaucratic organization is official, formal, machinelike, distant, and otherwise incompatible with man's gregariousness as a "social animal." But let us note again that Weber had conceptualized an ideal type of bureaucracy: *an abstraction.* Since Weber's day, sociologists have discovered, through empirical research, what Charles H. Page has called "bureaucracy's other face."

Bureaucracy's other face is a way of saying that no matter how much like a machine an organization may be, it will have also an inescapable human dimension. Much of what went wrong in the American middle school organization can be explained in terms of rationalistic causation, but not all. Chapter 11 will show that nonrational, or psychological, causes have also been at work. A return at this point to the view of organization as a social system, a view which was first mapped in Chapter 2, will enable us to see at closer range a category of experience in organizations which is explained by the concept of *informal organization.*[9]

[8] Weber, *Social and Economic Organization*, pp. 330–37.
[9] Charles H. Page, "Bureaucracy's Other Face," *Social Forces*, Vol. 25, 1946. As is the case with the concept of formal organization, a considerable literature has been produced around the concept of informal organization. For representative works in which the con-

The Source of Affective Orientations

Sociologists have been interested in the larger significance of psychological, or informal, behavior in society even before the twentieth century. We have already noted Ferdinand Toennies' work on the subject. However, it was well into the twentieth century when sociologists became aware that the dichotomy of formal–informal behavior also carried important functional significance for the administration of large-scale organizations. But once its significance was conceptualized, it became an important extension of contemporary organization theory.

Among the earliest to discover the function of informal behavior in the formal organization was Elton Mayo, who, with a group of associates, was invited by management of the Hawthorne Works of the Western Electric Company to conduct some in-plant efficiency studies. Up until the time of the Hawthorne studies in the late 1920's, it was generally believed that output in factories and employee satisfaction revolved around the problem of physical fatigue, a consequence of the accumulation of lactic acid in body muscles as the day moved along. Indeed, so general was this belief that in 1926 the Harvard Graduate School of Business Administration established a Fatigue Laboratory for the study of industrial fatigue.

Hawthorne management had initiated on their own some illumination experiments in connection with a motivation program which they had hoped would lead to increased production output. Soon, however, their experiments produced data for which they had no cogent explanation. It was at this point that Elton Mayo was brought in from Harvard's Department of Industrial Research.

Because of the currency of fatigue theory, it was altogether reasonable of the Harvard team to prepare a research design in which improvement in the physical environment was treated as the independent variable and production output as the dependent variable. An experimental group was selected, but, alas, not a matched control group, although careful *before* and *after* observations were made of the experimental group, the Relay Assembly Test Room group.

---

cept of informal organization is treated, in addition to that of Page and those which have been cited in connection with the discussion of bureaucracy earlier in this chapter, see Blau, *Bureaucracy in Modern Society,* Chapter 3; Blau and Scott, *Formal Organizations,* Chapter 4; but more especially the well-composed chapter by Laurence Iannaccone, "An Approach to the Informal Organization of the School," in NSSE *Yearbook,* Part II, 1964, Chapter 10.

In any event, the investigators discovered before very long, and to their great astonishment, that while experimental conditions *did raise* production, the empirical evidence was clear beyond a doubt that the independent, or experimental, variable was not the cause of it.   Once it was realized that some variable other than modification of the physical environment was responsible for the effect, a search was begun for the elusive variable.   In time, it was found and is now known to behavioral science as the "Hawthorne effect."

In still another of these Hawthorne studies, the investigators were puzzled at the relatively stable quota of output in one experimental group, the Bank Wiring Observation Room group, despite bonus pay inducements from management to exceed the quota.   This was the last of the studies and, in terms of research methodology, the best designed.

The experimental group was observed in a laboratory which simulated normal industrial conditions as much as these can be simulated for experimental purposes.   And of all observations that were recorded of this group, an obvious resistance to management inducements to exceed the quota was the most baffling.   For here was an empirical datum which ran in the face of the long-standing concept of an "economic man," of man the gain-seeker in rational pursuit of self-interest.

At this point of the research, the theoretical framework was enlarged and otherwise modified.   No longer was the focus on single variables in the physical environment, and their effect upon production levels, as it had been in the early phases of the research.   The investigators now conceptualized the experimental work group as a social group in a *social situation*.   By the time of the Bank Wiring Observation Room study, it had become axiomatic in the research that aspects of human behavior had to be defined in the context of a social situation: in *Gestaltist* terms, as a figure against some given background.

Once the research had taken this turn, a whole range of new insights opened up for the investigators.   They discovered, for example, that comments which were elicited in interview sessions with workers contained two important elements: *manifest content* and *latent content;* that which was *meant* and that which was *revealed* in a comment. When, therefore, the phenomenon of a quota in the Bank Wiring Observation Room manifested itself, it too was hypothesized as an aspect of human behavior in a social situation.

The sociological significance of a quota in the Bank Wiring Observation Room was eventually defined in psychological terms and not in the economic terms of rational gain-seeking. The group as a whole, it seemed, had determined *informally* the output of each member in accordance with a predetermined, but never overtly defined, standard which represented the group's judgment of a fair day's work, a standard which rarely corresponded with that of efficiency engineers. It was discovered that meanings which individuals in a group assigned to events external to the group, and their psychological response to these events, were important variables in the research.

The Hawthorne research has been reported and its results analyzed in many published works. Some social scientists have been critical of the research methodology, and others have questioned certain of the conclusions. But all grant the seminal value of the Hawthorne studies. Collectively, they stand as a landmark in modern industrial sociology. From these studies came the first substantive empirical evidence that Weber's machine model of formal organization fails to explain all aspects of behavior in administrative organizations. The significance for administrative process of informal, nonofficial, psychologically induced behavior in bureaucratically structured social systems was discovered along the way.

Elton Mayo published one of the earliest reports of the Hawthorne studies in 1933 under the title *The Human Problems of an Industrial Society*. However, the classic, and by far still the most elegant, report of the Hawthorne research is the one by participants Fritz J. Roethlisberger and William J. Dickson under the title *Management and the Worker*. These works mark the ascendancy in the United States of a Human Relations School of management and the decline of efficiency engineering, the dominant mode of the Scientific School of management.

What the Hawthorne research uncovered essentially was that *human beings* continue to function as *human beings* when they become components of a bureaucratic organization. Such an abstraction as economic man, the gain-seeker of traditional economics, fails to take into account that humans cannot be denied psychological responses to the environment in which they are, rules and regulations notwithstanding, and that this fact about people carries important administrative significance.

People, it seems, will take refuge from the harsh and official climate of organizations in a variety of informal and nonofficial relations. These informal relations were found in the Hawthorne research, and confirmed later by other empirical studies, to exert a powerful influence on the formal, or official, behavior of members in the organization. The following two illustrations are cases in point.

Elton Mayo discovered that informal relations in the Hawthorne organization retarded output, as was the case in the Bank Wiring Observation Room, or accelerated output, as was the case in the Relay Assembly Test Room. The critical variable, it seems, was how members in each group perceived the official organization.

Mayo's investigation was conducted in an industrial organization. But varieties of the same phenomenon were uncovered also in a public school organization. A sociological study in the public school system of Kansas City disclosed that informal, nonofficial elements were exerting a substantial influence upon such matters as teacher assignment to undesirable locations, the disciplining of younger teachers, freedom to exercise creativity by teachers, and more. Again, informal structure was shown to be a carrier of important meaning for administrative process.[10]

It does not help any to proscribe, or outlaw, informal elements within the organization. Proscription merely drives them underground. Informal structure will emerge in one way or another. However, the Structuralist School of management, a school which synthesizes human relations and rationalistic orientations in administration, holds that formal and informal organization can be joined to good advantage by means of skillfully devised administrative strategies. Skilled administrators can raise, to use Chester Barnard's terms, levels of *effectiveness* and *efficiency* in an organization by allowing informal structure controlled latitude to provide immediate social-psychological satisfactions for members of the organization as *compensation* for those they must surrender in the performance of official duties. This, in part, is what Barnard had in mind when he conceptualized an organization's capacity to maintain equilibrium as a balance of individual burdens and satisfactions. In the Structuralist approach to administration, it may be said that no other integrative function of management in complex organizations calls for greater administrative skill than the one which is required for effecting an optimum transaction of the two powerful, but countervailing, forces that are generated by formal and informal components of organization.

[10] Warren A. Peterson, "Career Phases and Inter-Age Relationships: The Female High School Teachers in Kansas City." Unpublished Ph.D. dissertation, University of Chicago, 1956, pp. 202, 211, 251.

Such a view of organization sees the exercise of bureaucratic authority restrained by administrative imperatives to fuse, in Parsons' terms, cognitive and cathectic motivation in the organization. Structuralists regard interpersonal relationships as desirable in the authority process. Obtaining a willing acceptance of authority relations within the organization is regarded by Structuralists as the skill of "mediating between the individual and the organization in such a way that both can obtain maximum satisfaction."[11]

Reference to the administrative imperative for integrating formal and informal orientational thrusts have been registered in the literature under different concepts. However, the ubiquity of the reference in the modern literature of administration attests to its importance in administrative process.

Talcott Parsons had in mind the conflict of formal and informal thrusts when, in his theory of social systems, he resorted to such paired contrasts as the gratification-discipline dilemma, instrumental orientation-expressive orientation, and two aspects of an actor's need-disposition system. Indeed, his conceptualization of pattern variables is perhaps the most sophisticated sociological tool that has been invented for the analysis of problems which stem from a conflict of orientations to the valuation of objects in an organization. Other references which turn on the formal–informal dichotomy, and are now a commonplace in administration literature, are group maintenance–group achievement, consideration-initiation of structure, and one which by this time should be most familiar of all to students of educational administration, the nomothetic-idiographic-transactional model of a formal system by Jacob W. Getzels and Egon G. Guba.[12] Of course, in the

---

11 Warren G. Bennis, "Revisionist Theory of Leadership," *Harvard Business Review,* Vol. 39, 1961. Also by Bennis, "Leadership Theory and Administrative Behavior: The Problem of Authority," *Administrative Science Quarterly,* Vol. IV, December 1959. For other references to this theme see Marshall E. Dimock, *Administrative Vitality: The Conflict with Bureaucracy* (New York: Harper & Row, 1959); Melville Dalton, *Men Who Manage: Fusions of Feeling and Theory in Administration* (New York: John Wiley and Sons, 1959); Robert Dubin, *The World of Work* (Englewood Cliffs, N.J.: Prentice-Hall, 1958); and Robert V. Prestus, "Authority in Organizations," in Sidney Mailick and Edward H. Van Ness (eds.), *Concepts and Issues in Administrative Behavior* (Englewood Cliffs, N.J.: Prentice-Hall, 1962).

12 The Getzels-Guba model will be found, among other sources, in Roald F. Campbell, John E. Corbally, Jr., and John A. Ramseyer, *Introduction to Educational Administration* (Boston: Allyn and Bacon, 1962), p. 187; and Jacob W. Getzels, "Administration as a Social Process," in Andrew W. Halpin, *Administrative Theory,* p. 156. Other representative works that treat formal-informal structures in depth are George C. Homans, *The Human Group* (New York: Harcourt, Brace and Co., 1950), which has value for

shorthand of theoretical symbolism, each of the foregoing concepts is saying that the *Gemeinschaft-Gesellschaft* dilemma of large-scale society is also the dilemma of large-scale organizations.

Business administration in the United States was the first to profit from accretions to administrative theory that have come from the Hawthorne studies. As more and more schools of business administration enriched their preparation programs with theoretical insights, business and industrial management gained sophistication. Educational administration has been following a similar pattern of enrichment since the 1950's.

Altogether, out of modern organization theory has emerged an awareness that complex organizations can assume more than one type of bureaucratic posture. Recent sociological scholarship has demonstrated that the bureaucratic posture a system of organization assumes is structurally determined by the character of its goals, the character of the technical tasks by means of which goals are attained, and the degree of specialization that is required of members who perform technical tasks in the organization. It has been found, for example, that Max Weber's pattern of line authority is dysfunctional for certain types of service organizations. Even the military organization—perhaps the most faithful replica extant in modern society of Weber's bureaucratic model—has been forced to modify its exercise of authority because of the greater technical expertise that is now required for military tasks.[13]

The enlarged sociological view of bureaucratic organizations has led Gouldner to propose that two types of bureaucracy are actually dominant in modern society: a punishment-centered type and a representative type. In a punishment-centered bureaucracy, all authority is in the hands of administrators. Decisions are made by them without con-

---

all fields of administration; Daniel E. Griffiths, *Human Relations in School Administration,* which has already been cited in Chapter 1, is of value in the specialized field of educational administration; Andrew W. Halpin, "The Superintendent's Effectiveness as a Leader," Midwest Administration Center, *Administrator's Notebook,* Vol. VII, October 1958. See especially in the latter the four-cell scheme for describing a leader's behavior on the "initiating structure" and "consideration" dimensions. Hereafter cited as "Superintendent's Effectiveness."

It is most gratifying to be able to add that Professor Halpin's major ideas are now available in one book, including the one which is developed in the latter citation. See Andrew W. Halpin, *Theory and Research in Administration* (New York: The Macmillan Company, 1966).

[13] See Roy G. Francis and Robert C. Stone, *Service and Procedure in Bureaucracy* (Minneapolis, Minn.: University of Minnesota Press, 1956); and Morris Janowitz, *The Professional Soldier* (Glencoe, Ill.: The Free Press, 1960), especially Chapters 1–4.

sultation with subordinates "on the line" and are enforced by means of coercive sanctions. Whereas in a representative bureaucracy, administrators acknowledge in their official relations an authority which is based on expertise in applying the technology of the organization, *the authority of competence.* In such an organization, major administrative decisions are made in consultation with those who are affected by them. In short, the exercise of line authority in this instance is *structurally restrained* by the authority of competence.[14]

Let us note quickly that this restraint is *qualitatively* different from the restraint which stems from informal influences. The sharp edge of bureaucratic authority is blunted in the informal context by psychological imperatives which spring from the organization as a *social system,* whereas the authority of competence blunts the sharp edge of bureaucratic authority precisely because the organization must function also as a *mechanistic system* if it is to be effective.

Parsons' Hierarchy of Primary Subsystems

A juxtaposition of the two concepts, line authority and authority of competence, provides us with an ideal transition to another major structural arrangement of complex organizations, one of which has been conceptualized by Talcott Parsons as a *hierarchy of subsystems in formal organizations.*

So far we have examined two major structural components of organization: the formal and, its matched opposite, the informal. But still more has to be known about the structure of complex organizations for our analysis of malfunction in middle school organization. Bureaucracy, to be sure, will explain the pattern of line authority in an organization, but it does not explain with enough specificity how, in actual system operations, administrative authority relates with the authority of competence.

Especially in a complex system of organization, such as a public school, where a highly specialized technology necessitates a network of high-order role specialization, we need to know more about the network of organizational roles and the administrative control which holds spe-

[14] Alvin W. Gouldner, *Patterns of Industrial Bureaucracy* (Glencoe, Ill.: The Free Press, 1954). See also the footnote reference on p. 125 in Merton, *Social Theory.* Another aspect of representative bureaucracy is referred to by Simon Marcson as "colleague authority." See Simon Marcson, "The Management and Mismanagement of Industrial Scientists," *Trans-action,* Vol. 1, January 1964.

cialists in technical roles accountable for their assigned duties. Parsons' conceptualization of a hierarchy of subsystems takes us to this cognition.

Parsons' reason for conceptualizing a hierarchy of subsystems is given by him in the following:[15]

> The theory of "bureaucracy" has been so strongly influenced by the conception of "line" authority that there has been a tendency to neglect the importance of what in some sense are qualitative breaks in the continuity of the line structure. There is much sound observation and comment on many relevant problems but little direct attempts to analyze them in a more formal way.

Before Parsons' reference to "qualitative breaks in the continuity of the line structure" is studied at closer range, it would be well to have his own definition of the formal organization in which "the line structure" exists. A formal organization, according to Parsons, is[16]

> . . . a mechanism by which goals somehow important to the society, or to various subsystems of it, are implemented and to some degree defined. But not only does such an organization have to operate in a social environment which imposes the conditions governing the processes of disposal and procurement, it is also part of a wider social system which is the source of the "meaning," legitimation, or higher-level support which makes the implementation of the organization's goals possible.

A careful examination of Parsons' definition of formal organization will show it to be of a piece with his theory of social systems. Parsons, we will recall again, has conceptualized only society as a "total social system" and the organizations of society as "partial social systems," or subsystems of society.

As a major building block of his theoretical framework, Parsons then postulates that, like society itself, complex organizations have as structural mechanisms a hierarchy of three primary subsystems which are distinguishable, especially in organizations where the division of labor is highly specialized, by the character of the roles that constellate in each of them. These subsystems, according to Parsons, should be treated analytically as functional differentiations in the organization's division of labor, just as organizations themselves are differentiated by

[15] Parsons, "Some Ingredients of a General Theory," p. 40.
[16] *Ibid.*, p. 44.

the character of the functions they perform in the division of labor in society.[17]

Guided by the character of the roles that constellate in each of the subsystems, Parsons proceeds to classify them as follows: *technical, managerial,* and *institutional.* These primary subsystems are the structural mechanisms with which an organization attends to four types of "exigencies," as Parsons calls them, in order to carry on its vital functions and maintain a stable posture. Parsons defines these exigencies as that of *adaptation, goal attainment, integration,* and *latent pattern-maintenance,* or, as he at times refers to the latter, of *latency.*

The organization ascribes to each hierarchy of roles in this interdependent network of subsystems *primary responsibility* for the resolution of *specific problems* that are generated *recurringly* by the four types of exigencies. When these problems are not resolved, the organization cannot perform its vital functions and is, therefore, threatened by failure in the pursuit of goals.

Thus, the *technical subsystem* is expected to orient itself to the performance of technical tasks which produce the organization's output. At this level of organization constellate the technical roles.

Incumbents of such roles have *primary responsibility* for the effectiveness of the organization's technology. They have been recruited by the organization for these roles because they have been judged to possess the required skills for the performance of technical tasks and for maintaining the organization's technical processes in a constant state of effectiveness. Problems that are generated by exigencies of adaptation and goal attainment have to be resolved at this level of the organization, *the level of technical competence.*

The test of effectiveness in the technical subsystem is the proficiency of technical procedures in the attainment of goal objects.

The *managerial subsystem* is expected to orient itself to the maintenance of optimum functional conditions in the organization through the integration of technical effectiveness and human efficiency. At this level of organization constellate the administrative roles.

Incumbents of such roles have *primary responsibility* for the decision making that is required to control and service the technical subsystem. They have been recruited by the organization for these roles because

---

[17] Parsons, *Essays,* p. 399. For how Parsons has used this concept methodologically, with society as his focus, see his "General Theory in Sociology," in Robert K. Merton, Leonard Broom, Leonard S. Cottrell, Jr. (eds.), *Sociology Today* (New York: Basic Books, 1959).

they have been judged to possess the required skills for the performance of those integrative tasks that will maintain the organization in a constant state of effectiveness and efficiency. Problems that are generated by exigencies of integration have to be resolved at this level of organization, *the level of managerial competence.*

Major managerial tasks include filling technical roles in the organization with those who possess required technical skills, defining organizational goals, establishing official role expectations, procuring the material resources of the organization, formalizing consummatory relations with other systems, coordinating system operations, mediating conflict between the technical subsystem and consumers of its output, and devising administrative strategies with which to induce the voluntary cooperation of members of the organization.

The test of effectiveness in the managerial subsystem is the attainment of organizational goals.

The *institutional subsystem* is expected to orient itself to the maintenance of the integrity of the cultural values that have been set in the organization's goal structure. At this level of organization constellate the institutional roles. These roles link the organization with the authority system of society. They are the roles which some legal authority has designated, in a charter of some type, to assume responsibility for the trusteeship of the organization. In most modern-day organizations such roles are known collectively as a board of directors, and in public school organizations as a board of education.

Incumbents of such roles have *primary responsibility* for maintaining the integrity of institutional values which guide goal orientations of the organization and, therefore, also its consummatory relations with the external environment. Society has placed them in these roles to assure itself that the organization will implement social values for which the goal structure of the organization serves as a receptacle. Problems that are generated by exigencies of latent pattern-maintenance have to be resolved at this level of organization, *the level of guardianship competence.*

Major guardianship tasks include selecting competent management for the organization, obtaining consensus—that is, legitimation—in the society on which emerging subvalues the organization shall fulfill, exercising broad guide-line control over the managerial subsystem, and mediating between the organization and society in matters that turn on the procurement of resources for the organization; that is, securing support for the organization from societal resources.

The test of effectiveness in the institutional subsystem is the maintenance of the integrity of institutional values.

Parsons' dimensional classification of primary subsystems is, of course, an abstraction, but one of extensive analytical usefulness. Parsons is well aware that, in the real world of system operations, "concrete structures do not follow the lines of differentiation of system-function exactly."[18] He is, therefore, quite explicit in directing attention to the fact that, in actual operation, primary subsystems of an organization are functionally interdependent and that they "will necessarily have connections and interchanges 'upward' as well as laterally and 'downward.' "[19]

Nevertheless, according to Parsons:[20]

> The functional or dimensional classification is a frame of reference in terms of which this differentiation may be analyzed, but because of the empirical interrelationships between the units, the segregation of their properties from each other does not neatly follow the lines of such a classification. The situation is closely analogous to that in the biological sciences. Without the categories of metabolism, respiration, locomotion, coordination and the like, it would be impossible to analyze the structure and functioning of complex organisms, but speaking of any one concrete organ-system as serving only one organic function is seldom legitimate. Exactly what the "blurrings" of the analytical lines we have drawn will be in any concrete case will vary with the type both of value system and of level of its differentiation as a social system.

Rights of Authority, Rights of Skill

Parsons' dimensional classification of primary subsystems opens a new window on the authority-skill dilemma of complex organizations. The dilemma is seen most sharply defined in organizations where the application of technical processes require the high-order specialization of professionals. Then the problem is: Who have rights of participation in decision making? In terms of Weber's conceptualization of bureaucratic line authority, administrators must hold this right. But what of subordinates in technical roles who are more expert in knowledge about technical processes in the organization—do they have rights in decision making?

18 Parsons, *Essays,* p. 399.
19 Parsons, "Some Ingredients of a General Theory," p. 69.
20 Parsons, *Essays,* pp. 399–400. It is interesting to note that Durkheim begins his discourse in *The Division of Labor in Society* with a similar physiological reference.

Parsons, of course, has not discovered a new structural pattern in complex organizations. The pattern of suborganizations in complex systems has been familiar to students of organization for some time. Barnard, for example, described complex organizations as "units of 'working' or 'basic' organizations, overlaid with units of executive organizations. . . ."[21] But Parsons' conceptualization has more than descriptive power. Its greater power is in the analytical light it throws on administrative strains in the decision-making process which stem from continuing sophistication of technical roles in an organization's division of labor.

Parsons has constructed an important extension of Max Weber's theory of bureaucracy, one which delineates points of interaction in complex systems where constraints of *competence* limit the exercise of so-called line authority. His conceptualization of hierarchical subsystems brings to the surface a reality in complex organizations which shows that when the conglomeration of roles in primary subsystems interact, as they must in actual system operations, the line of authority is not continuous from the top of the bureaucratic pyramid to the bottom. Instead, there occur "qualitative breaks in the continuity of the line structure."

These breaks in line authority occur because functions that are performed at the technical level of organization are not merely *simpler* than those that are performed at the managerial level, they are *different!* Actors in technical roles possess a *special kind of competence* which the organization requires in order to attain its goals.

Therefore, while administrators of a complex system of organization may define broad tasks for the technical subsystem, they have to acknowledge at the same time the *authority of competence* which resides there. Especially when technical roles are by necessity filled with highly skilled professionals, the ascribed primary responsibility of the managerial subsystem to *control and service* the technical subsystem cannot be fulfilled, without dysfunctional consequences, by merely "giving orders," by a resort to line authority. Interactions between the managerial and technical subsystems have to be governed by a quality of administration which is capable of fusing managerial authority with the authority of competence.

The problem of effecting such a fusion is changing the character of

---

[21] Barnard, *The Functions of the Executive*, p. 113.

administrative process even in most bureaucratically structured organizations. The military organization has already been cited as a case in point. Also to the point is a heightened interest in the professional, as reflected by recent sociological literature, in business and industrial organizations. The source of the problem is precisely the *rationalistic character* of complex organizations, although its presence is most immediately and directly discernible in the quality of human relations within the *social system* of organizations.

It is altogether important, therefore, to have it firmly established that the structural variable of technical competence which restrains the exercise of bureaucratic authority is rational in character. Restraints on bureaucratic authority which are explained by the concept of informal organization turn on *social-psychological* variables of organizational structure, whereas restraints of competence turn on *technical-rational* variables. These two concepts lose vigor as analytical tools when one fails to distinguish between them and their usefulness in analytical applications is diminished. In point of fact, we can readily observe in a system of school organization the structural constraint of *competence* on bureaucratic authority without *any reference* to informal aspects of structure in the organization.

Parsons himself provides us with a rare illustration.

Before a 1957 seminar, which was sponsored jointly by the University of Chicago and the University Council for Educational Administration, and whose theme was "Administrative Theory in Action," Parsons read a paper in which he treated his concept of primary subsystems, and he used the school organization most frequently for illustrative references. Excerpting the references to school organization only, Parsons said:[22]

> In the first place, every formal organization has certain "technical" functions. In an educational organization these are the actual processes of teaching. . . . There is, then, always a type of suborganization whose "problems" are mainly those of effectively performing this "technical" function—the conduct of classes by the teacher. . . . The primary exigencies to which this suborganization is oriented are those imposed by the nature of the technical task. . . .
> . . . Moreover, classrooms have to be provided; the teacher does not automatically control adequate facilities for performing the function. Furthermore, while it is taken for granted that a child should learn to

22 Parsons, "Some Ingredients of a General Theory," pp. 41–69.

speak the language of his parents, what should be taught in what schools to what children is by no means automatically given.

. . . When the division of labor has progressed beyond a certain point, decisions that pertain to this division must take precedence over those on the "technical" level. Thus it does not make sense to set up classrooms without having decided what children should be taught what things by what kinds of teachers, or without knowing whether specific teachers and specific physical facilities can be made available.

. . . We may say then that the most complex technical functions are performed by suborganizations controlled and serviced—in various ways and at a variety of levels—by higher-order organizations. The higher-order organization is sometimes called an "administration." . . . Perhaps a good name for this level of organization is . . . a "managerial" system.

The relations between such a managerial system and the technical system can be divided into two categories: mediation between the organization and the external situation, and the "administration" of the organization's internal affairs. Both involve . . . "decision-making" processes. . . .

At the level I have in mind, there are two main foci of the external reference and responsibility. The primary one is to mediate between the technical organization and those who use its "products"—the . . . pupils, or whoever. The second is to procure the resources necessary for carrying out the technical functions (i.e., financial resources, personnel, and physical facilities).

In one set of connections, decisions made in the management system control the operations of the technical system. This is certainly true for such matters as the broad technical task which is to be performed in the technical system—the scale of operations, employment and purchasing policy, etc. But, as in other cases of functional differentiation, this is by no means simply a one-way relation, for managerial personnel usually are only partially competent to plan and supervise the execution of the technical operations. The managers present specifications to the technical subsystem, but vice versa, the technical people present "needs" which constitute specifications to the management; on various bases the technical people are closest to the operating problems and know what is needed. Perhaps the most important of these bases is the technical *professional* competence of higher personnel in technical systems, a professional competence not often shared by the administrative personnel—who in the line sense—are the organizational superiors of the technicians.

. . . The organization which consists of both technical and managerial suborganizations never operates subject only to the exigencies of disposal and procurement from other agencies . . . as sources of supply. There is always some "organized superior" agency with which the organization articulates.

. . . Essentially, this means that just as a technical organization . . . is controlled and "serviced" by a managerial organization so, in turn, is the managerial organization controlled by the "institutional" structure and agencies of the community.

The ways in which the managerial system fits into the higher-order institutional system vary widely according to the character of the managerial system's functions and the organization's position on both the "lateral" and the "vertical" axes of the larger social system [society]. But it is a cardinal thesis of this analysis that no organization is ever wholly "independent." In terms of "formal" controls it may be relatively so, but in terms of the "meaning" [valuation] of the functions performed by the organization and hence of its "rights" [legitimation] to command resources . . . it never is wholly independent.

As noted, this third level of organization, which articulates with the managerial, may take many forms. I would put school boards with their representative functions in the local community in this category. . . . These . . . are the mediating structures between the particular managerial organization—and hence the technical organization it controls—and the higher-order community interests which, on some level, it is supposed to "serve." . . .

The teacher's role is primarily to educate in the *technical* sense. That of the school administration, i.e., the superintendent's office and the principal's, typically is to *organize* the educational process in the community, to make it, within the framework of community commitments to educate, as effective as possible and thereby to contribute to the level of performance-capacity in the community. But the superintendent is not the focus for determining the community's commitments to education in relation to other competing demands on its total resources. In community terms this is a "political" problem. In organizational terms this problem focuses on the school board. . . .

Given a high level of differentiation, perhaps one of the worst tendencies of organizational practice is for trustees or boards to attempt to control specific appointments in the organizations under their trusteeship. This function rests between the managerial and the technical aspects of organization. But trustees *must* be concerned with the question of how far and under what conditions their organization . . . has access to the type and quantity of performance capacity which is essential for the proper functioning of the organization.

It is crystal clear from Parsons' illustration of primary subsystems in school organization that the limitation which is imposed upon the exercise of bureaucratic authority therein is not a consequence of what so often is mistakenly called "democratic administration," or of kindness, or for that matter of any other informal condition in the structure of organization. It is a condition which arises from the division of labor of organizations in which the *esteem of technical competence* has important functional utility for the organization. When, therefore, implementing control and service relations between the managerial and technical subsystems lack a capacity for encouraging and stimulating technical competence, they inhibit effectiveness in the organization.

Here precisely is when *leadership* becomes a critical variable in an assessment of administrative behavior.[23] For now an administrator has to "come to terms with categories of other people" in the course of decision-making.[24] Finis E. Engleman, a long-time Executive Secretary of the American Association of School Administrators, provides a perceptive reference to this condition as it pertains to educational administration. He predicted in 1962 as follows:[25]

> A likely development during the next quarter-century is the appearance of the fully professional operator at all levels of education. The job of the teacher or the specialist in any administrative post is so comprehensive and complex that it calls for a person with the competence of the professional to do it. . . .
>
> If this development takes place in the profession of teaching, the school administrator in the next 25 years must abandon the notion that he, as an administrator with authority, can set goals for and direct or supervise the activities of his associates, whether first-grade teachers, guidance officers, or elementary-school principals. This implies a *whole set of new personal relationships between him and his associates.* [*Italics added.*]

One has merely to scan current professional literature for support of Engleman's prediction. Advancing professionalization at all levels in the network of technical roles in school organization continues to invest the skill variable with ever greater authority to determine the quality of interaction between teachers and administrators. The changing character of the elementary school principalship is a dramatic mani-

---

23 See Halpin, "Superintendent's Effectiveness."
24 Parsons, "Some Ingredients of a General Theory," p. 48.
25 Finis E. Engleman, "Editorial," *The School Administrator,* February 1962.

festation of how the authority of competence is now exerting itself in the elementary school. An enlarged complex of skills is required today for the role of elementary school teacher. Consequently, elementary school teachers have to master curriculum technology of the elementary school as specialists, whereas the principal does not. Similar manifestations of increasing authority for the skill variable also can be found in recent high school experience.[26]

Very much to the point also is the redefinition of administrative titles which is under consideration now in New York State. Two titles most particularly, "Instructional Administrator-Principal" and "Instructional Administrator-Curriculum," which the New York State *Ad Hoc* Committee on Administration and Supervisory Certification has considered are indicative of developing responses to the higher-order specialization that is now required in the technical subsystem of public school organization.[27]

Engleman leaves no doubt in his viewing of the passing scene that public school systems will be constrained to move "beyond bureaucracy" as the dominant mode of organization. Precisely because continuing change is now a constant in the external environment, obsolescence is fast overtaking the bureaucratic organization. Bureaucracy, according to Bennis, "thrives in a highly competitive, undifferentiated, and stable environment" wherein tasks can be routinized in social arrangements which follow the bureaucratic pattern.[28] But these conditions are characteristic of an American culture which is already more in the past than in the present and which, from all significant indicators now current, will be nonexistent in the future.

What this means essentially is that public school systems will be confronted in the future, and it has already begun, with constantly shifting conditions in consummatory relations with the external environment; that is, with other systems in society which require outputs of the public school organization for their own goal interests. This, in turn, will necessitate frequent redefinitions of policy decisions in public school

[26] See "A New Baby in the House," *Spotlight*, National Association of Secondary School Principals, September–October, 1964, p. 3; *Ibid.*, "The Drive to Be Heard and Heeded," p. 1. The latter is a current issue; no month and year of publication is shown.

[27] See "State Committee's Report on Supervisory Certification," *Bulletin*, New York City Council of Supervisory Associations, Vol. 2, May 1965, p. 4.

[28] Warren Bennis, "Beyond Bureaucracy," *Trans-Action*, Vol. 2, July–August 1965, pp. 33–35. The view of complex organizations of the future which Bennis spells out in this reference will be found elaborated in his *Changing Organizations* (New York: Holt, Rinehart and Winston Co., 1966).

systems. For decisions which set the conditions in consummatory relations between systems are phenotypic policy decisions for whose implementation executive roles are held responsible.

Frequent redefinition of policy decisions, on the other hand, will inescapably necessitate also frequent modifications of allocative and coordinating decisions. Hence, each executive role—from elementary school principal up to the superintendent—will be *constantly preoccupied* with executive responsibilities for decision-making and for defining and redefining goals of the system. There will be no time or tolerance for the administrivia which now characterizes much of public school administration at all levels of system operation. And because, as Engleman projects, *all technical roles* in the system will be filled by high-level professionals, school administrators, whether superintendent or principal, will find rules and regulations, the integrating power of now obsolescent bureaucratic organization, at best of only limited functional value.

Instead, they will have to resort to large quantities of leadership influence as the functional means for integrating the vast complex of an organizational mechanism. For *influence* is the generalized facility and institutionalized symbolic medium of exchange in leadership roles. It is the social capital of leaders. The exercise of leadership influence in the managerial subsystem of public school organization, following Parsons' conceptualization of a hierarchy of primary subsystems, will in all likelihood be the best strategy for attaining effectiveness in an administrative role. Indeed, because the integration of the organization in pursuit of its goals is an ascribed function of every administrative role, one may safely venture to hypothesize that with rising levels of expertise in the technical subsystem of public school organization, the integration variable on a polarized continuum will shift away from bureaucratic norms and move rapidly toward leadership influence.

But a resort to leadership influence, and not bureaucratic norms, for integrating the system does not mean the type of vulgar influence which is derived from a retailing of processed humor, or other personal relations which ensnare members of the organization in a web of private obligations to an administrator, and thereby divert them from obligations to the larger values of organizational goals. It means a type of influence which is derived from an expert mastery of communication and coordinating skills, from an ability to involve creatively the technical subsystem in the decision-making process, from a familiarity with the diverse languages of research, from a demonstrated ability to procure the necessary resources for the organization, from a trained capacity to be sensitive to emerging social aspirations and values in the external environment, and ultimately from a leadership capacity to redefine old goals of the organization in a new *milieu* and to propose new subgoals which the organization might pursue in the larger interests of society and, therefore, also of itself.

When technical roles are peopled by highly specialized professionals, and their *cooperative involvement and acquiescence* in decision-making contexts is crucial, this is the type of leadership influence that is required for administrative effectiveness. For such professionals, fiercely proud of their expertise, cosmopolitan in their orientation to the organization, will not suffer to have their ideas measured with village scales. The authority of official rank will count for little as influence in the interaction of managerial and technical roles in the public school organization of the future. What will count very much, however, is a mastery of the discrete skills which are required for effective role performance at each subsystem level of public school organization and mutual confidence in the quality of professional preparation for these roles. For the professional quality of conceptual frames in which value orientations to role tasks are shaped will be of equal importance with technical skills that are required for these tasks. This is the substantive meaning in Engleman's perceptive prediction of things to come in public school systems.

Insofar as it concerns the task of mapping the structure of middle school organization for the purpose of analysis, Parsons' classification of primary subsystems is now exceedingly useful. It can be employed for marking the *specific level* in the network of public school roles where difficult middle school problems have persevered unresolved over the years. Patchwork attempts to resolve these problems in the past have, as it turns out, failed. They have merely diverted the pursuit of organizational stability in the American middle school. Adjustments that are required for the future stability of middle school organization cannot very well be undertaken without identifying first the *character* of organizational problems that have been inducing instability.

It is not enough to say merely that the middle school organization in the United States is, and has been, afflicted by bureaupathology. This is just another way of saying that it is a sick organization. But is it a sickness of the machine-like formal system, the psychologically motivated social system, or of the guiding institutional system? With a cognitive map in hand, and with a framework of sensitizing concepts with which to elicit the deeper meaning of observed experience, we are now equipped to look at sources of organizational instability in the American middle school.

The clinical evidence, which the next chapter unfolds, reveals a syndrome of instability in the middle school to which, as we shall see, all subsystem levels of public school organization have contributed in ample measure.

11

DYSFUNCTIONS AND INSTABILITY

Manifestations of instability in the middle school organization recall to mind the myth of Sisyphus. Sisyphus, King of Corinth, was condemned by Zeus forever to roll a heavy stone up a steep hill in Hades only to have it roll down again whenever the summit was reached.

The Sisyphus-like behavior of middle school organization is suggested particularly by the great numerical increase of middle schools in the United States alongside an omnipresent threat to its existence as a unit of the public school system.

There were times when it seemed like the middle school unit was securely established by virtue of numbers. Briggs estimated in 1920, just one decade following the first middle schools at Berkeley, that there were upwards of 800 middle school units in the United States at that time; a numerical increase of an educational organization which, in his judgment, was "unparalleled in our history."[1] At the same time, Briggs also reported that he found considerable confusion in professional education as to what a middle school "is or ought to be."[2]

A national survey of secondary education some ten years later, for

[1] Briggs, *The Junior High School*, p. 60.
[2] *Ibid.*, p. 56. Briggs' estimate has been validated by others. See, for example, the *Digest of Educational Statistics*, 1963 edition, Bulletin No. 43, U.S. Office of Education, pp. 10 and 31.

which the Congress of the United States had appropriated $225,000, found 1,787 separately housed middle school units in the country, of which the three-year type was by far dominant.[3] Nevertheless, in the very year of the Congressional survey grant, a member of the Ohio State Department of Education declared before an audience of the North Central Association of Colleges and Secondary Schools, "We have not yet passed the stage, if we ever will, in which we are frequently confronted by the question, 'what do you mean by a junior high school?' "[4]

Despite a rapid numerical increase, the posture of middle school organization was sagging badly by the 1920's and 1930's. Its original institutional mission had become blurred, and consequently, its legitimation as a unit of public school organization was compromised.

Evidence of a compromised legitimation could be seen in the attacks which were directed at the middle school from different sectors of professional education. *The Elementary School Journal* attacked the unit from its editorial page.[5] Annual meetings of the National Education Association became an occasion for debates which questioned the instrumental effectiveness of the organization.[6] Educational journals of the 1920's and 1930's were filled with discussions which pointed sharply to the erosion of middle school legitimation.[7] On the eve of America's entry into World War II, *School and Society,* a journal of prestige in professional education, looked skeptically at the middle school and demanded editorially, "Let Us Have the Evidence!"[8]

These were more than idle disputations. Implied in the dialogue

[3] The 1930 National Survey of Secondary Education found the following quantities of middle school structures in the United States: 7–9 (1,288); 7–8 (204); 7–10 (196); others (99). See F. T. Spaulding and O. I. Frederick, "The Junior High School Movement In the Year 1930," *The School Review,* Vol. XLI, January 1933, pp. 20–21. See also Leonard V. Koos, "The National Survey of Secondary Education," *NCA Quarterly,* Vol. V, September 1930, pp. 219–20.

[4] T. Howard Winters, "The Chartering of Junior High Schools in Ohio," *NCA Quarterly,* Vol. IV, December 1929, p. 358.

[5] See the editorial "Reaction in the Junior High School Movement," *The Elementary School Journal,* Vol. 23, December 1922.

[6] See, for example, *Addresses and Proceedings,* NEA, 1920, Vol. 58, pp. 217–26; *ibid.,* 1921, Vol. 59, pp. 31–36.

[7] Typical of these articles were Charles H. Judd, "Recent Discussions of the Junior High School Problem," *The Elementary School Journal,* Vol. 19, June 1919; Joseph A. Fitzpatrick, "An Appraisal of Junior High Schools," *Journal of Education,* Vol. 110, September 1929; V. H. Hardin, "Facing a Vital Problem," *The Junior-Senior High School Clearing House,* Vol. 8, September 1933; Walter R. Hepner, "The Junior High School," *California Journal of Secondary Education,* Vol. 13, December 1938; T. J. Mahan, "Is the Junior High School Functioning?" *The Junior-Senior High School Clearing House,* Vol. 7, November 1932; [Anon.], "Incoordination Between Junior and Senior High Schools," *The School Review,* Vol. 35, November 1927.

[8] *School and Society,* Vol. 53, January 1941.

was the very point of middle school survival. Early in the 1920's, as one illustration, Superintendent L. C. Ward of Fort Wayne, Indiana, asked the hard-nosed administrative question, "Is the Junior High School Delivering the Goods?" His reply was, "Negative." Accordingly, he eliminated the middle school unit from his school system. In support of his decision, Ward made the following statement before an NEA audience:[9]

> What then is a junior high school? High school confessedly it is not, or there is no need for the "junior." Elementary school it cannot be for its organization apes too closely the plan of the high school to leave any doubt upon that point.

The "aping" theme was destined to become the hard core of attacks on middle school legitimation. But like Sisyphus, the middle school has survived these frustrations. Not only has it survived them, the middle school is now the second most numerous type of public secondary school organization in the United States.

A 1958–59 United States Office of Education survey of enrollment and organizational patterns in American secondary education found that of the 24,000 secondary schools which were then operational in the United States, 21.0 percent were separately housed middle school units, another 7.0 percent of three-year units were operating in the same plant with the high school of 6-3-3 systems, while still another 6.0 percent were two-year units which were operating in the same plant with the high school of 6-2-4 systems.[10] Moreover, separately housed middle school units *alone* were educating 25.0 percent of the 11 million pupils then enrolled in public secondary education. From these data, the survey directors concluded that "the strong upsurge of junior high schools in the past seven years, both in numbers of schools and in size of enrollment, may well be the dominant trend revealed by our survey."[11]

A glowing increase record of this sort could lead to the conclusion that the middle school organization had at last acquired stability, it had reestablished its original identity and legitimation. Surely, one might speculate, in the face of such robust numerical growth, there must now

---

[9] *Addresses and Proceedings*, NEA, 1921, Vol. 59, p. 836. See also L. C. Ward, "The Junior High School Abandoned at Fort Wayne, Indiana," *The Elementary School Journal*, Vol. 22, May 1922, pp. 647–49.

[10] Edmund A. Ford, "Organizational Pattern of the Nation's Public Secondary Schools," *School Life*, U.S. Department of Health, Education and Welfare, Office of Education, Vol. 42, 1960, p. 3.

[11] *Ibid.*, p. 4.

exist a commonly shared orientation to this unit of public school organization. Its link with the myth of Sisyphus is no more. Not so!

In the very year in which the United States Office of Education published the optimistic figures of middle school increase, there were sharp flashes of evidence which illuminated the still precarious status of the organization. The following is one such case in point.

The Educational Research Council of Greater Cleveland marked in 1960 the Golden Anniversary of the first middle school in America with a conference. It was an important conference; important enough to attract the attention of *The New York Times*. The latter newspaper reported the conference under the following lead: "The fiftieth anniversary of the junior high school in America has found considerable criticism focused on the 'stepchild' of public education."[12]

One of the principals on the program at that Cleveland conference was William T. Gruhn. The journalistic account of his participation has Gruhn ennumerating the following "critical problems and needs" of the modern-day middle school organization:[13]

1. There is a serious shortage of qualified talent for positions of professional leadership in the junior high school. . . .

2. There is a serious shortage of teachers prepared for teaching in the junior high school. . . .

3. The curriculum must be re-examined and priorities must be established concerning what should be taught. . . .

4. The influence of college entrance requirements, merit scholarship examinations and similar programs must be examined.

5. There must be more agreement on the "essential purpose" that the junior high school is to serve.

The foregoing five "critical problems and needs" combine as syndromic evidence of a still sick middle school organization. How ironic! After fifty years of existence as a unit of public school organization, and despite a vigorous increase in numbers, its "essential purpose" is today still a matter for speculation. The middle school, which in its early period was held forth as "the prodigy of American Progress," is demeaned in our own day by such sobriquets as "the problem child of the 1960's" and "tramp steamer of the educational fleet."[14]

12 *The New York Times*, Dec. 18, 1960. Copyright 1960 by the New York Times Company. Reprinted by permission.

13 *Ibid.*, Dec. 18, 1960.

14 Fred M. Hechinger, "The Junior Blues," *ibid.*, July 28, 1963; W. Dale Baughman, "The Awkward Age," *Educational Leadership*, Vol. 18, December 1960, p. 140.

Yet, in retrospect, the wonder of it all is that the unit was able to survive all these years in a sort of no man's land of public school organization. For at the root level of analysis, the instability which overtook the American middle school organization soon after it came into existence is traceable to an *ambiguous legitimation,* which, in turn, was a direct consequence of a diversion of its institutional mission. The larger empirical meaning of the latter will crystallize as it is set in the conceptual framework which has been prepared in earlier chapters.

Following the theoretical constructs of Weber, Durkheim, and Parsons, all organizations require the legitimation of society if they are to endure. Society legitimates organizations whose fulfilled goals are perceived as either direct or indirect value "inputs" to the commonweal. *Such goals have social value.* An organization, therefore, draws stability in a number of ways from the social value of its goals.

Functions of the organization are validated by the measure of their contribution to goal attainment. Role definitions and interactions are facilitated when an organization has a societally esteemed goal to hold up before its members and with which they can identify rationally, culturally, and affectively. Demands upon societal resources are more readily granted an organization when the social value of a goal is clearly in sight, and so forth.

Except for a brief period following its inception, the middle school organization has profited from none of these advantages. From the time of World War I, as we shall see, the middle school has been caught in a web of external conditions which have militated against its cultural development. But even the blows of an unkind fate might have been softened some had there not occurred a disastrous loss of institutional leadership in American school administration soon after the middle school was established. As a consequence, educational administration in the United States was turned into a vast dust bowl of empiricism. It is a catastrophe from which it is only now beginning to recover.

Harold Benjamin caught precisely this aspect of the middle school problem in his sights when he remarked in the early 1940's:[15]

> Although the junior-high-school idea is somewhat old and the institution itself is relatively young, the latter has aged more rapidly than the former. It is more than a half century since Charles W. Eliot officiated

[15] See "Editor's Introduction," Maurice M. Smith, L. L. Standley, and Cecil L. Hughes, *Junior High School Education: Its Principles and Procedures* (New York: McGraw-Hill Book Company, 1942), p. xiii.

at the birth of the idea and hardly more than half that time since Frank F. Bunker fathered the first seventh-eighth-ninth grade institution of modern type. Yet, today, the junior high school has a maturity in practical operation which it sometimes seems to lack in the theory underlying its operation.

There are compelling indications today that the middle school can no longer continue to exist in the limbo of organizations whose legitimation is ambiguous. It has been suggested in Chapter 3 that the middle school is now at a crossroads: one turn leads to survival, another to extinction. At least one school superintendent of the 1960's has already concluded that "the junior high school dream has not come to pass and is impractical."[16] He, like Superintendent L. C. Ward of the 1920's, did away with the middle school unit and has reverted to the 8-4 plan of organization.

The latter action would be of little consequence as an isolated administrative decision, except that it is indicative of what can follow once the values of an organization have been distorted. A superintendent of schools has in this instance stamped "impractical" the institutional commitment of the American middle school—his reference to it is as "the junior high school dream"—because "Whether we like it or not, today the emphasis (by public interest and public demand) is on scholastic achievement in all our schools."[17]

No professional educator is likely to dispute the need of scholastic achievement and scholastic excellence in a post-Sputnik world. But is the institutional commitment of the first American middle schools "impractical" in a post-Sputnik world? A preponderance of professional opinion in the nation's public schools, as such opinion has been ascertained by recent NEA surveys, does not seem to support such a judgment. But what is even more out of joint here is that the superintendent in point does not *actually* seem to believe this.

In essence, the administrative rationale for eliminating the middle school unit from his system is given by him in the following statement:[18]

The typical junior high school program today neglects the fundamental fact that a child needs the security of an environment in which he is well established while he is getting his physical and emotional growth.

16 J. H. Hull, "The Junior High School Is a Poor Investment," *The Nation's Schools,* Vol. 65, April 1960, p. 80. Reprinted with permission from *The Nation's Schools.* Copyright 1960, Modern Hospital Publishing Co., Inc., Chicago. All rights reserved.
17 *Ibid.,* p. 78.
18 *Ibid.,* p. 79.

The problems of early adolescence make him awkward, scared, confident, timid, infantile and adult all at the same time. [*Italics added.*]

What the foregoing statement seems to communicate is that the middle school "dream" of the 1910 period is "impractical" of attainment in the modern age because of ineffectual process in the middle school organization. But at least by strong implication, the statement *does acknowledge* the social value of protective intervention at early adolescence. The difficulty, then, is not of the institution but of the implementing organization! The technical subsystem, following Parsons' functional differentiation of organizational roles, has failed, and the middle school organization cannot carry on its vital functions.

But to say that an organizational mechanism has failed is one thing, to conclude therefrom that its institutional commitment is "impractical" is quite another matter. Of course, the argument is "Whether we like it or not, today the emphasis (by public interest and public demand) is on scholastic achievement in all our schools." There is an implication here that gratificational orientations of a middle school environment interfere with the hard tasks of learning. The "burden of proof" in such an instance is on the middle school curriculum.[19] Indeed, the matter of proof will be considered in the chapter to follow. But even if cultural conditions of the post-Sputnik world have made obsolescent the traditional middle school curriculum, as indeed they have, and if the social value of the American middle school is still culturally valid, then curriculum specialists are obliged in the educational division of labor to find innovative functional alternatives through curriculum reconstruction. The administrative alternative of eliminating the middle school organization altogether, the alternative which more than one superintendent has selected, serves as an example *ad horrendum* of the harsh consequences that can follow from a wrong turn at the crossroads.[20] But now, how did the American middle school get to a crossroads in the first place?

[19] Parsons, *The Social System,* p. 49.

[20] For cases of other educational organizations that are in difficult straits for some of the same reasons as is the middle school see Burton R. Clark, *Adult Education in Transition: A Study of Institutional Insecurity* (Berkeley: University of California Press, 1956); and Leland L. Medsker. *The Junior College: Progress and Prospect* (New York: McGraw-Hill Book Company, 1960). For variants of the same problem in other organizations see Philip Selznick, *TVA and the Grass Roots: A Study in the Sociology of Formal Organization* (Berkeley: University of California Press, 1953); and Andrew Gunder Frank, "Goal Ambiguity and Conflicting Standards: An Approach to the Study of Organization," *Human Organization,* Vol. 17, Winter 1958–59, pp. 8–13. See also James D. Thompson and William D. McEwen, "Organizational Goals and Environment: Goal-

How It Came to Pass

The first step toward a crossroads was taken when school boards countenanced a distortion of institutional values in American public education. It was a case of failure in pattern maintenance at the institutional level of public school organization. Ironically, it was the drive of institutional leadership at the managerial level to increase the holding power of American public school systems which latently precipitated failure in the institutional, or community, system.

It will be recalled from Chapter 8 that at the height of agitation for the revitalization of American secondary education, school administrators had become aware of appalling dropout rates which followed the eighth grade. Many school systems instituted procedures to attract larger numbers to secondary education, and at that time a number of systems turned to the six-year high school organization. Indeed, had not the Committee on Six-Year Courses endorsed the principle of a six-year high school because, among others, "the six years division would cause more pupils to enter the ninth year" than did the 8-4 plan of school organization?[21]

The impetus to broaden the base of educational opportunity in American secondary education, therefore, had been in high gear by the time of the first middle schools in 1910. As a result, while the increase in total national population between 1890 and 1910 was nearly 47 percent, the increase in secondary school enrollments for the same period was 208 percent.[22] One report gives the secondary school enrollment of the 1890's at about 4 percent of the public school population and by 1930 at better than 50 percent.[23]

These statistics could have been a source of great pride for American education had school construction and classroom facilities kept apace of the growing secondary school enrollment. But, alas, they did not! Many urban school systems were overcome by severe congestion. Then World War I intensified manifold the classroom shortage. The war put a halt to all schoolhouse construction. Construction costs were

Setting as an Internal Process," *American Sociological Review*, Vol. 23, February 1958; and Richard L. Simpson and William H. Gulley, "Goals, Environmental Pressures, and Organizational Characteristics," *ibid.*, Vol. 27, June 1962.

[21] See again Chapter 9 for the 1907 report of the Committee on Six-Year Courses.

[22] *Proceedings*, Association of Middle States, 1913, p. 51.

[23] *NCA Quarterly*, Vol. V, September 1930, p. 219. See also *ibid.*, Vol. II, April 1935, p. 468; *ibid.*, Vol. XIV, January 1940, p. 257; *Proceedings*, NCA, 1914, p. 18.

inflated, materials were scarce, and the labor force was needed for military service or essential war work.

The pinch of these conditions in the high school was felt mostly in the ninth grade. It was quite commonplace by the early 1920's to find as many pupils enrolled in the ninth grade alone as were counted in the combined three upper grades of a high school.[24] Teaching tasks in the ninth grade of many public school systems, as a consequence, degenerated to little more than that of custodial care. When at last peace did return, and the imbalance between bulging enrollments and schoolhouse construction could have been righted, American public school administration found itself trapped knee-deep in a morass which Raymond E. Callahan has conceptualized as the "cult of efficiency."[25]

School administrators of the early twentieth century, according to the cult of efficiency thesis, were cut from a different pattern than those of the nineteenth century. A transformation had begun by the early 1900's in the self-image of chief school administrators. Leading public school administrators of the nineteenth century had used the scholar and educational statesman as reference models. After 1900, it was the successful business executive who more and more became the reference model for public school executives.[26] With the transformation, there was a drying-up of institutional perspective in American public school administration.

The following exchange between two school superintendents at the 1908 Annual Meeting of the NEA is illustrative of what was happening to administrative perspective at about the time the middle school came into existence. Superintendent S. L. Heeter of St. Paul, Minnesota, apparently a confirmed "cultist," told his listeners:[27]

> The saving of time and energy—the opportunity for economy in the work of public education—must be sought, first of all, in an economy of aim looking toward education for efficiency in our industrial society. Economy in treating the course of study, economy in the selection, adaptation, and presentation of subject-matter presupposes an economy of aim.

24 Joseph K. Van Denburg, *The Junior High School Idea* (New York: Henry Holt and Co., 1922), p. 15.
25 Raymond E. Callahan, *Education and the Cult of Efficiency* (Chicago: University of Chicago Press, 1962). Hereafter cited as *Cult of Efficiency*.
26 *Ibid.*, pp. 7–8.
27 *Addresses and Proceedings*, NEA, 1908, p. 138.

The administrative values to which Heeter adhered were, to be sure, in the ascendancy by 1908, but they were not unchallenged. F. B. Dyer, Superintendent of Schools in Cincinnati, Ohio, not a "cultist," and one who apparently preferred the language of the scholar to that of the businessman, rose in response to Heeter's remarks and said:[28]

> Efficiency is a blanket term, efficiency in a democracy is a complex matter. While it includes vocational fitness, it includes much more. To be confidential, it seems to me that this term "efficiency," the slogan of recent educationists, has been sadly overworked of late. It has lost its special virtue, its *divinum quiddam*, its Socratic daemon, so to speak, and should be decently shelved in the museum of pedagogical cant.

But the tide was running against the type of administrator whom Dyer and M. G. Brumbaugh of Philadelphia personified. It was not long, therefore, before the transformation of the chief school administrator affected all administrative roles in public school organization. So rapid was this development that, by 1914, the Principal of Horace Mann School of Teachers College, Columbia University, felt no embarrassment in saying publicly, "I am not sorry to see the methods of the modern efficiency engineer applied to the school."[29]

The efficiency engineer, personified by Frederick W. Taylor of the Taylor System orientation to production management, made a dramatic entrance upon the American industrial scene the very year in which the first middle schools were opened in the United States. The scientific management movement was launched in 1910, and *efficiency* was made the most revered symbol in its litany.[30] Public school superintendents soon emulated Taylorism in educational administration, but in too many instances the desideratum of efficiency in the Taylor System was corrupted to mean a low budget as the true mark of a well-managed school organization. "The situation in American education after 1911," Callahan has concluded, "demanded leaders who were oriented toward the business side of education, not the social or philosophical side."[31]

The demand for a business orientation in public school administration was generated by school boards who were feeling the impact of

[28] *Ibid.,* 1908, p. 143.
[29] *Proceedings,* Association of Middle States, 1914, p. 21.
[30] Callahan, *Cult of Efficiency,* pp. 1–18; see also Leland H. Jenks, "Early Phases of the Management Movement," *Administrative Science Quarterly,* Vol. 5, December 1960.
[31] Callahan, *Cult of Efficiency,* p. 180. Quoted by permission. Copyright 1962 by the University of Chicago Press. All rights reserved.

problems which were brought on simultaneously by a rising tide of immigration, a vigorous natural increase in population, and burgeoning societal expectations of public education. Thousands of additional classrooms were needed desperately just to maintain the status quo, and most school boards of that period had little appetite for philosophical speculation about educational values. School boards, under such circumstances, wanted a business manager in the chief school administrator and not an educational statesman.[32] School board esteem of administrative performance no longer was measured by institutional criteria of pattern-maintenance and value fulfillment, but rather by the short cuts an administrator could find to lower budgets.

Here the usable past lays bare a grave *latent dysfunction* of local control. The corruption of school administration by the lure of the cult of efficiency seems in retrospect to have been almost inevitable once school boards, guardians of institutional values in the public school organization, made scientific management the *paramount value* in educational administration. The *instrumental value* of efficiency in school management was allowed to become a *terminal value:* an end in itself.[33]

The corruption of American school administration by so-called scientific management had been considerable by the early 1920's. However, it seems that not all public school administrators lost institutional perspective. P. W. L. Cox, for one, Principal of Ben Blewett Junior High School, St. Louis, Missouri, stood before the 1920 Annual Meeting of the North Central Association of Colleges and Secondary Schools and exposed as a pernicious influence in the educational enterprise a brand of scientific management which ignores guiding institutional orientations. He made the following points:[34]

Does Scientific Management require a Philosophy of Education? Schools may be run with great precision, with machine-like regularity, with no friction, with splendidly kept records, accurate knowledge of every diversion of energy and its results, every moment of time of every child

32 Raymond E. Callahan and H. Warren Button, "Historical Change of the Role of the Man in the Organization: 1865–1950," NSSE *Yearbook*, Part II, 1964, pp. 79, 80.

33 Merton, *Social Theory*, p. 199. Merton elaborates on the meaning of terminal value.

34 *Proceedings*, NCA, 1920, pp. 27–29. Philip Wescott Lawrence Cox received his AB(1905) and MA(1920) from Harvard College and Graduate School, respectively. In 1925, he received his PH.D from Teachers College, Columbia, where he wrote a dissertation on "Curriculum Adjustment in the Secondary School" under the direction of a committee consisting of Thomas H. Briggs, William H. Kilpatrick, David Snedden, and Harold O. Rugg. His cultural insights, as we shall see later, were a source of strength for the struggling middle school institution.

and teacher accounted for, and yet, if the organizer has not clearness of thought in terms of his institution and the problem that democracy is asking his school to help solve, his "scientific management" if not futile, is at most, of little direct value.

There may be such a thing as an abstract science not dependent on philosophy, but science functionally considered in relation to problems of administration and organization must grow out of and be checked up with the problems raised by philosophy. We must first know the road, the destination, the direction, before we can know how to measure our preparations to travel . . . on the route.

. . . Therefore secondary education must base its scientific management on a faith in democracy, and a determination to accept responsibility for all adolescent children of the community, fulfilling every need not better provided for thru [sic] other agencies.

A Diversion of the Original Middle School Goal

That a middle school principal should have denounced scientific management with such vehemence was more than an accident. For it was the middle school unit, more than any other structure in public school organization, which was victimized most by the cult of efficiency. Blinded by the fool's gold of efficiency, school boards sanctioned at the institutional level of public school organization a *diversion* of the original middle school goal by administrative surreptitiousness.

Now, there is nothing extraordinary about goal diversion in an administrative organization. An organization, for example, will have to find another socially useful goal, if it is to survive, precisely because it was successful in attaining the original goal which had been set for it. The National Foundation for Infantile Paralysis is in such a predicament at this time. The organization of the Progressive Education Association, for another, was disbanded entirely in 1955 because its leaders were satisfied that its goal had been achieved and there was no further need of the organization. Or, changing cultural conditions in society can sharply divert the original goal of an organization. However, this does not mean necessarily that the organization is handicapped, provided when the original goal is diverted another socially valued goal is found for the organization. A case in point is the summer school organization.

The summer school unit was first established in the City of Newark, New Jersey, during the 1880's because of mounting pressures from urban growth. For the problem of "what to do with the large number of children during the long summer vacation who cannot leave the city" the school superintendent recommended a summer school of six-week's duration. Thus, in 1886, the City of Newark became the first municipality in the United States to open a summer school with public funds.

Few, if any, public-supported summer schools exist today for such a custodial purpose. Today's summer school has as its paramount organizational goal pupil improvement through remedial, developmental, or enrichment programs, and its legitimation as a unit of public school organization is not questioned.[35]

However, the retreat from the original middle school goal fits neither of the foregoing conditions. In the case of the middle school, it was a *withdrawal* from a commitment to fulfill a social value in public education: the commitment to provide a protective and mediating school environment for the education of early adolescent youth. It was a period in the history of the American middle school when the social value of early adolescent education had been compromised badly by both *institutional* and *managerial* levels of public school organization.

Like Aaron's golden calf, the cult of efficiency took its toll in the schoolhouse of sanctioned educational values. Cultists could not be bothered with larger social values or with cultural problems of early adolescent youth, not when classroom space was scarce and success in school management was measured by how well a superintendent kept down school costs. It was, alas, a period in American public school administration when institutional perspective had been abandoned and the bureaucratic virtuoso was encouraged.[36]

Chief school administrators continued to pay lip service to the value of a separate school unit for early adolescent youth. Indeed, they established many middle school units during and after World War I. But although the *professed goal* of these middle schools was said to be the

---

[35] See Samuel H. Popper, "Urbanism and Early Growing Pains in the Newark Public School System," *Proceedings of the New Jersey Historical Society,* Vol. 282, July 1955, p. 162. The reader will find the larger concept of *goal displacement* exceedingly useful in the study of organizational behavior. For a helpful introduction to the subject see Peter B. Clark and James Q. Wilson, "Incentive Systems: A Theory of Organizations," *Administrative Science Quarterly,* Vol. 5, September 1961; Merton's discussion of goal displacement under the heading of "Bureaucratic Structure and Personality," in Merton, *Social Theory;* and the Blau and Scott discussion of the same theme under "Organizational Dynamics," in Blau and Scott, *Formal Organizations.*

[36] *Bureaucratic virtuoso,* it will be recalled, is Merton's expression. He employs it in the discussion of goal displacement. See Merton, *Social Theory,* p. 199.

special education of early adolescents, the *actual goal* was to relieve, at one and the same time, classroom shortages in the high school and lower instructional costs in the ninth grade.

High school teachers were at that time paid on a higher salary schedule than were those in the elementary school. By taking the ninth grade, with nearly half of the enrollment, from the high school and placing it in a so-called middle school unit, it at once relieved the severe classroom shortage in the high school and, by paying middle school teachers on a salary schedule lower than that of the high school, cut instructional costs.[37]

That this was a frequently employed administrative stratagem of efficiency cultists is attested to by James M. Glass, who it will be recalled from Chapter 3 had pioneered in middle school administration. Glass addressed the 1922 Annual Meeting of the NEA and he deplored:[38]

> The building need is accepted in most communities as the opportunity for inaugurating the educational reorganization offered by the junior high school. The history of the movement will doubtless reveal that the great majority of junior high-school organizations have had their origin in this twofold administrative objective of combining [a] building program with a program for education reorganization. . . .
>
> It is evident that no mere physical combination of grades 7 and 8 and first year high school can meet the demand. *This type of organization has already caused almost irrevocable harm to the development of the junior high school.* Such an organization can be a departmentalized intermediate grouping of grades 7, 8, and 9, but it is not a junior high school. [*Italics added.*]

Once the integrity of the middle school's value pattern had been compromised, repercussions which followed at the *technical level* were inevitable.

Because the school unit had not yet acquired a secure status in the public school organization and, more particularly, because technical roles within the unit had not yet been institutionalized, the surreptitious diversion of the middle school goal encountered little resistance from teachers. Middle schools were formed by simply lopping off

---

37 For a more extensive commentary on this administrative subterfuge see Van Denburg, *The Junior High School Idea*, pp. 8–20.

38 James M. Glass, "The Junior High School Program of Studies," *Addresses and Proceedings*, NEA, 1922, pp. 386, 387.

the seventh and eighth grades from the elementary school and adding to them the ninth grade.[39]

Almost forgotten now was the cultural concern for early adolescents which had occupied Bunker, Greeson, and others at the turn of the century. Little or nothing was done to prepare a special course of studies in consonance with affective and diffuse learning requirements of early adolescents. Seventh and eighth grade students were taught as they had been formerly in conventional elementary schools, and ninth grade students were taught as had been the custom in the ninth grade of traditional or six-year high schools.[40]

At least in midwestern United States, where the North Central Association had a permanent middle school committee to intervene in school systems as interpreter of middle school norms, an attempt was made to check the rate of middle school deterioration. Even so, the 1924 Annual Meeting of the Association was told by Leonard V. Koos, who reported for North Central's Commission on Unit Courses and Curricula that "careful scrutiny of program[s] of study in any number of Junior High Schools brings the inference . . . that large proportions of reorganizations are unaccompanied by profound curricular changes."[41]

The very fact that Koos had complained about a lack of "profound curricular changes" in North Central middle schools was in itself a mark of progress in that region. For the country at large, however, most of the middle schools that had been opened during and after the war could not boast of even *superficial* curricular changes. A curriculum had been improvised hastily in such schools, and teachers were reassigned from elementary and high schools to teach in them. More often than not, these teachers, especially from the high school, were marginal and were, therefore, unable to resist a reduction in salary which in many cases came with the transfer.

A Retreat to Technology

Retreat to technology is Philip Selznick's concept. Its theoretical kinship is traceable to the political sociology of Robert Michels, a German sociologist. In his studies of political parties, Michels discovered

---

[39] *Proceedings*, NCA, 1916, p. 141.
[40] *Ibid.*, 1916, p. 141. See also *ibid.*, 1921, p. 52.
[41] *Ibid.*, 1924, p. 95.

a type of behavior which social scientists have found to exist also in other organizations and even in small task-oriented groups.

Social scientists explain aspects of such behavior by variations of what has come to be known as a "maintenance" theme. Sometimes the reference is to a "maintenance orientation," sometimes, as in the case of Selznick, the reference is to a "retreat to technology." Merton prefers "technicism." Some analytical studies of small group behavior have treated aspects of this phenomenon as "group-maintenance behavior."

Variations of the "maintenance" theme have been used in organizational studies to explain a pattern of behavior which seems oriented to the preservation of the organization for its own sake without regard for its larger institutional mission. It is, in Selznick's words, "an excessive or premature technological orientation" which, because of its preoccupation with means activities, is a "threat to the integration of purpose and [institutional] commitment. . . ."[42]

A maintenance orientation of this type has been found to crystallize when goals of the organization are of uncertain social value, when goals are ambiguous, when there is conflict over goals, or when these conditions exist in combination. Members of the organization begin to justify their means activities in terms of immediate job requirements: "I am doing what I am doing because there is a job to be done." They stress the value preeminence of technical tasks. They see themselves as neutral instruments who do as their superiors wish them to do and, therefore, withdraw from a responsibility for defining and redefining the larger institutional mission of the organization.

A retreat to technology occurred in the American middle school when the primacy of a psychosocial orientation in early adolescent education was abandoned for the Essentialism of the premiddle school period. Essentialism had dominated American education until the time of the comprehensive high school, the middle school, and other educational reforms of the early twentieth century.

It is an orientation to educative process which regards a mastery of subject matter as the paramount value in learning. The essentials of

---

42 Selznick, *Leadership in Administration,* p. 74. For the best treatment of the "maintenance" theme see Robert Michels, *Political Parties,* translated by Eden and Cedar Paul (Glencoe, Ill.: The Free Press, 1949); also Robert Michels, *First Lectures in Political Sociology,* translated by Alfred de Grazia (Minneapolis, Minn.: University of Minnesota Press, 1949). For studies of small groups in which the "maintenance" variable is identified see among many others Dorwin Cartwright and Alvin Zander (eds.), *Group Dynamics* (Evanston, Ill.: Row, Peterson & Company, 1953); and Robert F. Bales, *Interaction Process Analysis.*

learning are defined as those cognitive skills which enable pupils to draw upon the organized knowledge from the past. The pupils' mind is viewed as a receptacle into which the teacher conveys a structured curriculum and which is tested periodically in order to ascertain its content.[43]

Empirical evidence of a retreat to technology in the middle school organization was to be seen soon after its original paramount goal had been diverted. Instrumental values of subject matter became ends in themselves rather than functional, or means, values of a larger goal. The American middle school, we will recall, was not meant to be an elementary school or a high school. What precisely, then, was its organizational purpose in the larger scheme of education? The consensus on middle school meaning which had marked the 1910 period was pretty well dissipated by the 1920's. Few middle schools of the post–World War I period could have made a cogent institutional case for existing in terms of their educative process. Therefore, soon after its original goal was diverted more and more in professional education came to question the meaning and, inferentially, the legitimation, of the middle school. But if goal ambiguity had made the organization institutionally vulnerable, survival of the unit was one goal around which all members of the unit could rally. Consequently, the retreat to technology became even more pronounced with the passing years.

Those psychosocial values which architects of the school had built into its environment were now assigned a low rank order of importance in the hierarchy of middle school values. No longer was the guiding orientation to educative process the human condition at early adolescence, but rather the importance of teaching subject matter for its own sake. As expressive values were drained out of the environment, and instrumental values of subject matter became increasingly dominant, the unit lost its institutional commitment in the division of labor of public school education.

The retreat to technology in the middle school, on the other hand, opened a Pandora's box of dysfunctions. Once the search for a discrete curriculum was abandoned in the middle school, a retreat to the terminal value of technicism had to come to terms with the question: a

---

[43] For a discussion in depth of Essentialism see Theodore Brameld, *Education for the Emerging Age: Never Ends and Stronger Means* (New York: Harper & Row, 1961), *passim.* See especially p. 25. Hereafter cited as *Education for the Emerging Age.*

retreat to which technology? Was it to be the curriculum of the elementary school or that of the high school? Both types had been brought lock, stock, and barrel into the middle school once it was turned into a money-saving device. Neither, as it turned out, was functional for early adolescent education.

The turn of events which eventually fixed the high school orientation to curriculum as the model for the middle school is best explained by drawing upon the theory of reference group behavior. Two concepts from this theory are especially germane for our purpose: the concept of "relative deprivation" and the concept of "anticipatory socialization." Relative deprivation came to reference group theory from empirical studies during World War II of the Army Research Branch, Information and Education Division. Social scientists who were associated with empirical investigations of morale in army ranks had employed relative deprivation as a conceptual tool with which to reconcile otherwise dissimilar findings.

The concept of relative deprivation explains the enigma of an individual who defines his situation not by the *reality* of his own deprivation, but rather by a *feeling* that he is more deprived than he ought to be when he compares his circumstances with others. He reacts to his estimate rather than the actual deprivation. These "others" with whom he compares is his *reference group*.

According to Merton, who, with other social scientists, has made a secondary assessment of "The American Soldier" research data, no new sociological insight would have been gained from mere discovery that a soldier will compare his own lot with others *in his own membership group.* The concept of "a social frame-of-reference" has, after all, been in sociological theory long before "The American Soldier." What is significant in "The American Soldier" studies, as accretion to reference group theory, is the discovery that an individual will also evaluate his lot by looking to groups, higher or lower in status than his own, of which he is *not a member,* and that this *does* affect his behavior in a given situation.[44]

Anticipatory socialization, on the other hand, is a concept which explains the orientation of an individual to a group of which he is *not a member,* but in which, as a response to upwardly striving behavior, he seeks membership. The concept of anticipatory socialization is

[44] Merton, *Social Theory,* pp. 233–424. All of Chapters 8 and 9 should be read for their importance to reference-group theory.

Merton's invention. He employs the concept to explain the behavior of an individual who, in anticipation of acceptance into membership by a higher-status group, seems to take on the values and behavior pattern of the higher-status group.

Of particular significance for an analysis of the middle school organization is Merton's caution that while anticipatory socialization may be *functional* for the self-interest of an individual who aspires to a higher status, it is *dysfunctional* for the group to which he belongs. For, according to Merton, the *solidarity* of the group is weakened when he defects from its values for the values of another group.[45] With these two concepts in tow, the turn of events which established the high school as the model for curriculum construction in the middle school can be explained with greater precision.

Teacher roles in elementary and high school units had been well defined by the time of the middle school. These units, moreover, had fairly well-defined goals, and even more important, nowhere in the profession was the legitimation of these goals in doubt: one was for childhood education, the other for postchildhood education. However, prestige and better pay always had been characteristic of high school teaching.

Longer professional preparation, for one thing, was required for technical roles in the high school. The compensation schedule was, accordingly, higher there than in either the elementary or middle school. When, therefore, the middle school came under attack in the profession, teachers therein began to compare their lot with teachers in other public school units, a comparison which sharpened the sense of deprivation of even those middle school teachers who, for one reason or another, could not aspire to move into the high school unit.

But in the social system of public school organization, which is an open system, mobility is possible for those who aspire toward what one regards as a higher professional status. Moreover, mobility in the public school organization is not limited to *interpositional* shifts, as when a teacher becomes a principal, *intrapositional* mobility is also possible; that is, a teacher can transfer as a teacher from one unit to another in the same system. Thus, with intrapositional mobility possible, as teachers in the middle school eyed the prestige and higher pay of teachers in the high school, both relative deprivation and anticipatory socialization took a heavy toll of middle school values.

[45] *Ibid.*, p. 266.

Middle school teachers began to model their professional behavior in the school system after that of high school teachers. Before long, educative process in the middle school turned into an inferior imitation of the high school program and, as a consequence, charges of "aping" the high school came with increasing frequency after World War I.[46]

Here is an instance of dysfunction in the organizational mechanism of the middle school which was triggered by a psychological irritant. Although the problem was of the social system, its effects disoriented essential functions in the formal system and corroded values in the institutional system. It is a condition not unlike the one which Philip Selznick, in *TVA and the Grass Roots: A Study in the Sociology of Formal Organization*, reports has occurred in the organization of the Tennessee Valley Authority during its early period.

The institutional commitment of TVA was to bring New Deal benefits to hard-pressed farmers. A large number of public relations specialists were employed to cultivate cordial relations between TVA agencies and local communities. But these public relations people, as a subgroup, tended to identify with the values of wealthier farmers. In time, their collective influence succeeded in having TVA policy modified in favor of wealthy farmers and at the expense of diverting the organization from its original goal.

Although a sociological definition of anticipatory socialization had not been formulated at that time, its empirical manifestations were nevertheless crystal clear to those who still esteemed the social value of the original middle school goal. Thomas W. Gosling, Supervisor of Junior High Schools in Wisconsin, urged by the 1920's that[47]

> . . . the tendency manifest in some places to establish a salary schedule that is intermediate between the schedule of the elementary school and that of the senior high school is to be resisted strongly, because it not only fails to recognize the importance of the junior high school and the significant contributions of its teachers to the development of a difficult piece of work, *but also it strikes at the stability of the institution by*

---

[46] The periodical literature from about the 1920's and onward has been replete with criticisms of curricular conditions in the middle school. The following are representative of the lot. J. Harvey Rodgers, "Junior High School Curricula and Programs," *School Review*, Vol. 29, March 1921; Anne Gilbert, "Junior High Schools Criticized," *ibid.*, Vol. 113, June 1931; V. M. Hardin, "Facing Vital Problems," *The Junior-Senior High School Clearing House*, Vol. 8, September 1933; Thomas H. Briggs, "Has the Junior High School Made Good?" *Educational Administration and Supervision*, Vol. 24, January 1938; Arthur J. Jones, "Appraising the Junior High School," *The Education Digest*, Vol. 9, May 1944.

[47] Quoted in Van Denburg, *The Junior High School Idea*, p. 10. Also see in this source the reference of a "money-saving device" applied to the post-1910 junior high schools.

*the subtle suggestion to teachers that they may regard their position
merely as a stepping-stone to the safe berth and the higher salary which
the senior high school offers.* In other words, the intermediate salary
creates a condition of unstable equilibrium, whereas fixedness, firmly
based in high purposes persistently followed, is needed to develop the
junior high school up to the full measure of its possibilities. [*Italics
added.*]

That the effects of anticipatory socialization had by the 1920's turned
the middle school into a *steppingstone organization* was also clear to
the North Central Association of Colleges and Secondary Schools. We
know already from Chapter 3 of some specific steps which the North
Central Association had taken to institutionalize a middle school organization. In the next chapter, we shall also look at a curriculum the
Association prescribed for middle schools which sought its official "recognition." But its pursuit of middle school stability went further still.

Before the Association had decided to abandon "accreditation" for
"recognition" as the stamp of a standardized middle school, it was
proposed:[48]

No school shall be accredited whose salary schedule does not insure the
attracting and retaining in the Jonior High School of teachers equal in
teaching ability to those selected for Senior High School teaching.

Of the standards that had been proposed in the North Central Association to institutionalize a middle school organization, the norm of a
salary schedule had aroused "the greatest interest on the part of Junior
High School Principals."[49]
According to North Central records:[50]

This standard was introduced in order to prevent the development of
the practice of using the Junior High School as a training school for
teachers intended for Senior High School work. . . . *The only criticism offered relates to the revision of the standard so as to demand more
attractive salaries in Junior High Schools rather than salaries equal in
attractiveness to those paid in Senior High Schools.* [*Italics added.*]

Other Dysfunctional Conditions

As the foregoing suggests, there were those who had hoped to combat
the corrosive effects of anticipatory socialization in middle schools with

48 *Proceedings,* NCA, 1920, pp. 16A–17A.
49 *Ibid.,* 1920, p. 16A.
50 *Ibid.,* 1920, p. 17A.

money. It is open to speculation, however, whether it would have been enough. For even had the middle school attained immediate salary parity with the high school, and it did not, there were still two other conditions at the technical level of its structure which were, at the very least, equally dysfunctional for the unit: *the professional preparation of middle school teachers and the old irritant of college entrance requirements.*

Teachers colleges had no formal preparation program for middle school teachers. Middle school principals, moreover, had not yet acquired sufficient administrative sophistication to evaluate the significance of this for their own managerial role obligations. Even in middle schools of the North Central Association, where pressure for salary parity with high schools was strongest, the aim of parity was not to obtain teachers who had been *specially prepared* for middle school roles but rather to *attract and retain* "teachers equal in preparation and ability to those in the Senior High School."[51]

Apparently, North Central middle school principals wanted salary parity for their teachers as a means of strengthening the competitive posture of their unit in teacher-placement bureaus. It is, after all, a managerial obligation to fill technical roles of an organization with those who are judged most competent for the performance of technical tasks. They had overlooked, however, the subtle, but crucial, sociological fact that a function of the teacher-preparation program is *to structure the teacher's role in an institutionalized pattern.* This, in turn, exerts a powerful influence upon an incumbent's internalization and externalization of norms that have been institutionalized in a given teacher's role. Consequently, because the high school, and not the middle school, was the dominant focus in secondary teacher-preparation programs, teachers entered the profession with a preconditioned bias for values of the high school.[52]

Then there was the matter of college entrance requirements. Despite many efforts, especially by the North Central Association, to eliminate ninth grade subjects from college entrance requirements, most of the nation's colleges and universities would have none of it. It is true that

[51] *Ibid.*, 1920, p. 17A.

[52] Talcott Parsons has provided some penetrating insights into the problem of "conflicting sets of legitimized role expectations" which have great relevance for the preparation of teachers for the several units of public school organization. See Parsons, *The Social System*, Chapter 7, "Deviant Behavior and the Mechanisms of Social Control"; see also Peter Blau's reference to the functional value of internalized organizational values in Blau, *Bureaucracy in Modern Society,* pp. 57–67.

a handful of North Central institutions of higher learning did acquiesce to North Central's urgings and eliminated the ninth year from entrance requirements. But as late as 1926, even after the more conservative New England Association of Colleges and Secondary Schools had formally joined North Central in efforts to free ninth-year subjects in the middle school from the external control of college entrance requirements, Superintendent Jesse H. Newlon of Denver, Colorado, believed that resolutions to this effect from both associations were still "dead letters."[53]

A latent dysfunction of the first water followed from this condition for educative process in the middle school. *For in organizational terms, it, in fact, gave the high school principal a decision-making control over the technology of a school unit for which another administrator was responsible.* It was a control in consummatory relations with the middle school which high school principals were not willing to surrender willingly. That such was the case, indeed, is suggested by an action of the 1927 Annual Meeting of the Association of Colleges and Secondary Schools of the Middle States and Maryland.

A four-part resolution was introduced at that meeting to the following effect:[54]

1. That the present fifteen units be retained as the minimum standard for college entrance.
2. That twelve of these units shall have been completed in the final three years of the secondary school course.
3. That the remaining three units may represent work completed previous to the final three years of the secondary school course either in a Junior High School or in the first year of a four-year secondary course.
4. *That the certifying principal shall be responsible for the validity of all units included in the credentials and shall be left free as to the method of determining the validity of the three marginal units in the case of units representing work done outside of his school.* [*Italics added.*]

The resolution was tabled following "considerable discussion" led by spokesmen for middle school interests, for, according to the pub-

[53] *Proceedings,* NCA, 1926, p. 261.
[54] *Proceedings,* Association of Middle States, 1927, p. 61.

lished proceedings of the Association, "Objection was made that there would be nothing gained as the principal of the Senior High School must still be responsible for preparation obtained by the student in another school outside of his control. . . ."[55]

Efforts by middle school men to free the mechanism of middle school organization from debilitating dysfunctional conditions became more vigorous as the 1930's approached. The muster of resistance to the foregoing resolution at the 1927 Annual Meeting of the Middle States and Maryland Association is illustrative of these efforts. But with the 1930's also came the Great Depression and because of it, what we shall refer to as the *latent marginality* of middle school organization was to become pronounced.

A Consequence of Marginality

Selznick has written:[56]

When institutional leadership fails, it is perhaps more often by default than by positive error or sin. Leadership is lacking when it is needed; and the institution drifts, exposed to vagrant pressures, readily influenced by short-run opportunistic trends. The default is partly a failure of nerve, partly a failure of understanding. It takes nerve to hold a course; it takes understanding to recognize and deal with basic sources of institutional vulnerability.

In all likelihood, had the Great Depression not come when it did, failures of institutional leadership in school administration, of which abandonment of the middle school unit to "short-run opportunistic trends" was one, might have been stemmed. A shift away from an all-out business orientation in American school administration was already discernible by 1930.[57] But dysfunctional conditions had by then too extensively compromised the original legitimation of the middle school organization. Consequently, with the onset of the Great Depression, "low functional autonomy," which from the beginning has been a structural characteristic of the middle school, combined with organizational ineffectiveness and institutional ambiguity to heighten the latent marginality of middle schools.

Low functional autonomy is a concept which, like many others, has

---

[55] *Ibid.*, 1927, p. 61.
[56] Selznick, *Leadership in Administration*, p. 25.
[57] Callahan and Button, NSSE *Yearbook*, Part II, 1964, p. 89.

enriched organization theory since the Hawthorne studies. It was developed by Gouldner. Its use at this point will shed light on a development which made manifest the latent marginality of the middle school organization as a mechanistic system.

As an organizational mechanism, the middle school exists within the complex structure of a public school system. Like the superordinate organization, the unit is goal-directed, a division of labor marks its tasks, and its professional members are certified personnel. It is governed by the same rules and regulations which ascribe roles and norms for all members of a public school organization.

However, two conditions impose *a high degree of system interdependence* upon the middle school unit. These conditions restrict it to a status of low functional autonomy. Foremost is its location in the structure of public school organization.

Because it is *a middle school,* and is physically wedged between the elementary school and high school, the input-output flow of middle school pupils—that is, consummatory relations with other systems—must move within the structural confines of the larger organization. Such a condition forces a Januslike character on middle school articulation with other units in the system. It means that educative process in the middle school has to articulate with the elementary school and the high school. This is one of the manifest functions of the unit. A second condition—one, however, which the middle school shares with all other units in the system—is that a central office authority controls the allocation of its resources and personnel.

The concept of functional autonomy of units in a large-scale organization has become a useful tool in organizational analysis. Its application here is of immediate value in that it directs attention to the predicament of a low functional autonomy unit. Modern-day middle school principals recognize, for example, that their unit "cannot sensibly stand alone even though they do wish to have it regarded as an organizational level in its own right."[58] But Gouldner's concept of *degrees* of functional autonomy also directs attention to the fact that some units may be separated from a system of organization and that the system can survive the separation.[59] Experience with the middle school unit illustrates this case.

[58] *NCA Quarterly,* Vol. XXXVI, Fall 1961, p. 199.
[59] A discussion in depth of functional autonomy will be found in Alvin W. Gouldner, "Reciprocity and Autonomy in Functional Theory," in L. Z. Gross (ed.), *Symposium on Social Theory* (Evanston, Ill.: Row, Peterson & Company, 1958).

For Gouldner's concept suggests that a unit of low functional autonomy may, under certain conditions, be relegated to a marginal status in the system. In turn, this can mean that when conditions in a system urge the separation of certain parts, then administrative judgment of the *effectiveness* of a low functional autonomy unit becomes crucial for that unit's survival. And, of course, basic in any judgment is some value orientation.

We already know of at least two instances when public school systems had eliminated the middle school unit. Ineffectiveness of the unit was given as the reason behind both decisions. And surely more than mere accident must account for the fact that while separate middle school units had increased between 1930 and 1938 by only 1.2 percent, five- and six-year high schools increased during the same period by 10 percent.[60] These statistics, juxtaposed with the school-budget crises of the 1930's, may be taken as muted evidence of the marginal status which can overtake an ineffective unit of low functional autonomy during periods of organizational stress.

Perhaps nowhere was this demonstrated during the years of the Great Depression with greater drama than in the City of Chicago.

On July 12, 1933, the Chicago Board of Education responded to pressure from a citizens' committee to cut school costs with a vote to abolish the middle school unit and to return the system of public school organization in Chicago to an 8-4 pattern. One day Chicago had a middle school division, with 1,385 teachers and some 48,000 pupils, the next day it had no middle school division. Pupils and teachers were reassigned to other divisions in the system.[61]

An editorial reaction in the *Grand Rapids Herald* of Grand Rapids, Michigan, to the middle school decision in Chicago plumbed the depths of irony. It showed up in bold relief the extent to which the retreat to technology in middle schools had brought about an "aping" of the high school. But even more important from the larger societal interest, it demonstrated from experience how an institutional adaptation is endangered when implementing organizational machinery is dysfunctional for its fulfillment. The editorial stated in part:

> The big slice that Chicago made in her school expenses was in abolishing the junior high school and reverting to the eight grades and a four-

---

[60] *Digest of Educational Statistics,* 1963 edition, Bulletin No. 43, Department of Health Education, and Welfare, U.S. Office of Education, pp. 10, 31.
[61] *The School Review,* Vol. XLI, September 1933, p. 483.

year high school. Of course this is entirely sensible. . . . Whether a student spends eight years in the grades and four in what is called a high school, or whether he spends six in the grades, followed by a junior and a senior high school, has nothing to do with what he learns. But it does make a mighty lot of difference to the taxpayer, who in effect is supporting *two high schools* with all their overhead and supervision and what not instead of one.[62] [*Italics added.*]

It is clear from the language of the editorial that, at least insofar as its author reflected community perception, no discrete organizational purpose distinguished the middle school from the high school. It had lost functional differentiation. That such an editorial should have been written in Grand Rapids, Michigan, highlights the value of effective implementing organizational apparatus for institutional commitments.

For among the earliest to advocate a separate middle school unit for the education of early adolescents, it will be recalled, was W. A. Greeson, who, during the early 1900's, served as Superintendent of Schools in Grand Rapids. It was Greeson who had pointed out the inadequacy of the six-year high school before the 1909 Annual Meeting of the North Central Association. It was he who had proposed at that time a structural blueprint for what was to become in Berkeley the first modern-day middle school. Indeed, in the applause of that *Grand Rapids Herald* editorial for the Chicago action, the ring of irony is unmistakable.

World War II and After

The long night of the Great Depression came to an end with the onset of World War II. American eyes were transfixed in the late 1930's on the events which followed the German invasion of Poland. When America was at last drawn into the war, school building construction came to a halt, and all educational programs accommodated themselves to a nation at war.

But the coming of war also put a halt to sharp attacks on the middle school. With a hard war to be prosecuted, there was no inclination anywhere to think about the middle school problem. Time was gained for the middle school organization.

With the war's end came a robust renaissance of interest in the

62 *Ibid.,* p. 487. By permission of the University of Chicago Press. All rights reserved.

middle school. No longer immediately marginal because of a budgetary pinch, it was, nonetheless, still vulnerable as a low functional autonomy unit so long as its goal remained unclear. Now, in the war's aftermath, the season returned when a decision would have to be made about the status of the middle school unit.

A reversion to the status quo antebellum was out of the question for the American middle school. More than ever before, its cultural purpose had to be redefined in cogent institutional and organizational terms. For school administration in the United States had taken a sharp turn toward professional sophistication in the years following World War II. It seemed altogether likely, therefore, that administrative judgment might again stamp the middle school marginal—budgetary crisis or no—unless it could be shown that it was capable of fulfilling a legitimate educational purpose.

The prospect of precisely such an eventuality caused the United States Office of Education to convene, in 1955, a conference on the middle school to which were invited thirty-seven established middle school specialists. In the "Foreword" to the published proceedings of that conference, the following is stated:[63]

> If the junior high school has failed to achieve fully the advantages originally claimed for it, the reorganization movement has nevertheless gone forward with accelerated speed. The 6 years from 1946 to 1952, for example, have produced annually about 100 new separately organized junior high schools and more than 350 junior-senior high schools. This must mean that such reorganization is popular, but more significantly it means a challenge to give closer study to this segment of education with a view to making it what it should become.

Two items of important significance are to be gleaned from the record of that conference. First, the rate of increase in postwar middle school units suggests that school boards at the institutional level of public school organization were again willing to make commitments to the middle school idea. Second, the fact that fifteen of the thirty-seven specialists who had been invited to the conference were principals of *separately housed* middle school units suggests also that the organization had acquired new strength at the administrative level.

[63] Walter H. Gaumnitz, *Strengths and Weaknesses of the Junior High School: Report of the National Conference on Junior High Schools*, Circular No. 441, Department of Health, Education, and Welfare, U.S. Office of Education, 1955, p. v. Hereafter cited as *Strengths and Weaknesses of the Junior High School*.

Beyond these, the 1955 United States Office of Education conference was to serve as the bellwether of postwar efforts to make things functionally right in the middle school organization. Fritz Redl, who at the time was Chief, Laboratory of Child Research, National Institute of Mental Health, and who in 1936 had come to the United States from Vienna Psychoanalytic Institute, where he specialized in child analysis, gave his *unqualified professional endorsement* to the social value of a *special school unit* for early adolescent education. In his address, Redl reviewed for the conference the complex psychological-physiological character of early adolescent development. These were his concluding remarks:[64]

> If you were not already in junior high school work, I wouldn't have spoken in this vein, because I would have feared that I might scare you off. But since you are already in this work and have enjoyed some of the fascinations of this job and recognize its importance as well, I have spoken as realistically as possible. . . . I hope that in reviewing some of the facts which we all know from practice, and which I tried to put together for us in one piece, I may have rendered you a service.

Redl may not have known it at the time, but he had rendered the American middle school the greatest service of all. After it had been languishing for many years in ambiguity, he reestablished the institutional purpose of the middle school unit on the *terra firma* of cultural and psychological values. He cast a powerful psychological light, as had G. Stanley Hall at the turn of the century, upon the *special school environment* that is required for early adolescent education. What greater service could anyone have rendered for the middle school organization at the time?

Two substantive resolves came out of that Office of Education conference. First, there was unanimous consensus that the only legitimate paramount purpose for a middle school is the education of early adolescents in a special school environment. The other resolve acknowledged that this purpose cannot be fulfilled without a process *specially* designed for the school and applied by teachers *specially* prepared for the school. The following excerpt from the summary of the conference, which, by the way, was given by William T. Gruhn, expresses the institutional significance of the foregoing two resolves:[65]

64 *Ibid.,* p. 10.
65 *Ibid.,* p. 46.

We should encourage principals and faculties to take a look at their junior high schools to see if they really function as transitional schools. The programs should be examined to make sure that they recognize the transitional nature of the early adolescent.

In structural-functional terms, what that conference did was to call upon incumbents of technical and managerial roles in the middle school organization to evaluate the middle school program by the pragmatic test of function: Is a given middle school program functional for fulfilling the legitimate paramount organizational purpose of the unit? Whether or not teachers at the technical level of middle school structure and principals at the managerial level were competent, or even inclined, to make such an evaluation is a question which strikes at the very core of middle school problems in the post–World War II period.

The Sometime Middle School Principal

True, the quality of administration in the middle school did improve after the war when more of the abler talents turned to middle school administration. But the old devils of relative deprivation and anticipatory socialization have done their best to minimize the gain. Simply put: Because high school principals in most school districts are paid at a better rate than are middle school principals, the lure of high school administration is too much to resist. Commitment to middle school values is bound to be tenuous when a middle school principal has one eye fixed on administrative vacancies in the high school. How is he to cope with the dysfunctional anticipatory socialization of his teachers when his own behavior is likewise motivated?

One statement of the dysfunction which stems from this modern-day condition is as follows:[66]

> Unhappily, not all of the professional good fortune which has come to the high-school principal in recent years is shared by his blood brother in the junior high school. In all too many school districts, the junior high-school principalship is still a way station in the frenetic climb from the classroom to high-school administration. It is rare to find in such districts talented aspirants for administrative posts who are willing to accept the junior high-school principalship as a lifetime career position.

[66] Samuel H. Popper, "Another Look at the Junior High School Principalship," *The Bulletin*, NASSP, Vol. 44, November 1960, pp. 125–26. Reprinted by permission. Copyright: Washington, D.C., National Association of Secondary School Principals. See also *The Junior High School We Need*, p. 11.

What accounts for the force of this upward mobility? More often than not, it is money!

As long as school districts persist in favoring the high-school principalship in the salary schedule, efforts to raise the professional status of the junior high-school principal will go unrewarded. The lure of the differential is too much to resist. Instance after instance can be cited of the able junior high-school principal who was rewarded with a *promotion* to the high school.

A School Without Teachers

Then there is still the problem of teachers who have not internalized middle school norms. Despite efforts in recent years to raise the quality of middle school teaching, progress at strengthening the technical subsystem of middle school organization has not been encouraging. The explanation for this turns on the fact that most teachers colleges, especially those of larger universities, still resist persistent pleas from the profession for a *discrete preparation program* for middle school teachers.

Nearly all such schools offer *some courses* that focus on the middle school. However, a gulf of deep significance separates *courses* from *a discrete preparation program* in the socialization of teachers. Consequently, although most urban school districts now have a single salary schedule for teachers at all grade levels, the professional behavior of middle school teachers is still affected by concomitants of relative deprivation and anticipatory socialization. Only now, the sense of deprivation is generated not by *money* but by the *greater prestige,* imagined or real, of the high school teacher.

Frederick H. Stutz, onetime Dean of Cornell University's School of Education, has put the problem in the following words:[67]

> The junior high school has been aptly described as the "school without teachers," because its teachers have been prepared for careers either in senior high schools or in elementary schools. It is most certainly the school without a sufficiently logical direction for programs of study and with a number of serious educational problems. . . .
>
> It is not a matter of salary that keeps secondary teachers out of junior high schools . . . because in most school systems the salary scales in junior and senior high schools are identical.
>
> It appears to be more a matter of prestige; the elementary teacher

---

[67] See "Educator Points Out Gap in Teaching," *Christian Science Monitor,* April 29, 1961. See also *The Junior High School We Need,* p. 11.

feels she is going up if she teaches in junior high school, while the secondary teacher feels that she is going down if she accepts a junior high school assignment.

There are a number of teacher-training institutions which have course work in junior high school work, but there are few institutions in this country which specifically train teachers for junior high school.

The loss of able middle school principals to better-paying high school administration is patently dysfunctional for goal attainment in the middle school organization. But perhaps even more dysfunctional is the frustration middle school principals encounter in teacher recruiting. They deplore the neglect in schools of education of an obligation to prepare middle school teachers. It is an obligation which schools of education have assumed in the division of labor and which, in the instance of middle school teachers, is grossly neglected. Modern-day middle school principals now know very well that this neglect in schools of education impinges sharply upon their own administrative obligation to obtain the most skilled personnel for technical tasks in their schools. A middle school principal, to be sure, can find many *technically* well-prepared teachers in placement offices, but he is sorely pressed to find teachers who possess the *discrete skills* which are required for middle school teaching.

What can be more frustrating for an administrator? *The middle school principal of today is in the unhappy predicament of an administrator who is held responsible for goal attainment in a functionally differentiated unit of a professional service organization whose technical personnel lack the special skills and institutional commitment for the performance of essential functions!*

Stephen A. Romine, Dean of the School of Education, University of Colorado, has spotlighted the frustration of modern middle school principals in the teacher market. In a report of two exploratory middle school studies which were undertaken by the North Central Association of Colleges and Secondary Schools in 1960, Romine states this:[68]

> One other suggestion of junior high school principals merits serious attention, namely, *the need for programs of preparation planned specifically for junior high school personnel.* Too few colleges and universities apparently offer programs of the type judged by the respondents to be adequate. Careful and thorough study of essential attributes of successful junior high school personnel will be basic to the development

[68] *NCA Quarterly*, Vol. XXXVI, Fall 1961, p. 200.

of sound programs. Proper assignment and use of personnel also relate to this problem, for the junior high school is often *a stepping stone* for teachers and administrators. . . . [*Italics added.*]

A similar note of support for the insistence that middle school teachers require a discrete preparation program has come from the United States Office of Education. When the 1958–59 survey of enrollment and organizational patterns of the 24,000 secondary schools in the United States revealed that 21.0 percent of them were separately housed middle schools which enrolled 25.0 percent of the 11,000,000 secondary school pupils, Edmund A. Ford, Specialist for School Organization and Administration in the Office of Education, used the occasion to make this comment: [69]

> Surely the tremendous implications of this significant figure can no longer be ignored by the curriculum specialists and the teacher-training institutions who have dichotomized public education, far past the limits of reality, into "elementary" and "high school."

The position statement of 1961 of the Association for Supervision and Curriculum Development, *The Junior High School We Need,* and which was cited in Chapter 1, has also contributed to the mounting pressure on teacher education to treat the middle school as a functionally differentiated unit of public school organization, just as it does with the kindergarten, elementary school, and high school. Indeed, similar position statements which the Association has published on the elementary and high school units tend to underscore this point.

First, there is the general character of the ASCD middle school statement itself. It mirrors in its orientation to educative process the middle school's institutional purpose. Then, at least by inference, it deplores the goal diversion by administrative fiat which has occurred in the middle school. The statement then abandons inference and goes on to assert the teacher's role prerogative, as a technical specialist, to participate in decisions which concern educative process in a middle school. Such a view of the teacher's role prerogative acknowledges the authority of competence and conforms with the Parsonian view of "connections and interchanges" which functionally link the institutional, managerial, and technical levels of school organization.

Even more forthright, however, is a reminder which is addressed to schools of education that they have an *institutional obligation* in the

[69] Ford, "Organizational Pattern of the Nation's Public Secondary Schools," p. 4.

division of labor to prepare teachers for *all units* of school organization. The concluding paragraph of the ASCD statement reads as follows:[70]

> Change by fiat has rarely been enduring in educational institutions. Teachers, as professional persons, may justly expect to be full participants in the study, planning and decision that must take place to change the institution of which they are a part. Teacher education institutions have an obligation here, of course, to prepare new teachers for the junior high school of the future and to help them want to be a part of new educational programs.

Perpetuating the Retreat to Technology

Insofar as colleges of education fail to recognize the differentiated function of the middle school unit, and prepare teachers for it accordingly, they help to sustain in the American middle school dysfunctional conditions which emerged during the World War I period and after. More directly, they perpetuate a *trained incapacity* in middle school teachers. Teachers, that is, tend to emerge from preparation programs in secondary education with a pronounced high school orientation and experience reality shock when they are later confronted by norm expectations in the middle school organization. Therefore, unless teachers have been especially prepared for middle school assignments, they are actually incapacitated by *professional preparation* for performing middle school tasks. Two recent empirical studies illumine this modern-day condition.

A 1964 report of the Association for Supervision and Curriculum Development, *The Junior High School We Saw: One Day in the Eighth Grade,* tells of a national *spot check* of the quality of educative process in American middle schools. As with *The Junior High School We Need,* this was a project of the ASCD Commission on Secondary Curriculum.

On May 3, 1962, a body of skilled curriculum personnel "shadowed" 102 eighth grade pupils in ninety-eight middle schools in twenty-six states "to see what happens to the pupil as he lives in a junior high school program on a typical day." Recordings were made of observations at ten-minute intervals.[71]

---

[70] Grambs, *et al., The Junior High School We Need,* p. 34.
[71] John H. Lounsbury and Jean V. Marani, *The Junior High School We Saw: One Day in the Eighth Grade* (Washington, D.C.: Association for Supervision and Curriculum Development, 1964), p. v.

"How," the question is put in the report of this ASCD project, "is the teaching-learning process to be described in the polyglot image of the junior high school which emerged on May 3rd?" And the answer:[72]

> The most prominent impression is of a classroom dominated by the teacher, in full direction of the learning complex. Lecturing was common and appeared in classes ranging from English to art.

Lecturing, as a dominant mode of instruction, has long since been abandoned by skillful teachers even in the high school where the primacy of instrumental values in educative process is altogether functional for goal attainment in that unit. But in a middle school, the dominance of lecturing in the classroom defines a school program whose primary value orientation is focused on the instrumentalism of subject matter, and not on the human problem of early adolescent development. Following a national tour of middle schools during his sabbatical year, Gruhn reported much of the same in 1960. "In spite of the attention that we have given for a quarter of a century to new and varied methods of working with boys and girls," Gruhn concluded, "methods of teaching the academic subjects in our junior high schools apparently have not changed a great deal."[73]

Teachers in modern-day middle schools are apparently still eager to be more like high school teachers, and, as a consequence, defect from middle school values for those of the high school. Such a tendency, one suspects, may have actually become a *structural variable* of the middle school organization: it may now be a built-in characteristic of the organization. Is there here a manifestation of what C. Robert Pace and George G. Stern have called "institutional press?"[74] Recent research seems to support the hypothesis that this may very well be the case.

Two investigators went into a separately housed middle school unit, grades 7-8-9 and a pupil enrollment of 1,025, to ascertain the degree of

[72] *Ibid.*, pp. 52–53.

[73] William T. Gruhn, "What Is New in Junior High School Education," *The Bulletin*, NASSP, Vol. 44, February 1960, p. 7.

[74] The concept of "institutional press" has been tested in empirical research by these two investigators and will be found reported in many places in the educational literature. See, for example, C. Robert Pace and George G. Stern, "An Approach to the Measurement of Psychological Characteristics of College Environments," *Journal of Educational Psychology*, Vol. 49, October 1958; C. Robert Pace, "Methods of Describing College Cultures," *Teachers College Record*, Vol. 63, January 1962; George G. Stern, "Characteristics of the Intellectual Climate in College Environments," *Harvard Educational Review*, Vol. 33, 1963.

consensus among *all professional members* in the organization on the middle school goal, and whether goal perception affected teacher orientations to the performance of official tasks.

A pretested structured interview of twenty-eight open-ended questions was used on forty-two of the forty-four teachers in the school, as well as on the principal, assistant principal, school social worker, guidance counselor, school psychologist, school librarian, and the system's assistant superintendent in charge of secondary schools.

When replies were subjected to a content analysis, they were found to consist overwhelmingly of two major kinds of statements: service-oriented and maintenance-oriented. Twelve major classificational categories were then developed from the character of these statements. Four of these were service-oriented categories and eight were maintenance-oriented.

Two competent "outsiders" were asked to classify the responses in interview protocols. Each was presented with definitions of the categories and sample statements. A coder-reliability test was performed in which two measures of agreement were employed. On "precise" agreement, only cases of perfect correspondence with some category were counted as agreement; here agreement was 63 percent. A measure of "gross" agreement referred to the degree of agreement between the classifiers that a reply was either service or maintenance-oriented; agreement here was 88 percent. Each classifier then went ahead and treated all responses independently. The analyzed responses were placed on punch cards, background data were added, and the cards were run on a computer.

A total of 1,407 categorized responses were secured. These were distributed as follows:

		Percent
Service-oriented responses	702	49.9
Maintenance-oriented responses	563	40.0
Other	142	10.0

The investigators concluded:[75]

[75] Edward Gross and Samuel H. Popper, "Service and Maintenance Orientation in a Junior High School Organization," *Educational Administration Quarterly*, Vol. I, Spring 1965, pp. 35–36. This is the first report of research which has been completed by the authors under the working title: "Goal Perception in the Junior High School by Professional Role Incumbents: A Case Study." The research was begun in 1962 and completed in 1964.

The figures of 49.9 percent for service-oriented responses and 40 percent for maintenance-oriented responses are, of course, totals and, therefore, in that sense, averages. However, when we examined our respondents in terms of background factors, a striking result occurred.

We analyzed our replies according to the following background variables: sex, religion, marital status, age, years of teaching experience, type of college attended, where practice teaching was done, whether respondent had any courses specifically related to the junior high school, degrees attained, years taught at this school, where respondent taught immediately before assignment here, other duties in school, and non-teaching experience.

Although there was some fluctuation, the results tended to mirror very closely the total figures; albeit, maintenance orientation was somewhat lower for certain background variables. We found, for example, that when we broke down the results by the sex of the respondent, men were not any more service oriented than women: both gave about one-half of their responses in a service-oriented category. Irrespective of sex, then, about half of the responses made reference to service orientation and around 40 percent to maintenance orientation. We got almost identical figures for all other background variables.

This suggests strongly that service and maintenance orientation are structural variables which are characteristic of the organization we have studied, as such, rather than of the particular people in it. For if they were characteristic of actors in the organization, we would surely expect them to vary in distribution, with men perhaps being differently oriented than women, those with degrees differing from those without degrees, and so on. The fact that no such differences were found suggests that, whoever the person, a teacher in a junior high school finds *certain constraints and obligations* imposed upon him by the organization.

The investigators concluded further from the analysis of the data:[76]

Our study suggests that a major structural preventive of technicism in the junior high schools is the professional orientation which preparation programs ought to provide prospective junior high school teachers. Professionals, who in their prior socialization have internalized a dedication to principles of their professional role, are in less danger of substituting mere technical means for ends.

As the chapter to follow will document, the dominant value orientation of middle school teachers has been a matter of concern from the

[76] *Ibid.*, p. 40.

beginning of middle school experience. Indeed, Frank Bunker of Berkeley would not assign high school teachers to his middle schools because he feared the thrust of their dominant orientation to pupils. He understood apparently that a teacher's professional orientation is first shaped in the value matrix of a preparation program which socializes to the norms of a teaching role.

Once in the profession, a teacher's socialization to role norms is continued through the influence of colleagues. For socialization to a professional role involves also the internalization of categories of meaning which conform to expectations of colleagues. As is revealed by the data, middle school teachers who were studied in the forecited Gross-Popper research seem to be ensnared by conflicting role expectations. It is altogether significant that the 49.9 percent of service-oriented responses from teachers was matched by 86.5 percent service-oriented responses from the principal, assistant principal, and the assistant superintendent of schools in charge of all secondary schools in the district. Teachers, after all, are the *technical experts* in a school, and according to reference group theory:[77]

> The "reference group" to which the expert looks in connection with his competence and the definition of its standards is not his "managerial" boss but his professional peers and colleagues.

Empirical evidence, therefore, is supportive of the continuing administrative concern for the professional preparation of middle school teachers. From accounts of proceedings in the National Association of Secondary School principals since the end of World War II, it would seem that middle school principals in the United States have taken the initiative to resolve Gruhn's five "critical problems and needs" of their administrative unit.

Initiative of this kind, however, left on its own, is not likely to overcome dysfunctional conditions in the organizational mechanism which frustrate the institutional purpose of the American middle school. Even if it were possible to eliminate overnight the pernicious effects of anticipatory socialization from middle school organizations, there is little likelihood that the primacy of the affective domain would be reestablished in the middle school curriculum. Chances of success would increase manifold were curriculum specialists, especially in schools of education, to respond innovatively to this administrative initiative.

[77] Parsons, "Some Ingredients of a General Theory," p. 47.

It is precisely the required diffuseness and affectivity in a middle school curriculum that seems to make many curriculum people apprehensive. They perceive in the middle school's protective intervention, and in its psychosocial orientation to educative process, a discontinuity in program articulation. A turn away from the road to scholastic achievement is seen here. And, in the manner of a self-fulfilling prophecy, such curriculum specialists persuade themselves to see the American middle school as little more than a custodial organization. No doubt, the growing demand of modern culture for well-mastered cognitive skills also contributes to the delusion.

Yet, unless the dominant educative focus is on the human condition at early adolescence, there is little point to a protective intervention in the educational program at the onset of adolescence. Here, indeed, would be an unwarranted discontinuity in program articulation without a compensating value. School districts, as we know, have eliminated the middle school unit precisely for this reason. The burden of proof, therefore, is with educative process in the middle school.

Proof that apprehensions about educative process in the middle school are unfounded must come to grips with the following two questions: Is a program which is capable of fulfilling the institutional commitment of the American middle school an obstacle to scholastic achievement? Is discontinuity in curriculum articulation an unavoidable built-in condition of such a program? Let us keep these two questions in mind as we trace the general evolution of a middle school program in the United States.

12

A MIDDLE SCHOOL PROGRAM
EVOLVES

Unlike middle schools in other countries, educative process in the American middle school was from the first dominantly oriented to the social and psychological problems of human development at early adolescence. A new social role was defined in American society about 1910, the role of *early adolescent,* and it was institutionalized in the normative framework of organizational systems which serve the adolescent subculture. One of these was the organization of public education.

Cultural conditions in American society, on which a section of the next chapter will focus, had catapulted a protective intervention in early adolescent socialization to the status of an important social value. Once this value was incorporated as an educational subgoal in the goal structure of public school organization, a middle school unit was designed to fulfill it.

Even as public school administrators were planning the implementing organization of a middle school, they called on specialists in educational technology to devise its curriculum. In their managerial "specifications to the technical subsystem" of public school organization, to use the Parsonian reference, curriculum builders were directed to be mindful of unique physiological, psychological, and social problems which attend the transitional period of early adolescence. Neither the subject-oriented high school curriculum nor the curriculum for childhood education would do. The new middle school required a discretely patterned educative process. The required middle school curriculum had to be capable of fusing instrumental and expressive values in keeping with the unit's organizational goal.

It was precisely the dominance of an instrumental orientation in the high school's process of education, it bears repeating, that decided Frank Bunker not to assign high school teachers to Berkeley's new middle schools, or "lower high school," as he referred to them for lack of a better name. It is clear that he wanted teachers whose internalized orientation to school process would not clash with the necessary psychosocial orientations of his middle school. The assignment of high school teachers to the middle school, he feared, would result in such a conflict in professional valuations of middle school objects:[1]

> The point of view of such teachers tends to be that . . . the subject and its contents are of paramount importance, often overshadowing interest in the pupil himself. . . . By selecting teachers for the lower high school who first of all have had successful experience in teaching in the grades, and who in the second place have taken enough advanced academic work to broaden their horizon somewhat beyond that of the grade teacher, the ideal combination is secured. Furthermore, by insisting that such teachers be assigned at least two different subjects rather than one, as often obtains in the larger high schools, *the tendency toward undue specialization* in those early years can be checked. [*Italics added.*]

Much of the same mood is to be found in the statement of disenchantment with the six-year high school which W. A. Greeson delivered before the 1909 meeting of the North Central Association of Colleges and Secondary Schools, but here it was because too much of the elementary school pattern was feared in middle school process. The following passage, which was given in Chapter 3 within a larger context, is directed to this point:

> Boys and girls of this age [early adolescence] are put into one room with one teacher, exactly as the method has been in previous years, and no

[1] Bunker, *Reorganization of the Public School System,* pp. 106–07.

attempt is made to broaden the curriculum and appeal to the new capabilities and abilities of this age. Boys of this age naturally crave for organization among themselves. They ought to have their debating clubs, their societies, their athletic games and contests, their baseball teams, their football teams.

. . . The seventh, eighth and ninth grades should be placed in schools separated from the primary grades.

These remarks by Bunker and Greeson shed light on the transitional and diffuse quality administrators wanted in a middle school curriculum. Bunker rejected subject-matter specialization in the curriculum of his "lower high school" to the point of barring from it teachers who had been prepared for the high school. Greeson, on the other hand, shunned patterns of curriculum construction in the elementary school. He wanted some of the departmentalization of a high school, and he wanted some of the high school's extracurricular program, but he wanted these patterned in a discrete curriculum for a middle school of grades seven, eight, and nine. His administrative prescriptions for a middle school program materialized eventually in the now familiar middle school benchmarks of limited departmentalization, a generalized curriculum which integrates elements of elementary and high school subjects, and the student-interest activity program.

As the idea of a middle school took on a sharper definition in the minds of American school administrators, they articulated those functions which are manifestly required for attaining the middle school's paramount goal. These manifest functions reflected in turn the transition theme which is central to the goal of protective intervention in the process of education at the onset of adolescence. Gruhn later conceptualized these manifest functions under the following six rubrics: Integration, Exploration, Guidance, Differentiation, Socialization, and Articulation.[2]

Apparently there was available by 1914 a discrete educational program which could discriminate between an organizational unit in which a mere rearrangement of grades seven, eight, and nine had been effected and one which was functionally oriented to the middle school goal. Chapter 1, it will be recalled, took account of a report to the 1914 meeting of the North Central Association of Colleges and Second-

2 See the "Questionnaire on Proposed Functions" in Gruhn, "Doctor's Thesis," Index. These six functions will be found discussed in depth in William T. Gruhn and Harl R. Douglass, *The Modern Junior High School* (New York: The Ronald Press Co., 1956), pp. 31–32.

ary Schools in which the following was said about middle schools in North Central's jurisdiction:

> In the beginning of this movement the subject matter of instruction was substantially the same as it had been before the movement was inaugurated but gradually, in many of these schools, a change has been effected until now not only is there a difference in organization, but also a change in subject matter. They have gradually become junior high schools.

Institutionalization Is Initiated

These remarks of 1914 suggest that, at least in school systems of the North Central Association, there had evolved by the time of World War I a definable middle school program. North Central, we know, was the first of the regional accrediting associations to endorse officially the middle school organization. It is no accident, therefore, that it should also have been the first within professional education to initiate the institutionalization of a discrete middle school program.

The Association considered a committee proposal for a patterned middle school program at its 1916 annual meeting. The proposal defined, among other things, functions of the program, the three grades which were to be included, subject matter for each grade, and the goal toward which the program was directed.

In addition to "mathematics, natural science, social science, language, fine and practical arts," the proposal called for "physical training" and "educational guidance." The committee also recommended "a measure of departmentalization," supervised study, laboratories, and libraries. "The committee recommends," so goes the concluding section of the proposal, "that the construction of junior high school buildings or the remodeling of old school buildings for junior high-school purposes shall make provision for an auditorium and for the adequate carrying into effect of the above recommendations regarding supervised study, physical education and the free and effective use of library and laboratory facilities."[3]

North Central took no formal action on the proposal of its committee. Nevertheless, the proposal was to serve as a frame of reference for subsequent discussions of educative process for the middle school. But several problems had to be resolved before the Association could

[3] *Proceedings*, NCA, 1916, pp. 171–74.

"standardize"—institutionalize—a middle school program. By far the most stubborn was the problem of the ninth grade.

Assistant Superintendent of Schools Frank G. Pickell of Cleveland, Ohio summoned the problem of the ninth grade into clear view when, as Chairman of North Central's Commission on Unit Courses and Curricula, he reported in 1921:[4]

> . . . colleges have not yet written their entrance requirements in terms of the three year high school, although we believe and have said that college dominance should not extend down into the junior high school. . . . Consequently, we find a troublesome joker in every three year junior high school in this territory. The seventh and eighth grades have been reorganized, but the ninth is the first year of high school taken over in toto and without change, and every senior high school regards itself a four year school. It at least maintains its sovereign rights over that ninth year.

Despite obstacles, North Central's efforts to establish defining norms for a middle school program continued unabated. Resolutions at annual meetings, a standing middle school committee, and overt support within North Central's Commission on Unit Courses and Curricula combined in 1924 to gain official status for a "Standard Junior High School."

The program of studies that was expected of a "Standard Junior High School" included the following:[5]

> The appropriate subjects to be offered by the junior high school are: English, Mathematics, Foreign Language, History and Civics, Geography and Elementary Science, Music, Art, Health Education, Vocational Information, and Practical Arts for both boys and girls, including commercial subjects.
>
> The program of studies shall be organized into a single curriculum with limited electives.
>
> Electives prior to the second semester of the 8th year are considered ill advised. Prior to this semester exploration and review of subject matter should be provided by the content of courses and the administration of the curriculum, and not by electives.
>
> Instruction shall be departmentalized.
>
> The school shall practice flexible promotion rather than promotion by subject.

4 *Ibid.*, 1921, p. 34.
5 *Ibid.*, 1924, pp. 98–99.

Flexible promotion means that pupils shall be promoted when the occasion arises and without restriction of subject promotion. It means pupil placement. It implies the use of opportunity classes and coaching teachers.

The school shall provide within the school day for pupil club and social activities under the direction of the faculty.

The school shall provide adequately for keeping in contact with the homes and home life of the pupils and introduce only gradually the freedom in discipline characteristic of the senior high school.

North Central's action of 1924 patterned a middle school program which defined in terms of educative process the transitional character of the middle school and its dominant value orientation. There is no mistaking the dominance of a psychosocial orientation in this program. The primacy of expressive values is clear. Such prescriptions in the North Central program as "flexible promotion rather than promotion by subject," "pupil placement," "opportunity classes," "provide within the school day for pupil club and social activities," and "keeping in contact with the homes and home life of the pupil" were meant to restrain subject-matter instrumentalism in the school's environment. Lest this intention should be missed in program prescriptions, North Central reaffirmed it in specifications for middle school plant facilities:[6]

Facilities should be provided adequately for instruction in academic subjects, in the practical arts, in health education, recreation, and in such subjects as may require the laboratory method. Adequate provision shall be provided for assembly programs, social activities, and for the supervision or direction of study.

Simultaneously with the drive in North Central circles to institutionalize a middle school, the very influential James M. Glass was striving toward the same end elsewhere. His experience with middle schools dated from the time of his principalship in 1915 of Washington Junior High School in Rochester, New York, to the end of his service as Director of Junior High Schools in the Commonwealth of Pennsylvania, Department of Public Instruction. Glass never lost sight of the dominant psychosocial orientation which founders of the American middle school intended for its structure and process. His influence in keeping alive the institutional commitment of the American middle school has to be measured by a high exponential factor indeed.

6 *Ibid.*, 1924, pp. 97–98.

A prolific contributor to professional and popular literature, in demand for consultation by such groups as the Commonwealth Fund and the National Council of Education, an acknowledged middle school authority in discussions of the North Central Association, and visiting summer lecturer at colleges and universities are representative of the activities through which he defined again and again the legitimate institutional purpose of a middle school in American culture.[7]

Glass and the North Central Association were of one mind about educative process in the middle school. The following passages from an address he delivered before the 1922 meeting of the NEA show the extent of agreement in their perception of a patterned middle school program:[8]

> The junior high-school program of studies should be a resultant of several forces. It should be made up, in part, of a continuation of the elementary school curriculum, but a review of these courses, i.e., a new view through articulation of elementary and secondary courses. . . . This transitional unit of the public-school system must preserve its contacts and become a composite product of the forces which precede and follow it.
>
> At the same time the program of studies of the junior high school is a self-contained unit. The point of view of the elementary curriculum towards its pupils is *en masse* to the end that all may receive a usable knowledge of the common branches and a sympathetic understanding of the social and civic structure of our democratic society. Differentiation of pupils into groups, so far as program of studies is concerned, prevails in the senior high school to the end that the individuals of each group may receive training in the types of work for which they have aptitudes.
>
> The junior high school "must help *each* child to discover his own aptitudes" in the transitional stage between the *en masse* organization of the elementary school and the group organization of the senior high

[7] For articles by Glass in professional and popular literature, in addition to those already cited, see J. M. Glass, "Library in Junior High Schools," *Library Journal,* Vol. 50, February 1925; J. M. Glass, "Careers in Education; Teaching in Junior High School," *Journal of the National Education Association,* Vol. 17, May 1928; J. M. Glass, "The Mission of the Junior High School Is in Articulation and Guided Exploration," *School Life,* Vol. 12, February 1927; J. M. Glass, "Recent Developments in the Junior High School Field," *High School Quarterly,* Vol. 14, October 1925; and James M. Glass, "The Junior High School," *The New Republic,* Vol. XXXVI, November 1923. See also Leonard V. Koos' citation of Glass as a middle school authority in *Proceedings,* NCA, 1924, p. 23. Glass conducted a curriculum study for the Commonwealth Fund in 1923.

[8] Glass, "The Junior High School Program of Studies," *Addresses and Proceedings,* NEA, 1922, pp. 386–97. Other passages from this address were given in Chapter 11.

school. It is the finding, testing, and trying-out period of the public-school system. The point of view is, therefore, the individual. Exploration of individual differences, guidance of educational or vocational choice, and stimulation of educational advancement are its primary objectives. The identity of the junior high school is, therefore, established in its purpose to treat each pupil as an individual problem.

. . . In brief, the junior high school must accomplish two purposes at the same time and each equally well—create and maintain its identity and preserve [a] close relationship with the elementary and senior high schools.

. . . The final objective of the junior high school program of studies must be to provide school socialization on a scale so extensive that adolescent youth may find in the school itself "the special field for their activities as (junior) citizens." It is vital to recognize that the organized activities of school socialization should be . . . motivated by accepted educational objectives to an extent equal to the motivation of the subjects of study by such objectives. When this recognition is once given, school activities will be dignified by a place in the program of studies and by a definite time allotment consistent with their rich educational possibilities. They must be as definitely planned as any other administrative or instructional facilities for the attainment of the objectives of secondary education.

. . . These activities will largely fail to contribute to the attainment of the objectives if they continue as incidental. They should, therefore, become integral parts of the program of studies. They deserve a higher recognition than that accorded by the designation extra-curricular. They are intra-curricular activities.

Glass, as did North Central's *official* middle school program of 1924, defined the American middle school in structural-functional terms which left no doubt what its legitimate institutional purpose is and what, therefore, its legitimate organizational goal must be. It is, to repeat Glass, a "transitional unit." It intervenes protectively in the process of socialization at the onset of adolescence in order to "help *each* child to discover his own aptitudes in the transitional stage . . . between the elementary school and the senior high school." "It is," Glass is quite explicit, "the finding, testing, and trying-out period of the public-school system." Functional educative process in a middle school, according to Glass, "must . . . provide school socialization on a scale so extensive that adolescent youth may find in the school itself 'the special field for their activities as junior citizens.' " In sum, the middle school was meant to be the early adolescent's own *special school*.

Glass, moreover, like Frank Bunker of Berkeley, was apprehensive about entrusting the middle school program in the hands of teachers who had not internalized institutional values of the American middle school. The protective guidance function, he specified, "would presumably be undertaken by a faculty serving primarily as counselors or advisers and not solely as 'subject teachers seeking only to lead pupils to mastery of subject matter.' "[9] Accordingly, Glass advocated this:[10]

> Since junior high school teachers are today almost wholly trained through service, it becomes a foremost administrative obligation to provide an educational program for the professional training of the teaching staff. This professional program is so vital to the clear vision of the primary function of guidance . . . and of other junior high school objectives that a weekly period, partly within school time in a six hour day, should be provided for professional meetings and discussions. The faculty conference period should become one of the organized activities of the school and to this extent part of the program of studies.

A value foundation for a patterned middle school program was laid in the 1910 period by means of administrative prescriptions to curriculum builders. Glass, among others, defined middle school values in more precise structural-functional terms, and North Central formalized a program in 1924. Out of these early developmental efforts began to emerge such now familiar middle school features as the parent-teacher conference, planned pupil-teacher conferences, the Core teacher, mainstay of many modern-day middle school staffs, and, as it is particularly clear in the Glass address of 1922, much of what was later incorporated in Gruhn's definition of six manifest functions.[11]

Institutionalization Is Thwarted

But, as it turned out, efforts to institutionalize a middle school program were frustrated by conditions in society which obstructed institutionalization. The years between the two world wars saw the American middle school engulfed in a miasma of confusion. Its legitimate institutional purpose was already a blur by the early 1920's, thanks in large

9 *Ibid.*, 1922, p. 392.
10 *Ibid.*, 1922, p. 392.
11 For references to the importance of Core teachers in a modern-day middle school program see Gertrude Noar, *The Junior High School Today and Tomorrow* (Englewood Cliffs, N.J.: Prentice Hall, 1961); Nelson L. Bossing and Roscoe V. Cramer, *The Junior High School* (Boston: Houghton Mifflin Company, 1965), Chapters 7 and 11.

measure to efficiency cultists. During most of this period, the North Central Association of Colleges and Secondary Schools was the only professional group in American education which persisted in attempts to arrest the erosion of middle school values. Then, by the late 1930's, it too succumbed to futility.

The combination of efficiency cultists, building shortages, the Great Depression, no preparation programs for middle school teachers and principals, and the adamantine refusal in higher education to release ninth grade subjects from college entrance requirements was too formidable to overcome. In such a climate, North Central's sanction for enforcing the institutionalization of its middle school program was of little effect. In many instances, indeed, it was of no effect. A member public school system could have its high schools accredited at the very same time that its middle schools were denied the official "recognition" of the Association. As for North Central's plea to have ninth year subjects excluded from entrance requirements into higher education, with rare exceptions the plea was ignored by its university and college members. The Association, it seems, was not prepared at that time to make censure of a member college or university one of the sanctions for enforcing its middle school norms.

But North Central's efforts were not entirely wasted. Its drive to institutionalize a middle school program was only temporarily thwarted. For during this long darkness in middle school experience, Keepers of the Institution led eventually to a reconstruction of North Central's 1924 pattern in the post–World War II period.

Keepers of the Institution

Keepers of the Institution were those in professional education who, between the two world wars, held fast to the legitimate institutional purpose of the American middle school either as a state of mind or through productive scholarship. Representative of these two categories are James M. Glass and William T. Gruhn.

Not many doctoral dissertations in education of the modern era have been privileged to exert an influence to match that of Gruhn's. The substantive matter of Gruhn's thesis made its way eventually into *The Modern Junior High School,* a book he coauthored with Harl R. Douglass, who directed Gruhn's dissertation at the University of North Carolina.

Publication of the book in 1947 could not have been better timed. World War II was in the past, and ahead waited a resurgent interest in the middle school. Cultural pressures which led to the middle school in 1910 intensified in the postwar period, and the social value of a middle school became even more commanding. But unlike middle schools of the 1910 period, post-World War II units had the advantage of a patterned program which was spelled out in *The Modern Junior High School.*

Gruhn's doctoral dissertation of 1940 rescued the American middle school from the miasma of confusion into which it had been cast some twenty years earlier. It redefined in the idiom of function three vital concepts of middle school organization: its legitimate institutional purpose, its manifest functions, and the qualitative relationship between a manifest function and the paramount goal. In terms of functional value, he explained as follows:[12]

> By a *function* of the junior high school we mean . . . the responsibility for providing conditions which will contribute to the realization of the ultimate aims of education. For instance, we may consider it the responsibility of the junior high school to provide for the guidance of pupils so that the ultimate aims of education may be more economically and more completely realized. Therefore, we may consider it a function of the junior high school to provide opportunities and facilities for guidance.

These redefined concepts were then later employed by Gruhn and Douglass to pattern a middle school program in *The Modern Junior High School.* In its essential features, the pattern was a reconstruction of North Central's 1924 program. Obsolescent parts of educative process were discarded, but fundamental middle school values of the earlier period were redefined and joined with modern social imperatives. From the perspective of institutional history, the most striking thing about the patterned middle school program in the Gruhn-Douglass book is its obvious organic kinship with Glass's address of 1922 and North Central's middle school program of 1924.

Gruhn's influence on post–World War II middle school experience has been ubiquitous. His name has become inseparably identified in professional education with the American middle school. Most contemporary middle school programs incorporate as a controlling norm

---

[12] Gruhn, *Doctoral Thesis,* Vol. I, p. 8.

in process development his definition of manifest functions in a middle school organization. And as is often the case with men whose ideas have exerted a powerful effect upon social experience beyond their own day, the influence of Glass's institutional definition of the American middle school is sharply imprinted on Gruhn's reconstructionist scholarship and on contemporary middle school program patterns as well.

Perhaps the finest specimen extant which illustrates the latter is the program pattern of the Southern Association of Colleges and Secondary Schools. The Southern Association's pattern is spelled out in *The Junior High School Program.* It was formulated by the Association's Commission on Secondary Schools and the Commission on Research and Service. The guiding value orientation to the program pattern was taken from a "philosophy of the junior high school" in the *Junior High School Manual,* Bulletin 248, of the Pennsylvania Department of Public Instruction, where, it will be recalled, Glass had served for many years as Director of Junior High Schools.[13] Gruhn's definition of six manifest functions were built into the pattern unchanged, and the following were taken as "Areas of Agreement":[14]

1. *The junior high school is a respectable, established and essential unit in the organizational pattern of public education.*

. . . 2. *The curriculum of the junior high school should be different from that of the senior high school or the elementary school.*

. . . 3. *The program of the junior high school basically should be a general education program.*

. . . 4. *The junior high school program should be geared specifically to the problems, concerns and interests of the pre-adolescents and early adolescents and to the impacts of society upon their lives.*

The Southern Association's *The Junior High School Program* was published in 1958, and it had a third printing by 1960. Its wide circulation in the nation may be taken as one index of the new consensus which has crystallized around the middle school in contemporary American education. Catalytic influences of Keepers of the Institution are clearly discernible in this consensus. A steadfast esteem of the American middle school's institutional commitment has led to a recon-

---

13 Maurice Ahrens, Durell Ruffin, and Raymond Wilson, *The Junior High School Program* (Atlanta, Ga.: The Southern Association of Colleges and Secondary Schools, 1958), p. 5.
14 *Ibid.,* p. 3.

struction of North Central's 1924 program pattern. It is this pattern which has now been institutionalized in norms of program construction for middle schools in the United States. The question is: How *practical* is this pattern in a post-Sputnik world?

The Burden of Proof

Questions of practicality constrain a modern middle school to prove that the primacy of expressive values in its educative process will not interfere with scholastic achievement, as this achievement is measured by current norms. At least one such American middle school has assumed the burden of proof and has produced the type of solid evidence which this proof requires.

The school is Como Park Junior High School of St. Paul, Minnesota. As luck will have it, its program is as faithful a replication in the modern idiom of North Central's 1924 pattern as will be found anywhere in the United States. Official role expectations of teachers in this school conform closely with the role expectations of Bunker and Glass which were given earlier. As an added stroke of good fortune, the influence of James M. Glass can be positively identified in the administrative decision to institute this program in St. Paul middle schools.

The manner in which Glass influenced middle school development in St. Paul has a touch of the dramatic. Glass would spend summer leaves from the Pennsylvania Department of Public Instruction teaching summer sessions at colleges and universities. One of these was the State University of Iowa.

There is no telling how many graduate students, future public school administrators, caught the institutional "spirit" of the American middle school from James M. Glass. It is known, however, that one of them was Forrest E. Conner, Superintendent of Schools in St. Paul from 1949 to 1963 and afterward Executive Secretary of the American Association of School Administrators. Conner links the Glass influence with the middle school program which was evaluated in St. Paul.

Conner received his doctorate degree from the State University of Iowa in educational administration. Following a period of service as high school principal and superintendent in several midwestern communities, he went to St. Paul in 1949 as superintendent of schools. St. Paul at that time had very little with which to attract a forward-moving superintendent, except a mountain-sized administrative challenge. The system had been politic-ridden for years. A starved and demoralized teaching staff turned to the picket line in 1946 out of desperation. School plants were in a state of gross disrepair. The City Council determined school budgets, and St. Paul was one of the last cities of the first class in the United States at the time without a board of education. However, Conner did find one great central office asset in the public school system of St. Paul: two first-line assistants in the persons of Nolan C. Kearney and Glenn F. Varner.

Kearney, an able theoretician, was Assistant Superintendent of Research and Curriculum. Varner, equally able as an administrative strategist, was Assistant Superintendent of Secondary and Vocational Education. Mutual respect for one another's talent, and friendship, welded these two into a strike force of great potential. Conner was to draw upon this potential on many occasions.

Conner assaulted the St. Paul challenge from three directions simultaneously: staff development, curriculum modernization, and plant rehabilitation. There was plenty of challenge left for general school administration in St. Paul when Conner left in 1963 to assume service with the American Association of School Administrators, but he did turn over to his successor a modern public school system which had a middle school program in the institutional tradition of the American middle school.

Conner was given an elected board of education in 1950. In pursuit of curriculum modernization, he committed the St. Paul public school system in 1952 to a predominantly 6-3-3 plan of organization. A successful bond referendum in 1953 gave him some $6 million of capital funds for three new middle school buildings, one of which was to be the Como Park Junior High School. Responsibility for implementing Conner's program in the division of secondary education fell to Varner.

Varner surrounded himself with able subordinates who, like himself, were also capable of institutional insight. Subordinates were given a free hand to fulfill assigned tasks. It was Varner's way of showing confidence and of encouraging administrative initiative in his division. In order to assure himself of a *permanent administrative cadre* in the middle schools, he obtained Conner's support in a recommendation to establish *a single salary schedule* for all secondary school principals in the system.

It was Varner's plan to assign technical tasks of program construction for the new middle schools to a representative committee of teachers, counselors, principals, and central office specialists. But first, Conner's direct participation was required in the task of defining a value framework for the committee. Would Conner support Varner's orientation to middle school education?

When Varner went to see Conner about the matter, he took along Roy O. Isacksen, into whose hands he meant to entrust the administration of Como Park Junior High School. What Varner and Isacksen did not know was that they had Conner's support even before the conference. As Conner tells it:[15]

> Glenn Varner asked me for a conference on the program we were to have in the three new junior high schools that were about to go on the drawing boards. Glenn brought Roy along to help him sell me a program he had in mind.
>
> For the better part of two hours, they told me about the virtues of Core, an activity program in the curriculum, problems of early adolescents, Gruhn's junior high school functions, and so on. They were going at it like True Believers. I just didn't have the heart to tell them that I had learned all these things about the junior high school program from James Glass at Iowa, where he used to teach the junior high school during summer session. All of what Glenn and Roy were telling me had a very familiar ring.

There is no mistaking the antecedent influences which have made their way into the middle school program of St. Paul. Values in "the program of studies and its administration" which are of immediate relevance in the transition period of early adolescence are given primacy, just as Superintendent Maxwell of New York City had wanted it in his 1903 address before the Middle States and Maryland Association. W. H. Greeson's prescriptions of 1909 are seen fulfilled in the St. Paul program by means of assembly programs, a program of student-centered interest activities which is built into the curriculum, and a separate school plant. Bunker would also find his caution against "undue specialization" heeded and teachers who are "assigned at least two different subjects."

The latter are Core teachers around whom *center* major guidance tasks in the program. A Core teacher, more than any other, comes closest to the teacher-counselor role which James M. Glass had advocated for middle schools in his 1922 address before the NEA. Core teachers in St. Paul middle schools, following the normative pattern of North Central's 1924 middle school program, are responsible "for keeping in contact with the homes and home life of the pupils." Altogether, the

---

[15] Interview with Forrest E. Conner, July 16, 1962. Verified by Conner.

role of Core teacher is the most demanding technical role in St. Paul middle schools and the most difficult to perform successfully.

Core teachers, unlike other teachers, are scheduled for twenty hours in the classroom out of a thirty-hour school week. Four hours are devoted to preparation, four to pupil or parent conferences, and two are consumed by assembly and student-interest activity programs. A representative weekly schedule of a middle school Core teacher in St. Paul might be shown as follows:

Monday	*Tuesday*	*Wednesday*	*Thursday*	*Friday*
Preparation (1 hr.)	Conference (1 hr.)	English-Social Studies Core (2 hrs.)	Preparation (1 hr.)	English-Social Studies Core (2 hrs.)
English-Social Studies Core (2 hrs.)	English-Social Studies Core (2 hrs.)	Assembly (1 hr.)	Speech (1 hr.)	Conference (1 hr.)
Speech (1 hr.)	Preparation (1 hr.)	Conference (1 hr.)	English-Social Studies Core (2 hrs.)	English-Social Studies Core (2 hrs.)
English-Social Studies Core (2 hrs.)	English-Social Studies Core (2 hrs.)	Speech (1 hr.)	Conference (1 hr.)	Preparation (1 hr.)
		Student-Interest Activity Program (1 hr.)	Speech (1 hr.)	

The primacy of expressive values in the St. Paul middle school program is most sharply delineated within the role structure by the Core teacher. Core teachers bear the "lion's share" of the burden in protective and mediating interventions. Their singular status in the role structure is defined in the following segment of an official statement:[16]

> In St. Paul's junior high schools, a plan has been devised to reduce the number of pupils which certain teachers are required to meet, and to give these teachers three to four guidance periods per week for parent and pupil conferences, in addition to their preparation periods. This is done by combining English and social studies into "core" classes, under the direction of a single teacher.
>
> . . . Core teachers perform counseling duties at a level just below that of a trained counselor for all students in their core classes—a total of

16 *The Organization and Curriculum of the New Junior High Schools in Saint Paul*, Office of Secondary and Vocational Education, Saint Paul Public Schools, St. Paul, Minnesota, Fall 1958, pp. 12–13.

approximately 66 students. The responsibility for training these teachers in counseling techniques, such as test interpretation, the pupil and the parent conference, falls upon the trained counselor in each school. He must have regular meetings with these teachers and give them the benefit of his experience, provide them with resource materials, and give them the opportunity to relate their experiences, each teacher knowing in advance that he will receive help and consideration from the counselor and the group.

Core teachers are provided with a good deal of background information on each child in their core classes—scores on standardized tests over a period of years, I.Q. scores, reading grade-level scores, health history, anecdotal reports by previous core teachers and by other people within the school who worked with the student. The core teacher is considered the advisor throughout the school year for the students in his classes. He will confer with other teachers about the progress of these students, and they with him; he will confer with the students themselves. With the help of the counselor, superior students are identified and guided into classes and activities from which they can profit most. For those students who are less talented academically and for those students who have special problems, the core teacher seeks the help of specialists such as the corrective mathematics teacher, the remedial reading teacher, psychologist, and other resource people in the school system.

In addition to this, the core teacher will have at least one conference per year with the parents of every youngster in his core classes. . . .

St. Paul's middle school program was unique in Minnesota when it was put into operation in 1955. Gruhn's definition of six manifest functions—Integration, Exploration, Guidance, Differentiation, Socialization, and Articulation—was built into its normative pattern for fulfilling the institutional purpose.[17] The program's orientation was made dominantly expressive, although values of cognitive learning were by no means neglected. But because gratificational values were to be dominant in the program, and because the program would depart from official State of Minnesota prescriptions for grades 7-8-9, the Minnesota State Department of Education approved it as an *experimental program* only, subject to the following condition: A rigorous evaluation was to be made of the program after it had been in operation for several years. Such an evaluation was made during 1961–62 of the program shown in the following:[18]

[17] *Ibid.,* pp. 1–2.
[18] *Ibid.,* pp. 4–5.

EVALUATED ST. PAUL MIDDLE SCHOOL PROGRAM
Grades 7 and 8

		Hours Per Week	Required or Elective
1. ENGLISH-SOCIAL STUDIES		8	Required
2. PRACTICAL ARTS:			
(a) Industrial Arts			
1. Wood Shop			
2. Metal Shop and Electricity	Approximately 12 weeks in each area	4	Required for Boys
3. Graphic Arts and Mechanical Dr.			
(b) Home Economics			
1. Foods			
2. Clothing	Approximately 12 weeks in each area	4	Required for Girls
3. Related Arts			
3. BAND	One year	4	Elective
or			
GENERAL MUSIC	18 weeks of Music	4	Required
ARTS, CRAFTS	Arts and Crafts rotates every 6 weeks with 3 Art-Crafts teachers		
4. MATHEMATICS		4	Required
5. PHYSICAL EDUCATION AND HEALTH		4	Required
6. GENERAL SCIENCE / SPEECH	One-half year of each	4	Required
7. SPECIAL INTEREST ACTIVITY		1	Required (Students elect activity)
Activities meet 1 hour per week Activities change 3 times during year			
8. CLUB AND ASSEMBLY PROGRAM		1	Required (Students elect club)
(Assemblies every other week; class meetings, interest clubs, and service clubs meet on alternate weeks)			

Before the completion of each grade, the student plans his next year's program with the help of his teachers, the school counselor, and his parents.

EVALUATED ST. PAUL MIDDLE SCHOOL PROGRAM
Grade 9

		Hours Per Week	Required or Elective
1. ENGLISH-SOCIAL STUDIES		8	Required
2. PRACTICAL ARTS 　(a) Industrial Arts 　(b) Home Economics	} Same as for 7th and 8th grades	4	Required
3. CHORUS OR BAND 　(one year in either) *or* ARTS, CRAFTS, SPEECH 　(approximately 12 weeks in each area)		4 4	Elective Elective
4. ALGEBRA* 　CONSUMER MATHEMATICS 　BASIC BUSINESS	} Choice of one of these	4	Required
5. GENERAL SCIENCE 　TYPING	} One half year in each	4	Required
6. PHYSICAL EDUCATION AND HEALTH		4	Required
7. SPECIAL INTEREST ACTIVITY	} Same as for 7th and 8th grades	1	Required (students elect activity)
8. CLUB AND ASSEMBLY PROGRAM 　(Assemblies every other week; 　class meetings, interest clubs, and 　service clubs meet on alternate weeks)		1	Required

* Only students who rank high in mathematical abilities will be permitted to take algebra. Factors considered before registration for algebra is approved include: achievement and aptitude tests, past performance, teacher and counselor recommendations. Since algebra is also offered in senior high school, students who may need additional drill in fundamentals are requested to register for consumer mathematics in order to acquire these needed skills.

During the ninth grade the student plans his senior high school program with the assistance of his teachers, the school counselor, senior high school counselors, and his parents.

No one in the St. Paul public school system had been aware of the existence of North Central's 1924 program pattern, although Varner had been active in the Association. Apparently the Association's action of 1924 was too far back in time for a chance recall. Nevertheless, the substantive process of North Central's 1924 middle school program is to be found in the program which was evaluated in St. Paul nearly forty years later. The mystique of cultural osmosis employs diverse channels for diffusing social experience. In the case of American middle school experience between two world wars, the principal channel was a handful of Keepers of the Institution.

After Conner had left St. Paul in 1963, he reminisced, "One of the things on which I look back with the greatest degree of satisfaction is that an excellent junior high school program was developed in St. Paul during my tenure."[19] And Conner had solid data of a rigorous evaluation to justify his satisfaction.

Program Evaluation

Limited evaluations of scholastic achievement in American middle schools have been made ever since World War I. But either because of inept methodological procedures or a lack of comprehensiveness, these evaluations have not been commanding.[20] Then, in 1961, the St. Paul Board of Education engaged the Bureau of Field Studies and Surveys of the University of Minnesota to perform a comprehensive evaluation of its middle school program. So far as is known, no other middle school program of a large American city has been as comprehensively evaluated before.

The statistical design of the evaluation was constructed by Robert J. Keller, who in 1964 became Dean of the College of Education, University of Minnesota. William T. Gruhn was brought into the evaluation as the consulting middle school specialist. The following four items explain why the evaluation was requested.[21]

To help clarify the goals and objectives of the new junior high school program in St. Paul. . . .

19 Letter from Forrest E. Conner to author, June 5, 1964.

20 For several of these evaluations see Gruhn and Douglass, *The Modern Junior High School*, pp. 49–52; also, Leonard V. Koos, *The Junior High School*, pp. 88–102.

21 *St. Paul Junior High School Study: A Progress Report and Preliminary Tabular Findings of the St. Paul School Report, Number 25*, Bureau of Field Studies and Surveys, College of Education, University of Minnesota, September 1962, p. 4. Hereafter cited as, *St. Paul Junior High School Study*.

To evaluate rather specifically the way in which the St. Paul junior high school program departs from usual practices. More specifically this involves the four-class-meetings-per-week schedule, seven subject areas, the regularly scheduled club and assembly programs, and the special interest activities in which all students engage. In this instance the St. Paul Public Schools are under obligation to the State Department of Education to appraise the adequacy of instruction under this departure from normal scheduling.

To make an intensive appraisal of a single junior high school as it operates within its given community as a functional unit in the St. Paul School System. . . .

To establish techniques, materials, and practices which might have usefulness in evaluating other junior high schools in St. Paul or elsewhere. . . .

Como Park Junior High School was the "single junior high school" which was selected for the evaluation. According to the evaluation report:[22]

An early decision was reached that the junior high school study be largely concentrated upon Como Park Junior High School. Several factors led to this choice: (1) the program of studies and activities at Como Park well represent the major elements in the new junior high school program which is developing in St. Paul; (2) opening in the fall of 1956, Como Park has been operating long enough to have students who have completed three full years at that junior high school in the 1962 graduating class, principally at Washington High School; and (3) the principal . . . [and] staff were willing to engage in such [a] study; and (4) the accessibility of that school to the University made it a good choice.

The attendance area of Como Park Junior High School includes industrial, railroad, commercial, and residential property. Homes range from the modest and minimal to the upper middle class. Occupational roles of family heads span the continuum of professional and unskilled categories. More, Como Park Junior High School pupils are "a fairly representative cross-section of the general population" in levels of ability. As a group, therefore, the evaluated pupils were "neither more able nor less able than students in other junior high schools across the country."[23] But, as the evaluation revealed, they were *more motivated.*

Five separate instruments were constructed for obtaining judgments

22 *Ibid.,* p. 2.
23 *Ibid.,* p. 13.

from pupils, parents, teachers, and graduates of Como Park Junior High School. However, only scores that have been made by pupils on the *Iowa Tests of General Educational Development* and the *Iowa Tests of Basic Skills* were used to ascertain gains in scholastic achievement. According to the report:[24]

> These tests included information about the achievement of students only in academic subjects. Such information was not available for the ˉachievement of students in art, music, industrial arts, home economics, speech, physical education, and health. Furthermore, information was not available concerning the development of students in citizenship, leadership, and personality qualities, all of which are an important part of the educational program. The scores of students on achievement tests were compared with national norms, and students who spent three years at Como Park Junior High School were compared with those who were there for only one or two years. Numerous analyses were made to identify strengths and weaknesses in the school program.

Usable instruments were returned by 983 pupils in grades 7-8-9, by 747 in grades 10-11-12, and by 665 parents of Como Park Junior High School pupils then enrolled—approximately a 75 percent response from families. Keller recalls, "We used a 'rake' rather than a 'comb' to establish significance for the literally thousands of possibilities for testing by pairs."[25] And then:[26]

> Responses for the several groups or subgroups were translated into comparable percentage form so that differences between groups could be treated to determine their levels of significance. A nomograph developed by Nicholas Fattu was used to determine levels of significance for differences between percentages. This technique took into account the size of samples. The customary one and five percent levels of probability were employed in rejection and acceptance respectively for the null hypothesis.
>
> In an effort to determine level of achievement on standardized tests for comparable groups of students, the mean and standard deviations for the norm groups were used to establish confidence limits within which sample means would be expected to fall based on chance expectation. This generalized approach was substituted for computation of individual tests of significance between norm and sample means.

24 *Ibid.*, p .8.
25 Letter from Robert J. Keller to author, October 27, 1964.
26 *Ibid.*, October 27, 1964.

More than 2,600 respondents, among whom were teachers of Como Park Junior High School, feeder elementary schools, and Washington High School, had each contributed from 70 to better than 300 items of information to the evaluation. Information items were coded and punched on IBM cards. Cross classifications were made to catch differences between grades and between sexes. The evaluation was then reported through 170 tables, graphs, and interpretive commentary. The following are excerpted passages from the report:[27]

The overall finding of this study is the high level of satisfaction generally expressed by parents, students, former students, and teachers on the different aspects of the school's program. Despite the different vantage points from which these individuals looked upon the school —its program of studies, its activities, services, policies, and practices, and the character of its students, teachers, and administrators—the results were positive and favorable. Every effort was made by the survey staff and advisory committees to provide numerous alternatives in the evaluation of the program. Participants were usually offered choices ranging from strong support to positive rejection. They tended to choose or endorse the favorable reactions and to avoid or reject the negative ones. A positive tone to special write-in responses was most evident.

. . . The six general functions previously accepted for St. Paul junior high schools (integration, exploration, guidance, differentiation, socialization, and articulation) seem to be well accepted by faculty members at Como Park, the feeder elementary schools from which students come, and the senior high school they later attend. Furthermore, teachers at all school levels indicated that, in their opinion, these functions are well demonstrated at Como Park Junior High School.

. . . The survey results provide more than adequate evidence that in the academic areas in which achievement tests were given, Como Park students are achieving as well as or better than might be expected on the basis of their ability. The scores of Como Park students in the ten areas covered by the Iowa Tests of Educational Development show that, with class meetings four days per week rather than five, the achievement of these students is as good as or better than that of pupils of comparable ability in other schools in the United States where these tests have been used. Moreover, students at Como Park have the benefit of a richer program because they carry seven subjects, and yet continue to maintain satisfactory achievement in the basic learnings.

[27] *St. Paul Junior High School Study,* pp. 17–19.

The Meaning for Motivation

We are constrained by the rule of parsimony in scholarship to treat results of this evaluation as *partial evidence* only. Conclusive evidence that needed environmental gratifications in American middle schools, where psychosocial orientations are dominant in pursuit of the paramount goal, do not interfere with scholastic achievement will have to await replications of the St. Paul evaluation in other systems. Nevertheless, even by a most parsimonious interpretation of the evaluation, there is substantive significance for middle school process in the St. Paul evaluation which should not be obscured. Performance and achievement are, after all, aspects of one type of behavior in the cognitive domain. The evaluation of Como Park Junior High School is, therefore, also a measure of its capacity to motivate performance and achievement.

Quite apart from demonstrating with the empirical evidence of scores made on standardized tests that local and national norms of scholastic achievement are attainable in the special psychosocial environment of a middle school, this evaluation in St. Paul has also produced evidence of validation for the middle school program which North Central had institutionalized in 1924. For the organization of Como Park Junior High School, as was stated earlier, implements a middle school program which is as close to a modern prototype of North Central's 1924 program for a "Standard Junior High School" as will be found anywhere in the United States. It would seem, therefore, that, at least since 1924, the United States has not been lacking for educative process which is functional for fulfilling the institutional purpose of the American middle school.

Out of 665 responses from Como Park Junior High School parents, 93.4 percent responded: "The parent-teacher conferences help parents understand what is happening at school"; 82.0 percent: "The school program fits my child's abilities and interests"; 77.9 percent: "The activity program helps my child gain confidence . . . "; 70.2 percent: "The activity program helps my child learn how to make better use of . . . free time"; 80.5 percent: "The activity program helps my child make new friends"; 82.6 percent: "The activity program helps my child to learn how to work with others"; and so on.[28]

Gains in poise and self-confidence, mastering the skill of using leisure time constructively, an ability to cultivate qualitative human relations—

[28] *Ibid.*, Tables 5.01, 5.02, 5.03.

what Erich Fromm calls "the art of loving"—and the like, are social skills which are not measured by standardized tests of scholastic achievement. But in St. Paul, these are apparently *regular dividends* of the middle school program. In a society wherein problems of leisure time, mental health, and human relations have turned into stubborn social ills, such dividends have to be weighted as very *practical* indeed. But this is not all.

The evaluation of Como Park Junior High School does more than allay apprehensions of the special psychosocial environment in which scholastic skills are taught in a middle school. Empirical evidence has been uncovered by the evaluation which supports a claim that early adolescents are significantly *more responsive* to scholastic motivation in the special psychological environment of a middle school than they would be in the environment of an elementary school or high school.

The graded system in American public schools assumes that children of normal intelligence will grow in mental development over the years at an ascending rate. Each grade builds upon the preceding grade. Pupils are expected to attain higher levels of mental growth in correspondence with chronological age.

Cross-sectional studies of achievement at different school age seem to confirm the general correctness of the assumption behind the graded system, up to about age twelve. Longitudinal studies of normal groups, such as the Harvard Growth Study of 1922 to 1934, have revealed that the line of mental growth, when it is graphed, is not constant in the upward climb. Gerald T. Kowitz and Charles M. Armstrong have discovered, for example, that in the population of pupils they studied the middle school period "was generally a low point in the patterns of academic development." They go on to say, however, that "test results suggest that the depression is momentary." Pupils seem to catch up later in the high school.[29] And then also, a reanalysis of the Harvard Growth Study data disclosed a "gap between the end of the childhood cycle of mental growth and the beginning of the adolescent cycle. . . ."[30]

Ethel L. Cornell and Charles M. Armstrong, the investigators who performed the reanalysis, found that many pupils in the Harvard

29 Gerald T. Kowitz and Charles M. Armstrong, "Patterns of Academic Development," *Journal of Educational Measurement,* Vol. 2, December, 1965, p. 208.

30 Ethel L. Cornell and Charles H. Armstrong, "Forms of Mental Growth Revealed by Reanalysis of the Harvard Growth Data," *Child Development,* Vol. 26, September 1955, p. 200.

Growth Study showed "little or no growth in mental age" during two or three years before age sixteen.[31]   Discovery of this phenomenon led them to speculate:[32]

> The question of *whether the gap between the end of the childhood cycle of mental growth and the beginning of the adolescent cycle,* marked by a period of no mental growth in early adolescence, . . . *is an inherent phenomenon of certain patterns of mental growth or is the result of the kind of school curriculum provided should . . . be further explored.*   In either case it should have a profound influence upon our thinking about the needs of young adolescents.   If it is an inherent phenomenon of growth, then those who develop according to patterns of this type must undergo a period of exceptional stress and strain under a school program set up on the theory of increasing learning difficulty from year to year during this period.   Such an interpretation might explain some of the adolescent breakdowns which appear to be increasing in frequency at the same time that the holding power of the high school is also increasing.   If it is not an inherent phenomenon of growth but is the result of certain types of experience, then the school program for at least half of the school population does not provide appropriate experience.

Two items in the evaluation of Como Park Junior High School suggest that "the gap between the end of the childhood cycle of mental growth and the beginning of the adolescent cycle" *is not* "an inherent phenomenon of certain patterns of mental growth."   The evaluation report states: "Senior high school students who spent three years at Como Park Junior High School seem to perform better on achievement tests than those who spent only a year or two there or whose previous education was secured in other schools."[33]   More significant, however, is the disclosure of a *similar pattern* of scholastic achievement within the ninth grade of Como Park Junior High School.

The ninth grade which was evaluated consisted of 421 pupils.   A scholastic evaluation was made of the entire group and of the following subgroups: those who were in the Como Park Junior High School program for three years and those who were in the program from one to two years only.   Although the *median intelligence quotient* on the Otis

31 *Ibid.*, p. 202.   A gap has been found to occur in some individual cases even before early adolescence, but the reference to a gap in this study relates to a significantly large segment of the group.
32 *Ibid.*, pp. 200–01.
33 *St. Paul Junior High School Study,* p. 20.

Gamma for the two subgroups was almost identical, 105 and 102, the *median composite score* of tests I-VIII on *The Iowa Tests of Educational Development* was 62 for the three-year subgroup and 53 for the other. Even more pronounced was the gap on Test IX, *Use of Sources.* The *median score* for the three-year subgroup was 65, and 50 for the other.[34]

In an age when the more valid test of scholastic development turns on the skill of self-learning beyond the period of formal education, the level of achievement which separates the three-year subgroup from the other subgroup on Test IX, *Use of Resources,* is of important social significance.

But precisely because there is such important significance in the St. Paul evaluation, both for American society and its systems of education, a latent, but higher-level, meaning in the evaluation of Como Park Junior High School should not be overlooked. From the larger cultural perspective, even more important than results of the evaluation is the imperative of adapting middle school programs to social conditions of the post-Sputnik world. Como Park Junior High School, after all, produced its impressive output with a structure and process which had been little modified since it was patterned in 1924. Is it unreasonable to assume that innovative modifications in middle school structure and process at this time will enhance the unit's potential for even larger quantities of qualitative output? Latent in St. Paul's evaluation is, therefore, the problem of obsolescence.

Of course, the intensive evaluation of Como Park Junior High School is unique in American middle school experience. Indeed, it is for this reason that so much has been shown of it here. It would be better to have many such evaluations for assessing outputs of the American middle school. But in studies of organizational experience, significance is sometimes gleaned from the unique. Important insights into the political democracy of union organizations have been gleaned, for example, from a study of the International Typographical Union. This union is the only International in the United States which has a two-party system built into its organizational pattern and is, therefore, unique.[35]

[34] *Ibid.;* medians are estimated from percentile norms shown in Figures 6.01, 6.15, and 6.16.

[35] For the organizational study of this union, and the significance of its unique features see Seymour M. Lipset, Martin A. Trow, and James S. Coleman, *Union Democracy* (New York: The Free Press, 1956).

Como Park Junior High School has demonstrated with rigorously evaluated experience that the special school organization for early adolescents can hold its own in *gross scholastic achievement,* as measured by national norms, in the course of performing its *differentiated function* within the larger school system. Moreover, its program seems to articulate successfully with the elementary school and the high school. Discontinuity, therefore, is not a built-in condition of this program. It was Philip W. L. Cox, another Keeper of the Institution, and Professor of Secondary Education at New York University from 1923 to 1949, who wrote in 1926:[36]

> It is not that pupils from vital junior high schools know more or can do more than pupils from conventional schools—though I am sure that they do and can; the important point is that they desire to do more, to know more, to be more, and *that they feel adequate* to fulfill these desires.

The evaluated results of middle school education in St. Paul give such claims of motivation potential in the American middle school a credible ring. Yet despite the many verified and unverified claims that have been made for the social good of this unit of public school organization since its inception, the American middle school—its structure, process, and clientele—still has to beggar for attention in colleges of education.

Wattenberg, who has given much serious thought to middle school education, sees two paradoxical elements in this predicament of the American middle school:[37]

> First, its clientele is composed of so bewildering an assortment of young people at crucial turning points in their lives as to defy orderly description. Second, at colleges of education there is a tendency to make believe that there is no such institution [as a middle school]: schools are considered either elementary or secondary; young people, either are children or adolescents.

Such references to the enigma of middle school education in the United States have also a touch of poignancy about them. It has been

---

36 Philip W. L. Cox, "Problems of College Entrance Arising from the Development of the Junior High School," *NCA Quarterly,* Vol. I, December 1926, p. 296. Cox, it will be recalled from Chapter 11 was also a onetime Principal of Ben Blewett Junior High School in St. Louis, Missouri.
37 William W. Wattenberg, "The Junior High School—A Psychologist's View," *The Bulletin,* NASSP, Vol. 49, April 1965, p. 34. Copyright 1965, Washington D.C. Reprinted by permission from the Bulletin of NASSP.

known for a long time now that there is *something special* about youth in American society at the "pivotal psychological" period of early adolescence. The "gap between the end of the childhood cycle of mental growth and the beginning of the adolescent," which was discovered in a significant number of cases by the reassessment of Harvard Growth Data, is similar to phenomena which have been observed in early adolescent development at the Fels Research Institute, the Adolescent Growth Study at the University of California, Berkeley, and elsewhere.[38]

But schools of education have paid scant attention to these clues of a special condition at early adolescence and have, therefore, neglected middle school education. But early adolescents, like *all pupil clients* of a school organization who require differentiated treatment in the process of education, are entitled to have their *special condition* defined and known. A definition of the special condition of early adolescents in American society is, therefore, the subject of the next chapter.

[38] *Ibid.,* pp. 40–41.

13

ADOLESCENCE IN AMERICAN SOCIETY

The legend of Antaeus has fascinated mankind through the ages. Antaeus, so Greek mythology has it, was the giant son of Poseidon. He was of great strength and he was indestructible. His secret? Antaeus drew his strength from earth, Gaea, his mother. So long as his feet touched earth, Antaeus could not be overcome. Then one day, Hercules lifted Antaeus into the air and destroyed him.

Roots of an educational system, like those of Antaeus, draw strength from their source of origin. Detached from life in the society, their source of origin, they wane and their yield of social good diminishes. Emile Durkheim had just this axiom of culture in mind when he lectured at the Sorbonne that each society has its own educational system "as it has its own moral, religious, economic system, etc." Durkheim merely transmitted to students what has been axiomatic in education from the time of ancient Greece.[1]

Culture, as it is defined by anthropologists, includes all material and nonmaterial things which are used directly or indirectly to satisfy

[1] See George S. Counts, *The Social Foundations of Education* (New York: Charles Scribner's Sons, 1934), p. 1.

human needs in a society. Customs, habits of body and mind, commodities, instruments, modes in the social division of labor, and so forth are, therefore, parts of a society's cultural complex. Institutions are cultural patterns that have acquired a considerable degree of permanence.

Culture, then, is the way of life in a society. In its diverse structures and processes are imbedded what Clyde Kluckhohn referred to as "its own assumptions about the ends and purposes of human existence." It summarizes behavioral phenomena which have evolved in the society and which have been transmitted from generation to generation. It is absorbed, or internalized, by members of society either through habituation or formal education. Anthropologists think of this as *enculturation*. In modern Western societies especially, because their cultural patterns have become enormously complex, formal schooling is the dominant mode of learning the culture. However, learning the ways of its life style begins in every society with the pattern of childrearing in the family.[2]

Patterns of childrearing are themselves projections of culture. Comparative anthropological studies have shown that each society has its own institutionalized pattern which is followed from the instant of birth. In the United States, as an example, it is estimated that 70 percent of babies are born in the sheltered environment of hospitals, and even mothers don't get a good look at the baby until the anesthesia wears off, whereas the new baby in New Guinea is on view to adults, children, and even household animals, within minutes after birth.[3]

The uncomplicated pattern of childrearing in primitive societies is a cultural manifestation of a simple social structure just as the complicated pattern of childrearing in advanced societies is a cultural manifestation of a complex social structure. Relative uniformity which anthropologists have observed *within* childrearing patterns of primitive

[2] Footnote 3 of Chapter 2 has already cited several sources which deal with aspects of culture. The sophistication of anthropology since the turn of the century is reflected in the specialization of its modern-day research and literature. There are now specialists in social anthropology, cultural anthropology, physical anthropology, and even psychological anthropology. In a word, the anthropological literature is vast. For representative introductions to studies of culture see Bronislaw Malinowski, *The Dynamics of Culture Change* (New Haven, Conn.: Yale University Press, 1945); Ashley Montague, *Man's Most Dangerous Myth* (New York: Harper and Bros., 1952); George D. Spindler, *Education and Culture* (New York: Holt, Rinehart and Winston, 1963); and A. F. C. Wallace, *Culture and Personality* (New York: Random House, 1961).

[3] L. Joseph Stone and Joseph Church, *Childhood and Adolescence* (New York: Random House, 1957), p. 2. Copyright Random House, Inc.

cultures is contrasted in advanced cultures by a diversity which reflects the heterogeneity of modern social structures. Middle-class mothers, again in the United States, practice considerably less breast feeding than do lower-class mothers. Scheduled feeding is more in keeping with the orderly routine of middle-class existence than is feeding on demand. Babies of middle-class families are weaned earlier than are those of lower-class families.[4]

Illustrations *ad infinitum* can be invoked to demonstrate that the pattern of childrearing in a given society is culturally determined. It is neither a biological inheritance nor a universal absolute. Adolescence is in the same way a *cultural invention*. The social role of adolescent projects a cultural condition in the role structure of a society at a given period of its history.

As an illustration: Shakespeare defined the seven ages of man without any mention of adolescence. The social role of teenager was unknown to his culture. Children assumed adult roles at fourteen or fifteen as they became biologically capable of parenthood. In the cultural idiom of today, Romeo's Juliet would be defined as an adolescent. Social roles, therefore, are projections of cultural conditions in a society.

Cultural conditions also account for the fact that American school systems had no patterned middle schools before the twentieth century. Yet the biological and physiological course of human development was much the same in the nineteenth century as it is now. Indeed, with due allowances for variations caused by climate and food, biological and physiological attributes of human development are the same everywhere in the world, in Samoa and New Guinea as well as the United States. But neither Samoa nor New Guinea even now require the protective intervention of a social agency to shield early adolescent youth from the pressures of culture, whereas the United States of the twentieth century does. Obviously, an explanation for this has to be sought within the structure of American society. As a point of departure, the address of Superintendent J. H. Francis of Los Angeles before the An-

---

[4] These facts are so well established in the literature of anthropology and child development that documentation of them is almost superfluous. For illustrative references, however, see John M. Whiting and Irvin L. Child, *Child Training and Personality: A Cross-Cultural Survey* (New Haven, Conn.: Yale University Press, 1953); Victor Barnouw, *Culture and Personality* (Homewood, Ill.: Dorsey Press, 1963); Allison Davis and Robert J. Havighurst, "Social Class and Color Differences in Child Rearing," in Clyde Kluckhohn, Henry A. Murray, and David M. Schneider (eds.), *Personality in Nature, Society, and Culture* (New York: Alfred A. Knopf, 1953); and Allison Davis, "American Status Systems and the Socialization of the Child," in the foregoing work.

nual Meeting of the NEA of 1912 will serve well. It is the same address to which a reference was made in Chapter 1.

Culture and Early Adolescence

Francis, in defense of the new American middle school, said at the time: "The three divisions of the school system are physiologically, psychologically, sociologically, and logically correct." Unfortunately, Francis neglected to leave for posterity an explanation of what he meant by "logically correct." What could Francis have had in mind? Could he possibly have meant *rationalistically* or *administratively* "correct"?

Let us posit the following conjecture: Francis had made his way to a position in 1912 which held that some rationale in school administration, supported by the sciences of physiology, psychology, and sociology, justified the decision to establish a middle school division in public school systems. In a test of validity, let us deal first with the sociological variable in the hypothesis.

Modern American society is highly industrialized, urban, mobile, pluralistic, and it is still rapidly developing. The economic aspect of this society evolved in a matrix of free enterprise. It is a society of large-scale organizations: medicine, government, industry and business, education, national defense, penology, and so forth. All sciences, but more especially, the physical and biological sciences, have recorded spectacular advances since the turn of the century, and these have affected every sector of American society.

The United States is an open society. Mobility of persons, in pursuit of a shift in either social or economic status, is, in a legal sense, unrestricted. It is a society which, since the 1880's, has assimilated successfully millions of immigrants who have come from a diversity of cultures.

But it is also a society of continuing rapid change in which problems of personal choice in the selection of an occupational role have been getting increasingly complex. For youth especially, these conditions of contemporary society combine to generate "many elements of strain" which, according to Parsons, "may be considered normal for this type of society."[5] He explains:

[5] Parsons, "Youth in American Society," pp. 238–39, 254, by permission of Houghton Mifflin Company. Copyright © 1964 by the National Vocational Guidance Assoc., a Division of the American Personnel and Guidance Assoc. All of this essay by Parsons is of value for sociological insights into those problems of youth in contemporary American

There seems to be an important reason why this source of strain and disturbance bears rather more heavily on the younger generation than on others: The major agents for initiating processes of change lie in other sectors of the society—above all, in large-scale organization, in the developments of science and technology, in the higher political processes, and in the higher ranges of culture. Their impact tends to spread, and there is a time lag in change between the locations of primary change and the other parts of the social structure.

Then Parsons goes on to say:[6]

> . . . If we are right in thinking that special pressures operate on the younger generation relative to the general pressures exerted by social change, there are factors on the other side of the relationship which make for special sensitivity in youth. The residue of early dependency . . . constitutes one such factor. In addition, the impact on youth of the general process of social differentiation makes for greater differences between their position and that of both children and adults than is true in less differentiated societies. Compared to our own past or to most other societies, there is a more pronounced and increasingly long segregation of the younger groups, centered above all on the system of formal education.[6]

The "many elements of strain" which bear upon youth in contemporary American society are, in Parsons' view, a product of cultural conditions. We shall mark later how these culturally induced strains combine at early adolescence with the stress of rapid physiological change. At this point, however, still another Parsonian observation of youth in American society is important:[7]

> Broadly speaking, youth in a developing society of the American type, in its deepest values and commitments, is likely to be favorable to the activist side. It is inculcated with the major values of the society and strongly impressed with the importance of its future responsibilities.

The dominant pattern which is formed by "the major values" of American society is defined by Parsons, it will be recalled from Chapter 4, as one of instrumental activism. Moreover, instrumental activism in

---

society which are indigenous and which, therefore, have to be regarded as normative in societies of the American type. See also D. C. McClelland, *The Achieving Society* (Princeton, N.J.: D. Van Nostrand Co., 1961); and S. N. Eisenstadt, *From Generation to Generation* (New York: The Free Press, 1956).

6 Parsons, "Youth in American Society," pp. 247–48.

7 *Ibid.*, p. 254.

the American case "implies that for cultural reasons the society is oriented to mastery of the environment, but it is at the same time individualistic in a very important sense." The American value system impresses upon members of society a "primary obligation" to make the most of personal opportunities, not out of a motivation to gratify "hedonistic wants," but rather "to make a maximal contribution to the implementation of the values by helping to make it in the relevant sense *a better society*."[8] The idealism which defines the legitimate thrust of American individualism is not of the kind that is spelled out in *What Makes Sammy Run*, but of the brand which is portrayed in *The Fountainhead*.

This is why Parsons holds that youth in American society "is likely to be favorable to the activist side." Activism and individual responsibility for making the most of one's opportunities "is inculcated with the major values" from the earliest stages of socialization. Even in the early phases of childrearing, as we have already noted before, there is a tendency in American society to inculcate independence and self-responsibility. Youth is very early in the socialization process habituated to the esteem which American culture attaches to self-initiative and achievement: the ethos of effort optimism!

Later, beginning at age six, what has been learned of the culture through habituation is reinforced and continued by formal education. The value pattern of society is impressed upon the school's own value system. Society's dominant value orientations are institutionalized in its role structure. For the source of educational life, following Durkheim again, is the society. "Educational practices," he lectured students, "are not phenomena that are isolated from one another." Behavior that is esteemed and rewarded in society is also esteemed and rewarded in the schoolhouse. So does culture, in one of many ways, condition social reflexes and shape personality.

A remarkably clear glimpse of this phenomenon of culture was captured in a study of elementary schools in five school districts of a west coast state. Children in these schools came from neighborhoods which "ranged from a relatively low socio-economic area to one of the most select residential districts in the entire geographic area."[9] The children of one school were largely Mexican-American. But cues of the

---

8 The reader's return to the section in Chapter 4 where Parsons' discussion of the American value pattern is given will facilitate recall of Parsons' main points.

9 Marie M. Hughes and associates, *A Research Report: Development of the Means for the Assessment of the Quality of Teaching in Elementary Schools* (University of Utah, 1959), p. 21.

dominant culture were transmitted in the classroom to all alike. The investigators reported:[10]

> A basic conclusion to be drawn from our study is that the relationship of teacher to child reflects to a marked degree the adult-child relationship of our culture. There are common expectations of how a teacher performs the teaching role. Contrary to opinions articulated by a few, the classrooms are distinctly controlled by the teacher; there is drill; there is a tight holding of the child to completion of his work; there is pressure on the child for him to learn to read and to meet other standards for his grade.

Cues of the culture, however, are not always clear to youth, and this leads to confusion and the distress of value dissonance. Honesty is taught in the school as a cherished virtue, yet *stealing a base* is applauded by thousands of adults at a baseball game. Violence is abhorred, but a good football game or boxing match is hardly possible without violence. The school prohibits smoking, but advertising budgets in the millions of dollars encourage it. Schools teach social democracy and the world of adults discriminates. Good government is extolled in schools, but the intellectual in the real world of politics is an *egghead*. Teachers are to be respected because, like parents, they guide one's path to the good life, but in society's reward system undertakers, and not teachers, drive Cadillacs. Such examples can go on and on.

Moreover, *within patterns of socialization,* American youth encounters paradoxical adult expectations. During the pliable years of latency, from the age of six to twelve, relationships with adults are good. Children of these years covet the approbation of adult authority figures; parents, teachers, spiritual leaders, and so forth, and are eager, therefore, to demonstrate that sanctioned values have been internalized and the rewards of approbation have been earned. But when these same children approach the pubertal period, and are ready to move out of their well-ordered environment to explore on their own the bewildering world of adults with values they have been taught, they soon discover a host of frustrating cultural restraints. They discover, for one thing, that conditions of culture and parental authority combine to limit

---

10 *Ibid.,* p. 299. Helen Heffernan, Chief of Elementary Education in the California State Department of Education, reported to the Eleventh Annual Institute in Curriculum and Supervision in Minneapolis that "children literally are killing themselves for good grades in school." Forty-one childhood suicides in New Jersey between 1960–1963 were traced directly, according to Heffernan, to "pressure to achieve academic success." Moreover, she informed her audience that "suicide is the sixth leading cause of death among children in California." Minneapolis *Tribune,* November 17, 1964.

severely the exercise of independence which they have been taught in childhood. Parental control which had been psychologically welcome in childhood and latency is now, in early adolescence, uncomfortably binding. As if this alone were not enough, their innocent idealism is then further assaulted by realties of social, economic, and biological adult existence in American society which run counter in many respects to values young adolescents have internalized.

Frustrations and disillusionment generate psychological strain. Psychological strain is compounded for early adolescents by the first realization that adult expectations of achievement are difficult to fulfill in a highly differentiated society whose choicest rewards go to those who have mastered some màrketable specialization.

Nonetheless, they are surrounded by cultural reminders of the critical decisions they must soon make about the future. At the very time when a "physiological revolution" is afflicting them with an assortment of inner turmoil and self-doubt, pressures of culture force them to begin to think about a future role in a complex society.[11] They have to begin speculating about the first tentative commitments to some future adult role at a time when their psychological security has been weakened by a sudden onset of rapid physiological change. Not yet competent to exercise sound judgment, confused by value conflict all around them, the potential for harm can be great without the protective intervention of some agency at this point of their socialization. The middle school is the primary social agency which performs this protective function in American society.

The physiological revolution at early adolescence is universal, but the manner in which the behavioral response to it is tolerated by different cultures is not. Americans are culturally conditioned to what Parsons, in his conceptualization of pattern variables, calls "affective neutrality." The cultural *Geist,* or existential mood, of the American social system has been strongly influenced by ascetic values of the Puritan fathers. Their commitment to asceticism, to be sure, was articulated first through sacred patterns. But in mundane pursuits, their asceticism was also articulated through affectively neutral secular patterns.

Affective neutrality in the social environment of the United States has been functional for its development from a frontier society to its present industrial might. The achievement drive of dominant Ameri-

---

11 The reference to a "physiological revolution" is from Erik H. Erikson, *Childhood and Society* (New York: W. W. Norton and Co., 1963), p. 261.

can values is a cultural thrust which in a climate of affective neutrality can run its course with least resistance. Norms of affective neutrality, on the other hand, have also been a source of social problems in the American social system.

Many of these problems sprang out of value conflict. The pluralization of American society was intensified in the late 1840's by the first wave of German immigrants. These were later followed by waves of Italian, Russian, and other East European nationals. Some values which these immigrants brought with their cultural baggage did not mix well with the affective neutrality of dominant native patterns. In the interplay of values, social conflict resulted. A remarkably clear historical illustration of this phenomenon is to be found in the development of Newark, New Jersey.

Newark was the last theocracy which Puritan fathers founded in the new world. A band of Puritans from the Connecticut River Valley established the community in 1666. Until the 1840's, it remained little more than a village, peopled for the most part by descendants of original settlers. Beginning in the 1840's, however, it became a haven for thousands of European immigrants who were drawn there by wage-earning opportunities. The first of these newcomers were Germans.

By 1870, German-Americans were well entrenched in the economy of Newark, either as wage earners or as factory owners. They published a German newspaper, and they were a power in clubs of the Republican Party. The instrumental activism of the American value pattern complemented their own values, but not entirely.

German esteem of music, dancing, and beer was exhibited through expressive behavior in the community which encountered native antipathy. The high-level of asceticism in the dominant community climate was inhospitable to the affective patterns of Germanic culture. As a result, mutual social aloofness between these two cultures erupted eventually into open conflict when Germanic concepts of Sabbath observance clashed head on with native concepts. A Sunday *Saengerfest* in the German community was denounced by Puritan-oriented Sabbatarians as clear proof of the presence in Newark of "a great menacing, living, curse." A leading churchman thundered: "The breach [of the Sabbath] was too extensive and influential to pass unnoticed by any clear-eyed, single-hearted, 'watchman' on the wall of Zion."[12]

---

[12] For a full account of this episode of culture conflict in the United States see Samuel H. Popper, "New Tensions in Old Newark," *Proceedings of the New Jersey Historical Society*, Vol. LXX, April 1952.

Social problems of another kind, however, have sprung out of the conflict between affectively neutral social patterns in the United States and human gratificational needs. And a singular instance of such a social problem is the early adolescent in the pattern of formal education.

Psychological strains which follow from the physiological revolution at early adolescence require expressive adjustments which are incompatible with patterns of affective neutrality. At a time when the young adolescent craves sleep and more sleep to allay the fatigue of rapid physiological change, even the most tenderhearted family will roust him to make an eight o'clock class. Expressive adjustments which young adolescents require as motivational stimuli for satisfying cultural expectations have to be provided, therefore, within a relational system where a dominance of expressive symbolism is normative. In the protective environment of a middle school, early adolescents can explore and continue to learn the culture in a network of expressive relations.

Studies of adolescent behavior in other cultural systems have demonstrated that cultural variables do account for differences in the behavioral response to adolescence. This theme will be enlarged later in the discussion where the psychological response to the physiological revolution at the onset of adolescence is treated. But several brief cross-cultural references are in place at this point.

A study of suburban Montreal has revealed a community in which the quality of interactions within the nuclear family serve to minimize the psychological trauma of early adolescent development.[13] A comparative study of youth in the United States and China has also shown that cultural patterns in these two countries account for differences in the behavior of adolescents.[14] Then there is Margaret Mead's study of adolescence in *Coming of Age in Samoa.*

"Coming of age in Samoa" is a stage of human development which, apart from certain rites of passage, requires no special attention in Samoan society. However, none of the diversity and heterogeneity which is a marked characteristic of American society is known there. Life in Samoa, in contrast to our own, is simple and homogeneous. Against these contrasts, Mead speculated why it is that "coming of age"

---

13 Frederick Elkin and William A. Westley, "The Myth of Adolescent Culture," *American Sociological Review,* Vol. 20, October 1955.

14 See Francis L. K. Hsu *et al.,* "Culture Pattern and Adolescent Behavior," in Robert E. Grinder (ed.), *Studies in Adolescence* (New York: The Macmillan Company, 1952).

in modern America is fraught with deep psychological strain, whereas in Samoa the onset of adolescence is relatively placid and free of anxieties.

At the heart of the matter, Mead concluded, is the value system of Samoan society and its implementing agencies. Agencies of socialization in Samoa; that is, education, the family, rituals, taboos, the village, and so on, combine in support of "attitudes toward life" that would be repugnant to the American value pattern. The casualness of the Samoan life style, Mead has noted, is esteemed as a *social value* and has, therefore, been institutionalized in patterns of childrearing, family relationships, sexual behavior, attitudes toward birth and death, the social division of labor, and so forth.

American society, on the other hand, is pronouncedly heterogeneous. Subgroups of an ethnic, racial, or religious character abound in large numbers, each with its own subculture. However, regulative, or ascriptive, systemic patterns in American society are supportive of *the dominant culture*. One is expected to be a success in American society—to achieve, to compete, to be aggressive—and the earlier in life one makes choices about the future the better.

These, then, are the more salient cultural conditions in American life which exacerbate the psychological response to the coming of age in the United States. The physiological revolution of adolescence in both Samoa and the United States is natural. American society, however, is constrained to intervene with a protective agency in socialization at the onset of adolescence, whereas Samoan society is not.[15] Erikson has expressed this cultural imperative in a concise context when he wrote, "We have learned not to stunt the child's growing body with child labor, we must now learn not to break his spirit by making him the victim of our anxieties."[16]

Superintendent J. H. Francis, so it would seem, had sensed correctly the social implications of early adolescence in American culture. Institutionalizing the early adolescent role in the social system of the public school seemed to him, from an institutional point of view, the logical course to follow. Moreover, as the following overview of the physiological revolution will show, the rationality of his course was indeed sustained by physiological facts of early adolescence.

[15] All references to Samoan society are from Margaret Mead, *Coming of Age in Samoa* (New York: The New American Library, 1963), especially Chapters 13 and 14.

[16] Erik H. Erikson, "Growth and Crises of the 'Healthy Personality,'" in Clyde Kluckhohn, Henry A. Murray, and David M. Schneider, *Personality in Nature, Society, and Culture* (New York: Alfred A. Knopf, 1953), p. 224.

The Physiological Revolution

L. Joseph Stone and Joseph Church, specialists in child development, have written:[17]

> By the end of the school years, the child has found a way of life that is essentially satisfactory. And then, with the coming of adolescence, he discovers that he has it all to do over again. He stops being a child (although he does not wholly want to) and is not yet an adult (although he may think that he is). Adolescence, it appears, is a way station in development, neither this nor that, but something of both.

If the early adolescent is "neither this nor that," as Stone and Church have indicated, then how is American society to deal with him? Soon after the onset of adolescence, as Crampton's table in Chapter 9 shows, some adolescents are already sexually mature and most of them become sexually mature by the time they reach age fifteen. Yet sanctioned sexual activity has to be deferred in American society until marriage. This, however, is but one aspect of a larger social problem. Sexual maturity, in the sense of becoming capable of procreation, is preceded in adolescence by all other maturation leading to adulthood. But in the gap of years between the onset of adolescence and adulthood, the period of early adolescence is the most difficult to endure both by the individual and by society.

The central social problem which confronts the early adolescent is finding answers to such questions as "Who am I?", "What is happening to me?", and "What will become of me in this complex and bewildering society?" Society, on the other hand, is also confronted with a problem. At this stage in the socialization process, what demands can be made of early adolescents? What shall be the norms of expectation? Dominant cultural patterns in American society are oriented toward activism, achievement, and responsible individualism, but early adolescents do not seem capable of conforming to these norms.

Mead, as was indicated before, has given much attention to cultural phenomena of adolescence in her anthropological studies. Of early adolescence in the United States, she stated before the 1963 First Annual Indiana State College Conference on the Junior High School:[18]

---

[17] Stone and Church, *Children and Adolescence*, p. 268. Permission of Random House, Inc. Copyright Random House, Inc.

[18] Mead, "The Early Adolescent in Today's American Culture," p. 5. The reader will recall Mead's earlier comment in Chapter 3 which was cited by footnote 8.

The main task of this period, is related to the physical changes when one shifts from being a child, through puberty, into an at least sexually mature being, not a psychologically mature or sociologically mature, but sexually mature being. This means that with the tremendous number of changes which are going on in the human body, the thing that children need most is a chance to get used to themselves—to their own bodies—to the fact that when they reach here it hits there and a glass of milk gets upset on the other side of the table, bodies that they don't know yet are theirs. The growth spurt comes on them very suddenly. They need time to get used to it and they need time to sleep and they need freedom from pressure—freedom from choosing their careers, freedom from being told that if they don't pass this exam they won't ever get anywhere.

When Mead insists that what young adolescents "need most is a chance to get used to themselves—to their own bodies," she echoes a dominant theme in the modern scientific literature on early adolescence. The finding-of-self theme is as a leitmotif in the literature which deals with the meaning of adolescence.

Another dominant theme in the modern literature on adolescence is a general agreement upon the urgency for protective mediation between the natural stress and strain of early adolescence and pressures of the achievement-oriented American culture. Chapter 3 has already registered Mead's view of the American middle school as an implementing social agency which was "set up to protect young adolescents. . . ." One of the mediating functions of the middle school, as Mead sees it, is to protect early adolescents from social embarrassment during a period when they are most vulnerable to embarrassments; embarrassments which are capable of leaving lasting psychological scars upon the human personality.

Early adolescence has been defined by humorists as the period in a child's life when parents begin to be most difficult, when boys discover girls and girls discover they have been discovered. It is the "awkward age," the "terrible teens," the age when cherubic soprano voices of boys take on some of the timbre of a baritone. These are some of the surface indications that the pea-sized pituitary gland, or master gland, at the underside of the brain has triggered puberty. Nature has begun the cycle which will change boys and girls into men and women.

Profound physiological changes that occur during the circumpubertal years have been scientifically observed and reported in a voluminous literature and, therefore, no more than some of the more general characteristics need to be reviewed here. However, it is most important to keep in mind that the *entire structure* of the organism is affected by these changes. There may be variations in time when these changes will occur in each sex, but the sequential order of the occurrence is more or less constant in both sexes.

Boys will show a spurt in height between twelve and thirteen, while girls will begin rapid develoment one to two years earlier. Some boys will shoot up as much as six inches in one year. The rate of growth will decelerate, however, after the onset of puberty. It has been established by medical science that the initial growth spurt is a response to the endocrine regulation of genital structure and function. There is cause for embarrassment during this spurt because of the disproportionate growth of extremities. A sudden acquisition of long legs, long arms, and large feet is often accompanied by the social ineptness to which Mead has alluded.

Patterns of coordination are further disturbed by the uneven growth of bone and muscle structure. Muscle cramp is not unusual when bone enlargement precedes the growth of adhering muscle. The general "asynchrony"—the uneven growth rate of organs, extremities, bone and muscle structure—which characterizes the onset of adolescence also accounts for changes in the contour of the body and in facial proportions. Secondary sex characteristics appear in the form of enlarged breasts, pubic hair, deposits of subcutaneous fat, enlarged testes and scrotum, and others.

Along with the sudden growth spurt comes an increased craving for food intake and sporadic explosions of muscular energy in the form of hypermobility. Hypermobility and the growth spurt then combine to cause frequent periods of fatigue. Indeed, rapid growth, abundance of muscular energy, hypermobility, and fatigue are elements of the syndrome that is responsible for the "sleep and sleep" early adolescents seem to require and to which Mead referred.

Nature jolts the child out of the calm and contentment of latency and hurls him mercilessly into the turmoil of early adolescence. The body which has been familiar for years suddenly becomes a stranger and a source of deep personal anxiety.

A quickened heartbeat, shortness of breath, an increase of systolic blood pressure, oily secretions from sebaceous glands, resulting susceptibility to acne and blackheads, strong body odors brought on by more active sweat glands and the altered composition of sweat—and in girls also by menstruation—are some of the new conditions of existence which are known to stampede emerging adolescents to inner anxiety, self-doubt, and a "negative body image."[19]

And with it all, there is an acceleration of body stress. The stress factor is often overlooked in the physiological revolution of early adolescence because it cannot itself be perceived. It is a sort of index to the wear-and-tear effect of changes in the body. As one writer has put it, stress is the "speedometer of life."[20] A speedometer reading at early adolescence will show that the tempo of wear and tear in the body is fast, a physiological fact of deep sociological significance in American society.

For the physiological turbulence of early adolescence which has been sketched descriptively is more or less the same in all cultures. However, not all cultures are constrained to *invent* a social mechanism in order to give it sanctioned expression. Some societies, Samoa for one, have cultural patterns which provide normative channels for the acting-out of early adolescent turbulence. But in the developing urban-industrial culture of twentieth-century America, neither the family nor other established socializing agencies seemed capable of this function.

It was not always so in the United States. A host of social problems which were unknown before the Civil War were seeded and came to fruition in the urban-industrial milieu of the postwar period. The difficult social response to the onset of adolescence, relatively placid in the well-ordered society of the nineteenth century, was one of them. Once it was recognized as a social problem, American society turned to

[19] William A. Schonfeld, "Body Image Disturbances in Adolescents with Inappropriate Sexual Development," *American Journal of Orthopsychiatry*, Vol. XXXIV, September 1961; Douglas Hubble, "The Problems of Puberty," *British Medical Journal*, No. 5064, January 1958; Beverly Rutherford, "Junior High School Girls and the Feminine Role," *The Clearing House*, Vol. 35, March 1961; Margaret Silver Faust, "Developmental Maturity As a Determinant in Prestige of Adolescent Girls," *Child Development*, Vol. 31, March 1960; Elizabeth Lee Vincent, "Physical and Psychological Aspects of Puberty and Adolescence," *Journal of the National Association of Deans of Women*, Vol. 19, October 1955. Beyond a voluminous periodical literature on early adolescence, there has been published an almost equally voluminous book literature. The following are representative: Caroline B. Zachry and Margaret Lighty, *Emotion and Conduct in Adolescence* (New York: Appleton-Century-Crofts, 1940); William W. Wattenberg, *The Adolescent Years* (New York: Harcourt, Brace and Co., 1955), especially the section on "Pre-Adolescence"; Mary Jane Loomis, *The Preadolescent* (New York: Appleton-Century-Crofts, 1959); Arthur Witt Blair and William H. Burton, *Growth and Development of the Preadolescent* (New York: Appleton-Century-Crofts, 1951).

[20] Hans Seyle, *The Stress of Life* (New York: McGraw-Hill Book Company, 1956), pp. 273–74.

the European invention of a middle school, adapted it to its own cultural imperatives, and provided through the organizational mechanism of this middle school a channel for the acting-out of early adolescent turbulence.

Had there been no model of a middle school in any other cultural system by the early 1900's, the United States in all likelihood would have had to invent one of its own. But societies do frequently borrow and adapt one another's cultural inventions. As is the case with individuals, imitation is easier than invention.

The educational imperative of a transitional middle school to mediate between early adolescent stress and the strain-producing culture had apparently so deeply impressed Francis of Los Angeles, it was for him by 1912 a matter of *administrative logic* to restructure public school organization in three divisions. And, as with the sociology and physiology of early adolescence, he was also correct in invoking the science of psychology in defense of his logic.

The Psychological Response

Basic to the concept of "psychological man" is a behavioral principle which holds that man in his pursuit of equilibrium will respond emotionally to himself and to others in his environment. The response may be conscious or unconscious, selective or random, intense or superficial, but he does make some response. Surely, then, there ought not to be anything extraordinary about the discovery that in *every culture* there seems to be some psychological response to the physiological revolution at the onset of adolescence. In point of fact there isn't.

Sociologically, however, three variables are crucial in the phenomenon of a psychological response to the physiological revolution of adolescence. These are the intensity of the response, behavioral manifestations of the response, and the manner in which behavioral manifestations of the response are accommodated by cultural norms in the society. These three variables, coupled with the productive usefulness of the adolescent in the economic sector, determinatively define the status of adolescents in a given society.

G. Stanley Hall's second volume of *Adolescence* chronicles the social behavior through which the psychological response to adolescence has manifested itself through the ages. The behavior of adolescents has also been a subject of interest to writers of fiction. What seems to be a common element in all accounts of early adolescent behavior is an exaggerated sense of idealism. The adolescent onset seems to set off a phantasmagorian idealism in which adults, especially parents, are the villains. In a commentary on this phenomenon, Erikson has written:[21]

> In their search for a new sense of continuity and sameness, adolescents have to refight many of the battles of earlier years, even though to do so they must artifically appoint perfectly well-meaning people to play the role of enemies; and they are ever ready to install lasting idols and ideals as guardians of a final identity.

The cultural pattern of some societies has allowed adolescent idealism to run its course through sanctioned modes of behavior. Hall found, for example, that adolescent idealism found expression through mysticism in cultures where the dominant value pattern was religious in character. And during the period of German romanticism, Goethe has young Werther in *Leiden des jungen Werthers* vent his adolescent idealism through *Weltschmerz*, a form of brooding over the suffering of mankind. The *Sturm und Drang* theme—storm and stress—which Goethe employed to explain the adolescent behavior of Werther was also used by Thomas Mann to explain Tonio Kröger, the adolescent in *Stories of Three Decades*. The acting-out of early adolescent turmoil in these cultures presented no special social problem and, therefore, required no special socializing agency. However, in American society, committed as it is to a pattern of instrumental activism, a withdrawal for too long from the expectations of society can result in a "Magic Mountain" effect: a neurotic type of escape to within oneself.

Nor was the meaning of adolescent existence a social problem in American society before factory and city had become dominant landmarks of the culture. Expectations of achievement in the American culture of the rural period did not exacerbate the human condition at the onset of adolescence. Adult roles were for the most part learned in the nuclear family; the father's occupational role served as a model for the son, and girls suffered no uncertainty about a future adult status. And the land itself abounded in an idealism of which both adolescent and adult could share.

American idealism of the pre-Civil War period was a residue of the Revolution. Transcendentalism and Manifest Destiny had served well as socially sanctioned channels of expression for adult idealism. The

---

21 Erikson, *Childhood and Society*, p. 261.

Great West and its romantic heroes, vast stretches of open country, un-contaminated rivers, and unspoiled mountains and forests were adequate for the acting-out of adolescent restlessness and idealism. Mark Twain's *The Adventures of Huckleberry Finn* has captured for posterity facets of that idyllic adolescent existence.

Then came what Frederick Lewis Allen has called "the big change."[22] Even while the big change was in progress, and had not yet run its course, adolescence assumed already the proportions of a major social problem in American culture; not alone in the large cities of the eastern seaboard, where the social impact of the big change was first felt, but in the American midwest as well.

A prominent educator addressed the Minnesota Education Association in the 1890's and, with deep adult frustration, declared:[23]

> The bad boy of America has no counterpart in any other part of the world . . . ; he is savagery growing up in the midst of civilization, impiety mocking at religion, lawlessness whistling defiance at law and order, and license masquerading in the costume of liberty.
>
> His language is slang and profanity, his amusement is violence, his education a blank and his name a terror to society. . . .
>
> What shall be done with them and for them? Philanthropists, reformers, humanitarians and statesmen have given this question their most serious attention, and yet the problem seems still to vex them.

No doubt, a certain allowance must be made in the meaning of the foregoing passage for oratorical zeal. Nonetheless, its deeper sociological significance is not to be escaped. It had been spoken in 1898 and not in the 1960's, not from a platform in Hell's Kitchen of New York City, but in the Capital City of Minnesota. "The decline of parental control, the lessening of the restraints of the home, the decay of that tremendous responsibility which fathers and mothers ought to feel," so stated a 1903 editorial of the St. Paul *Globe*, "have exposed the new generation to dangers that it is unfit either to cope with or to escape."[24]

All of what the editorial writer had deplored in the foregoing came with the big change. New conditions in the American culture transformed the Huckleberry Finns of yesteryears into the juvenile delinquents of the 1900's. The restlessness and romantic adventurism of adolescence, for which there were socially sanctioned channels of ex-

22 Frederick Lewis Allen, *The Big Change* (New York: Harper & Row, 1952).
23 St. Paul *Dispatch*, January 3, 1898.
24 "Editorial," St. Paul *Globe*, November 29, 1903.

pression in the nineteenth century, had become deviant behavior in the culture of the twentieth century.

After the census of 1890, Americans were informed by the United States Census Bureau that for the first time since the founding of the Republic, the nation no longer had a frontier. The Wild West had been tamed, and the age of the automobile, motion picture, and jukebox was waiting in the wings to come on stage. No longer children, but not yet accorded an adult status in any sphere of the now complex industrial society of the 1900's, American adolescents evolved a subculture of their own. They discovered their own channels for acting-out internal turmoil. For many this took the form of school dropouts, others sought status and psychological gratification in the gangs of street-corner society, and still others escaped from the inner anxieties of adolescence through the excitement of juvenile crime. "Go to the streets in any city night or day," the St. Paul *Globe* of 1903 directed, "and you will find them crowded with children who have no more business to be there than they have in a cage of wild beasts."[25]

In the interest of its organic solidarity, and in defense of the social welfare, American society invented social agencies, or adapted some of other cultures, to intervene in the condition of adolescence in modern culture. One such agency which was invented is the now familiar juvenile court.[26] Other intervening social agencies which were brought into existence are, in fact, institutional substitutes for now lost natural channels for the acting-out of adolescent behavior. The American settlement house, an adaptation of England's Toynbee Hall, the comprehensive high school with its interscholastic athletics and a variety of other extracurricular activities, junior achievement, scouting, church and synagogue-sponsored youth groups, and the like, serve as implementing structures of institutionalized adolescence in modern American culture. But the implementing structure of the American middle school attests most particularly to the *special case* of early adolescence.

Contrary to legend, no malevolent scheme in American school administration had transformed the Huckleberry Finns of the nineteenth

---

25 *Ibid.*, November 29, 1903. See also A. B. Hollingshead, "A Sociological Perspective on Adolescence," *Pediatrics Clinics of America*, Vol. 7, February 1960; and Friedrich H. Tenbruck, "Contemporary Adolescence," *Diogenes*, Winter 1961.

26 For more on social conditions late in the nineteenth century which had necessitated the first juvenile courts in the United States see Samuel H. Popper, *Individualized Justice: Fifty Years of Juvenile Court and Probation Services in Ramsey County, Minnesota* (St. Paul, Minn.: Bruce Publishing Co., 1956).

century into the high school athletic heroes of the twentieth century. The transformation occurred with *the institutionalization of an adolescent subculture* in modern America. Some adults do deplore certain patterns of this adolescent subculture. But like it or not, modern-day high school athletic heroes and pompom girls are merely the gaudier figures of an adolescent subculture which twentieth-century American society has sanctioned through institutionalization.[27]

The Special Case of Early Adolescents

Early adolescents, on the other hand, stand for a special category within the adolescent subculture. The early adolescent is physiologically no longer a child, yet his status in the adolescent subculture is marginal. So-called teenage culture in the United States begins at about age twelve and ends at about age eighteen. For cultural reasons, the period of adolescence is long in the United States, and seems to be getting even longer. Therefore, because adolescents are mostly in school during this period, many relational patterns in the adolescent subculture form within the social system of the school. But for psychological reasons, and because of the norms in adolescent subculture, most adolescents are not fully integrated in their subculture until about age fifteen.

During this period of marginality, early adolescents are *dangerously vulnerable to deviant influences*. Left on their own, and without the protective intervention at this period in socialization of an agency which is capable of neutralizing deviant influences, there is danger that young adolescents will make qualitatively inferior first commitments to some future adult role, as such quality is measured by the broad values of American society.

The function of socialization, as it is summarized by Parsons, is to develop in youth "commitments and capacities which are essential prerequisites of their future role-performance."[28] Then he goes on to

27 For more on this theme see James S. Coleman, *The Adolescent Society* (New York: The Free Press, 1961); and Willard Waller, *The Sociology of Teaching* (New York: John Wiley and Sons, 1932), especially Chapters 9–13 of Part III; Jessie Bernard, "Teen-Age Culture: An Overview," *The Annals of the American Academy of Political and Social Science*, Vol. 338, November 1961; James S. Coleman, "The Adolescent Subculture and Achievement," *The American Journal of Sociology*, Vol. LXV, June 1960; James S. Coleman, "The Competition for Adolescent Energies," *Phi Delta Kappan*, Vol. XLII, March 1961.

28 Talcott Parsons, "The School Class as a Social System," *The Harvard Educational Review*, Vol. 29, Fall 1959, p. 298.

propose that these commitments are composed of two categories: a commitment to implement "the broad *values* of society," and a commitment to perform some future adult role within the society. But modern psychological science, we will now mark, alerts us to the vulnerability of early adolescents to deviant influences. Therefore, again, without the protective intervention of a specialized agency during this period of adolescence, first commitments can easily be made to the *wrong values.*

In Sophocles' *Antigone,* the chorus chants: "Many things are wonderful—terrible." Is it possible the clairvoyant Sophoclean chorus glimpsed in passing the early adolescent in twentieth century American culture?

Wattenberg's contention in Chapter 3 that middle school pupils "are so 'special' that to abandon the idea of separate schools for them would be a mistake" now becomes a crucial point in our analysis of middle school organization. Irene M. Josselyn, formerly of the Chicago Institute of Psychoanalysis, a specialist in child psychiatry and a prolific contributor to the clinical literature in adolescent psychiatry, supports Wattenberg's view of early adolesecents in the school system.

She reports that young adolescents become psychologically disoriented, not *psychopathically* disoriented, but disoriented enough to set them apart as a psychologically vulnerable group in society. She regards the sudden growth spurt as a major source of the confusion. Moreover, according to Josselyn, a feeling of strangeness to the body makes them apprehensive and induces insecurity. Many conceal feelings of insecurity by resorting to brash, bravado posturing. Others may seek escape from their discomfiture by engaging intensively in sports, creative expression, or reading. In either of these patterns, it is a case of *psychological overreacting.*

It is also during this period of *Sturm und Drang* that early adolescents strive desperately to attain independence. Childhood controls, once psychologically comforting, now turn into irritants. They struggle for freedom from parental control—to be on their own—but cultural conditions of modern society, especially those of an economic character, keep them in a state of dependence. Fear of failure, and failure is a proscription of near-taboo strength in American culture, deters many of them from accepting responsibility even while they are striving for independence.

One of the more vexing enigmas of early adolescent behavior, Josselyn reports, is the craving for peer approval. Even as they stand in rebellion of parental controls, they will slavishly submit to the controls of a peer code. However, Josselyn cautions that adult society need not be concerned as much with the rigid conformity of young adolescents to a peer group as it should be to the *type of peer group* to which they conform.[29]

Josselyn obviously supports Wattenberg's view that *there is something "special"* about early adolescents. Moreover, in her reports of work with adolescents, Josselyn has urged as a social imperative the special protection of young adolescents in modern culture. Illustrative of the urgency she advocates for protective intervention in the socialization of early adolescents is the reference which follows. Indirectly, she points to the social value of a *separate school* in American society for early adolescents, although in the reference itself there is no mention made of education. Josselyn writes:[30]

> It is frequently pointed out in a discussion of adolescence that one of the characteristics of this age group is the confusion of the individual in regard to his self-image. As the adolescent attempts to structure a concept of the *self* he not only looks into himself, and in so doing finds many apparently unresolved contradictions, but also strives to become a mirror to give back a reflection of those about him. The mirror he makes of himself, however, is a selective one, reflecting back primarily those individuals whose behavior-image satisfies some aspect of the internal facets that are so chaotically disarranged during this period. Having found the individual, or individuals, whose pattern of behavior

[29] Irene M. Josselyn, "Psychological Changes in Adolescence," *Children*, Vol. 6, March-April 1959, pp. 43–47. Josselyn has reported her clinical experience with early adolescents before many professional societies; mostly, however, before professional groups in psychiatry and social work. Representative of these are Irene M. Josselyn, "Social Pressures in Adolescence," *Social Casework*, Vol. 39, May 1952; "The Ego in Adolescence," *American Journal of Orthopsychiatry*, Vol. 24, April 1954. For other representative medical-psychiatric references to early adolescence see Joseph D. Teicher, "Normal Psychological Changes in Adolescence," *California Medicine*, Vol. 85, September 1956; Oscar B. Markey, "A Study of Aggressive Sex Misbehavior in Adolescents Brought to Juvenile Court," *American Journal of Orthopsychiatry*, Vol. 20, October 1950; Richard E. Wolf, "Variations in Personality Growth During Adolescence," *Journal of Pediatrics*, Vol. 59, November 1961; George A. Constant, "Adolescence: Its Perspective and Problems," *Journal of the Mississippi State Medical Association*, Vol. IV, January 1963; Marynia F. Farnham, *The Adolescent* (New York: Harper & Row, 1951); and, of course, perhaps the best-known medical literature on young adolescents in lay circles, Arnold Gesell, Frances L. Ilg, Louise Bates Ames, *Youth, The Years from Ten to Sixteen* (New York: Harper & Row, 1956).

[30] Irene M. Josselyn, "A Type of Predelinquent Behavior," *American Journal of Orthopsychiatry*, Vol. 28, July 1958, p. 606. Copyright The American Orthopsychiatric Association, Inc. By permission of the American Orthopsychiatric Association.

if imitated offers such promise of gratification, the adolescent may then choose that person with whom to identify.

Josselyn is alerting society to the imperative of keeping the phenomenological world of early adolescents free of what one sociologist has conceptualized as the "antimodel": "A way of performing that is to be avoided."[31]

From the time of Kurt Lewin, social psychology has been aware of selective screening phenomena in perception.[32] The concept of selective screening explains the behavior of an individual whose marginal status in a given social situation causes him to *screen out* supportive elements in the situation and to *focus* on those elements which are perceived as threatening. But Josselyn's clinical observation of early adolescents cautions of another kind of selective screening in early adolescent perception.

According to Josselyn, a young adolescent left on his own will tend to reflect in his social behavior "primarily those individuals whose behavior-image satisfies some aspect of the internal facets that are so chaotically disarranged during this period." The meaning of this points to a potential social hazard: the hazard of an *antimodel* being selected by a young adolescent as a *model* for his own behavior, because the antimodel stands for a "pattern of behavior if imitated offers . . . promise of gratification."

It is a social hazard which exists, of course, in and out of school. But especially in the public school, where most early adolescents *must spend* the greater part of each school day in the ascriptive social role of pupil, the hazard is particularly acute. For in a school community where no protective organizational barrier separates the social system of young adolescents from that of older adolescents, antimodels are provided with *accommodating environmental conditions* for materializing a potential influence. As early adolescents seek escape from their childhood identification, and as they strive for a secure status in their new adolescent subculture, social and psychological motivations to emulate older adolescents are strong.[33]

31 Roy G. Francis, "The Antimodel as a Theoretical Concept," *The Sociological Quarterly,* Vol. 4, Summer 1963, p. 198.
32 See Kurt Lewin, *Principles of Topological Psychology* (New York: McGraw-Hill Book Company, 1936).
33 Josselyn's *caveat* here is directed to the latent hazards of antimodels in the environment of young adolescents. It seems, however, that psychiatrists have discovered also a latent *functional* value in antimodels in their treatment of very young children. Ac-

Fritz Redl is another in the profession who is in accord with Wattenberg that there is great social value in dealing with early adolescents as a special category of pupils in the process of education. In his graphic description of early adolescent psychosocial conditions at the United States Office of Education middle school conference in 1955, Redl laid great stress upon the social meaning of "a group psychological break" which is induced by what he conceptualizes as "organismic disorganization."

According to Redl:[34]

It is a characteristic of many preadolescents or young adolescents that for a while they really go through a phase which I might call organismic disorganization. It is not true that in growing the child just stretches and becomes bigger and better, all the time developing nicely and smoothly with a few things being added like sex and so forth as he goes along. The truth is that it is normal, even for wonderful children, to go through a temporary stage of partial individual disorganization.

Then Redl goes on to say:[35]

A second area of changes which we know happens even to the most wonderful of these boys and girls is what I would call a group psychological break. Again, I'm not now talking about the problem child. Him we already know or else we wouldn't call him a problem child. Until the late years in elementary school it is normal for children to consider their families as the main base. That does not mean that they don't continue to form groups with other kinds of children which they started with much earlier. They play with such groups and we want them to do so. But on the whole their greatest security comes from being in line and in conformance with those figures who are most important in their life, their parents, their teachers, and of course the family pattern. There is also some branching out into other areas during this age period just before they reach junior high school. Most of them however move into something rather different.

They move into a terrific dependence on what psychologists call the

---

cording to a newspaper report, psychiatrists in Los Angeles are hanging on walls of their office waiting rooms paintings of children pulling cat's tails, washing the cat in a salad bowl, and other such scenes of misbehavior. Their rationale is that all children misbehave, normal and abnormal alike, and the mere sight of other children acting out deviant behavior is "soothing" and "relieves guilt feelings." From the "Insider's Newsletter," Minneapolis *Tribune,* January 31, 1965.

34 Fritz Redl, "Some Psychological Facts About Junior High School Children," in Gaumnitz, *Strengths and Weaknesses of the Junior High School,* p. 5.

35 *Ibid.,* pp. 6–7.

peer code in which the behavior patterns are set by the "older children." Probably, too, they will play up to children 1 to 2 years older than they are. It is certain at any rate that they now become more strongly dependent on the behavior code of the other kids, even at the expense of a conflict within themselves. We find many instances of junior high school youngsters who do have real internal conflicts. . . . This means there is a deep seated need for a terrific dependency on the opinions and practices of others in their group.

The "terrific dependency on the opinions and practices of others in their group" of which Redl spoke seems to be a psychological characteristic of early adolescents which teachers have observed even in pupils who are restricted by some physical handicap from pursuing social gratifications on even terms with others. A teacher of the blind, it is of interest to note in this regard, insists that blind middle school pupils ought to be taught script writing as well as typewriting because, among other reasons,[36]

I feel that early adolescence is the time for the concerted teaching of this skill to a blind student because it is at this age that it becomes important for him to do things in the same manner as that of his seeing peers.
So, if there were no other reason, most of the blind students that I have seen in junior high school become very excited when they are offered the opportunity to learn to write with a pencil the scriptwriting which the peers are using daily.

Redl, moreover, agrees with Josselyn that early adolescents are subject to a short-lived psychological disorientation. It is not serious, and it will pass with the reacquisition of stability in later adolescence:[37]

They get a little bit paranoid. . . . I do not really mean there is serious paranoia, but there is often a tendency to think somebody is after them, somebody has done them wrong; somebody does not appreciate how well they can do things, etc.

The theme of a temporary psychological disorientation leads directly to Erikson's concepts of ego diffusion and ego identity. Erikson follows Erich Lindemann, Psychiatrist-in-Chief of Massachusetts General Hospital, in holding to a "crisis theory" in the development of identity.

[36] Letter from Gay Garey to author, February 10, 1964. Mrs. Garey is Itinerant Teacher of the Blind in the Robinsdale, Minnesota, School District.
[37] Redl, "Some Psychological Facts About Junior High School Children," in Gaumnitz, *Strengths and Weaknesses of the Junior High School,* p. 9.

Ego synthesis and resynthesis is also central in the theory of "positive disintegration" of Kazimierz Dabrowski, of the Institute of Child Psychiatry and Mental Hygiene of Warsaw, Poland. Dabrowski explains this phenomenon as a "disintegration and secondary integration in personality development."[38] Indeed, aspects of the crisis theory are now the most frequent thematic references to adolescent development both in preventive psychiatry and in psychoanalytical literature.

Erikson holds that human personality takes form in a crucible of psychosocial crises which accompany stages of maturation, and which have to be resolved for each discrete stage of human development from infancy through adulthood. It is the onset of adolescence, according to Erikson, which triggers what has come to be known as the "adolescent crisis." Ego identity in normal children is positive. They have a secure sense of themselves and have structured for themselves a strong self-concept. However, with the coming of adolescence, their ego identity comes apart. They lose their secure childhood sense of self and must make their way to a new self-concept.

Escape from a state of ego diffusion to the psychological security of a new ego identity, following Erikson, is one of the principal problems of personality development that have to be resolved during the adolescent crisis. The type of psychological *anomie* which accompanies ego diffusion is by no means a light burden for young adolescents. Erikson suggests, as does Dabrowski, that the process of ego diffusion may well serve as a buffer against *potentially more serious* psychological disorientation.

Erikson insists, therefore, that young adolescents be granted by society a *psychosocial respite,* a moratorium as it were, from cultural pressures. They require freedom to explore in new behavioral patterns without fear of social embarrassment or harsh reproach. Early adolescents require freedom from compounding psychosocial pressures while they make their painful way toward a new ego identity. Erikson is asking essentially that complex urban and industrial society grant its young adolescents a haven from cultural pressures while they master what Robert J. Havighurst thinks of as the "developmental tasks" of early adolescents.[39]

[38] See Jason Aronson's "Introduction" to Kazimierz Dabrowski, *Positive Disintegration* (Boston: Little, Brown and Co., 1964). Aronson, the editor, is a member of the Department of Psychiatry, Massachusetts General Hospital and Harvard Medical School.

[39] Erikson's major ideas have been presented in an extensive literature. Perhaps the best known of his published works include *Childhood and Society,* which has been cited

Havighurst's concept of developmental tasks converts into imperatives of socialization the Erikson-Dabrowski-Redl view of adolescent development in modern psychological science. From infancy to adulthood, according to Havighurst, man has to master a host of physical-psychological-social tasks that are associated with each stage of human development. At the heart of Havighurst's thesis is the hypothesis that when developmental learnings are mastered successfully at each stage of human development, there is satisfaction and a foundation is laid for learning other developmental tasks that lie ahead. Conversely, unsuccessful, or inadequate, mastery of developmental tasks impedes progress toward optimum human development.[40]

Havighurst found his hypothesis partly confirmed in data which the Midwest Community Study Research Project of the University of Chicago had been gathering since 1942. Recorded data of early adolescent development were analyzed on the following five-point scale of developmental tasks:[41]

1. Learning an appropriate sex role.
2. Achieving emotional independence of parents and other adults.
3. Developing conscience, morality, and a set of values.
4. Getting along with age-mates.
5. Developing intellectual skills.

Among conclusions that were drawn from this empirical study are the following:[42]

> The hypothesis that good achievement on one task tends to be associated with good achievement on other tasks at the same age appears to be correct. . . . The results of this empirical study tend to show the hypotheses about adjustment and achievement implicit in the concept of developmental tasks to be correct.
>
> The evidence seems clear-cut that the early period of adolescence is

---

before; *Identity and the Life Cycle* (New York: International Universities Press, 1959), and *The Psychoanalytic Study of the Child* (New York: International Universities Press, 1946). A host of other published works by Erikson will be found listed in the 1963 edition of *Childhood and Society*.

[40] See Robert J. Havighurst, *Human Development and Education* (New York: Longmans, Green and Co., 1953); Robert J. Havighurst and Hilda Taba, *Adolescent Character and Personality* (New York: John Wiley and Sons, 1949).

[41] Aileen Schoeppe and R. J. Havighurst, "A Validation of Developmental and Adjustment Hypotheses of Adolescence," *The Journal of Educational Psychology*, Vol. 43, October 1952, p. 339.

[42] *Ibid.*, pp. 348, 352.

the crucial one in which changes in levels of accomplishment of these tasks are taking place, that levels of achievement are largely determined by age thirteen on these specific tasks.

A Return to the Paramount Middle School Goal

If J. H. Francis of Los Angeles did not have available in 1912 most of the scientific evidence which has been reviewed here to demonstrate the special case of early adolescents in the process of education, then he must have had remarkably correct intuitive insights about the matter. From the larger institutional view of society, the paramount cultural mission of the American middle school is to guide pupils to a mastery of what Havighurst has defined as the developmental tasks of early adolescents.

When this mission was defined in Chapter 3 by principles of functional differentiation which govern the division of labor in a modern public school organization, it was expressed as follows:

The differentiated function—hence, the paramount goal—of the American middle school is to intervene protectively in the process of education which was begun in the elementary school, mediate between the human condition at the onset of adolescence and the pressures of culture, and continue the general education of early adolescents with a curriculum applied in a psychosocial environment which is functional for learning at this stage of socialization.

Gruhn's conceptualization of six manifest functions through which this goal can be fulfilled is as valid today as it was in 1940 when he formulated it. What is most desperately needed, however, is a middle school process more in consonance with cultural conditions today and a teaching staff which has the necessary expertise and commitment to apply such a process. It does not fare well at all for middle school education in modern America that most middle schools have to resort to a program of the 1920's with which to perform Gruhn's six manifest functions, only because nothing more sophisticated is available. But if much of contemporary middle school technology is outdated, the functions of integration, exploration, guidance, differentiation, socialization, and articulation are not. These have to continue in the modern era as the manifest functions of a middle school program if the social value of a protective intervention in early adolescent education is to be maximized.

Of course, no occult vision is required to recognize instantly that these are also functions of the elementary school and of the high school. Indeed, even a partial organizational analysis of any other functionally differentiated unit of public school organization will show that each of these functions is required for fulfilling that unit's goal. But further analysis will also show that the *qualitative and quantitative character* of these functions will differ from unit to unit in accordance with the primacy of values which differentiate one unit from another in a school system's division of labor.

A comparison of the guidance function in a high school and a middle school illustrates the empirical significance of this distinction. Rank order of emphasis in high school guidance is given first to educational goals following graduation from high school, then to vocational goals, and last to immediate personal problems. Whereas, rank order of emphasis in middle school guidance is given first to immediate personal problems, then to educational goals in high school, and last to distant vocational aspirations in the world of work.

It will be recalled from Chapter 13 that James Glass in his address before the MEA in 1922 had delineated a similar qualitative distinction between an elementary school and a middle school. "The point of view of the elementary curriculum towards its pupils," he said, "is *en masse* to the end that all may receive a useable knowledge of the common branches and a sympathetic understanding of the social and civic structure of our democratic society." Whereas the middle school "must help *each child* to discover his own aptitudes" during the transitional years between childhood and adolescence.

And of the six manifest functions in an American middle school, guidance has to be given first place in a ranking of importance. *For the protective intervention which is required of a middle school in the United States is not for a special category of psychotic pupils, but for the entire population of early adolescents, regardless of ethnic-social-economic distinctions, who in the normal course of healthy personality development are disadvantaged in the culture by a temporary psychological disorientation.* The consensus in preventive psychiatry is that cultural pressures in American society *do exacerbate* psychological strains which accompany physiological stresses of emerging adolescence. And such a compensation in the process of education for a disabling condition conforms entirely with basic orientations of the institutionalized American value pattern.

Because individuals within normative patterns of American society *are expected* to aspire toward higher levels of personal development and achievement, they must be equipped in youth with essential cultural prerequisites for satisfying these expectations. Without such essential cultural prerequisites individuals suffer a deprivation and will either fail to aspire altogether or be frustrated in the attempt. Either case leads to alienation from the broad values of society. An opportunity-deprived Negro reveals such alienation when he insists that learning is a white man's value. American society has now learned through bitter experiences with all opportunity-deprived groups that the social cost of alienation from its values can come exceedingly high.

It is frequently overlooked, therefore, that the middle school is not the *only* structure in contemporary American public school organization which compensates in educative process for a handicap in pupils. The wide range of programs in Special Education perform precisely such compensatory functions. Neither handicaps of the body nor of opportunity are now permitted by American society to keep youth from acquiring essential cultural prerequisites for fulfilling its expectations of personal development, achievement, and the internalization of commitment to the institutionalized value system.

A section of Public Law 88-452, Economic Opportunity Act of 1964, enables the Congress to fund 90 percent of local programs whose goal is to socialize opportunity-deprived youth to *employer expectations.* Only after normative responsive behavior has been learned in school programs of the Neighborhood Youth Corps are youths moved into out-of-school programs under the Manpower Development and Training Act to learn a marketable skill. These programs, together with sections of Public Law 89–10, the Vocational Act of 1962, Project Head Start, and others, are expressions in American society that youth must be given every chance in the process of socialization to acquire the essential cultural prerequisites for fulfilling its values.[43]

In the instance of these programs in particular, and through Special Education in general, American society equips its instruments of socialization with compensatory capacities as a means of lessening burdens of a debilitating disadvantage. Special Education, however, is directed at *discrete* categories of pupils at all phases of schooling. But because

---

[43] For more on the theme of compensatory education, see B. S. Bloom, A. Davis, and R. Hess, *Compensatory Education for Cultural Deprivation* (New York: Holt, Rinehart, Winston, Inc., 1965).

the psychosocial problems at early adolescence are a cultural universal, the middle school is made available in a public school system to *all pupils* who are at the threshhold of adolescence. Programs in Special Education mediate between deprivation or physical vulnerability and culture, whereas a middle school mediates between temporary psychological vulnerability and culture.

The institutional case of early adolescents in the social system of public school organization, moreover, conforms in some important respects to Parsons' definition of the sick role in society. Parsons conceptualizes sickness as a type of deviant behavior. A sick person, according to Parsons, withdraws from the expectational norms of society to a dependent relationship with others who are asked to make him well. Society legitimizes the *right* to such a dependency during periods of illness, and the *right* to a passive evasion of an obligation to conform, contingent on an implied "admission that it would be a good thing to get well as expeditiously as possible."[44]

A patient in the hospital organization does not alienate himself permanently from expectational norms of the larger society, but only so long as it takes to get well. Within the social system of a hospital organization, therefore, the otherwise deviant behavior of patients is not "punished" because the legitimation of their *right* to be "helped" has been institutionalized in the normative framework of hospitals.

An early adolescent, of course, is not a sick person, nor is the public school organization a hospital. But the role of an early adolescent within the relational network of public school organization, like the sick role in society, is a special case. Despite significant differences which distinguish between these two in a typology of social roles, there are, nevertheless, some important points of similarity between them.

As is the case with the sick person who is disabled during a period of illness, the early adolescent is disabled by a temporary psychological disorientation which has been brought on by radical physiological change. During the period of disability at early adolescence, pupils find it difficult to conform to the expectational norms of the school. They ask essentially for a temporary moratorium from the pressure of obligations to conform as they have before. They ask for a haven where they will be helped to work things out in their own way. Once the dis-

---

44 Parsons' remarkable conceptualization of the sick role in society will be found under "The Social Structure of Deviant Behavior Tendencies," in *The Social System,* pp. 283–97.

ability is resolved, however, there is an implied admission of an obligation to conform as before.

Since 1910, American society has legitimized the early adolescent's *right* to such a claim. It has institutionalized this legitimation in a middle school of public school organization. Within the relational system of a middle school, therefore, the otherwise deviant behavior of pupils is not "punished," because their *right* to be "helped" is affirmed in the normative framework of middle school structure. Authority figures within this relational system warrant the validity of an early adolescent's right to this moratorium by the manner of their interactions.

Does it mean, then, that the protective intervention of a middle school in the secondary phase of education reduces it to the status of a custodial organization? It does not! Nor, moreover, does it mean a discontinuity in the learning of cognitive skills will follow from the dominance of psychosocial orientations in middle school education. Evaluated middle school experience in St. Paul has demonstrated, albeit with limited evidence, that it does not. The next chapter reaffirms, therefore, the social value of America's middle school in the modern era, proposes that its potential to motivate early adolescent pupils is greater today than ever before, and urges revitalizing innovations in its structure and process.

The unhappy past of middle school education in the United States can well serve as prologue to a brighter future, provided administrators cast out what has become obsolescent in the middle school and introduce patterns which are functionally better attuned to the imperatives of life in a post-Sputnik world. But as innovations are effected in middle school structure and process, the touchstone of validity must continue to be the human condition at early adolescence. For as in the legend of Antaeus, American society will provide its middle school organization with strength so long as its structure and process is discretely identified with problems of early adolescent development. From the point of view of institutional imperatives, history leaves no doubt that this is the only commitment of enduring social value which is capable of sustaining over the years middle school legitimation in a system of public school organization.

14

THE TURN AHEAD

Social conditions following World War II have triggered a movement of educational revitalization in the United States. The movement is dynamic, it is pervasive, and it is already transforming traditional patterns of structure and process at all levels of education. No system of education is likely to escape its confrontation: not graduate school, not college, and certainly not systems of public school education. For the revitalization of public school systems has been set by society in the lead position of a still larger endeavor at self-renewal through social reconstruction.[1] The United States, in short, is now confronted by a set of cultural conditions which have accelerated imperatives for its rapid adaptation.

Only once before was American education caught up in a similar wave of revitalization because society had turned highly adaptive. It began in higher education soon after the Civil War, and it ended on the eve of World War I with a so-called reorganization of secondary

[1] The concept of a "revitalization" as it has been used heretofore and as it is used in this context follows the definition of Anthony F. C. Wallace: "A revitalization movement is . . . a deliberate, organized, conscious effort by members of a society to construct a more satisfying culture." See Anthony F. C. Wallace, "Revitalization Movements," *American Anthropologist*, Vol. 58, April 1956, p. 264.

education. Between these two peaks of an earlier revitalization, American educational systems were turned toward the twentieth century.

Chapters 7 to 9 mapped the broad contours of that earlier revitalization within the larger context of social reconstruction. The revitalization of public school education after Appomattox was projected as of a piece with the reconstruction of institutional patterns for the expression of American values. Organizational innovations in the institutional network of society had facilitated a revitalization of the American value system in the emerging culture of factories and cities. A built-in political capacity in the structure of American society for self-renewal had accommodated transformations in social, economic, and political patterns without revolutionary upheavals. Out of that period of social reconstruction, we will recall, came the American middle school.

President Lyndon B. Johnson, in his education message to the 89th Congress of the United States on January 12, 1965, explained why education has been made the bellwether of contemporary social reconstruction. "We are now embarked on another venture," he said, "to put the American dream to work in meeting the new demands for a new day." And, continued the President, "Once again we must start where men who would improve their society have always known they must begin —with an educational system restudied, reinforced, and revitalized." The speed with which the Congress responded to the President's message with enabling legislation to initiate new educational ventures expressed in political terms the cultural urgency for educational revitalization.

In its own certain confrontation with contemporary imperatives for revitalization, the middle school will be pressed to redefine its discrete institutional character and, therefore, the social value through which its *right* to a differentiated structure and process in a public school system is legitimized. Institutional leadership in American school administration of an earlier period had defined this social value in the cultural idiom of early twentieth century. It has to be redefined now in the cultural idiom of a post-Sputnik world. And the incantation of warmed-over middle school shibboleths will not do.

For the turn ahead will test the cultural value of middle school organization as never before, but the turn ahead will also afford unprecedented opportunities to reaffirm the institutional integrity of the American middle school. Society, in a word, will demand of middle school organization solid demonstrations of its capacity to perform a discrete function of social value in the culture of a post-Sputnik world.

But the still-sagging posture of the middle school is not equipped for the confrontation that awaits it. Our analysis has pinpointed dysfunctional conditions at the institutional, managerial, and technical levels of public school organization which have compromised the institutional integrity of the American middle school and which have robbed its organizational mechanism of what Selznick has called "distinctive competence." These conditions will have to be eliminated in order to restore its distinctive competence and, therefore, also its institutional integrity. And in line with Selznick's dominant thesis, holding to the distinctive competence of an organization is at the same time a defense of its institutional integrity.[2]

By "the defense of institutional integrity" Selznick does not propose a defensive administrative posture; he does not equate such a defense with defensiveness. Quite the contrary, what Selznick has in mind is bold and sure-footed administrative action when legitimate organizational goals are threatened with corruption by external conditions.[3]

Accordingly, a broad strategy of three large-scale tasks is proposed as a means of restoring a distinctive competence to the American middle school: the organized body of middle school administrators, in alliance with other organized groups in education, has to have the middle school's unique institutional mission reaffirmed at the school board—that is, the community—level of public school organization; it has to effect the internal integration of middle school organization with this mission; and it has to quicken the pace of dynamic innovation in the middle school in accordance with modern-day social imperatives. Although a treatment of the last of these three tasks is left for the concluding chapter, it is the first which is most important of all. Indeed, because of its history, it would be futile to undertake any other task of strengthening the organizational posture of the modern-day middle school without a reaffirmation first of its institutional legitimation at the school board level of public school organization.

Institutional Reaffirmation

The middle school organization in the United States, as we know, has been in trouble from the earliest stages of its development. It began when school boards, influenced by what Selznick has characterized as

2 Selznick, *Leadership in Administration,* pp. 119 and 139.
3 *Ibid.,* p. 119.

"short-run opportunistic trends," sanctioned administrative corruptions of the middle school's institutional commitment as a means of relieving the school plant pinch of the World War I period and after. Historically, this episode in American education should not be viewed as a case of "good guys versus bad guys," but rather as a case study of school boards and school administrators made vulnerable by a social climate permeated with the cult of efficiency.

All that, however, is in the past. Modern-day school board members are by and large more enlightened about their institutional role, thanks in large measure to the National School Boards Association and its state affiliates, and, therefore, are less vulnerable to the corruption of terminal values. The making of broad, long-term school policy is an institutional prerogative of school boards, and according to the Executive Director of the National School Boards Association, no one interest group "should be permitted to dictate the policy of school operation."[4] Moreover, interactions between associational systems of school board members, administrators, and teachers are of a better quality today, and they are more frequent. These are assets which can be mobilized in a concerted action to reaffirm the institutional mission of the middle school.

Then there are the regional accrediting associations. The Southern Association of Colleges and Secondary Schools has already reaffirmed the middle school's legitimate institutional pattern in its publication *The Junior High School Program*. The North Central Association of Colleges and Secondary Schools, we will recall from Chapter 3, was the first organized body in American education to grant what Harry Stack Sullivan has called "consensual validation" to the middle school of the 1910 period. North Central has now reactivated its former concern with institutional definition in middle school structure and process by establishing a Junior High School Accrediting Committee. Regional accrediting associations have a large capacity for influencing school board orientations.

Now, therefore, as educational revitalization in the United States shifts into high gear, is the propitious season for the defense of institutional integrity in middle school administration. What is needed for

4 Harold Webb, "Community Pressures on School Boards," in *Proceedings*, Seventh National Conference on School Finance, 1964, National Education Association, p. 110. It is altogether significant that among the "special interest clinic topics" at Annual Conventions of the National School Boards Association such topics as "The School and Social Problems," "Goal Priorities for Public Schools," "Policy-Making or Administration," and "Effecting Educational Change" are now quite commonplace.

making the most of this opportunity are bold actions of middle school leadership at local and national levels. By and large, however, the Committee on Junior High School Education of the National Association of Secondary School Principals will have to spark-plug this leadership and sustain its momentum.

The permanent Committee on Junior High School Education was established by the Executive Committee of NASSP shortly after World War II. William T. Gruhn has headed the committee for a number of years, and its very existence attests to the growing strength and influence of middle school administrators within the National Association of Secondary School Principals. Annual meetings of NASSP and its publications, particularly *The Bulletin,* have been giving more and more attention to problems of middle school administration since the inception of this committee.

Perhaps most important of all, the Committee on Junior High School Education has initiated a program of biennial regional middle school conferences which, in all sections of the country, have been of a high quality. Altogether, the Committee on Junior High School Education has demonstrated a capacity to provide leadership for the organized body of middle school administrators in the United States. It is this leadership which must come to grips now at the national level with the weighty challenge of institutional definition and legitimation in middle school organization.

The challenge is weighty on several counts. Institutional definition is first and foremost an exercise in social value definition, and this is always difficult. But the social value of a protective intervention in early adolescent education with a differentiated structure and process is particularly difficult to define. A school board, after all, consists for the most part of lay members who have successfully satisfied societal expectations of instrumental achievement. They have internalized the norms of the larger value pattern. Many school board members, therefore, find it difficult to understand why early adolescents require, in the interest of the larger social welfare, a moratorium from cultural pressures and a right to withdraw temporarily from obligations to satisfy adult expectations of achievement. Then too there is the matter of administrative protocol in public school systems. Middle school principals of a given school system cannot under normal conditions initiate communication with the school board except through the agency of higher-level administrators.

These, and more, make the institutional definition of middle school organization exceedingly difficult at the school board level. But however difficult this task may be, and no matter how long it takes to get it done, it has to be done and done effectively. *For the decisive differentiation of middle school structure and process must begin with a clear value differentiation in the orientation to early adolescent education at the institutional level of public school organization.* Otherwise, middle school functions and resources, especially those of a social and psychological character, will be difficult to justify within the superordinate system so long as their valuation at the institutional level is ambiguous. But once the legitimizing value of a differentiated program for early adolescent education is clearly defined at the institutional level, problems of institutional corruption in the middle school will lose their now formidable cast.

School boards, for one thing, are likely to become less inclined to sanction administrative diversions of the middle school from its legitimate institutional purpose as a means of resolving building problems, integration problems, political problems, athletic problems, and what not. They might ask, as their role in school organization behooves them to ask, where is the institutional warrant for starting middle school education before the onset of adolescence? The legitimation of the American middle school from the first has been as a school for early adolescents. Grades 7–9 were assigned to this school not out of accommodation or chance, but because the years from twelve to fifteen were defined by science as the transitional period between late childhood and postpubescent adolescence. Our citations of Bunker, Greeson, Francis, Glass, and other middle school pioneers leave no doubt of that. Therefore, in terms of middle school legitimation, scientifically ascertained knowledge about child growth and development alone should determine which grades are functionally appropriate for this unit of public school organization. This, then, is an empirical problem which has to be solved by scientific means and not as an issue for debate. *Any other motive for starting middle school education earlier than the onset of adolescence is institutionally unwarranted.*

So far at least there is at best extremely nebulous research evidence in the general field of child growth and development in support of administrative schemes to change grades 7–9 as the period of early adolescent education. Nonetheless, there is a growing inclination abroad to begin middle school education as early as the fifth grade, usually for reasons which, by institutional definition, are not legitimate.

Comparative statistics in child growth suggest that advances in medical science, better diet, and a greater control of environmental conditions do affect the rate of physical development.[5]   J. M. Tanner of Great Britain has reported that children of Western Europe and the United States are maturing earlier at the rate of nearly twelve months every forty years.[6]   But, according to Luella Cole, recent studies show that for most youth the circumpubertal period is still the age span from twelve to fifteen.   And then, as Wattenberg cautions, early adolescents perhaps do mature somewhat earlier because of improved nutrition, and may even show greater intellectual sophistication because of improved educative processes, but because of diverse other cultural conditions they "are more dichotomized than any previous generation."[7]

About the most generous judgment that can be made about current evidence of an earlier pubescent development, because of changing environmental conditions, is to propose that the subject requires commanding scientific investigations of an extensive and intensive character.   Of course, the period of American middle school education would indeed have to be reconsidered once it is established by definitive research evidence that the onset of adolescence in the general population does begin at a significantly earlier age than was the case at the turn of the century.   But despite a lack of such evidence, there is an emerging tendency to revive in a new guise an old pattern of middle school misuse by "gerrymandering" its present grades.

A New Pattern of Misuse

Most middle school organizations in the United States have been, and still are, of grades 7–9.   Some are of grades 7–8, or 6–8, because of some political *rapprochement* which separates high school districts from elementary school districts in a state.   One state passionately devoted to basketball has many middle schools of grades 7–8 because basketball coaches in the high school want to begin training their charges for

---

[5] See especially "Children: Bigger and Better," *Journal of School Health*, Vol. 27, November 1957; C. J. Hale, "Changing Growth Patterns of the American Child," *Education*, Vol. 78, April 1958; and Kai Jensen, "Physical Growth," *Review of Educational Research*, Vol. 25, December 1955.

[6] J. M. Tanner, *Growth at Adolescence* (Oxford: Blackwell Scientific Publications, 1955).

[7] Luella Cole, *Psychology of Adolescence* (New York: Rinehart and Co., 1959), pp. 69–70. Cole shows 69 percent of the girls as still "immature" at age twelve.   See also, William W. Wattenberg, "Today's Junior High School Students," *Educational Leadership*, Vol. 23, December 1965, p. 190.

competitive play at the ninth grade. And a school district here and there in the United States will begin middle school education at grade five because the middle school is still a convenient way of getting out from under a building problem, although, as in the 1920's, this is seldom acknowledged in the public record. For the most part, however, these misuses of middle school organization have been around for some time, and their opportunistic character is easily recognized. Now, in the larger context of social reconstruction, a variation in the pattern of old misuses is rapidly taking shape, and it portends ill for institutional integrity in the middle school of tomorrow.

At the heart of the matter is once again, as it was after World War I, an inclination to divert the middle school organization from its legitimate goal. Public school systems, especially of large cities, have been struck since *Brown v. the Board of Education of Topeka* in 1954 by one racial integration crisis after another. The problem is essentially one of the social consequences of de facto racial segregation in the housing pattern of American cities. Nevertheless, despite the obvious community-wide moral and psychological character of the problem, pressure on school boards to eliminate de facto racial segregation in large urban school systems has been sustained and increased from year to year. These boards of education are enmeshed in what Gunnar Myrdal chose to call "an American dilemma."

One solution which school boards are now considering seriously is a change of pattern in school system organization from 6-3-3 to 4-4-4. Racial segregation is most pronounced in elementary schools, where school and home are within walking distance of each other, and less so in the larger attendance areas of the middle school and high school. The pattern shadows essentially the housing pattern of a community. The 4-4-4 strategy is to start middle school education at grade five, bring pupils out of the elementary schools two years earlier, have open enrollment in the middle school and high school divisions, and thereby facilitate the racial integration of a school system. Excellence in education, team teaching, nongradedness, creativity in teaching and learning, and other inducements of this kind are used in administrative strategies as persuasion to obtain school board sanction of the 4-4-4 plan.

What the 4-4-4 plan of school organization seems to ignore is that the social roots of de facto racial segregation in public schools are external of the system. School boards, therefore, ought to regard it more as a temporary escape from the pressures of a deeply rooted social problem than as a solution. Moreover, as Karl Taeuber, a specialist in the construction of segregation indices, has pointed out, "Discrimination is the principal cause of Negro residential segregation, and there is no basis for anticipating major changes in the segregated character of American cities until patterns of housing discrimination can be altered."[8] A more direct assault on de facto racial segregation in public schools, and on the larger problem of exclusion because of social prejudice, might be *open enrollment throughout a school system* and busing elementary school pupils to the attendance unit of their choice. Research in intercultural attitudes "has documented again and again, in many different social groups and geographical areas, the fact that young children (at preschool years and in the primary grades) have learned social prejudices."[9] A 4-4-4 plan of organization without open enrollment in *all* school units will indeed give the appearance of a racially integrated system, but the hard core of racial segregation in elementary schools would remain intact.

Myrdal's American dilemma has been sustained from generation to generation through patterns of social, political, and economic alienation. These have denied to many in the United States the beneficence of values which the Founding Fathers, out of "a decent respect to the opinions of mankind," have declared as the legitimizing values of the American separation from English political authority. American society, bent on self-renewal by putting "the American dream to work," to borrow the President's language, is now determined to strike down these deviant patterns.

Boards of education do indeed satisfy institutional obligations when they come to grips with problems of racial integration in public school systems. They link implementing organizations of public-supported education with the larger institutional network of society in attempts to correct social inequities which do violence to guiding American values. It is a social problem which a public school organization, as one of the principal agencies of socialization in society, should be functionally equipped to attack in accordance with its discrete competence. At the same time, however, school boards weaken the institution of

---

[8] Karl E. Taeuber, "Residential Segregation," *Scientific American*, Vol. 213, August 1965, p. 19.
[9] Helen G. Trager and Marian Radke Yarrow, *They Learn What They Live* (New York: Harper and Bros., 1952), p. 351.

public school education when they fulfill one societal obligation at the expense of another. Such is the case when the pursuit of racial integration is allowed to divert the middle school from its legitimate goal.

All of this shows up with striking force the crucial importance of institutional insight at the school board level of public school organization at the time when broad policy decisions are made. Especially for the middle school, the best first line in the defense of its institutional integrity is a school board which will insist that administrative plans for racial integration have to be formulated within a framework of alternatives which do not corrupt institutional values. Such a stance at the institutional level of public school organization will at once stimulate the cultivation of executive statesmanship at the managerial level and head off "short-run opportunistic trends."

A general letter from the President of the American Association of School Administrators, August 31, 1965, to the membership contained the following observation: "If any question mark hangs over the superintendency today, it is whether the superintendent is astute enough and tough enough to stand the heat which attends his decision-making role." Executive statesmanship, by Selznick's definition, is the intellectual stuff of a chief school administrator who is "astute enough and tough enough" to conceptualize alternative courses of action within the larger context of institutional values. Rather than compromise the integrity of institutional patterns in a public school system, executive statesmanship will instead mobilize institutional strengths in support of administrative strategies for a qualitative integration of the system with an external society "now embarked on another venture to put the American dream to work in meeting the new demands for a new day."

In administrative terms, an effective external integration of a public school system means essentially that its outputs, or what Parsons thinks of as disposal, satisfy input requirements of other systems in society; in the same way as a business organization is said to be integrated with a market when its output satisfies customer demands. Such an external integration of the system is a superintendent's responsibility and it summarizes the quality of consummatory relations between public school organization and other systems in the larger society. When, therefore, American society confronts its educational systems with "new demands for a new day," it is asking for *new* educational outputs. Society is not asking for institutional discontinuity, for the institutions of a society are repositories of esteemed values which have sprung from the experience of its development, but only that systems of education innovate their organizational mechanisms and equip themselves to produce outputs which are required "for a new day." Lacking these, society would suffer what Parsons refers to as a "deprivation."

The American middle school has sprung from the exigencies of life in modern industrial and urban society. It has been legitimized by society as an agency which intervenes protectively in the process of education at a time when a group psychological break, induced by the physiological revolution, occurs in early adolescent pupils. Within the larger design of the American value system, it is the social value of this *differentiated function* in a system of public school education, *and of this function alone,* which sustains the legitimation of middle school structure and process.

Cultural pressures which had brought the American middle school into existence as a differentiated school for early adolescent education have intensified and multiplied since the 1910 period. The new Department of Housing and Urban Development attests to that. Will the larger social welfare be served, now or in "the new day," by abandoning this institution for any other purpose? What other social value is capable of sustaining the legitimation of a middle school's *right* to exist once its differentiated function is no longer early adolescent education? To be sure, even open enrollment in elementary schools, and the busing of pupils, will not resolve the larger problem of de facto segregation in American society, but it would be more tolerable *as an alternative* first step in pursuit of a racially integrated public school system. Deviant intercultural attitudes, after all, should no more be countenanced in elementary schools than in any other unit of public school organization. Why, then, divert the middle school from its legitimate goal by tampering with its grade structure?

And society wastes its resources in unrewarding duplication when a middle school is diverted from the paramount goal of early adolescent education. Once the human condition at early adolescence ceases to be the dominant focus of middle school education, then the old pattern of 8-4 school organization would have *a more valid* administrative rationale for existing than a 4-4-4 pattern. Such disposal as positive intercultural and interracial attitudes, excellence in education, the cultivation of creativity, acquisition of cognitive skills are indispensable outputs of all school units, from first grade through the twelfth, and it does not matter whether the pattern of system organization is 8-4, 6-3-3, or 4-4-4.

No doubt, the external integration of public school systems with the new demands of society will necessitate not only larger quantities of these outputs, and of a superior quality, but also new outputs. What this means, however, in terms of structure and process, is that public school systems will have to innovate internally in order to obtain an effective integration with external aspirations for social reconstruction. It is the weight of *this task* which now rests heavily on the three primary subsystems of public school organization—institutional, managerial, technical—and there is no easy way of getting out from under its weight: not for boards of education, not for school administrators, and not for teachers.

Each of these subsystems, through its ascribed functions, must share in this task. The task is of a piece with the larger social reconstruction in which all of American society is now engaged. For the middle school organization there has never before existed the opportunity it now has for casting off its former handicaps, of undertaking its own revitalization, and of restoring its distinctive competence. Therefore, what institutional leadership in middle school administration makes of this opportunity now will determine whether the American middle school of tomorrow shall be a vigorous educational institution in the service of a renewed society or an organizational relic of a one-time institution.

Internal Integration

And the American middle school of tomorrow can be made into a vigorous educational institution. Its organizational mechanism has a potential of producing outputs which a space-age society would highly esteem as stabilizing inputs to its social welfare. First, however, to recapture the central argument in the preceding discussion, its *right to exist* as the implementing organization of a unique educational institution has to be reaffirmed at the school board level of public school organization. The next large-scale task then is to effect a qualitative internal integration of middle school organization with its unique institutional mission: restoring to it a distinctive competence.

Such a task entails for the most part a return to the nascent stage of middle school development in the United States. Patterns which over the years have been obstructing the internal integration of the middle school would have to be *deinstitutionalized*. This requires a resumption of the direction in middle school development which has been set before the World War I period. It is a direction which the North Central Association of Colleges and Secondary Schools had unsuccessfully attempted to hold after the war and to which the Southern Association of Colleges and Secondary Schools has committed itself in the 1950's. A revitalization of the American middle school, as with the self-renewal of society itself, calls for doing away with patterns of development which have been obstructing its internal integration. Deinstitutionalizing such patterns, either in the larger society or in any of its institutional systems, is no ordinary feat, but neither is institutional leadership ordinary or it would not be in short supply. As Selznick has put it, "It takes nerve to hold a course; it takes understanding to recognize and deal with the basic sources of institutional vulnerability."[10]

Our analysis has uncovered two "basic sources of institutional vulnerability" in middle school development: an ambiguous legitimation which settled around the middle school soon after it came into existence, and an inferior internal integration of the middle school with its institutional mission. Problems that have sprung from these sources, in the manner of a self-fulfilling prophecy, have reinforced each other in sustaining an image of the American middle school as "the tramp steamer of the educational fleet."

Middle school administrators now have to deal with these "basic sources of institutional vulnerability" in arenas within and without systems of public school organization. These are the contexts of consummatory relations of the middle school organization with other systems. Most problems which stem from an ambiguous legitimation can best be dealt with at the institutional level of public school systems. But the hard-core problems of internal integration originate outside of public school systems. The manner in which colleges qualify secondary school programs for the admission of pupils to higher education is one of these.

The Carnegie Unit

Chapter 7 has shown that, in accordance with a declaration of the Carnegie Foundation, Carnegie units "were never intended to constitute a rigid form of college admission, but merely as a means of comparing high schools." Moreover, by the time of World War I, the

[10] Selznick, *Leadership in Administration,* p. 25.

Foundation held that Carnegie units "have served their main purpose." Nevertheless, we will recall, 60 percent of the nation's colleges were reported in 1953 as still using the Carnegie unit for quantifying secondary school subjects in admission to higher education.

The Carnegie unit had preceded the middle school in American education. It came into use at a time when, by the authority of tradition, the ninth grade was in the high school. The Carnegie unit was at that time a functional mechanism for the goal of standardizing college admission in the United States. However, because the Carnegie unit had not anticipated the *differentiated function* of a middle school in secondary education, its continued use beyond 1910 obstructed the internal integration of the new middle school organization.

Colleges continued to count work of the ninth grade in their assessment of whether or not a high school program was completed. It had taken Charles Eliot and other college leaders nearly twenty years to standardize college entrance requirements in the United States. Then the collaboration between colleges and public school systems took a different turn. Secondary education broke the grip of college domination and innovated high school structure and process in accordance with its own institutional imperatives. When the 6-3-3 pattern of public school organization came on the scene, higher education had its own house well in order. Admission to college had been standardized around the four-year high school and stewards of higher education in the United States were of one mind with Voltaire's Dr. Pangloss that this was the "best of all possible worlds." Colleges continued to apply the Carnegie unit to ninth grade work as if the middle school never happened.

That an unmodified use of the Carnegie unit was obstructing middle school integration became apparent early. It will be recalled that the meeting of the North Central Association of Colleges and Secondary Schools in 1921 was told:

> . . . Colleges have not yet written their entrance requirements in terms of the three year high school. . . . Consequently, we find a troublesome joker in every three year junior high school in this territory. The seventh and eighth grades have been reorganized, but the ninth is the first year of high school taken over in toto and without change. . . .

The "troublesome joker" of the 1920's has persevered and has been obstructing internal middle school integration to this day. Too many colleges still calculate a grade point average based on ninth grade work or count Carnegie units in the ninth grade. It takes legerdemain to integrate the ninth grade with Gruhn's six middle school functions when subjects are measured by a Carnegie unit for college admission. The Carnegie unit and grade point averages are predominantly instrumental in orientation, whereas middle school functions are predominantly expressive in orientation. Consequently, many middle schools have given up the attempt and those which have not, at best, effect a poor integration of the ninth grade with middle school functions. Thus, failure to integrate fully the ninth grade has put a powerful leverage in the hands of those who would misuse the organizational mechanism of a middle school.

The middle school has to be freed of this predicament. Legitimation by society of its right to exist as a unique educational institution entitles the middle school to a differentiated educative process which, in accordance with rationalistic dictates of administration, has to be integrated with the manifest functions of its own institutional mission. Its articulation with the high school, one of its manifest functions as a transitional school, includes an *implied right* to certify a pupil as ready for high school, just as the high school has an explicit right to certify a pupil as ready for college.

Although the functions of a middle school do indeed have to articulate with functions of high school education, they are, nonetheless, *qualitatively different*. Educational experiences which early adolescent pupils have in a middle school ought to facilitate their study in high school, but it is a manifest function of the high school, and not of the middle school, to prepare pupils for college.

Regional accrediting associations, as they contemplate giving an accredited status to the middle school, might borrow an idea from Alfred North Whitehead as a guide to the preparation of institutionally warranted accreditation criteria. In an address of 1916 before the Mathematical Association of England, Whitehead urged reforms in English education and he said:[11]

> Each school should grant its own leaving certificates, based on its own curriculum. The standards of these schools should be sampled and corrected. But the first requisite for educational reform is the school as a

---

[11] Alfred North Whitehead, "The Aims of Education," in Stan Dropkin, Harold Full, and Ernest Schwartz, *Contemporary American Education* (New York: The Macmillan Company, 1965), p. 15.

unit, with its approved curriculum based on its own needs, and evolved by its own staff. If we fail to secure that, we simply fall from one formalism into another, from one dung-hill of inert ideas into another.

A "leaving certificate" is, of course, out of the question for a school which is by design transitional in character. Many public school systems do not have a graduation exercise in the middle school, or issue a certificate of graduation, precisely because even the inference of middle school education as terminal is to be avoided. There is, however, a deep universal insight in Whitehead's counsel that "the first requisite for educational reform is the school as a unit, with its approved curriculum based on its own needs, and evolved by its own staff." Those who devise strategies for strengthening the institutional and organizational posture of the American middle school ought to ponder it reflectively.

Inputs as Procurement

The Carnegie unit problem, and for that matter all other middle school problems which stem from gate-keeping procedures in higher education, can be viewed in still another light by applying Parsons' concept of disposal and procurement. The instrumentalism of having to count credits in a middle school, dysfunctional because it obstructs internal middle school integration, stands out in this light as an *input* to middle school organization and is, therefore, one aspect of the larger problem of *procurement*.

Parsons' conceptualization of disposal and procurement has been used before in Chapter 10 and at other points of our analysis. At a general level of definition, Parsons thinks of disposal as *any output* of the organization, whether the output is tangible or intangible. Qualitative disposal is output which contributes to the organization's external integration with other systems which require the output for their own input and without which they would "suffer a deprivation." Procurement, in the same way, is *any input* to the organization, whether the input is tangible or intangible, and without which it would suffer a deprivation in the pursuit of goals. Therefore, qualitative procurement is input which contributes to the organization's *internal integration* and, hence, its equilibrium.

It is useful to recall at this point that Parsons' classification of primary subsystems, in accordance with the function of roles, ascribes procurement as a *primary* responsibility of the managerial subsystem. Thus, middle school administrators, by definition of their role, have a primary responsibility for the procurement of resources which their organization requires for goal attainment, equilibrium, and for necessary adaptations. Consequences of gate-keeping procedures in higher education which obstruct middle school integration are patently dysfunctional inputs and, therefore, can be conceptualized as a procurement problem. In such a theoretical context, the Carnegie unit can be dealt with at a higher level of abstraction. For the problem is no longer the Carnegie unit per se, in isolation from other inputs, but the *quality of middle school procurement* in general.

Two important benefits accrue to middle school administration by conceptualizing inputs to middle school organization in a framework of procurement. First, the Carnegie unit is set in proper perspective as *one* input variable which has to be eliminated, but at the same time others of a similar character are not overlooked because of a simplistic attack on the problem. Second, *the right to eliminate dysfunctional inputs* is sustained by an administrative responsibility for procurement. It is now not a matter of tilting at windmills when middle school principals come to grips with the likes of a Carnegie unit problem.

For the use of the Carnegie unit in early adolescent education is not the only input variable which has been dysfunctional for the internal integration of middle schools. Some inputs, like the application of the Carnegie unit to ninth grade subjects, is manifestly dysfunctional, but there are others which are also dysfunctional because of their *latent characteristics*. When inputs are conceptualized as procurement, a cogent assessment can be made of latent and manifest characteristics in all input variables by a weighting of their integrative capacity and their ultimate contribution to goal attainment. A singular case in point is the use of evaluative criteria.

Evaluative Criteria

Two types of evaluative criteria are employed for self-evaluation in middle schools. One type, such as the Texas *Criteria for Evaluating Junior High Schools* and Connecticut's *An Assessment Guide for Use in Junior High Schools,* has been constructed from the ground up for the middle school. Another type, such as the 1963 *Evaluative Criteria for Junior High Schools* of the National Study of Secondary School Evaluation, has been *adapted* from the high school. As an input, what assessment shall be made of evaluative criteria which are indigenous to the institution of early adolescent education and those which have been adapted from the high school? And any mechanism which is employed for the self-evaluation of norms in a middle school organization has to be treated analytically as another input variable of procurement.

An inherent, and inescapable, weakness of *adapted* evaluative criteria for middle schools is that they have been meant for another educational institution. Evaluative criteria perform an institutionalizing function. They spell out a normative framework through which the institutional mission of a middle school is to be fulfilled by the implementing organization. There is, therefore, an inference in adapted evaluative criteria that the institutional mission of a middle school can be fulfilled in an *adapted* high school organization.

Both from the more distant institutional perspective and the immediate administrative concern for the quality of middle school procurement, there is much to be said for evaluative criteria which have been built from the ground up for the middle school. Indigenous evaluative criteria have attributes of quality, as an institutionalizing mechanism, which adapted criteria do not have. They are, for one thing, more likely to detect *latent deviance* in middle school structure and process than would adapted criteria. But even more important, unlike adapted criteria, indigenous evaluative criteria are at all points of evaluation infused with the "institutional spirit," precisely because they have evolved from the empirical development of the institution.

Indigenous evaluative criteria can be attuned from the ground up to the distinctive competence of middle school organization. Equipped with such institutional sensitivity, they can then guide dynamic adaptations of the organization to changing conditions in the external environment and, at the same time, serve as a raised-from-a-pup watchdog over its institutional integrity. No such confidence can be reposed, however, in evaluative criteria which have been adapted from the high school.

What Selznick calls "organization engineering" is not likely to be taken as an acceptable substitute for institutional middle school administration when expectations of evaluative criteria in administrative process include this: "The principal strives to make this school the specific type of school early adolescents need."[12] Nor are functional and institutional values of a discrete preparation program for middle school teachers likely to be overlooked by evaluative criteria which measure technical competence in a middle school by the criterion, "The teacher has had training for the junior high school."[13] It was George Santayana who warned, "Those who do not remember the past are condemned to relive it." If Santayana is right, then indigenous evaluative criteria, even without any other differentiating quality, would have to be stamped as of premium quality. And what is this premium? It is the guide of institutional experience!

The Input of Commitment

The guide of institutional experience will remind middle school administrators of a past which leaves no doubt whatsoever that the *single most important input* to middle school organization is the quality of an internalized commitment to early adolescent education which teachers bring with them. Frank Bunker, it will be recalled, had decided in 1910 against using high school teachers in his middle schools because "the point of view of such teachers tends to be that . . . the subject and its contents are of paramount importance, often overshadowing interest in the pupil himself." He did not want the instrumentalism of a "tendency toward undue specialization" in the high school as input to his middle school organization.

The distinctive technical competence of middle school teachers, it will also be recalled, was of such important input for James Glass that he regarded in-service programs "for the professional training of the teaching staff" as a "foremost administrative obligation." Institutional experience, as we know from Chapters 11 and 12, has confirmed over and over the correctness of his judgment.

There was a time when salary parity with teachers in the high school was believed to be the key to effective internal middle school integration. Indeed, we will recall, there were those in the North Central Association of the early 1920's who wanted "more attractive salaries in

---

[12] *An Assessment Guide for Use in Junior High Schools.* The Connecticut State Department of Education, Bureau of Elementary and Secondary Education, June 1960, Hartford, Conn., p. 15.

[13] *Ibid.*, p. 18. See the same references in criteria 1 and 2 of *Criteria for Evaluating Junior High Schools.* Research Study Number 21, The Texas Study of Secondary Education, 1956, pp. 6 and 19.

Junior High Schools rather than salaries equal in attractiveness to those paid in Senior High Schools" as a means of driving out the pernicious effects of anticipatory socialization and relative deprivation from middle schools. But the investigation in 1962 by Gross and Popper, conducted in a middle school of a North Central Association member school system, and whererin middle school teachers have attained salary parity with high school teachers, showed that salary parity alone was not enough.

"A teaching body without pedagogical faith," Durkheim held, "is a body without a soul."[14] More than in any other organizational unit of a public school system, the internal integration of the middle school has been obstructed by teachers who bring little or no "pedagogical faith" to their assignment. The notion of a "school without teachers" is a contemporary figurative derivation of Durkheim's "teaching body without pedagogical faith." It has come to symbolize the darkest frustration of middle school administration in the post-World War II period.

Most state departments of education do not require a discrete certification for middle school teachers. Middle school teachers are certified either as elementary or secondary school teachers and are allowed to teach in middle school grades by some arrangement in certification procedure. Their socialization, therefore, has been to the norms of either the elementary school or high school. And because the professional preparation of middle school teachers is still "a no man's land" in American teacher education, most middle school teachers in the United States are neither equipped with the required skills for the role nor have they internalized an institutional commitment to the role.[15]

They know little more than a layman about the human condition at early adolescence. The professionalization of the American teacher has crystallized three skill dimensions around the role of teacher: cognitive, psychological, and social. A teacher is prepared for a role in the educational enterprise in accordance with a commitment to apply these skills on clients who have attained a given stage of development. Each school unit, moreover, has its own norms for applying these skills, and teachers in each unit are socialized to these norms in the preparation program. The self-contained classroom, as an example, is a structural

---

[14] Durkheim, *Education and Sociology*, p. 144.
[15] For a discussion of the current status of this problem in teacher education see "Symposium: The Junior High School Teacher," *The Clearinghouse*, Vol. 40, October 1965.

norm of the elementary school, whereas departmentalization is the norm in high schools.

Neither of these, however, is the norm in middle schools because the articulation function of a transitional school calls for a fusion of these norms. Teachers who have not been socialized to the normative framework of a middle school are overcome by frustration after frustration because, as was put in Chapter 11, of a trained incapacity to conform, in accordance with administrative expectations, to middle school norms. Frustrated middle school teachers, so the guide of institutional experience will attest, retreat to the technicism of the "job." They encounter difficulty in identifying with values of early adolescent education, either because they have already internalized a commitment to other values or because they do not know precisely what these values are. Such teachers retreat to lecturing, an emphasis on grades, piling on of homework, and other such practices with which they can identify professionally. They are teachers without pedagogical faith, and consequently, the middle school is turned into a school without teachers and suffers a deprivation.

The frustration of middle school principals is, therefore, altogether understandable. They deplore the neglect of middle school organization in teacher education. It is a neglect which impinges sharply upon their administrative role. When, however, the quality of a teacher's professional preparation is conceptualized as an important ingredient of procurement, middle school principals are expected to do more than deplore.

A responsibility for middle school procurement obliges them to enter the sector of higher education and attend to the manner in which the Carnegie unit is applied. The same responsibility obliges them also to expect a qualitative output from teacher education. It is the differentiated function of schools of education in the social division of labor to produce disposal which school organizations require as inputs and, again, without which they would suffer a deprivation. Middle school administrators have a right, therefore, to expect disposal from schools of education which is functional as input to their own organization.

Schools of education are by *social definition* obliged to fulfill the input requirements of the middle school in the same way as they now fulfill input requirements of other school units. To merely deplore the neglect of middle school organization in schools of education is not enough. Middle school administrators are derelict in a major executive function, by role definition, when they fail to "go on the line" for the procurement their organization requires.

In the same vein, a middle school is entitled to all of the input values of teacher certification that accrue to other units of public school organization. State departments of education confess to an abysmal ignorance of early adolescent education, and they are remiss thereby in an obligation to protect the public welfare, when they certify middle school teachers on less than the successful completion of *a discretely differentiated preparation program.*

A principal function of certification in education, as with licensure in medicine, law, pharmacy, and other professions, is to protect clients from incompetence. High school teachers are not allowed to teach elementary school pupils nor are kindergarten teachers allowed to teach high school pupils. Their discrete certification means to assure kindergarten, elementary, and high school clients of a *competent* professional service, and this is as it should be. But early adolescents, who during the period of transition endure the physiological stress and the psychological strain of the most difficult stage in human development, are abandoned by many state departments of education to teachers who, despite a course here and there in early adolescent education, are nonetheless professionally unequipped to render the required service in a middle school. A qualitative and discrete teacher certification for early adolescent education is, therefore, another ingredient of procurement for which middle school administrators have to be prepared to go on the line in the performance of major executive functions.

But, of course, whether or not a middle school principal will go on the line for the procurement his organization requires for goal attainment and a stable existence turns on how he perceives executive functions as well as the strength of his own institutional commitment to the middle school. It is because of this that the quality of his own preparation for middle school administration, and his own internalized commitment to early adolescent education, are also a crucial category of inputs to middle school organization. Again, as Selznick has put it, "It takes nerve to hold a course; it takes understanding to recognize and deal with the basic sources of institutional vulnerability." Only middle school principals who have an institutional commitment to couple with nerve, who are equipped with conceptual strength in getting a fix on middle school problems, and who have cultural insights with which to infuse administrative functions are likely to go on the line and deal with the basic sources of institutional vulnerability.

Administration as an Input

The quality of middle school administration in the United States has been rising perceptibly since World War II. Much of the credit for this can be claimed rightfully by the National Association of Secondary-School Principals. Its Executive Committee, aware of the talent drain from middle school administration because of the better pay in high school administration, has come to grips with the problem by recommending three categories of secondary schools, determined by enrollment size, as differentiating variables in the compensation scale of secondary school administration.[16] Although many school boards have followed this recommendation, many have not. Consequently, effective middle school principals in all too many public school systems are still, we recall from Chapter 11, "rewarded with a *promotion* to the high school."

But even if all school boards in the United States were to abide by the Association's recommendation, it would still not assure a qualitative administrative input to middle school organization. It is inherently defective as a mechanism for strengthening the middle school because it differentiates *quantitatively* between executive functions. Executive functions of a middle school principal are no different from executive functions of a high school principal. Certain administrative tasks of "running the school" are, to be sure, different, but not basic executive functions as these are defined by Barnard, Selznick, Parsons, Dimock, and others.

A high school principal, as an example, has to arrange administratively for an extracurricular athletic program, whereas a middle school principal does not. But coaches, and not the principal, conduct the athletic program, in the same way as teachers, and not the principal, conduct in a middle school the student-interest activity program, scheduled parent-teacher and teacher-pupil conferences, and other such nonacademic instructional activities. Although, here again, it is the middle school principal who has to arrange for these administratively. The administration of a middle school which provides a proper professional service for "x" early adolescent pupils can be as demanding of time and energy as is the administration of a high school which provides a proper professional service for "y" pupils. Other illustrations can be cited which show up the weakness of a quantitative differentation. En-

[16] See *What Salary for You?* Statement approved by the Executive Committee of the National Association of Secondary School Principals, October 1, 1957.

rollment size and the number of administrative tasks are valid as quantitative variables in a determination of how many *administrative subordinates* a principal will require for the performance of basic executive functions, but they are not valid as differentiating variables between these functions; not when the principal in secondary school administration is conceptualized as an executive role.

What this suggests is that qualitative, rather than quantitative, variables have to be assessed in a determination of the middle school principal's status, not alone on a salary scale, but in American secondary school administration generally. A qualitative differentiation between middle school and high school organizations would have to treat the variable of *distinctive competence* in each and thereby protect the *institutional integrity* of both. With such a frame of reference to the middle school principalship, an alternative course is at once available for dealing with the problem of a salary scale for middle school principals *vis-à-vis* high school principals. Basic salary parity with high school principals can be justified for middle school principals in this frame of reference because middle school and high school organizations are implementing mechanisms of differentiated, but culturally necessary, institutions in secondary education which require an equally high order administrative expertise for the attainment of their respective goals.

Such an approach to the middle school principalship is manifestly functional for the infusion of institutional commitment into middle school administration. No longer will the lure of better pay in the high school drain the American middle school of its best administrative talents. Middle school administration would become a lifetime career for those who have responded to the mystique of motivation with a commitment to early adolescent education. But apart from its intended function, such an approach to the middle school principalship suggests a latent value which the National Association of Secondary School Principals might explore with profit for all of secondary school administration in the United States.

The American Association of School Administrators advanced the professionalization of general school administration after World War II by establishing the Committee for the Advancement of School Administration. It was the work of this committee which led the AASA to decide that after January 1964 only those who have successfully completed a sixth year of graduate study in educational administration at an AASA accredited school of education would be eligible for membership. The National Council for the Accreditation of Teacher Education was engaged by the AASA to serve as its accrediting agency.

Perhaps the time is at hand for a Committee for the Advancement of Secondary School Administration. The National Association of Secondary School Principals might commission such a committee to undertake, among other assignments, a comprehensive study of preparation requirements for secondary school administration in the modern period and adjust its qualification of new members accordingly. A required sixth year in the preparation program for secondary school administration at NASSP accredited schools should focus on a program which is infused with interdisciplinary and theoretical enrichments, it should advance the professionalization of secondary school administration, and it should allow for necessary differentiations at the sixth year between high school and middle school administration.

A mastery of administrative mechanics alone should no longer qualify for middle school administration. Contemporary middle school administration requires an intellectual capacity which transcends mere organization engineering. A capacity for relating middle school structure and process to the dynamics of culture calls for deep intellectual insights into that powerful bond between school and society which is defined in the works of Durkheim, Dewey, Counts, and other social theorists. It is a bond of many strands. Each strand is a projection of culture which, through the diverse symbolism of human aspiration, esteem, and endeavor, is intertwined with the others in a socially significant way. It is no longer realistic to expect that one year of professional preparation in educational administration can equip middle school principals with the necessary technical skills of administration and also with those intellectual insights which distinguish between an administrative technicist and institutional leader. Closer to the point, principals who are devoid of institutional insight are not likely to be the ones who will initiate the innovations of a dynamic adaptation which will lead to the middle school of tomorrow.

15

THE MIDDLE SCHOOL OF
TOMORROW

Unlike Pallas Athena, sprung full-grown from the forehead of Zeus, the middle school of tomorrow will not materialize overnight. It is more likely to evolve from a continuing process of self-revitalization. Tomorrow, in all likelihood, will see the institution of a middle school for early adolescent education. A wrong turn at the crossroads, where it now stands, may indeed jeopardize its existence as an institutional type, but not for long. A wrong turn will only necessitate the eventual reversal of its course, or American society will have to invent some institutional substitute for it.

But the developmental course of middle school organization need not take a wrong turn at the crossroads. A commitment to the social value of a differentiated early adolescent education, a willingness to go on the line for the innovations which are required for the middle school of tomorrow can spell the difference between a right and wrong turn. It all hinges on the strength of institutional insight in contemporary public school administration. For the *mobilization of forces* in defense of distinctive competence in middle school organization and, therefore, also of institutional integrity, is the administrative obligation of middle school principals.

And institutional insight begins with an intellectual awareness of the powerful cultural bond between school and society. It is precisely because of this bond that the consequences of accelerated cultural change in society are laid as problems at school doors. These are the problems whose thrusts move systems of public school organization to undertake innovations.

Innovations, however, can take several directions. An innovation can be revolutionary and destructive of institutional values, it can be reformistic and rehabilitate corrupted institutional values, or it can be dynamically adaptive and discard organizational patterns of an old environment and evolve new patterns for the expression of institutional values in the new environment. All three directions have been advocated in American education at one time or another in the pursuit of progress.

An adaptive orientation to progress, unlike revolution, follows the principle of institutional continuity. Adaptive innovations are aimed at the revitalization of an institutional system through a new integration of its values with a changing society. Accelerated cultural change generates pressures on society, intensifies old problems, and unhinges its stability at vital points. Dynamic institutional adaptations infuse society with new stabilizing inputs at such a time and thereby obviate the necessity of *radical* institutional breaks with past social experience. None of this is possible, however, without corresponding innovations in the implementing organizational mechanism of institutions. Formal organizations, even those which are classifiable in the pattern-maintenance category on a typology, when they thus innovate their structure and process enable society to move from one stability to another as it pursues higher stages of progress. For when a society turns highly adaptive, as is now the United States, all of its categories of organization have to be responsive.

Following the principle of institutional continuity, then, the drive of adaptive innovations in middle school organization is toward a new institutional integration with a changing society. Central, and important above all else, is, therefore, the institutional focus. For such organizational innovations which do not have an institutional focus can easily turn revolutionary in character. Witness, as an example, the loss of institutional integrity which is threatened by a 5-8 middle school organization that has emerged in response to the problem of de facto racial segregation.

The Guiding Institutional Focus

Innovations which aim at a new institutional integration are, therefore, adaptive responses to pervasive cultural change in society. When the function of innovation is seen in such a light, it suggests the theoretical formulation of Ferdinand Toennies, *Gemeinschaft und Gesellschaft,* as a useful framework for speculating about middle school innovations in the still larger context of social reconstruction. *Gemeinschaft und Gesellschaft* it will be recalled, conceptualizes a deep social problem which afflicts modern society and which was touched upon in Chapter 10. The "loss of community" which Toennies had perceived in the purposive-rational orientations of modern society is a social problem which has intrigued social scientists ever since, and it has yet to be resolved. At the heart of the problem is the dehumanization of society by the rationalistic efficiency of bureaucratically structured organizations. Society is being drained of important human values when the primary group relations of "community" are weakened. Their loss raises the specter of an anomic society, of rootlessness, of large-scale alienation from the idealism of society. President Johnson voiced a revealing insight when, in May 1964, he said to a University of Michigan audience, "The Great Society is a place where the city of man serves not only the needs of the body and the demands of commerce, but the desire for beauty and the hunger for community." In the shorthand of political symbolism, "The Great Society" expresses through a slogan the best of American social idealism. It embodies in its meaning aspirations for the social and aesthetic attributes of High Civilization. It is, moreover, in close kinship with what Alfred North Whitehead had in mind when he wrote in *Science and the Modern World* that our problem is not the lack of great men, but of great societies. "The great society," Whitehead believed, "will put up the great men for the occasion."

It has been proposed by social scientists that society now has to invent new types of social organization whose function it will be to restore the sense of community that is lost by a weakening of kinship, friendship, and residential groups. But, except during periods of violent revolutionary upheaval, a mature society rarely invents, *de novo*, new types of social organization. New patterns of interaction usually evolve within established institutions to perform new functions, or society might borrow a social invention of another culture and adapt it for its own use. One such case in point is the middle school, another is Toynbee Hall of London, and yet still many other instances of cultural borrowing can be cited.

When an institutional projection of the American middle school is juxtaposed to the "loss of community—quest for community" dichotomization of Toennies' classic formulation, then the course of adaptive innovation in middle school organization becomes almost self-directing. From the institutional point of view, a middle school organization provides the normative framework for fulfilling the social value of a differentiated educational program for early adolescents. But in its structure is also what William J. Goode has conceptualized as "community within a community."[1]

Goode's reference to community means to direct attention to social patterns within purposive-rational systems which have evolved in the modern period as a response to the *Gemeinschaft-Gesellschaft* dilemma. Goode sees a gratificational element of community within the professions and he speaks of it as community within a community. Aspects of the same phenomena can be observed, however, in other systems as well. It can be seen, for example, in the tendency of employee relations departments of large industrial organizations to plan family recreation for employees, engage in community fund drives, and otherwise encourage employees to accept calls for community service. These activities are far removed from the rationalistic character of the organization, and they are, moreover, a relatively recent social development. This suggests that modern American society, in its quest for community, is evolving new social patterns within occupational systems as a means of replenishing its community values. Our institutional projection supports a view of the American middle school as still another type of social response to the *Gemeinschaft-Gesellschaft* dilemma.

The evolution of a community dimension within American sys-

---

1 William J. Goode, "Community Within A Community: The Professions," *American Sociological Review*, Vol. 22, April 1957. For others on the same problem see Robert A. Nisbet, *The Quest for Community* (Fair Lawn, N.J.: Oxford University Press, 1953); R. M. MacIver, *Community* (New York: The Macmillan Company, 1917); Don Martindale, *American Social Structure* (New York: Appleton-Century-Crofts, 1960); and Maurice R. Stein, *The Eclipse of Community* (Princeton, N.J.: Princeton University Press, 1960).

tems of public school organization can be observed at several points of reference and, in each instance, in a parallel course with the rationalization of society. Curriculum development, as one point of reference, has been so markedly affected by the intervention of activities which once were the province of community that no treatment of modern curriculum can be taken as complete without such a reference. W. L. Wrinkle and R. S. Gilchrist have written of the manner in which athletics came into the physical education program of high schools when "downtown sports enthusiasts" engaged a coach to direct boys in after-school athletics. They also note that instruction in instrumental music was at one time the exclusive province of either a private teacher or the village band. Now, however, it has been incorporated in the process of public school organization.[2] Others have also written on this theme.

As educative process endeavored to provide more and more of those gratifications which once were the province of community, the structure of public school organization, originally an extension of purposive-rational society, became increasingly fused with an extension of random community. The familiar legal doctrine of *in loco parentis* defines a teacher's role in formal instruction, but the rationalization of modern society has increasingly extended the doctrine of *in loco parentis* so that, insofar as it concerns the socialization of youth, one may before very long also speak of public school organization as *in loco communitatis*. Extensions of community into formal public school organization have been, in the manner of social evolution, almost imperceptible, but extensions there have been nonetheless.

Elementary school organization was from the beginning oriented to the rationalistic imperatives of society; namely the formal instruction of children in the cognitive skills which open what William T. Harris liked to think of as the "five windows of the soul."[3] High school organization was essentially an enlargement of the same orientation. Its goal is still predominantly oriented to the instrumentalism of higher education or the world of work. Not until after the Civil War, when Harris added a kindergarten to the public school organization of St. Louis, did an organizational unit materialize in a system of public education whose goal was the fulfillment of individual gratifications which theretofore

2 W. L. Wrinkle and R. S. Gilchrist, *Secondary Education for American Democracy* (New York: Farrar and Rinehart, 1942), p. 339. See also Dorothy M. Fraser, *Deciding What to Teach* (Washington, D.C.: National Education Association, 1964), p. 16.

3 Curti, *Social Ideas*, p. 315.

had been the exclusive province of the family. Then came the middle school.

Superintendent Harris added the kindergarten unit to public school organization as a means of compensating in the socialization process for a deterioration he perceived in the quality of family life.[4] Superintendent Bunker of Berkeley added the middle school as a means of intervening protectively in the socialization process at the onset of adolescence and to "warm up" the instrumental school climate with necessary psychological gratifications.

"The school system," according to Bunker's view as it was given in Chapter 2, "in its organic form, and in the articulation of its parts, completely ignores the significant physiological and psychical changes which are ushered in with the advent of adolescence." And Superintendent Greeson of Grand Rapids, whose view was also given in Chapter 2, saw early adolscence as an age when "boys are becoming men; the girls are becoming women; and a flood of new impulses, new ideas, new emotions are crowding up in them, making it a very critical and important period of their lives." But, he continued, in "our schools, . . . we do not take this into account."

What Bunker and Greeson did was to assume administrative responsibility in the case of early adolescents not alone for the rationalistic demands of society but also for individual human needs of community. Early adolescents, Greeson held, "naturally crave for organization among themselves," they "ought to have their debating clubs, their societies, their athletic games," and so forth. But because these gratifications "are impossible with the present organization," he proposed in 1909 that "the seventh, eighth and ninth grades" should be set in separate schools.

Middle schools of the 1910 period were products of the social reconstruction which followed Appomattox. Their process extended an incipient integration of community and society in public school organization which was initiated with the kindergarten. Liberal Darwinism had triumphed over the dehumanizing ideology of social Darwinism, and social reconstruction, as a way of self-renewal, took firm hold in the American mind. World War I, to be sure, put a halt to social reconstruction, but its direction was by then well defined in social experience.

It is a direction which has now been resumed after two world wars and a severe economic depression of long duration. The United States

4 *Ibid.,* p. 324.

has turned once again to social reconstruction because continuing confrontations between human needs of community and society's demands for conformity to its rationalistic patterns have made it crystal clear that the qualitative integration of these two orientations no longer can be left to *ad hoc,* day-to-day measures. These confrontations are at the root of grave cultural problems, and the best of social engineering is now required to join community and society in a compatible integration as a means of conserving valuable human resources. This in essence is the foremost social challenge which faces modern America.

Society has to effect what throughout this discussion has been referred to as a "dynamic adaptation" of its structure and process as a means of coming to terms with human needs and society's functional imperatives.[5] A start has been made in the institution of public education. The middle school is one of its manifestations. Indeed, in terms of the dynamic adaptation to external conditions which is now needed in systems of public school organization, the middle school of Bunker's day can now be seen retrospectively as an early stage in the evolution of what is generally referred to as "the community school."

The idea of a community school is not new to the subculture of education. But beyond a lighted schoolhouse program for youth, evening adult education classes, or some other community use of a public school facility after school hours, the idea of a community school has made little developmental progress in American education, although major facets of the idea have been advanced in contemporary literature with increasing urgency. Nevertheless, responsive internal strivings to satisfy external demands for new outputs are inexorably moving public school systems in the direction of the community school idea. "The institutionalized school system," wrote Van Miller, onetime editor of *Educational Administration Quarterly,* "will have to find ways of accommodating modern man and society or the educational needs of both will be pursued through other channels."[6]

---

[5] The sense in which *dynamic adaptation* is used here follows Selznick's meaning. See Selznick, *Leadership in Administration,* pp. 29–38.

[6] Van Miller, "Understanding and Respect Between 'Traditionalists' and Newcomers," *Educational Administration Quarterly,* Vol. II, Winter 1966, p. 4. For references in the literature to the community school concept, see, as examples, Chapter 3, "The Farmville Community School," in *Education for All American Youth* (Washington, D.C.: The Educational Policies Commission, 1944); W. E. Armstrong, Maurice R. Ahrens, William H. Bristow, and E. T. McSwain, "Conditions Compelling Curriculum Change," in *Action for Curriculum Improvement, Yearbook* (Washington, D.C.: Association for Supervision and Curriculum Development, 1951), pp. 33–34; also Samuel H. Popper, "The Challenge to the Two Professions," in Robert H. Beck (ed.), *Society and the Schools: Communica-*

A mature community school is still in the distant future. But when it does materialize, *a coordinate family of professions* will be required to apply *a multiple-skills process* with a capacity to satisfy both community and society. Such a school will evolve from adaptive responses in public school systems to new consummatory relations with society. And it will be more than a school in the traditional sense, it will be a Center for Human Development. Not all units of a public school system, however, are equally equipped for these adaptive responses. Here is where the middle school unit has the advantage of an orientational readiness.

A multiple-skills process is precisely what the middle school has been striving to attain all along. Organically, it is best equipped in public school organization to initiate an efficient adaptive response to new social conditions. Therefore, with the guide of institutional experience, adaptive middle school innovations at this time could lead to two highly desirable ends: the revitalization of the American middle school as a unique cultural system, and, in the course of its own revitalization, it can function as a social laboratory in which the superordinate system can perfect the complex communications network which a multiple-skills process, applied by a coordinate family of professions, will surely require.

The Past Is Prologue

No one was more keenly aware than James M. Glass of how required categories of community and societal values had to be integrated in the process of middle school organization. His intuition about this was exceeded by no known contemporary of his period. Both the gratificational orientation of community and the rationalistic orientation of society were captured in his definition of middle school structure and process.

Glass understood well enough that each school unit differentiates its structure and process in accordance with some differentiated function in the division of labor of a public school system. A middle school unit, Glass held, is differentiated by the dominance of its psychosocial

---

tion Challenge to Education and Social Work (New York: National Association of Social Workers, 1965). Hereafter cited as *Society and the Schools*. Flint, Michigan, Winchester Elementary School of New Haven, Connecticut, and the Children's Center of the Mount Vernon, New York public school system perhaps have given the most advanced developmental expression to the community school idea.

values. Middle school organizations have to effect an integration of community and society in which community is dominant. It is, therefore, the singularity of this differentiation which should govern orientations to middle school structure and process.

According to Glass, the dominant orientation of middle school organization is to "the individual" and not to mass society: "The identity of the junior high school is, therefore, established in its purpose to treat each pupil as an individual problem."[7] Glass left no doubt that his reference to "an individual problem" was directed at the human condition of early adolescents in modern society. The middle school phase of education, he said, is the "finding, testing, and trying-out period of the public-school system."

Glass had thus spelled out the norms of middle school education. These norms were later incorporated in the 1924 middle school pattern of the North Central Association. It is a pattern which evolved from institutional experience, and it had survived the test of critical North Central consideration for some eight years before it was officially adopted.[8] In all of its larger essentials, this pattern has been the normative framework of middle schools in the United States to this day. Hence, if Herodotus, father of history, was right and "the past is prologue" in human affairs, then the middle school of tomorrow will in all likelihood take its shape from this pattern.

Directly to the point then is *The Junior High School Program* of the Southern Association of Colleges and Secondary Schools. The middle school pattern of the Southern Association embodies the critical norms of North Central's pattern, but redefines them in a modern idiom. It is a pattern which expresses the most advanced stage of middle school development in the United States.

Protective intervention in the process of education at the onset of adolescence is legitimized, as heretofore, by the social value of attending to the human needs of this period. But these human needs are now explicated through Havighurst's conceptualization of developmental tasks at early adolescence and their relevance to mental health. Moreover, the singularity of a middle school is defined by six manifest functions, as these were intuited by Glass and later delineated by Gruhn.

---

[7] These remarks are taken from the same 1922 address before the NEA which was cited in Chapters 11 and 12.

[8] See "Committee Recommendations Regarding the Organization and Administration of Junior High Schools," in *Proceedings,* NCA, 1916, pp. 171–74.

But, again, these functions are scaled to early adolescent exigencies of today. The socialization function serves as an illustration.

Whereas Glass spoke abstrusely of socialization as an "objective" in "junior citizenship," the Southern Association's pattern focuses directly on particularistic primary group relations:[9]

> The junior high school has very important responsibilities which it should assume in helping early adolescents satisfy their need for friendships and, in particular, their relationships with the opposite sex. During this transitional period students must develop new social skills which will help them be comfortable in the presence of the opposite sex. Moreover, there are new, more mature, understandings in the area of social relationships which schools can assist students to acquire.

And, as in the case of other manifest middle school functions, socialization comes to grips in this pattern at "the teachable moment," to use Havighurst's expression, with the difficult matter of sex education:[10]

> As sex interest increases it is a topic of conversation among members of the same sex, with a pooling of sex information and misinformation. Smutty stories which survive from generation to generation, sex words and words on elimination become a part of the vocabulary. The more sexually mature often introduce the immature to the act of masturbation. Recent studies indicate that while masturbation is common among early adolescent boys, it is practiced much less by girls. Authorities believe this is not harmful physically but that there may be emotional harm should a guilt complex develop because of the practice. Young adolescents are disturbed by the seemingly unfounded causes for sexual stimulation. . . . With the change from childhood to adulthood, there comes an awakening of the sex drive. . . . Adjustment of young people to this change, while primarily the responsibility of the home, has implications for the junior high school program.

The Southern Association's pattern blueprints a middle school which embodies the continuity of institutional experience, but at the same time is also attuned to the modern social scene. Bunker, Greeson, and Glass would recognize on sight institutional hallmarks in this middle school, despite the modernity of its process. It is a process which is oriented to human needs at early adolescence, but at the same time does not neglect purposive society. "The instructional program," when the Southern Association's pattern is followed, "should be designed to pro-

[9] *The Junior High School Program,* p. 12.
[10] *Ibid.,* p. 13.

vide for needs of early adolescents and of society."[11]   But, and in keeping with its unique institutional character, "needs of early adolescents" come before "society," even in the instructional program.

The instructional program, like the larger pattern, bears a close institutional and organic resemblance to the middle school program of 1924 from the North Central Association.   However, the Southern Association has modernized the instructional program by means of two innovations: block-of-time scheduling coupled with a Core approach to curriculum organization.   These two innovations have added cognitive values to the learning experience without jarring the centrality of a psychosocial focus in middle school process:[12]

> Scheduling students to one teacher for an extended period of time provides increased opportunity for the needs, abilities, and interests of individual students to be identified and dealt with satisfactorily.   It also affords a gradual and effective means of adjusting to transition from the self-contained classroom of elementary schools and makes possible better guidance of students.   These are a few of the many increased advantages which teachers have by virtue of being with the same students over a longer period of time along with the newer approaches to teaching which are a characteristic of the block and constitute its chief advantage.
>
> Effective core classes make extensive use of teacher-student planning and of problem-solving techniques.   The specific curricular experiences which are dealt with through the problem solving approach are identified through teacher and total staff study and planning, and through careful planning with students to determine the problems which are significant and of concern to them.   These problems are real and are derived from what we know about the growth and development of early adolescents, their developmental tasks, their common and individual concerns, the demands of our democratic society, and the most significant clues we can distill from research.

In sum, the six manifest functions of a middle school are built into every facet of structure and process in the Southern Association's pattern.   Few, if any, American middle schools have succeeded in giving full operational expression to this pattern.[13]   Some, like Como Park

11 *Ibid.,* p. 37.
12 *Ibid.,* pp. 40–41.
13 John H. Lounsbury provides a supporting footnote to this contention.   He sampled, in 1954, developmental trends in 251 middle schools for his doctoral dissertation.   A resampling, in 1964, of 202 schools in the original study led him to conclude: "In the majority of the practices there were few differences between the practices in 1964 and

Junior High School of St. Paul, have come closer than others. But when a middle school organization does move toward the Southern Association's pattern, it equips itself developmentally to use past institutional experience as prologue to the middle school of tomorrow.

Toward a Dynamic Adaptation

The Southern Association has patterned a middle school organization which is implementable now and which, by means of a dynamic adaptation, can be tomorrow's middle school. For a middle school which already embodies the administrative and technical processes of the Southern Association's pattern stands in what Selznick thinks of as "the shadowy area where administration and policy meet" and where dynamic adaptation, as distinct from routine adaptation, takes place.[14] And any projection of a future development which can be sustained by what is already feasible has to be set apart from crystal gazing.

The notion of a "shadowy area" conforms to Selznick's conceptualization of leadership in administration. He thinks of it as a zone of interaction between the institutional and managerial subsystems where agreement has crystallized about the organization's long-range future and where "organizational processes profoundly influence the kinds of policy that can be made."[15] And conversely, policy decisions can now be made about innovations which will move the total organization to a dynamic adaptation.

Such innovations, however, have to be substantive and not routine. Routine innovations are not what Selznick has in mind when he speaks of a dynamic adaptation. Tomorrow's middle school will no doubt introduce many new procedures which will transform the *modus operandi* of early adolescent education. These, however, have to be seen in a projection of future middle school developments as *implementing routines of a more substantive innovation.* Assuming, by way of an illustration, a dynamic adaptation has been effected in some middle school which adhered to norms of the Southern Association's pattern, then what follows is a likely image of implementing routines that will be employed.

---

the practices followed ten years earlier." See John H. Lounsbury and Harl R. Douglass, "Recent Trends in Junior High School Practices, 1954–1964," *The Bulletin*, NASSP, Vol. 49, September 1965, p. 88.

14 Selznick, *Leadership in Administration*, p. 35.

15 *Ibid.*, p. 36.

Neither bell ringing nor competitive report cards will be allowed in the psychologically protective environment of that middle school. There will be no need actually of these pressure-generating devices. Modular scheduling, an invention made possible by computer technology and already operational, will regulate a program in which a large number of exploratory experiences materialize through short courses, student-interest activities, learning laboratories, and frequent excursions into the community to observe first hand its patterns of culture.[16]

Likewise, no instrumental value will be associated with conventional report cards because pupil progress in mastering the larger developmental tasks will be conveyed to the home through regularly scheduled parent-teacher conferences. And because this unit will function as an organizational component of a Center for Human Development, grading practices which are ego destroying, and, hence, are dysfunctional for building a positive self-concept, will be replaced by a "satisfactory" or "unsatisfactory" evaluation of completed short-range tasks. Even higher education, it is significant to note, is beginning to back away from anxiety-laden letter grades as a means of encouraging the intellectual traits of creative and critical thinking.[17] Motivation in this middle school will stress the stimuli of an upwardly spiraling self-competition and not fears of failure or embarrassment. Early adolescents, in the throes of a hyperidealism characteristic of this age, will not be expected to compete with classmates for grades at the same time as their school attempts to teach what Mary Parker Follet, a noted industrial human relations counselor of the pre-World War II period, has called "the art of cooperative thinking."

Procedures of this character proclaim that central to all things in our middle school of tomorrow is the human condition at early adolescence. Every aspect of middle school structure and process has been differentiated in accordance with the centrality of this orientation. Consequently, all of middle school organization, including its physical plant, is functionally equipped to fuse social-psychological gratifications of

---

16 See, among many others on modular scheduling, Robert N. Bush and Dwight W. Allen, *A New Design for High School Education* (New York: McGraw-Hill Book Company, 1964); Judith Murphy, *School Scheduling by Computer: The Story of GASP* (New York: Educational Facilities Laboratories, 1964). Modular scheduling in middle schools is already in use and reported in the literature. See Almon G. Hoy, "Flexibility and the RMS Program," *Minnesota Journal of Education*, Vol. 44, February 1964.

17 Prestigious Carleton College of Northfield, Minnesota, for example, has instituted a "pass-fail" evaluation of courses taken outside of a student's major field.

community with purposive-rational imperatives of society. *The singular institutional purpose of the American middle school has remained the same, but its social value has been enhanced by a pattern of organization whose structure and process is now adapted to new social conditions.*

Although a host of such new routines are likely in tomorrow's middle school, essentially only *two substantive innovations* are required for the dynamic adaptation of a middle school which is already structured in the Southern Association's pattern. But these two innovations will necessitate an enlargement of its role structure, they will expand administrative expectations of technical roles, they will require a communications network of unprecedented complexity, and they will in all likelihood accelerate the developmental pace of nongradeness in all units of a public school system. In short, the total organization will be modified by these innovations. These innovations, moreover, are feasible now, because each has already secured a beachhead in the middle school. As each is expanded, and gains in developmental maturity, the service capacity of the American middle school will be enlarged and even infused with new attributes of social usefulness.

A Family of Professions

One of these substantive innovations is the assignment of *a coordinate status* to all "helping" professions which contribute to the process of a middle school. Education is, of course, a long-established helping profession. Central to all formal education, from the Greeks to this day, is a helping function. A teacher in ancient Greek society was expected to guide the footsteps of his pupils on pathways leading to the good life. Some two millennia and more later, and many transformations in the world community, the social role of a teacher is still the same, albeit, technologies of education have changed. But since the steam engine, then electricity, and now nuclear power, pathways to the good life have become increasingly difficult to transverse. Many pupils falter, give up the effort altogether, and, to the detriment of themselves and society, never attain the good life. A teacher can no longer help such pupils singlehandedly. Consequently, teachers in time had to enlist other professions as auxiliaries.

Now, a public school system in the United States is considered derelict if it does not have a family of professions to service its pupils.

Doctors, social workers, psychologists, guidance counselors, and nurses perform *auxiliary* functions in formal socialization. Education, to be sure, is still the dominant profession in this family, but exigencies of modern society are rapidly transforming education into a multiple-skills process in which the role of teacher has to be coordinated with other professional roles within a complex communications network.

Society characteristically evolves temporary structures, usually within established systems, in response to new cultural conditions. A host of such temporary structures have mushroomed in modern educational systems in which other professions, now no longer in subordinate auxiliary functions, are *coordinated* with the classroom. In addition to the usual complement of teachers, these emerging structures also consist of social workers, youth activities counselors, guidance counselors, nurses, doctors, psychologists, and parent- education specialists.[18]

Temporary structures, however, have a way of becoming permanent. They are the trial-and-error stage of new social patterns that lead to dynamic adaptation. Especially when social problems which initially materialize them persist and intensify, society will institutionalize those that have demonstrated their adaptive utility. In anticipation of this development, the National Association of Social Workers convened in 1964 a group from the professions of education and social work to contemplate its implications for these two professions in a public school organization.

Social work, more than any other profession, has become indispensable in the process of education. Therefore, the conference was altogether timely. Indeed, it may in time be viewed as an historical landmark in both education and social work. Pressures of the community-society dilemma have brought these two professions together early in the twentieth century and points of interaction between their processes have multiplied since.[19] Public school systems seem to be integrating skills of social work and education in a new type of social process.

It soon became obvious in the four days of conference that the evolving process is modifying the character of interactions among the pro-

---

18 One account of such a temporary structure is provided by Louise G. Daugherty, "Working with Disadvantaged Parents," *NEA Journal*, Vol. 52, December 18, 1963. This reports on the Special Project of the Great Cities Program for School Improvement in Chicago's District Eleven. See also, *The Community School and Its Administration*, Vol. IV, February 1966. The Board of Education of Flint, Michigan, and the Mott Foundation.
19 Popper, *Society and the Schools*, pp. 162–63.

fessions in public school organization. Werner W. Boehm, Dean of the School of Social Work, Rutgers University, captured the essence of this dynamic in a view of social work in education which he illustrated with two models:[20]

> Model I reflects the residual view of social work. In this model the teacher is the major agent of service, and the social worker together with other professions such as the guidance counselor, the school psychologist, the nurse, the doctor, etc., perform a subordinate role.
>
> Model II . . . represents the institutional view of social work, it describes the family of professions, all of which are deemed necessary on a coordinate basis rather than on a subordinate one to carry out the teaching-learning mission of the school. In this model, the principal occupies the center because the principal is the administrative locus of school personnel deployment, and on the periphery of the circle are the teacher, the school social worker, the guidance counselor, the school psychologist, the nurse, etc., all deployed on a coordinate basis in accordance with the mission the principal assigns to them and performing the functions which, by virtue of their professional training, they are equipped to perform.

The pattern of the second model is already in the making. It has been evolving, *ad hoc,* in emerging temporary school structures. Now, however, *planned design* has become urgent. The communication challenge which already confronts education and social work is but one manifestation of this urgency. It is of a piece with the larger social phenomenon which is shifting the source of human gratifications from weakened primary systems to rationalistically structured secondary systems. More and more of the quest for community is being satisfied for youth in public schools. But a public school, no matter how much of community may be built into its structure, still has to "fulfill the teaching-learning mission," or else forfeit its distinctive competence. This means that each unit of public school organization, in congruence with its differentiated function in education, will have to devise its own pattern for integrating on a "coordinate basis" the multiple skills of a "family of professions." Such a pattern would constitute a dynamic adaptation in each unit. Out of these adaptations is likely to emerge a mature community school—a Center for Human Development—in

---

[20] Letter from Werner W. Boehm to author, June 4, 1964. Dean Boehm's paper for the conference is given in *Society and the Schools,* although these two models are not in it. They were presented by him during one of the early discussion sessions, and a reference to them will be found on pp. 132–33.

which, as ASCD's *The High School We Need* puts the matter, each pupil will be treated as "a resource of our nation." And this straightaway leads to the special adaptive capability of middle school organization.

A New Middle School Pattern

For the middle school unit this is a season of great opportunity. Organically, it is best equipped to initiate efficient adaptive responses to contemporary cultural conditions. Its inherent capability of moving toward a multiple-skills pattern is now a principal adaptive asset in the public school system. Unlike elementary and high school units, the middle school has been striving internally from its inception in American education to develop precisely such a pattern. External pressures for a dynamic adaptation of the public school system now favor the fulfillment of this striving. A middle school which has already assumed the pattern of the Southern Association is organically and orientationally ready for the more sophisticated pattern of a coordinate family of professions and a multiple-skills process.

Spurred on by its unique institutional mission in education, the American middle school has made its way, falteringly to be sure, toward the pattern of the Southern Association. It is a pattern in which the teacher, following Boehm's first model, "is the major agent of service" while other professionals perform in "a subordinate role." But even in this pattern, because of its dominant psychosocial orientation to early adolescent education, skills of other professions are drawn upon more extensively than in any other unit of public school organization. A bold adaptation of this pattern would change service relationships among the family of professions to a coordinate basis, in line with Boehm's second model, without inducing a discontinuity.

Primary evaluative orientations would continue to be toward the special case of early adolescents in American society. At the center is a principal who, following norms of administrative leadership, deploys professionals, "on the periphery of the circle," on a coordinate basis in accordance with requirements of technical tasks. All professionals are familiar with the communications network of this pattern and, therefore, interact with one another without strain. Each has been socialized to its norms in a preparation program for the middle school, and each has satisfied discrete middle school certification criteria.

The process of education in this school is an integration of skills which are provided coordinately by the following professionals:

1. Teachers who, regardless of the teaching field, have mastered skills of the Core curriculum. These include, in addition to those engaged in formal classroom instruction, remedial reading and mathematics specialists, a teacher of the educable, a director of a learning laboratory in which teachers work with pupils engaged in individual or small-group study, and a librarian under whose charge is the library and a materials center and who dispatches on carts large quantities of books to classrooms as they are requested by teachers. Extensive team planning is done, but teachers do from time to time improvise a union of classes for some special school experience; as when a class presents a play in one of the larger spaces to one or two other classes who at the time have a learning interest in the same play. Team teaching is one of several instructional methodologies which are employed. However, no master teacher heads a team. The skill of each team member is regarded of coordinate importance to the task and, therefore, such team teaching does not mean that two or three teachers combine to do collectively what each would do alone. Core teachers, and not guidance counselors, provide individual guidance in classes which are scheduled in multiple modules of time.

2. Guidance counselors who administer all routine testing, construct test profiles, and take on pupils with difficult problems. They attend to the intake of pupils from feeder elementary schools and to their departure for high school. In line with these articulation tasks, they arrange scheduled contacts during the school year between middle school teachers and those of feeder schools and the high school. All other time is devoted to the preparation of in-service guidance clinics for teachers and to parent workshops. By means of these in-service guidance clinics, teachers sharpen already learned guidance skills for use in classrooms. Parent workshops, on the other hand, mean to enlighten parents about the psychological and physiological characteristics of early adolescence. Some of these parent workshops, moreover, are scheduled during the school day and evenings, and they are conducted by a team which includes, in addition to a guidance counselor, a Core teacher, social worker, and the clinical psychologist.

3. School social workers who are equally skilled in case work technique and family education. They take charge of pupils who are referred by a guidance counselor. Many of these pupils, especially in

cities, are likely to come from multiple-problem families who are known to one or more social agencies in the community. The school social worker, therefore, is the liaison between the middle school and other social agencies. He enlists their help on behalf of a pupil whose home conditions can be improved by means of special family education procedures. The pupil's self-concept is central to everything he does professionally. Together with others in the school, but more especially the Core teacher, he initiates procedures for strengthening it.

4. An activities director who has mastered fundamentals of group work, as these are defined in the social work profession. He organizes and directs the pupil-interest activity program in which all teachers and pupils participate during school hours at least once each week. Pupils are placed in three activities of their choice each year in which they explore with teachers a large variety of leisure time and, for ninth graders, potential vocational interests. This pupil-interest activity program enlarges upon other exploratory and socialization functions of the middle school. The activities director also arranges for all field trips which teachers schedule, a weekly assembly program, after-school activities and clubs, and the election of a student council. The communications network of the school facilitates his interaction with teachers and school social workers, and his own tasks are therefore coordinated with theirs. He too conducts in-service clinics from time to time as a means of enlarging the group work capacity of teachers.

5. A school nurse, with an R.N. certification, who watches over the physical well-being of pupils. She supervises a dispensary and quiet rooms to which pupils come for short periods of rest when, in a teacher's judgment, this is salutary. She arranges for the annual examination of each pupil by a doctor and dentist who come to the school and makes necessary follow-up referrals. Her tasks necessitate frequent interactions with all other members of the professional staff. Indeed, she participates coordinately with teachers in the planning of programs for health and sex education.

6. A clinical psychologist who administers diagnostic tests to pupils that are referred by guidance counselors. His special concern is with pupils who display difficult adjustment or learning problems. His time is equally divided between individual testing and programs of the guidance department for teachers and parents.

Optimum ratios between professionals and pupils in each service field is determined in this pattern by social conditions of the attendance area in which the school exists. Also, social conditions in the attendance area, and not central-office prescriptions, govern technical decisions in educative process. Moreover, performance time of the professional staff is husbanded with care by means of a large number of back-up clerks, readers, and other helpers. The principal keeps a sharp eye on the flow of demand for service from each professional member of the school team, and at no time is it allowed to become excessive.

The foregoing is suggestive of how Boehm's second model might be followed in the middle school of tomorrow. Four professional services —education, social work, medicine, and psychology—are controlled from the administrative hub of a complex communications network and coordinately mixed in educative process. Elements of this pattern are already embodied in the Southern Association's middle school. Gradually, some middle schools are taking first steps beyond it. Skokie Junior High School of Winnetka, Illinois, as an example, has in operation a learning laboratory, while General Wayne Junior High School of Berwyn, Pennsylvania, has a library which also serves as a materials center and which is closely coordinated with classroom activities. Others are experimenting with a breakfast program. Much bolder, however, is the Higher Horizons project of New York City. It is one of the emerging temporary structures which embodies in nascent form the two principal elements of Boehm's second model: a coordinate family of professions and a multiple-skills process.

Higher Horizons originated in a middle school organization during 1959, and now it has been extended downward to elementary schools. In this project:[21]

> An attempt is made to build a cooperative relationship between the school and the family so that parents will encourage the school careers of their children.
>
> The same spirit of teamwork also is characteristic of the teaching and guidance personnel involved in the project.

The dominant focus of Higher Horizons is academic motivation. A family of professions is coordinately involved in such activities as parent workshops, remedial services, frequent excursions into the community for the enlargement of cultural experiences, family education, physical and mental health programs, and more. A similar multiple-skills pat-

---

[21] *Curriculum and Materials*, Board of Education of the City of New York, Vol. XIV, Winter 1960, p. 10.

tern, in microcosm, has been employed in St. Paul middle schools even before Higher Horizons in the form of a permanent Committee on Pupil Problems. Social worker, teacher, nurse, and guidance counselor convene at least once a week as a coordinate professional team and attend to hard-core pupil problems.

These forms, and others like them, are temporary structures which are still lacking in definition, but there is no mistaking their central inclination. They mean "to build a cooperative relationship between the school and the family." They are, in sum, idiomatic of the modes through which public school systems are attempting to bring more of community into educative process. Contemporary cultural conditions are now supportive of innovations in public school systems which heretofore have been anathematized as radical. The middle school is, therefore, singularly served by this turn of events. More of community in school structure and process would blend naturally with the institutional character of a middle school.

Here, then, is one of the two substantive innovations which America's middle school will require for tomorrow's tasks and which in an inchoate form has already secured a beachhead in its organization. Boehm's second model, fleshed out by planned collaboration between schools of education and social work, could take the middle school to a developed multiple-skills process and the coordinate family of professions for which it has been groping since its inception in American education. Similarly, its extensive experience in the use of Core technology performs the beachhead function for the second of these substantive innovations.

Core in Middle Schools

"In a very real sense," Paul Woodring claims, "all education *is* applied psychology."[22] But, he points out, "recent reform movements" in education have paid scant attention to this all-important verity of the teaching-learning process. Woodring deplores this trend, as well he should. At the same time, however, he has pinpointed, by indirection, the reason why a Core curriculum has been used more extensively in the middle school than in any other unit of public school organization. For central to Core is the psychological motivation of the learner.

---

22 Paul Woodring, "Reform Movements from the Point of View of Psychological Theory," in Ernest R. Hilgard, *Theories of Learning and Instruction*, NSSE *Yearbook*, Part I, 1964, p. 303.

Therefore, like social gratifications of community, the diffuseness and particularism of Core blends naturally with the institutional character of a middle school.

But despite this affinity, Core curriculum is one of those innovations in American education which heretofore has been anathematized as radical. Its theoretical origins can be traced to John Dewey's pioneering theory of learning, it has been gaining in sophistication ever since, but to this day the Core curriculum is still struggling for general acceptance. From all indications at hand, however, it now appears that curricular modes which are employed by Core are also favored in current efforts at curriculum revitalization.

Core, or "common learnings," as the Educational Policies Commission has characterized it in *Education for All American Youth* (1944 and revised in 1952), is a flexible, but nonetheless complex, pattern of curriculum organization which follows the Organismic Field theory of learning. In its larger orientation, Core curriculum follows John Ruskin's dictum: "Education does not mean teaching people to know what they do not know—it means teaching them to behave as they do not behave." But because the guiding theory of Core clashes head on with patterns of curriculum organization which still reflect influences of the long-time discredited Mental Discipline theory, or faculty psychology, advocates of Core curriculum have had a difficult time of it. Core curriculum has been demeaned, and its pioneers have been denied honors in places where they should have been honored.[23] Despite an uphill struggle, however, Core technology has grown in influence, most especially in middle schools, and according to one survey of the results, "The people who have had experience with core have overwhelmingly approved of the program."[24]

---

[23] One of the pioneers of Core in the United States is Nelson L. Bossing. He has published a vast literature in which the principles of Core are defined. For representative titles see Roland C. Faunce and Nelson L. Bossing, *Development of the Core Curriculum* (Englewood Cliffs, N.J.: Prentice Hall, 1958); Nelson L. Bossing, *Teaching in Secondary Schools* (Boston: Houghton Mifflin Company, 1952), especially Chapter 3. See also Emma Marie Birkmaier, "The Core Curriculum: A Promising Pattern for the Education of Adolescents," *The School Review*, Vol. LXIII, September 1955.

[24] Wayne B. Jennings, "What Is the Effectiveness of the Core Program?" Unpublished Master's thesis, University of Minnesota, Minneapolis, Minn., 1961, p. 77. This is perhaps the most complete survey extant of Core evaluations, as these have been reported in the literature up to 1961. See also, among many others which report on the use of Core technology in middle school education, Grace S. Wright, *Block-Time Classes and the Core Program in the Junior High School* (Washington, D.C.: U.S. Office of Education, Bulletin No. 6, 1958); and John M. Mickelson, "What Does Research Say About the Effectiveness of the Core Curriculum?" *The School Review*, Vol. LXV, Summer 1957.

Core stresses problem solving, critical thinking, the use of creative capacity, exploration, teacher-pupil planning, and other learning activities of this character. Upon his retirement from a long and distinguished career as "Teacher of Teachers," Earl C. Kelley used the occasion to highlight one particular Core value which has a direct bearing upon the community-society dilemma of our age. He noted:[25]

> It is most difficult to change method in the light of new understandings about the nature of learning and of the learner. We bring to this problem an enormous baggage of habit and custom. I believe that the biggest problem in education today is how to move from a method to which we are habituated to one which is indicated by the democratic ideal and the findings of research on learning.
>
> The core curriculum has the advantage of over thirty years of experience. It has a considerable literature on what is meant by core, and a good deal of evaluative data as to its success. It has built into its very structure the tenets of democracy and humanness. That is why I commend it to all who want to change in the direction of humanizing education.
>
> We should not, I think, pretend that we can change method without changing outcomes. With the core method, I believe that students will learn more than they do now, but what they learn will not necessarily be what the teacher cherishes. The biggest gain will be that young people will learn the problem-solving method. They will learn to have a better view of themselves, their peers, their teachers, and all other people. They will become better human beings.

The humanization of education: there is the rub! A host of "projects" have produced in recent years new courses in mathematics, science, English, social studies, and more are in the offing. These courses assault the monolithic curriculum, they follow Cognitive Field theory, they show a pronounced predilection for some Core methods, but, following Kelley's reference, they fail to incorporate Core's humanizing values. Moreover, directors of these projects are either unaware, or choose to ignore, that "the core method" of curriculum organization "has the advantage of over thirty years of experience" in the use of interdisciplinary curricular materials. Nevertheless, the *Gemeinschaft-Gesellschaft* dilemma of modern society which is forcing more of com-

---

[25] Earl C. Kelley, "Core Teaching—A New Sense of Adventure," in *Teaching Core*, Vol. XIV, June 1965. General Education Committee of Metropolitan Detroit Bureau of School Studies.

munity upon the purposive-rational scheme of school organization also seems to be fusing Organismic Feld and Cognitive Field theories of learning in what Jerome S. Bruner has called a "spiral curriculum." Imperatives for humanizing education, it appears, can no longer be ignored by curriculum builders.

A Humanizing Spiral Curriculum

A fusion of these two theories in curriculum revitalization is altogether feasible because they both employ methods which follow the same general school of psychology. Both, moreover, will not tolerate "that most common blight on human thinking: clutter."[26] But whereas the dominant orientation of Cognitive Field theory is to rationalistic skills, the dominant orientation or Organismic Field theory is to humanistic skills. Both, however, are anchored in *Gestalt* psychology, and *Gestalt* is empirically most congenial to the concept of common learnings. In the new age of probabilistic knowledge, the methodologies of *Gestalt* are best equipped for training pupils in what William J. Cory, a nineteenth-century English schoolmaster and lyric poet, has characterized as "the art of assuming at a moment's notice a new intellectual posture."

The press of the *Gemeinschaft-Gesellschaft* dilemma in curriculum revitalization efforts has been caught by John I. Goodlad in a survey of current curriculum projects which he prepared for the Fund for the Advancement of Education. Goodlad was a sharp observer and his impressions are penetrating. One of these states:[27]

> There is a striking similarity in the aims and objectives of nearly all projects. Objectives, as they are defined in various descriptive documents, stress the importance of understanding the structure of the discipline, the purposes and methods of the field, and the part that creative men and women played in developing the field. One of the major aims is that students get to explore, invent, discover, as well as sense some of the feelings and satisfactions of research scholars, and develop some of the tools of inquiry appropriate to the field. When more remote aims are implied, the impression is created that the student should prepare for intellectual and academic survival in a com-

---

26 Jerome S. Bruner, "How Can Schools Provide a Liberal Education for All Youth?" *Addresses and Proceedings*, NEA, 1965, p. 44.
27 John I. Goodlad, *School Curriculum Reform in the United States* (New York: The Fund for the Advancement of Education, 1964), p. 54.

plex, scientific world. Such social aims as preparation for citizenship or intelligent participation in decisions facing the community are only rarely mentioned.

Elsewhere Goodlad also reports:[28]

In all this agitation—some of it denoting progress, some of it not—a faint glimmer of light is growing stronger: the belief that, increasingly, curriculum reform will be based on the cultivation of the individual and the assurance of a self-renewing society, whereas the curriculum revisions of the past were largely a result of pressures for societal preservation.

The "faint glimmer of light" which Goodlad perceived, it is important to underscore, was a growing awareness that curriculum revitalization in the United States has to join "the cultivation of the individual and the assurance of a self-renewing society." Here is the *Gemeinschaft-Gesellschaft* dilemma in a curricular context. Goodlad reports that the universalistic orientation of "a complex, scientific world" is sharply defined in these projects by new courses which spiral "ideas in increasing depth," whereas "the cultivation of the individual"—the particularistic orientation of community—is but "a faint glimmer of light." One detects in Goodlad's mood an optimistic: but a light nonetheless!

Altogether, Goodlad saw much that augurs well for tomorrow's curriculum, but he also saw a lack of planning which is characteristic of temporary structures. "The current curriculum reform movement," he writes,[29]

has refurbished shockingly outworn courses and has given us a fresh way of approaching various subject fields—a fresh way as regards school practice, if not curriculum theory. But planning from the top down has in some instances brought with it a strait jacket, a strait jacket that is incongruously ill-suited to childhood schooling. A really significant reform movement . . . looks ahead to a time when the curriculum will be planned from the bottom up, with knowledge of students and their achievements built into the sequence of subject matter in the curriculum design. This movement will be marked by experimentation and by the emergence of curricular alternatives far exceeding the number of alternatives that have emerged so far through the current curriculum projects.

28 *Ibid.*, p. 51.
29 *Ibid.*, p. 59.

In line with Goodlad's assessment, then, what is coming out of these curriculum projects is not acceptable as the curriculum of the future. He is on this point in the large company of other curriculum specialists who regard the output of these projects as *ad hoc* responses to the sudden onset of a space-age world. Much of what these projects offer is important, but what they *fail to offer* is also important. The curriculum of tomorrow will have to have a structural unity and a multidimensional design which, as Goodlad proposes, shall have to be "planned from the bottom up." Even so, a rapidly developing consensus about the curriculum of the future suggests that Organismic Field theory and Cognitive Field theory are likely to fuse in a design whose controlling norms already can be anticipated.

Norms of its design, we can be certain, cannot ignore the vast body of knowledge about human development which science has produced. And also for sure, the curriculum of the future would be dysfunctional for fulfilling "the American dream" should it fail to integrate particularistic orientations of community with universalistic orientations of society; it must come to effective grips with the ubiquitous social problem of individual and society in conflict.

On the other hand, what Bruner has called the clutter of "irrelevant detail" will have to be displaced by a spiral arrangement of curricular content so that pupils could move to higher levels of abstraction in the mastery of "basic ideas, attitudes, and skills."[30] Grading of classes in the old Prussian manner would have no functional value in such a curriculum design, because pupils will progress on the spiral, within each unit of public school organization, at a pace in keeping with individual capacity. Finally, a built-in flexibility would have to provide for the many "curricular alternatives" in Goodlad's reference.

And of all public school units, the middle school, again, is organically best equipped to accommodate the substantive innovation of such a curriculum design. The following "notebook sketch" by Emma M. Birkmaier anticipates the more salient characteristics of tomorrow's curriculum and and helps to illustrate the point:[31]

In the past half century both the macrocosmic and microcosmic communities have been undergoing tremendous stresses and strains, almost

---

[30] Bruner, *Addresses and Proceedings,* NEA, 1965, pp. 42 and 44.
[31] Emma M. Birkmaier, "Notebook Sketch of the Curriculum of the Future." Birkmaier, a curriculum specialist, has prepared this introspective "notebook sketch" for use here. The author gratefully acknowledges the courtesy.

to the point of disintegration. The worker lives far from his work. The quality of the work done is hidden from sight. Today's vast field of service operations are hidden from the public eye. Many occupations have so altered the control and the satisfaction of men at work that youth has been excluded from direct observation of an important phase of human experience: aspiration and fulfillment.

The shuttling between home and the world of work, the mobility of the American family are weakening the fabric of community life. The definition of a community as a place where residents live, work, vote and interact has become obsolete. This dilemma in our society gives great importance to the school and the agencies with which it must work, the design of its curriculum, and the close interaction of the school personnel with the youth it serves.

As a result, the school must provide the institutional and organizational resources to meet the large proportion of youth's needs. But most of all it must also provide the small flexible organizational units in which the individual's needs are observable, where he manifestly matters, where the tasks are large enough to be a challenge yet small enough to give importance to his energies, where problems are within his direct experience and comprehension, where he lives with others who share his heritage or who come from quite different backgrounds.

The concepts of teaching the whole child, of teaching subject matter, of preparing students for life, of having students participate in life's daily activities, of teaching through solving problems, through learning abstract ideas are not concepts to be pitted one against the other. They are a part of a *Gestalt* in which each plays a significant role at certain times but interacts constantly with the others in the maturity and development of the individual.

With the increase in knowledge, skills, and insights needed for today, learning must be developed in as efficient and economical a way as is possible. Subjects must telescope and fuse. Others must be eliminated. The field of English can no longer be taught separately from modern languages. Mathematics becomes a communications science, social studies can not keep within its confines and must work hand in hand with the sciences. In a world which in the near future will seem no larger than the megalopolis of today, the nature of language and communications demands an entirely new approach—a contrastive approach in the analysis of one's mother language with that of other languages. This means that young people, the earlier the better, will be exposed to the field of descriptive linguistics and cultural anthropology. In the future, cultures must be analyzed and contrasted and insights must be developed to break narrow monolingual and monocultural backgrounds which promise no good for the future. Youth must understand that language is a verbal manifestation of culture but which at the same time also confines the thinking of a people. Youth must also realize that culture, created from an environment which develops its own habits and customs, creates its own verbal symbolism —language. Insights and concepts such as these can only come about when teachers are educated through a cross fertilization of courses which differ from those usually seen in our colleges and university prescriptive programs.

Nor is one pattern for teacher training enough. Some teachers will be spending their time presenting facts and information over mass media, and films and tapes become an integral part of the learning situation. Some teachers will spend a greater portion of their time working with small groups and individuals in analyzing, developing, synthesizing and challenging the creative potential of the individual student or the small group.

Such telescoping and interdisciplinary approaches demand a different concept of the classroom, of the teaching act, and of the learning act. School programs must foster the creative potential of each individual. Content information and skills can be more effectively taught by teaching machines and mass media, but the actual development of the individual is nurtured only through face-to-face, person-to-person communication and interaction individually and in small group situations.

Birkmaier's sketch reflects the general consensus which is crystallizing around the design of tomorrow's curriculum. Elements of this design, as it applies to the middle school phase of education, are already incorporated in the middle school pattern of the Southern Association. The singularity of the American middle school can be impressed upon variations of this pattern, and nothing in Birkmaier's sketch would compromise the institutional integrity of the middle school. It anticipates an innovation which, as in the earlier case, a middle school of the Southern Association pattern is equipped to undertake forthwith. Its implementation but awaits the curriculum maker's art.

Even the *general design* of a plant for the middle school of tomorrow already exists. As the following sketches show, it is a design which, in the relative disposition of its parts, is capable of accommodating the normative framework which is anticipated for tomorrow's middle school program.

Acknowledgments

These architectural sketches were prepared by C. William Brubaker in consultation with Stanton Leggett. They stem from the proceedings of a middle school conference which was convened in 1960 under joint sponsorship of the editors of *School Management* and the architectural firm of Perkins and Will. The following were the participants: Bernard Donovan, now Superintendent of Schools in New York City; Felix Festa, Superintendent, New City, New York; William Gragg, Superintendent, Ithaca, New York; Philip Koopman, Superintendent, Lower Merion, Pennsylvania; C. William Brubaker, Architect; James D. Lothrop, Architect; A. Whitney Murphy, Architect; Lawrence B. Perkins, Architect; Stanton Leggett, Consultant; and Willard W. Beatty, Consultant. See "Five Superintendents Plan a Junior High School," *School Management,* Vol. 4, November 1960. By permission of *School Management.* Variations of this general design are already incorporated in middle schools that have been built since 1960 and can be seen in Judith Murphy, *Middle Schools* (New York: Educational Facilities Laboratory, 1965); see especially "Three Houses Around a Court," pp. 33–38.

"Middle School" *for tomorrow*

Program • *Each middle school provides for the [psychological], social, and academic needs, interests and desires of 720 students.*

Organization • *Three "houses," each with 240 seventh, eighth, and ninth grade students, plus common facilities.*

Design Components • *A "house" of varied, flexible classrooms. A "machine" for service and supply functions. A "barn" for creative assembly and exercise.*

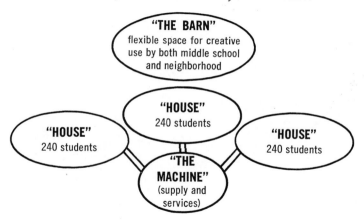

The key to middle school design is flexibility. As needs change, so do programs. Enrollments vary, too, and groupings change with them. Adaptable facilities, therefore, are essential. Rigid schedules have no place here. Emphasis is placed, instead, on the individual. The components are designed with this in mind.

Each "house" consists of 240 students of middle school age, plus a team of teachers. The three houses share common facilities: "the barn," an adaptable shelter (theatre space and swimming pool) to encourage the natural creativity of pupils; and "the machine," to provide supplies and services. Mechanical and electrical aids will be used liberally in order to free teachers for program planning and individual student contact.

341

"The House" *component 1*

Each house provides spaces adaptable to large and small group work as well as individual study. While details can vary with the particular school, these are the general space and facility requirements:

Homeroom area • Seventh graders will spend about 75% of their time here. Space allowances should be made for about 80 students in the typical house.

Seminar and classroom space • Eighth and ninth graders, in sections of various sizes and class hours, will need flexible learning areas.

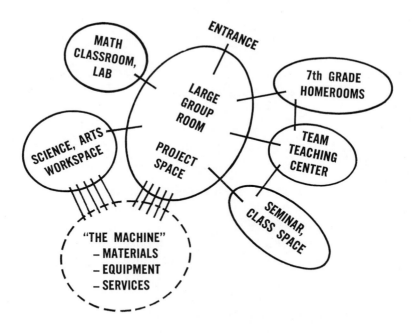

Work space • Two areas are allotted for this purpose: a combined science and unified arts work space and a smaller, combined science and math classroom and laboratory. Emphasis here is on small group and individual study, experiment, and project work.

Large group meeting room • Assembly, dining, lectures, films, group projects, and social affairs are carried on here.

Team teaching center • A headquarters for teachers and a place for their equipment.

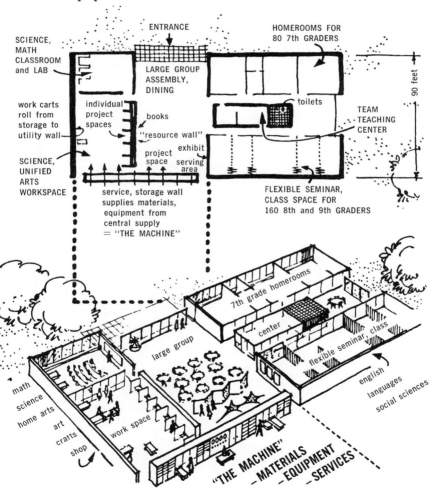

SCIENCE, MATH CLASSROOM and LAB

ENTRANCE

HOMEROOMS FOR 80 7th GRADERS

LARGE GROUP ASSEMBLY, DINING

work carts roll from storage to utility wall

individual project spaces

books

"resource wall"

project space

exhibit

serving area

toilets

TEAM TEACHING CENTER

90 feet

SCIENCE, UNIFIED ARTS WORKSPACE

service, storage wall supplies materials, equipment from central supply = "THE MACHINE"

FLEXIBLE SEMINAR, CLASS SPACE FOR 160 8th and 9th GRADERS

7th grade homerooms

center

flexible seminar class

english

languages

social sciences

math

science

home arts

art

crafts

shop

large group

work space

"THE MACHINE"
—MATERIALS
—EQUIPMENT
—SERVICES

"The Machine" *component 2*

One side of each house is attached to "the machine," the school's storage, supply, maintenance, and control center. The house is serviced through this common wall separating its work space and large group meeting areas from the machine. Teaching aids, electronic equipment, and learning materials are passed over as needed. Food, prepared in central kitchens, is delivered to the machine and rolled on carts into the dining areas of each house at lunch time. Heating and cooling equipment is located in the machine. Centered here, too, might be the school's administrative offices.

[**Added note:** Testing facilities of the guidance department, as well as other professional services, can be located here.]

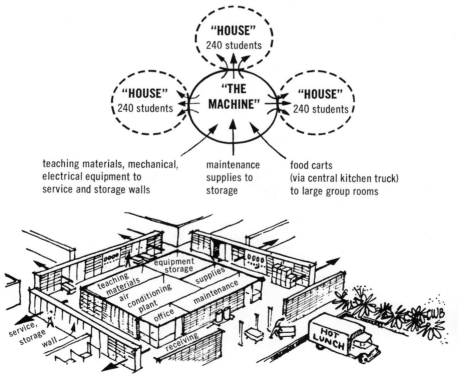

"HOUSE" 240 students

"HOUSE" 240 students   "THE MACHINE"   "HOUSE" 240 students

teaching materials, mechanical, electrical equipment to service and storage walls

maintenance supplies to storage

food carts (via central kitchen truck) to large group rooms

equipment storage · teaching materials · air conditioning plant · supplies · maintenance · office · service, storage wall · receiving · HOT LUNCH

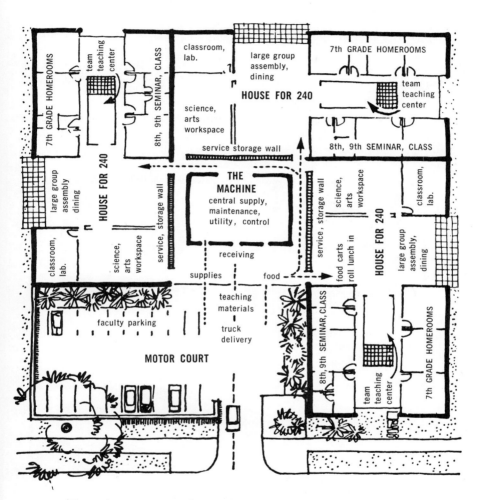

Three houses around the machine create a middle school for 720 students

"The Barn" *component 3*

"The barn" is actually a large building divided in two by a central, covered social area. On one side is the theatre and exhibit hall with dressing rooms, work spaces, and a flexible floor. On the other, are the swimming pool and locker rooms. Both school and neighborhood share these facilities. Space for community parking is provided near the barn for the convenience of the public. Students use the pool area lockers before going out to the playing fields next to the building.

[**Added note:** As determined by climatic factors, or social conditions in the attendance area, this area can be enlarged to include a

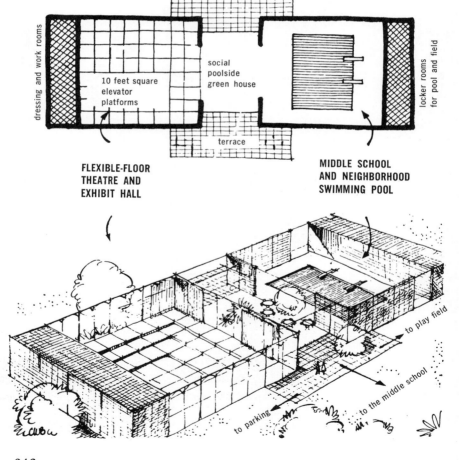

FLEXIBLE-FLOOR
THEATRE AND
EXHIBIT HALL

MIDDLE SCHOOL
AND NEIGHBORHOOD
SWIMMING POOL

Suburban Middle School
the components assembled

This example of a typical, available, flat suburban site presents one way a middle school can be laid out. The arrangement of its elements can vary with . . . needs and desires and the limitations imposed by the shape and location of . . . site. The houses, however, must surround the machine on three sides. In effect, they are treated as one large unit. In the plan given here, the barn faces a major street, making it easily accessible to residents who needn't pass through the rest of the school to reach it.

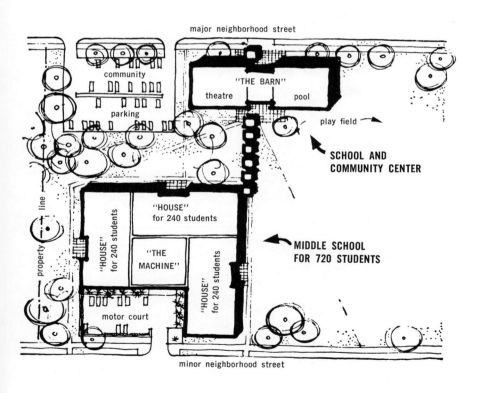

major neighborhood street

community

parking

"THE BARN"

theatre

pool

play field

SCHOOL AND
COMMUNITY CENTER

"HOUSE"
for 240 students

"HOUSE"
for 240 students

"THE
MACHINE"

"HOUSE"
for 240 students

MIDDLE SCHOOL
FOR 720 STUDENTS

property line

motor court

minor neighborhood street

Urban Middle School
in the city

Restricted by a small gridiron site in a crowded city area, the urban middle school expands upward rather than outward. Components still have the same relationship to each other, but the two house-machine units, built on separate levels, serve twice as many students. The larger barn is necessary for the same reason. In this case, it has been extended to include a gymnasium, since climate and site limitations restrict the size and number of outdoor playing fields. School and community parking space is underground.

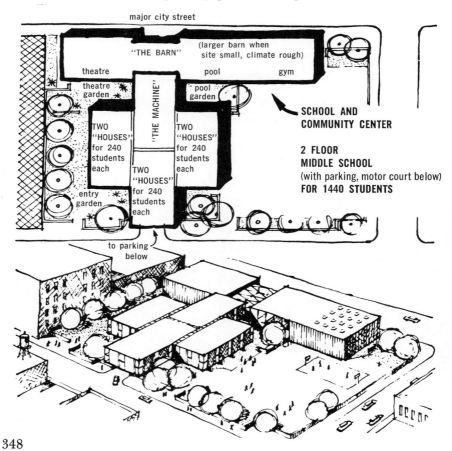

major city street

"THE BARN"   (larger barn when site small, climate rough)

theatre   pool   gym

theatre garden   pool garden

"THE MACHINE"

TWO "HOUSES" for 240 students each

TWO "HOUSES" for 240 students each

TWO "HOUSES" for 240 students each

entry garden

to parking below

SCHOOL AND COMMUNITY CENTER

2 FLOOR MIDDLE SCHOOL (with parking, motor court below) FOR 1440 STUDENTS

Exurban Middle School
in the country

Unhampered by a cramped site, the middle school of the exurbs spreads over an ample, wooded, rolling area set beside a lake. More freedom is possible here in the design, size and location of the school's components to take advantage of natural features. But whatever the geography, the interrelationship of the middle school's components remains the same.

theatre
"THE BARN"

pool

"HOUSE"
for 240 students

"THE MACHINE"

motor court

"HOUSE"
for 240 students

"HOUSE"
for 240 students

road

To Antaeus Again

American society has not maximized the social value of its middle school because, all too often, its organizational mechanism has been used for improper ends. It has béen abused by short-run opportunism, abandoned by schools of education, and neglected in serious research. A pity! For the middle school can be endowed with attributes of social usefulness it does not now possess and which contemporary American society needs more than ever before.

In 1932, George Sylvester Counts shocked American education with the query: "Dare the school build a new social order?" And, of course, he was branded a radical forthwith. Indeed, there were those at the time who misconstrued Counts' question altogether; they understood it as a political question. Actually, the thrust of his question was conservative and reconstructive in character. He, like President Johnson now, also talked of fulfilling the American Dream, of High Civilization—"the most humane, the most beautiful, the most majestic civilization ever fashioned by man"—but, as is frequently the case with men who have the power of vision far beyond their own time, Counts could muster only a handful of "buyers" for his bold proposition. Now, however, it is society which is commanding American education into the lead position of a revitalizing drive to build a new social order. This is the latent meaning of Public Law 89–10 and other such legislation. To miscalculate now the latent meaning of these Congressional enactments would be tantamount to a declaration of social bankruptcy in public school education. But this need not come to pass. Bold innovations, aimed at the dynamic adaptation of public school organization to new cultural conditions, can spell the difference between catastrophe and self-renewal in systems of public education. The middle school has an important place in this development.

Especially in large urban centers, where the *Gemeinschaft-Gesellschaft* dilemma of modern society manifests itself among youth in rising mental health problems, high rates of delinquency, and a lack of quality in the constructive use of leisure time, the middle school has a yet untapped built-in capacity for contributing to social processes which conserve human values in a mass culture. The middle school, so we have noted, is not an American invention, but its adaptation in the urban culture of the United States is essentially one of the social responses to the *Gemeinschaft-Gesellschaft* dilemma which is expressed in David Riesman's euphemism "the lonely crowd."

An innovated middle school can serve both community and society well. None of the curriculum innovations which are anticipated by Goodlad, Birkmaier, and others who share their orientation to curriculum design, are incompatible with the institutional commitment of the middle school. Such innovations would merely articulate the necessary cognitive values of a middle school curriculum in a modern idiom and thereby enhance their social utility.

Indeed, Birkmaier's analytic "contrastive approach" to the study of English would put modern language back into the middle school curriculum, as it was in the North Central middle school pattern of 1924, without displacing any of the nonacademic subjects which are important to the middle school phase of education. "Study after study based on objective testing rather than actual writing," reads a report of the National Council of Teachers of English, "confirms that instruction in formal grammar has little or no effect on the quality of student composition."[33] One can imagine the blessed relief from boredom when an innovated, concept-oriented curriculum will spare middle school pupils the irrelevant detail of such grammar instruction. Surely, whatever keeps boredom out of effective classroom learning serves society.

In a like manner, a multiple-skills process applied by a coordinate family of professions would serve community well. It would be a more functional utilization of what Birkmaier refers to as "institutional and organizational resources" for attending to the human needs of early adolescents. More than that, it can accelerate the pace of socialization research which focuses on early adolescence and which is now retarded by a lack of suitable laboratory conditions. Such research in public school systems under present norms produces deterring strains. But when every tenth middle school of a large city school system is designated as a research center, experimentation in the use of a multiple-skills process could be established as standard operating procedure. And whatever the price, returns in social value from such experimentation would justify the cost. The rising tide of juvenile delinquency provides a dramatic illustration.

Recent empirical studies of deviant behavior in the adolescent sub-

---

[33] Richard Braddock, Richard Lloyd-Jones, and Lowell Schoer, *Research in Written Composition* (Champaign, Ill.: National Council of Teachers of English, 1963), p. 37.

culture suggest that the quality of a self-concept at early adolescence might be a *critical variable* in the containment of juvenile delinquency. A study of the early 1950's revealed that 22 percent of the boys and 8 percent of the girls in the ninth grade of a metropolitan public school system have had a *first* official contact with either the police or juvenile court, or both, during the preceding two years, years of the adolescent onset.[34] Revealing as these statistics are, they assume even deeper sociological significance when they are juxtaposed to conclusions that have been drawn from a longitudinal study at The Ohio State University and also started in the 1950's.

Walter C. Reckless, a specialist in criminal sociology, headed the investigation. The investigators set out to study the phenomenon of "good boys" in high delinquency areas of the city who seem to be impervious to influences that lead to delinquency. What accounts for the immunity?

Reports of the investigation have been published since 1956 and on into the 1960's. One very significant conclusion that has been drawn from the data is that the internalization *at early adolescence* "of a favorable self-concept is the critical variable in the 'containment' of delinquency."[35] The investigators report:[36]

> In our quest to discover what insulates a boy against delinquency in a high delinquency area, we believe we have some tangible evidence that a good self concept, undoubtedly a product of favorable socialization, veers slum boys away from delinquency, while a poor self concept, a product of unfavorable socialization, gives the slum boy no resistance to deviancy, delinquent companions, or delinquent sub-culture. We feel that components of the self strength, such as a favorable concept of self, act as an inner buffer or inner containment against deviancy, distraction, lure, and pressures.

One might speculate at this point, if, as the foregoing suggests, self-concept is of such significance in the quality of social behavior, why not

34 Starke R. Hathaway and Elio D. Monachesi, *Analyzing and Predicting Juvenile Delinquency with the MMPI* (Minneapolis, Minn.: University of Minnesota Press, 1953), p. 109. A more recent report of this research is Starke R. Hathaway and Elio D. Monachesi, *Adolescent Personality and Behavior* (Minneapolis, Minn.: University of Minnesota Press, 1963).

35 Frank R. Scarpitti, Ellen Murray, Simon Dinitz, and Walter Reckless, "The 'Good' Boy in a High Delinquency Area: Four Years Later," *American Sociological Review*, Vol. 25, August 1960, p. 558.

36 Simon Dinitz, Frank R. Scarpitti, and Walter C. Reckless, "Delinquency Vulnerability: A Cross Group and Longitudinal Analysis," *American Sociological Review*, Vol. 27, August 1962, p. 517.

intervene earlier in school life and spot behavioral trends? According to Reckless and his associates, such interventions would be "unrealistic" before age twelve. They claim:[37]

> . . . Spotting behavioral trends of children at 12 years of age for purposes of predicting delinquency or nondelinquency in the next four or five years of their life is certainly superior to case spotting at 6 years of age. The 12 year-old is closer to the problem in time. The child himself can be the focus of the assessment rather than his family. . . . He is old enough to be mobilized in his own behalf for direct prevention and treatment.

Age twelve marks the beginning of the middle school phase of education. The Ohio State University research, therefore, has a special relevance for middle school organization. Granted, conclusions of a single inquiry are tentative. But when conclusions tend to support cumulative findings of other social science research, they have to be reckoned with as significant clues to the explanation of phenomena.

Reckless and his associates tend to confirm the self-esteem thesis of Albert K. Cohen who, like the Ohio State investigators, has also taken a social-psychological, rather than a psychoanalytical, approach to juvenile delinquency.[38] And according to I. Richard Perlman, Chief, Juvenile Delinquency Statistics of the United States Childrens Bureau:[39]

> Most studies indicate that the juvenile delinquent who comes to the attention of juvenile courts is more likely to be a boy than a girl (chances are 5 to 1); he is generally about 14 or 15 years old when referred although he had exhibited behavior problems considerably earlier. His attitude is hostile, defiant, and suspicious. He is usually retarded in school work and in reading ability and shows a chronic history of truancy.

But in order to ascertain the true worth of these clues, they would have to be tested as hypotheses in longitudinal research. Assuming, then, experimental and control groups in a middle school which has

---

37 Edwin L. Lively, Simon Dinitz, and Walter C. Reckless, "Self-Concept As A Predictor of Juvenile Delinquency," *American Journal of Orthopsychiatry*, Vol. XXXII, January 1962, p. 168. Copyright the American Orthopsychiatric Association, Inc. By permission of the American Orthopsychiatric Association.

38 See Albert K. Cohen, *Delinquent Boys: The Culture of the Gang* (New York: The Free Press, 1956).

39 I. Richard Perlman, *Delinquency Prevention: The Size of the Problem*, U.S. Department of Health, Education, and Welfare, Social Security Administration—Children's Bureau, 1960, p. 4.

been designated as a research center, promising intervention techniques might be designed by a coordinate family of professions which are aimed at strengthening pupil self-concept. Intervention procedures would constitute the experimental variables and the record of social behavior through high school, and even beyond, the dependent variable.

Here are clues which suggest that the middle school might well fulfill a value in the urban culture far beyond the expectations of its founders; it is, after all, a product of the modern urban environment. Moreover, the follow-up research that is capable of testing the actual social worth of these clues is also feasible now by means of delinquency proness scales that have been developed. Prediction instruments of this type include the Kvaraceus KD Proness Scale, De and Re scales from Gough's California Personality Inventory, which were employed in the Ohio State research, and the Glueck Social Prediction Table for Identifying Potential Delinquents. The reliability of the Glueck scale has been tested experimentally since the 1940's and, according to its designers, with good results.[40]

Despite these promising clues, both from psychoanalytical and social-psychological approaches to the problem, very little has been done in the American middle school to test them empirically in educative process. But where, as in Higher Horizons, such action research has been conducted, it is of singular significance that the pattern of a multiple-skills process and a coordinate family of professions was used.

The expanding subculture of juvenile delinquency confronts contemporary American society with a host of social problems. Society is now searching desperately for means of containing it. Research evidence points to the self-concept at early adolescence as a critical variable in the containment of deviant behavior. Such evidence does more, however, than just point to a promising strategy in the control of juvenile delinquency. It supports Josselyn, Redl, Erikson, and others from the psychoanalytic field, who hold that early adolescence in American society is a special case; even as it supports Wattenberg and Havighurst in educational psychology.

The middle school in mass American society intervenes protectively in socialization and by means of its six manifest functions helps early adolescents to achieve what Kelley has called "the self." For the self

---

[40] Eleanor Touroff Glueck, "Efforts to Identify Delinquents," *Federal Probation,* Vol. XXIV, June 1960.

cannot be achieved apart from significant others; "it is not given."[41]
The self, therefore, has to be achieved by social definition in interaction
with significant others. " 'Self and other,' " Kelley holds, "is not a
duality, because they go so together that separation is quite impossible."[42] But in mass society "self and other" do become separated,
and, especially during the psychologically vulnerable years of early
adolescence, the intervention of a social agency becomes necessary for
achieving the self.

All of which leads to one conclusion. Should the turn ahead bring
to extinction the middle school which Bunker, Greeson, Francis, and
other educational statesmen of the 1910 period founded, then American
society will have to reestablish it or invent some institutional substitute. But no matter what the outcome of that turn ahead may be, one
fact of middle school development in the United States stands out
above all others: Like Antaeus of Greek legend who was made vulnerable once he came detached from the source of his strength, so does the
American middle school turn vulnerable when its *primary orientation*
veers from the social meaning of early adolescence in modern society.

[41] Earl C. Kelley, "The Fully Functioning Self," in Arthur W. Combs (ed.), *Perceiving,
Behaving, Becoming* (Washington, D.C.: Association for Supervision and Curriculum
Development, Yearbook, 1962), p. 9.
[42] *Ibid.*, p. 9.

BIBLIOGRAPHY

Books and Monographs

ANONYMOUS, *Education for All American Youth.* Washington, D.C., The Educational Policies Commission, 1944.

AHRENS, MAURICE, DURRELL RUFFIN, and RAYMOND WILSON, eds., *The Junior High School Program.* Atlanta, Ga., The Southern Association of Colleges and Secondary Schools, 1958.

ALLEN, FREDERICK LEWIS, *The Big Change.* New York: Harper and Bros., 1952.

ANDERSON, C. M., "The Self Image: A Theory of the Dynamics of Behavior," in Lester D., and Alice Crow, eds., *Readings in Child and Adolescent Psychology.* New York, Longmans, Green and Co., 1961.

ANDREWS, CHARLES M., *The Colonial Period of American History.* New Haven, Conn., Yale University Press, 1934, 4 vols.

ARMSTRONG, W. E., MAURICE R. AHRENS, WILLIAM H. BRISTOW, and E. T. McSWAIN, "Conditions Compelling Curriculum Change," in *Action for Curriculum Improvement.* Washington, D.C., Association for Supervision and Curriculum Development, 1951.

AYRES, LEONARD P., *Laggards in Our Schools.* New York, Russell Sage Foundation, 1909.

BAKER, RAY STANNARD, *American Chronicles.* New York, Charles Scribner's Sons, 1945.

BALES, ROBERT FREED, *Interaction Process Analysis.* Reading, Mass., Addison-Wesley Publishing Co., 1951.

BARNARD, CHESTER I., *The Functions of the Executive.* Cambridge, Mass., Harvard University Press, 1947.

BARNOUW, VICTOR, *Culture and Personality.* Homewood, Ill., Dorsey Press, 1963.

BARUCH, DOROTHY WALTER, *New Ways to Discipline.* New York, McGraw-Hill Co., 1960.

BEARD, CHARLES A., *An Economic Interpretation of the Constitution of the United States.* New York, The Macmillan Co., 1946.

356

BENDIX, REINHARD, *Max Weber: An Intellectual Portrait*. New York: Doubleday and Co., 1960.

BIERSTEDT, ROBERT, "The Problem of Authority," in M. Berger, T. Abel, and C. H. Page, eds., *Freedom and Control in Modern Society*. New York, Van Nostrand, 1954.

BLACK, MAX, ed., *The Social Theories of Talcott Parsons*. Englewood Cliffs, N.J., Prentice-Hall, 1962.

BLAIR, ARTHUR WITT, and WILLIAM H. BURTON, *Growth and Development of the Preadolescent*. New York, Appleton-Century-Crofts, 1951.

BLAU, PETER M., *Bureaucracy in Modern Society*. New York, Random House, 1956.

————, and W. RICHARD SCOTT, *Formal Organizations*. San Francisco, Chandler Publishing Co., 1962.

BOEHM, WERNER W., "The Social Work Profession," in Robert H. Beck, ed., *Society and the Schools: Communication Challenge to Education and Social Work*. New York, National Association of Social Workers, 1965.

BOSSING, NELSON L., and ROSCOE V. CRAMER, *The Junior High School*. Boston, Houghton Mifflin Co., 1965.

BRADDOCK, RICHARD, RICHARD LLOYD-JONES, and LOWELL SCHOER, *Research in Written Composition*. Champaign, Ill., National Council of Teachers of English, 1963.

BRAMELD, THEODORE, *The Cultural Foundations of Education: An Interdisciplinary Exploration*. New York, Harper and Bros., 1957.

————, *Education for the Emerging Age: Newer Ends and Stronger Means*. New York, Harper and Bros., 1961.

BRIGGS, THOMAS H., *The Junior High School*. Boston, Ginn and Co., 1927.

BUNKER, FRANK FOREST, *Reorganization of the Public School System*. Washington, D.C., Bureau of Education, Department of Interior, Bulletin No. 3, Government Printing Office, 1916.

CALLAHAN, RAYMOND E., *Education and the Cult of Efficiency*. Chicago, University of Chicago Press, 1962.

————, and H. WARREN BUTTON, "Historical Change of the Role of the Man in the Organization: 1865–1950," in Daniel E. Griffiths, ed., *Behavioral Science and Educational Administration*. The Sixty-third Yearbook of the National Society for the Study of Education, Part II, 1964.

CAMPBELL, OLIVE DAME, *The Danish Folk School*. New York, The Macmillan Co., 1928.

CAMPBELL, ROALD F., JOHN E. CORBALLY, JR., and JOHN A. RAMSEYER, *Introduction to Educational Administration*. Boston, Allyn and Bacon, Inc., 1962.

————, LUVERN L. CUNNINGHAM, and RODERICK F. MCPHEE, *The Organization and Control of American Schools*. Columbus, Ohio, Charles E. Merrill Books, Inc., 1965.

CARLSON, RICHARD O., "Environmental Constraints and Organizational Consequences: The Public School and Its Clients," in Daniel E. Griffiths, ed., *Behavioral Science and Educational Administration*. The Sixty-third Yearbook of the National Society for the Study of Education, Part II, 1964.

CARTWRIGHT, DORWIN, and ALVIN ZANDER, eds., *Group Dynamics*. Evanston, Ill., Row Peterson, 1953.

CHAMBERLAIN, JOHN, *Farewell to Reform*. New York, Liveright, Inc., 1952.

CLARK, BURTON R., *Adult Education in Transition: A Study of Institutional Insecurity*. Berkeley, University of California Press, 1956.

COCHRAN, THOMAS C., and WILLIAM MILLER, *The Age of Enterprise*. New York, The Macmillan Co., 1943.

COHEN, ALBERT K., *Delinquent Boys: The Culture of the Gang*. Glencoe, Ill., The Free Press, 1965.

COLE, LUELLA, *Psychology of Adolescence*. New York, Rinehart and Co., 1959.

COLEMAN, JAMES S., *The Adolescent Society*. New York, The Free Press of Glencoe, 1961.

COMMAGER, HENRY STEELE, *The American Mind*. New Haven, Yale University Press, 1959.

COUNTS, GEORGE S., *The Social Foundations of Education*. New York, Charles Scribner's Sons, 1934.

CREMIN, LAWRENCE A., *The Transformation of the Schools*. New York, Alfred A. Knopf, 1961.

CROLY, HERBERT, *The Promise of American Life*. New York, The Macmillan Co., 1918.

CURTI, MERLE, *The Growth of American Thought*. New York, Harper and Bros., 1943.

——, *The Social Ideas of American Educators*. Patterson, N.J., Littlefield, Adams and Co., 1959.

DABROWSKI, KAZIMIERZ, *Positive Disintegration*. Boston, Little, Brown and Co., 1964.

DALTON, MELVILLE, *Men Who Manage: Fusions of Feeling and Theory in Administration*. New York, John Wiley and Sons, 1959.

DAVIS, ALLISON, "American Status Systems and the Socialization of the Child," in Clyde Kluckhohn, Henry A. Murray, and David M. Schneider, eds., *Personality in Nature, Society, and Culture*. New York, Alfred A. Knopf, 1953.

——, and ROBERT J. HAVIGHURST, "Social Class and Color Differences in Child Rearing," in Clyde Kluckhohn, Henry A. Murray, and David M. Schneider, eds., *Personality in Nature, Society, and Culture*. New York, Alfred A. Knopf, 1953.

DAVIS, CALVIN OLIN, *Junior High School Education*. New York, World Book Co., 1926.

DEWEY, JOHN, *Freedom and Culture*. New York, C. P. Putnam's Sons, 1939.

DIMOCK, MARSHALL E., *Administrative Vitality: The Conflict with Bureaucracy*. New York, Harper and Bros., 1959.

——, *The Executive in Action*. New York, Harper and Bros., 1945.

DORFMAN, JOSEPH, *The Economic Mind in American Civilization, 1606–1865*. New York, The Viking Press, 1946, 2 vols.

DOWNEY, LAWRENCE W., and FREDERICK ENNS, *The Social Sciences and Educational Administration*. Edmonton, Alberta, The University of Alberta and the University Council for Educational Administration, 1963.

DUBIN, ROBERT, *The World of Work.* Englewood Cliffs, N.J., Prentice-Hall, Inc., 1958.

DURKHEIM, EMILE, *Education and Sociology,* translated by Sherwood D. Fox. Glencoe, Ill., The Free Press, 1956.

——, *Sociology and Philosophy,* translated by D. F. Pocock and J. G. Peristiani. Glencoe, Ill., The Free Press, 1953.

——, *The Division of Labor in Society,* translated by George Simpson. New York, The Free Press of Glencoe, 1964.

EISENSTADT, S. N., *From Generation to Generation.* Glencoe, Ill., The Free Press, 1956.

ELIOT, CHARLES WILLIAM, *Educational Reform.* New York, The Century Co., 1901.

ERIKSON, ERIK H., *Childhood and Society.* New York, W. W. Norton and Co., 1950.

——, "Growth and Crises of the 'Healthy' Personality," in Clyde Kluckhohn, Henry A. Murray, and David M. Schneider, eds., *Personality in Nature, Society, and Culture.* New York, Alfred A. Knopf, 1953.

——, *Identity and the Life Cycle.* New York, International Universities Press, 1959.

——, *The Psychoanalytic Study of the Child.* New York, International Universities Press, 1946.

FARNHAM, MARYNIA F., *The Adolescent.* New York, Harper and Bros., 1951.

FAULKNER, HAROLD UNDERWOOD, *The Quest for Social Justice, 1898–1914.* New York, The Macmillan Co., 1931.

FAUNCE, ROLAND C., and NELSON L. BOSSING, *Development of the Core Curriculum.* Englewood Cliffs, N.J., Prentice-Hall, Inc., 1952.

FOSTER, GEORGE, *Traditional Cultures and the Impact of Technological Change.* New York, Harper and Bros., 1962.

FRANCIS, ROY G., and ROBERT C. STONE, *Service and Procedure in Bureaucracy.* Minneapolis, Minn., University of Minnesota Press, 1956.

FRASER, DOROTHY M., *Deciding What To Teach.* Washington, D.C., National Education Association, 1964.

GABRIEL, RALPH HENRY, *The Course of American Democratic Thought.* New York, The Ronald Press Co., 1940.

GASSET, JOSE ORTEGA Y, *Man and Crisis,* translated by Mildred Adams. New York, W. W. Norton & Co., 1958.

GAUMNITZ, WALTER H., *Strengths and Weaknesses of the Junior High School: Report of the National Conference on Junior High Schools.* Washington, D.C., United States Office of Education, Department of Health, Education and Welfare, Circular No. 441, Government Printing Office, 1955.

GEHNT, WILLIAM J., *Our Benevolent Feudalism.* New York, The Macmillan Co., 1902.

GERTH, H. H., and C. WRIGHT MILLS, eds., *From Max Weber: Essays in Sociology,* translated by the editors. New York, Oxford University Press, 1946.

GESELL, ARNOLD, FRANCES L. ILG, and LOUISE BATES AMES, *Youth, The Years From Ten to Sixteen.* New York, Harper and Bros., 1956.

GETZELS, JACOB W., "Administration as Social Process," in Andrew W. Halpin, ed.,

Administrative Theory in Education. Chicago, University of Chicago Midwest Administration Center, 1958.

GOLDMAN, ERIC F., *Rendezvous with Destiny.* New York, Alfred A. Knopf, 1952.

GOODLAD, JOHN I., *School Curriculum Reform in the United States.* New York, The Fund for the Advancement of Education, 1964.

GOULDNER, ALVIN W., *Patterns of Industrial Bureaucracy.* Glencoe, Ill., The Free Press, 1954.

————, "Reciprocity and Autonomy in Functional Theory," in L. Z. Gross, ed., *Symposium on Social Theory.* Evanston, Ill., Row, Peterson and Co., 1958.

GRAFF, ORIN B., and CALVIN M. STREET, "Developing a Value Framework for Educational Administration," in Roald F. Campbell and Russell T. Gregg, eds., *Administrative Behavior in Education.* New York, Harper and Bros., 1957.

GRAMBS, JEAN D., CLARENCE G. NOYCE, FRANKLIN PATTERSON, and JOHN ROBERTSON, *The Junior High School We Need.* Washington, D.C., Association for Supervision and Curriculum Development, 1961.

GRIFFITHS, DANIEL E., *Administrative Theory.* New York, Appleton-Century-Crofts, 1959.

————, *Human Relations in School Administration.* New York, Appleton-Century-Crofts, 1956.

GRUHN, WILLIAM T., and HARL R. DOUGLASS, *The Modern Junior High School.* New York, The Ronald Press Co., 1956.

HAIRE, MASON, ed., *Organization Theory in Industrial Practice.* New York, John Wiley and Sons, 1962.

HALL, G. STANLEY, *Adolescence: Its Psychology and Its Relations to Physiology, Anthropology, Sociology, Sex, Crime, Religion, and Education.* New York, Appleton-Century Co., 1905, 2 vols.

HALPIN, ANDREW W., ed., *Administrative Theory in Education.* Chicago, University of Chicago Midwest Administration Center, 1958.

————, and DON B. CROFT, *The Organizational Climate of Schools.* Chicago, University of Chicago Midwest Administration Center, 1963.

HATHAWAY, STARKE R. and ELIO D. MONACHESI, *Adolescent Personality and Behavior.* Minneapolis, Minn., University of Minnesota Press, 1963.

———— and ————, *Analyzing and Predicting Juvenile Delinquency with the MMPI.* Minneapolis, Minn., University of Minnesota Press, 1953.

HAVIGHURST, ROBERT J., *Human Development and Education.* New York, Longmans, Green and Co., 1953.

————, and HILDA TABA, *Adolescent Character and Personality.* New York, John Wiley and Sons, 1949.

HAYAKAWA, S. I., *Language in Action.* New York, Harcourt, Brace and Co., 1939.

HOFSTADTER, RICHARD, *Social Darwinism in American Thought, 1860–1915.* Philadelphia, University of Pennsylvania Press, 1945.

HOLMES, OLIVER WENDELL, JR., *The Common Law.* Boston, Little, Brown and Co., 1881.

HOMANS, GEORGE C., *The Human Group.* New York, Harcourt, Brace and Co., 1950.

HSU, FRANCIS, "Culture Pattern and Adolescent Behavior," in Robert E. Grinder, ed., *Studies in Adolescence.* New York, The Macmillan Co., 1952.

HUGHES, MARIE M., *A Research Report: Development of the Means for the Assessment of the Quality of Teaching in Elementary Schools.* University of Utah, 1959.

HUNTER, FLOYD, *Community Power Structure.* Chapel Hill, N.C., University of North Carolina Press, 1953.

IANNACCONE, LAURENCE, "An Approach to the Informal Organization of the School," in Daniel E. Griffiths, ed., *Behavioral Science and Educational Administration,* the Sixty-third Yearbook of the National Society for the Study of Education, Part II, 1964.

JANOWITZ, MORRIS, *The Professional Soldier.* Glencoe, Ill., The Free Press, 1960.

KELLEY, EARL C., "The Fully Functioning Self," in Arthur W. Combs, ed., *Perceiving, Behaving, Becoming.* Washington, D.C., Association for Curriculum Development, 1962.

KOOS, LEONARD V., *The Junior High School.* Boston, Ginn and Co., 1927.

LANDSBERGER, HENRY A., *Hawthorne Revisited.* Ithaca, N.Y., Cornell University Press, 1958.

LARKIN, OLIVER W., *Art and Life in America.* New York, Holt, Rinehart, and Winston, 1949.

LEFEBVRE, GEORGES, *The Coming of the French Revolution,* translated by R. R. Palmer. Princeton, N.J., Princeton University Press, 1947.

LEWIN, KURT, *Principles of Topological Psychology.* New York, McGraw-Hill Co., 1936.

LIPSET, SEYMOUR M., MARTIN A. TROW, and JAMES S. COLEMAN, *Union Democracy.* Glencoe, Ill., The Free Press, 1956.

LLOYD, HENRY DEMAREST, *Wealth Against Commonwealth.* New York, Harper and Bros., 1884.

LOOMIS, MARY JANE, *The Preadolescent.* New York, Appleton-Century-Crofts, 1959.

LOUNSBURY, JOHN H., and JEAN V. MARANI, *The Junior High School We Saw: One Day in the Eighth Grade.* Washington, D.C., Association for Supervision and Curriculum Development, 1964.

LYND, ROBERT S., and HELEN M. LYND, *Middletown in Transition: A Study in Cultural Conflict.* New York, Harcourt, Brace and Co., 1937.

MACIVER, R. M., *Community.* New York, The Macmillan Co., 1917.

MALINOWSKI, BRANISLAW, *The Dynamics of Culture Change.* New Haven, Yale University Press, 1945.

MANNING, WILLIAM, *The Key of Liberty—Shewing the Causes Why a Free Government has Always Failed, and a Remidy Against it.* Billerica, Massachusetts, The Manning Association. Notes and foreword by Samuel Eliot Morison.

MARCH, JAMES G., and HERBERT A. SIMON, *Organizations.* New York, John Wiley and Sons, 1958.

MARTINDALE, DON, *American Social Structure.* New York, Appleton-Century-Crofts, 1960.

MARX, LEO, *The Machine in the Garden: Technology and the Pastoral Ideal in America.* New York, Oxford University Press, 1965.

MASON, ALPHEUS THOMAS, *Brandeis: A Free Man's Life*. New York, The Viking Press, 1946.

McCLELLAND, D. C., *The Achieving Society*. Princeton, N.J., D. Van Nostrand Co., 1961.

McCLURE, SAMUEL SIDNEY, *My Autobiography*. New York, Frederick A. Stokes Co., 1913.

MEAD, MARGARET, *Coming of Age in Samoa*. New York, The New American Library, 1963.

MEDSKER, LELAND L., *The Junior College: Progress and Prospect*. New York, McGraw-Hill, 1960.

MERTON, ROBERT K., *Social Theory and Social Structure*. Glencoe, Ill., The Free Press, 1959.

———, and ALISA P. GRAY, BARBARA HOCKEY, and HANAN C. SELVIN, eds., *Reader in Bureaucracy*. Glencoe, Ill., The Free Press, 1953.

———, and PAUL F. LAZARSFELD, eds., *Continuities in Social Research: Studies in the Scope and Method of "The American Soldier."* Glencoe, Ill., The Free Press, 1950.

MICHELS, ROBERT, *First Lectures in Political Sociology*, translated by Alfred de Grazia. Minneapolis, Minn., University of Minnesota Press, 1949.

———, *Political Parties*, translated by Eden and Cedar Paul. Glencoe, Ill., The Free Press, 1949.

MONTAGUE, ASHLEY, *Man's Most Dangerous Myth*. New York, Harper and Row, 1952.

MOORE, HOLLIS A., JR., *Studies in School Administration*. Washington, D.C., American Association of School Administrators, 1957.

MORISON, SAMUEL ELIOT, *Three Centuries of Harvard*. Cambridge, Mass., Harvard University Press, 1936.

———, and HENRY STEELE COMMAGER, *The Growth of the American Republic*. New York, Oxford University Press, 1942, 2 vols.

MYRDAL, GUNNAR, *An American Dilemma*. New York, Harper and Bros., 1944.

NEVINS, ALLAN, *The Emergence of Modern America, 1865–1878*. New York, The Macmillan Co., 1927.

NISBET, ROBERT A., *The Quest for Community*. Fair Lawn, N.J., Oxford University Press, 1953.

NOAR, GERTRUDE, *The Junior High School Today and Tomorrow*. Englewood Cliffs, N.J., Prentice-Hall, Inc., 1961.

PARRINGTON, VERNON LOUIS, *Main Currents in American Thought*. New York, Harcourt, Brace and Co., 1930.

PARSONS, TALCOTT, *Essays in Sociological Theory*. Glencoe, Ill., The Free Press, 1963.

———, "General Theory in Sociology," in Robert K. Merton, Leonard Broom, and Leonard S. Cottrell, Jr., eds., *Sociology Today*. New York, Basic Books, 1959.

———, *The Social System*. Glencoe, Ill., The Free Press, 1963.

———, "Some Ingredients of a General Theory of Formal Organizations," in

Andrew W. Halpin, ed., *Administrative Theory in Education.* Chicago, University of Chicago Midwest Administration Center, 1958.

————, *Structure and Process in Modern Societies.* Glencoe, Ill., The Free Press, 1963.

————, "Youth in the Context of American Society," in Henry Borow, ed., *Man in a World at Work.* Boston, Houghton Mifflin Co., 1964.

PECHSTEIN, L. A., and A. LAURA McGREGOR, *Psychology of the Junior High School Pupil.* Boston, Houghton Mifflin Co., 1924.

PERLMAN, I. RICHARD, *Delinquency Prevention: The Size of the Problem.* Washington, D.C., United States Department of Health, Education, and Welfare, Social Security Administration—Children's Bureau, 1960.

PHENIX, PHILIP H., *Man and His Becoming.* New Brunswick, N.J., Rutgers University Press, 1964.

POPPER, SAMUEL H., *Individualized Justice: Fifty Years of Juvenile Court Services and Probation in Ramsey County, Minnesota.* St. Paul, Minn., Bruce Publishing Co., 1956.

————, "The Challenge to the Two Professions," in Robert H. Beck, ed., *Society and the Schools: Communication Challenge to Education and Social Work.* New York, National Association of Social Workers, 1965.

PRESTUS, ROBERT V., "Authority in Organizations," in Sidney Malick and Edward H. Van Ness, eds., *Concepts and Issues in Administrative Behavior.* Englewood Cliffs, N.J., Prentice Hall, Inc., 1962.

REGIER, C. C., *The Era of the Muckrakers.* Chapel Hill, N.C., University of North Carolina Press, 1932.

ROETHLISBERGER, FRITZ J., and WILLIAM T. DICKSON, *Management and the Worker.* Cambridge, Mass., Harvard University Press, 1939.

SCHLESINGER, ARTHUR MEIER, *The Rise of the City, 1878–1889.* New York, The Macmillan Co., 1933.

SELZNICK, PHILIP, *Leadership in Administration.* Evanston, Ill., Row, Peterson and Co., 1957.

————, *TVA and the Grass Roots: A Study in the Sociology of Formal Organization.* Berkeley, University of California Press, 1953.

SEYLE, HANS, *The Stress of Life.* New York, McGraw-Hill Co., 1956.

SIMONS, A. M., *Social Forces in American History.* New York, The Macmillan Co., 1911.

SMITH, MAURICE M., L. L. STANDLEY, and CECIL L. HUGHES, *Junior High School Education: Its Principles and Procedures.* New York, McGraw-Hill Co., 1942.

SMITH, WILLIAM A., *The Junior High School.* New York, The Macmillan Co., 1927.

SPENCER, HERBERT, *The Principles of Sociology.* New York, D. Appleton and Co., 1876–92, 3 vols.

SPINDLER, GEORGE D., *Education and Culture.* New York, Holt, Rinehart and Winston, 1963.

STEIN, MAURICE R., *The Eclipse of Community.* Princeton, N.J.: Princeton University Press, 1960.

STONE, JOSEPH L., and JOSEPH CHURCH, *Childhood and Adolescence.* New York, Random House, 1957.

STRAYER, GEORGE D., *Age and Grade Census of Schools and Colleges.* Washington, D.C., Bureau of Education, Department of Interior, Bulletin No. 5, Government Printing Office, 1911.

SUMNER, WILLIAM GRAHAM, *Folkways.* Boston, Ginn and Co., 1940.

———, *What Social Classes Owe to Each Other.* New York, Harper and Bros., 1883.

TANNER, J. M., *Growth At Adolescence.* Oxford, Blackwell Scientific Publications, 1955.

TERMAN, LEWIS M., *The Intelligence of School Children.* Boston, Houghton Mifflin Co., 1919.

THOMPSON, VICTOR A., *Modern Organization: A General Theory.* New York, Alfred A. Knopf, 1961.

THORNDIKE, E. L., *The Elimination of Pupils From School.* Washington, D.C., Bureau of Education, Department of Interior, Bulletin No. 4, Government Printing Office, 1907.

TOENNIES, FERDINAND, *Community and Society,* translated by Charles P. Loomis. East Lansing, Mich., Michigan State University Press, 1957.

TRAGER, HELEN G., and MARIAN RADKE YARROW, *They Learn What They Live.* New York, Harper and Bros., 1952.

VAN DENBERG, JOSEPH K., *The Junior High School Idea.* New York, Henry Holt and Co., 1922.

WALLACE, A. F. C., *Culture and Personality.* New York, Random House, 1961.

WALLER, WILLARD, *The Sociology of Teaching.* New York, John Wiley and Sons, 1932.

WARD, LESTER F., *The Psychic Factors of Civilization.* Boston, Ginn and Co., 1893.

WARREN, CHARLES, *The Supreme Court in United States History.* Boston, Little, Brown and Co., 1923, 3 vols.

WASHBURN, NORMAN F., *Interpreting Social Change in America.* New York, Random House, 1954.

WATTENBERG, WILLIAM W., *The Adolescent Years.* New York, Harcourt, Brace and Co., 1955.

WEBER, MAX, *The Protestant Ethic and the Spirit of Capitalism,* translated by Talcott Parsons. London, George Allen and Unwin, Ltd., 1930.

———, *The Theory of Social and Economic Organization,* translated by A. M. Henderson and Talcott Parsons. Glencoe, Ill., The Free Press, 1947.

WERTENBAKER, THOMAS JEFFERSON, *The First Americans: 1607–1690.* New York, The Macmillan Co., 1927.

WHITEHEAD, ALFRED NORTH, "The Aims of Education," in Stan Dropkin, Harold Full, and Ernest Schwartz, *Contemporary American Education.* New York, The Macmillan Co., 1965.

———, *Science and the Modern World.* New York, The Macmillan Co., 1926.

WHITING, JOHN M., and IRVING L. CHILD, *Child Training and Personality: A Cross-Cultural Survey.* New Haven, Yale University Press, 1953.

WILES, KIMBAL, and FRANKLIN PATTERSON, *The High School We Need.* Washington, D.C., Association for Supervision and Curriculum Development, 1959.

WOODRING, PAUL, "Reform Movements from the Point of View of Psychological

Theory," in Ernest R. Hilgard, ed., *Theories of Learning and Instruction.* The Sixty-third Yearbook of the National Society for the Study of Education, Part I, 1964.

WRIGHT, GRACE S., *Block-Time Classes and the Core Program in Junior High School.* Washington, D.C., United States Office of Education, Bulletin No. 6, 1958.

WRINKLE, W. K., and R. S. GILCHRIST, *Secondary Education for American Democracy.* New York, Farrar and Rinehart, 1942.

ZACHRY, CAROLINE B., and MARGARET LIGHTY, *Emotion and Conduct in Adolescence.* New York, Appleton-Century-Crofts, 1940.

Periodicals

ANONYMOUS, "Annual Stockholders Report," *NEA Journal,* Vol. 51, May 1962.
———, "John Graham, 1881–1961," *Art News,* September 1961.
———, "The Junior High School Today," *NEA Research Bulletin,* Vol. 39, May 1961.
———, "Incoordination Between Junior and Senior High Schools," *The School Review,* Vol. 35, November 1927.
———, "Principals' Opinions," *NEA Research Bulletin,* Vol. 40, May 1962.
———, "Reaction in the Junior High School Movement," *The Elementary School Journal,* Vol. 23, December 1922.
———, "Children—Bigger and Better," *Journal of School Health,* Vol. 27, November 1957.
———, "Five Superintendents Plan a Junior High School," *School Management,* Vol. 4, November 1960.
ABBOTT, MAX G., "Intervening Variables in Organizational Behavior," *Educational Administration Quarterly,* Vol. I, Winter 1965.
ALSOP, STEWART, "Presidents Don't Lose," *The Saturday Evening Post,* November 2, 1963.
BAUGHMAN, DALE W., "The Awkward Age," *Educational Leadership,* Vol. 18, December 1960.
BECK, ROBERT, "Perception of Individualism in American Culture and Education," *Educational Theory,* Vol. XI, July 1961.
BENNIS, WARREN G., "Revisionist Theory of Leadership," *Harvard Business Review,* Vol. 39, February 1961.
———, "Beyond Bureaucracy," *Trans-Action,* Vol. 2, July–August 1965.
BERNARD, JESSIE, "Teen-Age Culture: An Overview," *The Annals of the American Academy of Political and Social Science,* Vol. 338, November 1961.
BIERSTEDT, ROBERT, "An Analysis of Social Power," *American Sociological Review,* Vol. XV, December 1950.
BIRKMAIER, EMMA MARIE, "The Core Curriculum: A Promising Pattern for the Education of Adolescents," *The School Review,* Vol. LXIII, September 1965.
BRIGGS, THOMAS H., "Has the Junior High School Made Good?" *Educational Administration and Supervision,* Vol. 24, January 1938.
CAMPTON, C. W., "Physiological Age," *American Physical Education Review,* March–June 1908.

CLARK, PETER B., and JAMES Q. WILSON, "Incentive Systems: A Theory of Organizations," *Administrative Science Quarterly*, Vol. 5, September 1961.

COLEMAN, JAMES S., "The Adolescent Subculture and Achievement," *The American Journal of Sociology*, Vol. LXV, June 1960.

———, "The Competition for Adolescent Energies," *Phi Delta Kappan*, Vol. XLII, March 1961.

CONSTANT, GEORGE A., "Adolescence: Its Perspective and Problems," *Journal of the Mississippi State Medical Association*, Vol. IV, January 1963.

CORNELL, ETHEL L., and CHARLES H. ARMSTRONG, "Forms of Mental Growth Revealed by Reanalysis of the Harvard Growth Data," *Child Development*, Vol. 26, September 1955.

COUNTS, GEORGE S., "Dare the Schools Build the Great Society?" *Phi Delta Kappan*, September 1965.

COX, PHILIP W. L., "Problems of College Entrance Arising from the Development of the Junior High School," *North Central Association Quarterly*, Vol. I, December 1926.

DAUGHERTY, LOUISE G., "Working With Disadvantaged Parents," *NEA Journal*, Vol. 52, December 1963.

DEWEY, JOHN, "Discussion," *The School Review*, Vol. XI, January 1903.

DEXTER, EDWIN C., "Ten Years' Influence of the Report of the Committee of Ten," *The School Review*, Vol. XIV, March 1906.

DINITZ, SIMON, FRANK R. SCARPITTI, and WALTER RECKLESS, "Delinquency Vulnerability: A Cross Group Longitudinal Analysis," *American Sociological Review*, Vol. 27, August 1962.

ELIOT, CHARLES W., "What Has Been Gained in Uniformity of College Admission Requirements in the Past Twenty Years?" *The School Review*, Vol. XII, December 1904.

ELKIN, FREDERICK, and WILLIAM A. WESTLEY, "The Myth of Adolescent Culture," *American Sociological Review*, Vol. 20, October 1955.

ETZIONI, AMITAI, "Two Approaches to Organizational Analysis: A Critique and a Suggestion," *Administrative Science Quarterly*, Vol. 5, September 1960.

FAUST, MARGARET SILVER, "Developmental Maturity as a Determinant in Prestige of Adolescent Girls," *Child Development*, Vol. 31, March 1960.

FITZPATRICK, JOSEPH A., "An Appraisal of Junior High Schools," *Journal of Education*, Vol. 110, September 1929.

FORD, EDMUND A., "Organizational Pattern of the Nation's Public Secondary Schools," *School Life*, Vol. 42, May 1960.

FRANCIS, ROY G., "The Antimodel as a Theoretical Concept," *The Sociological Quarterly*, Vol. 4, Summer 1963.

FRANK, ANDREW GUNDER, "Goal Ambiguity and Conflicting Standards: An Approach to the Study of Organization," *Human Organization*, Vol. 17, Winter 1958–9.

GILBERT, ANNE, "Junior High Schools Criticized," *Journal of Education*, Vol. 113, June 1931.

GLASS, JAMES M., "The Junior High School," *The New Republic*, Vol. XXXVI, November 1923.

———, "Careers in Education; Teaching in Junior High School," *NEA Journal,* Vol. 17, May 1928.

———, "Library in Junior High Schools," *Library Journal,* Vol. 50, February 1925.

———, "The Mission of the Junior High School Is in Articulation and Guided Exploration," *School Life,* Vol. 12, February 1957.

———, "Recent Developments in the Junior High School Field," *High School Quarterly,* Vol. 14, October 1925.

———, "Tested and Accepted Philosophy of the Junior High School Movement," *Junior-Senior High School Clearing House,* Vol. 7, February 1933.

GLUECK, ELEANOR TOUROFF, "Efforts to Identify Delinquents," *Federal Probation,* Vol. XXIV, June 1960.

GOODE, WILLIAM J., "Community Within a Community: The Professions," *American Sociological Review,* Vol. 22, April 1957.

GRAZIA, ALFRED DE, "The Science and Values of Administration," *Administrative Science Quarterly,* Vol. 5, December 1960.

GRINDER, ROBERT E., and CHARLES E. STRICKLAND, "G. Stanley Hall and the Social Significance of Adolescence," *Teachers College Record,* Vol. 64, February 1963.

GROSS, EDWARD, and SAMUEL H. POPPER, "Service and Maintenance Orientation in a Junior High School Organization," *Educational Administration Quarterly,* Vol. I, Spring 1965.

GRUHN, WILLIAM T., "What Is New in Junior High School Education?" *The Bulletin, National Association of Secondary School Principals,* Vol. 44, February 1960.

HALE, C. J., "Changing Growth Patterns of the American Child," *Education,* Vol. 78, April 1958.

HALLECK, REUBEN POST, "Why Do So Many Pupils Leave the Public High School During the First Year?" *The School Review,* Vol. XIII, September 1905.

HALPIN, ANDREW W., "The Superintendent's Effectiveness as a Leader," *Administrator's Notebook,* Vol. VII, October 1958.

HARDIN, V. H., "Facing a Vital Problem," *The Junior-Senior High School Clearing House,* Vol. 8, September 1933.

HAVIGHURST, ROBERT J., "Poised at the Crossroads of Life: Suggestions for Parents and Teachers of Young Adolescents," *The School Review,* Vol. LXI, September 1953.

———, "A Validation of Developmental and Adjustment Hypotheses of Adolescence," *The Journal of Educational Psychology,* Vol. 43, October 1952.

HEIRONOMOUS, N. C., "Is This the Earliest Known Junior High School?" *The Clearing House,* Vol. 14, May 1940.

HEPNER, WALTER R., "The Junior High School," *California Journal of Secondary Education,* Vol 13, December 1938.

HOLLINGSHEAD, A. B., "A Sociological Perspective on Adolescence," *Pediatric Clinics of America,* Vol. 7, February 1960.

HOY, ALMON G., "Flexibility and the RMS Program," *Minnesota Journal of Education,* Vol. 44, February 1964.

HUBBLE, DOUGLAS, "The Problems of Puberty," *British Medical Journal,* No. 5064, January 1958.

HULL, J. H., "The Junior High School Is a Poor Investment," *The Nation's Schools,* Vol. 65, April 1960.

Jenks, Leland H., "Early Phases of the Management Movement," *Administrative Science Quarterly,* Vol. 5, December 1960.

JENSEN, LAI, "Physical Growth," *Review of Educational Research,* Vol. 25, December 1955.

JOHNSON, CHARLES HUGHES, "The Junior High School," *Educational Administration and Supervision,* Vol. II, 1916.

JONES, ARTHUR J., "Appraising the Junior High School," *The Education Digest,* Vol. 9, May 1944.

JOSSELYN, IRENE M., "A Type of Predelinquent Behavior," *American Journal of Orthopsychiatry,* Vol. 28, July 1958.

———, "The Ego in Adolescence," *American Journal of Orthopsychiatry,* Vol. 24, April 1954.

———, "Psychological Changes in Adolescence," *Children,* Vol. 6, March–April 1959.

———, "Social Pressures in Adolescence," *Social Casework,* Vol. 39, May 1952.

JUDD, CHARLES H., "Fundamental Educational Reforms," *Elementary School Journal,* Vol. XIII, January 1923.

———, "Recent Discussions of the Junior High School Problem," *The Elementary School Journal,* Vol. 19, June 1919.

KNIGHT, EDGAR W., "The Southern Association: Retrospect and Prospect," *The Georgia Review,* Vol. I, Spring 1947.

Koos, Leonard V., "The National Survey of Secondary Education," *North Central Association Quarterly,* Vol. V, September 1930.

KOWITZ, GERALD T., and CHARLES H. ARMSTRONG, "Patterns of Academic Development," *Journal of Educational Measurement,* Vol 2, December 1965.

LIVELY, EDWIN L., SIMON DINITZ, and WALTER C. RECKLESS, "Self-Concept As A Predictor of Juvenile Delinquency," *American Journal of Orthopsychiatry,* Vol. XXXII, January 1962.

LORTIE, DAN C., "Change and Exchange: Reducing Resistance to Innovations," *Administrator's Notebook,* Vol. XII, February 1964.

LOUNSBURY, JOHN H., and HARL R. DOUGLASS, "Recent Trends in Junior High School Practices," *The Bulletin of the National Association of Secondary School Principals,* Vol. 49, September 1965.

MAHAN, T. J., "Is the Junior High School Functioning?" *The Junior-Senior High School Clearing House,* Vol. 7, November 1932.

MARCSON, SIMON, "The Management and Mismanagement of Industrial Scientists," *Trans-Action,* Vol. I, January 1964.

MARKEY, OSCAR B., "A Study of Aggressive Sex Misbehavior in Adolescents Brought to Juvenile Court," *American Journal of Orthopsychiatry,* Vol. 20, October 1950.

MICKELSON, JOHN M., "What Does Research Say About the Core Curriculum?" *The School Review,* Vol. LXV, Summer 1957.

PACE, C. ROBERT, "Methods of Describing College Cultures," *Teachers College Record,* Vol. 63, January 1962.

———, and George G. Stern, "An Approach to the Measurement of Psychological Characteristics of College Environments," *Journal of Educational Psychology,* Vol. 49, October 1958.

PAGE, CHARLES H., "Bureaucracy's Other Face," *Social Forces,* Vol. 25, 1964.

PARKER, FRANKLIN, "A Golden Age in American Education: Chicago in the 1880's," *School and Society,* Vol. 89, March 25, 1961.

PARSONS, TALCOTT, "Suggestions for a Sociological Approach to the Theory of Organizations," *Administrative Science Quarterly,* Vol. I, April 1956.

———, "The School Class As a Social System," *The Harvard Educational Review,* Vol. 29, Fall 1959.

PETTIGREW, THOMAS F., "Continuing Barriers to Desegregated Education in the South," *Sociology of Education,* Vol. 38, Winter 1965.

POPPER, SAMUEL H., "Another Look at the Junior High School Principalship," *The Bulletin of the National Association of Secondary-School Principals,* Vol. 44, November 1960.

———, "Urbanism and Early Growing Pains in the Newark Public School System," *Proceedings of the New Jersey Historical Society,* Vol. 282, July 1955.

———, "New Tensions in Old Newark," *Proceedings of the New Jersey Historical Society,* Vol. 269, April 1952.

RICE, J. M., "Our Public School System: Schools of Buffalo and Cincinnati," *The Forum,* Vol. XIV, November 1892.

RODGERS, J. HARVEY, "Junior High School Curricula and Programs," *The School Review,* Vol. 29, March 1921.

RUTHERFORD, BEVERLY, "Junior High School Girls and the Feminine Role," *The Clearing House,* Vol. 35, March 1961.

SCARPITTI, FRANK R., ELLEN MURRAY, SIMON DINITZ, and WALTER RECKLESS, "The Good Boy in a High Delinquency Area: Four Years Later," *American Sociological Review,* Vol. 25, August 1960.

SCHONFELD, WILLIAM A., "Body Image in Adolescents with Inappropriate Sexual Development," *American Journal of Orthopsychiatry,* Vol. XXXIV, September 1916.

SIMPSON, RICHARD L., and WILLIAM H. GULLEY, "Goals, Environmental Pressures, and Organizational Characteristics," *American Sociological Review,* Vol. 27, June 1962.

SMITH, TIMOTHY L., "Progressivism in American Education 1880–1900," *Harvard Educational Review,* Vol. 31, Spring 1961.

SPAULDING, F. T., and O. I. FREDERICK, "The Junior High School Movement In the Year 1930," *The School Review,* Vol. XLI, January 1933.

STERN, GEORGE G., "Characteristics of the Intellectual Climate in College Environments," *Harvard Educational Review,* Vol. 33, Winter 1963.

TAUEUBER, KARL E., "Residential Segregation," *Scientific American,* Vol. 213, August 1965.

TEICHER, JOSEPH D., "Normal Psychological Changes in Adolescence," *California Medicine,* Vol. 85, September 1956.

TENBRUCK, FRIEDRICH H., "Contemporary Adolescence," *Diogenes,* Winter 1961.
THOMPSON, JAMES D., and WILLIAM D. McEWEN, "Organizational Goals and Environment: Goal-Setting As an Internal Process," *American Sociological Review,* Vol. 23, February 1958.
TOMPKINS, ELLSWORTH, and WALTER GAUMNITZ, "The Carnegie Unit: Its Origin, Status, and Trends," *The Bulletin of the National Association of Secondary School Principals,* Vol. 48, January 1964.
TURNER, RALPH H., "Sponsored and Contest Mobility and the School System," *American Sociological Review,* Vol. 25, December 1960.
VINCENT, ELIZABETH LEE, "Physical and Psychological Aspects of Puberty and Adolescence," *Journal of the National Association of Deans of Women,* Vol. 19, October 1955.
WARD, L. C., "The Junior High School Abandoned at Fort Wayne, Indiana," *The Elementary School Journal,* Vol. 22, May 1922.
WATTENBERG, WILLIAM W., "The Junior High School—A Psychologist's View," *The Bulletin of the National Association of Secondary-School Principals,* Vol. 49, April 1965.
———, "Today's Junior High School Students," *Educational Leadership,* Vol. 23, December 1965.
WEET, HERBERT S., "Rochester's Junior High School," *Educational Administration and Supervision,* Vol. II, 1916.
WINTERS, T. HOWARD, "The Chartering of Junior High Schools in Ohio," *North Central Association Quarterly,* Vol. IV, December 1929.
WOLF, RICHARD E., "Variations in Personality Growth During Adolescence," *Journal of Pediatrics,* Vol. 59, November 1961.

Newspapers

ANONYMOUS, "Educator Points Out Gap in Teaching," *Christian Science Monitor,* April 29, 1961.
HECHINGER, FRED M., "The Junior Blues," *The New York Times,* July 28, 1963.
Minneapolis *Tribune,* November 17, 1964; January 31, 1965.
St. Paul *Dispatch,* January 3, 1898.
St. Paul *Globe,* "Editorial," November 29, 1903.

Miscellaneous

Addresses and Proceedings of the National Education Association, 1899–1921.
An Assessment Guide for Use in Junior High Schools. The Connecticut State Department of Education, Bureau of Elementary and Secondary Education, June, 1960, Hartford, Conn.
Como Park Junior High School Orientation Bulletin
Criteria for Evaluating Junior High Schools. Research Study of Secondary Education, 1956.

Curriculum Materials. Board of Education of the City of New York, Vol. XIV, Winter 1960.

St. Paul Junior High School Study: A Progress Report and Preliminary Tabular Findings of the St. Paul School Report, Number 25. Minneapolis, Minn., Bureau of Field Studies and Surveys, College of Education, University of Minnesota, September 1962.

The Organization and Curriculum of the New Junior High Schools in St. Paul. St. Paul, Minn., Office of Secondary and Vocational Education, Fall 1958.

Birkmaier, Emma M., "Notebook Sketch of the Curriculum of the Future."

Bruner, Jerome S., "How Can Schools Provide a Liberal Education for All Youths?" *Addresses and Proceedings of the National Education Association,* 1965.

CALKINS, N. A., "Prefatory Note," *Report of the Committee of Ten on Secondary School Studies: With the Reports of the Conferences Arranged by the Committee.* New York, The American Book Co., 1894.

COY, E. W., "A Readjustment of the High School Curriculum," *Addresses and Proceedings of the National Education Association, 1903.*

Digest of Educational Statistics. Washington D.C., U.S. Office of Education, Department of Health, Education, and Welfare, Bulletin No. 43, Government Printing Office, 1963 edition.

ENGLEMAN, FINIS E., "Editorial," *The School Administrator,* February 1962.

GLASS, JAMES M., "The Junior High School Program of Studies," *Addresses and Proceedings of the National Education Association, 1922.*

GOLDSTEIN, LOUIS, "The Social Agency Executive—A Study of Organizational Isolation." Unpublished Ph.D. dissertation, University of Minnesota, Minneapolis, Minn., 1960.

GOFFMAN, ERVING, "The Characteristics of Total Institutions," in *Symposium on Preventive and Social Psychiatry.* Washington, D.C., Walter Reed Institute of Research, 1957.

GRUHN, WILLIAM T., "An Investigation of the Relative Frequency of Curriculum and Related Practices Contributing to the Realization of the Basic Functions of the Junior High School." Unpublished Ph.D. dissertation, University of North Carolina, Chapel Hill, 1940.

HALL, G. STANLEY, "Recent Advances in Child-Study," *Addresses and Proceedings of the National Education Association, 1908.*

JENNINGS, WAYNE B., "What Is the Effectiveness of the Core Program?" Unpublished M.A. thesis, University of Minnesota, Minneapolis, Minn.

KELLEY, EARL C., "Core Teaching—A New Sense of Adventure," in *Teaching Core,* Vol. XIV, June 1965. General Education Committee of the Metropolitan Detroit Bureau of School Studies.

MAPHIS, CHARLES, "A Decade of Growth," *Proceedings of the Nineteenth Annual Meeting of the Association of Colleges and Preparatory Schools of the Southern Association, 1913.*

McCLURE, S. S., "Editorial," *McClure's,* Vol. XX, January 1903.

MEAD, MARGARET, "The Early Adolescent in Today's American Culture and Implications for Education," *Junior High School Newsletter,* Indiana State College, Terre Haute, Ind., Vol. I, February 1963.

MURPHY, JUDITH, *Middle Schools.* New York, Educational Facilities Laboratories, 1965.

————, *School Scheduling by Computer: The Story of GASP.* New York, Educational Facilities Laboratories, 1964.

NULL, ELDON JAMES, "The Relationship Between the Organizational Climate of a School and Personal Variables of Members of the Teaching Staff." Unpublished Ph.D. dissertation, University of Minnesota, Minneapolis, Minn., 1965.

PETERSON, WARREN, "Career Phases and Inter-Age Relationships: The Female High School Teacher in Kansas City." Unpublished Ph.D. dissertation, University of Chicago, Chicago, Ill., 1956.

Proceedings of the Annual Convention of the Association of Colleges and Preparatory Schools of the Middle States and Maryland, 1889, 1892–1927.

Proceedings of the Second Annual Convention of the College Association of Pennsylvania, 1888.

Proceedings of the Annual Meeting of the North Central Association of Colleges and Secondary Schools, 1895–1926.

Report of the Committee of Fifteen on Elementary Education; with the Reports of the Sub-Committees: On the Training of Teachers; On the Correlation of Studies in Elementary Education; On the Organization of City Schools Systems. New York, The American Book Co., 1895.

STAMBLER, MOSES, "The Democratic Revolution in the Public High Schools of New York City." Unpublished Ph.D. dissertation, New York University, New York City, 1964.

STICKNEY, LUCIA, "The Homes of our Down-Town Children," *Addresses and Proceedings of the National Education Association, 1899.*

The Community School And Its Administration, Vol. IV, February 1956. The Board of Education of Flint, Michigan and the Mott Foundation.

TURNER, FREDERICK JACKSON, "The Significance of the Frontier in American History," *Proceedings of the State Historical Society of Wisconsin, 1893.*

WEBB, HAROLD, "Community Pressures on School Boards," in *Proceedings of the Seventh Annual Conference on School Finance.* Washington, D.C., National Education Association, 1964.

World Survey of Education. Paris: UNESCO, 1955.

SUBJECT INDEX

NAME INDEX